Music and Musicians in the Medieval Islamicate World

The Early and Medieval Islamic World

Published in collaboration with the Society for the Medieval Mediterranean

As recent scholarship resoundingly attests, the medieval Mediterranean and Middle East bore witness to a prolonged period of flourishing intellectual and cultural diversity. Seeking to contribute to this ever-more nuanced and contextual picture, *The Early and Medieval Islamic World* book series promotes innovative research on the period 500–1500 AD with the Islamic world, as it ebbed and flowed from Marrakesh to Palermo and Cairo to Kabul, as the central pivot. Thematic focus within this remit is broad, from the cultural and social to the political and economic, with preference given to studies of societies and cultures from a socio-historical perspective. It will foster a community of unique voices on the medieval Islamic world, shining light into its lesser-studied corners.

New and forthcoming titles

Cross Veneration in the Medieval Islamic World: Christian Identity and Practice under Muslim Rule, Charles Tieszen (Fuller Theological Seminary/Simpson University)
Power and Knowledge in Medieval Islam: Shi'i and Sunni Encounters in Baghdad, Tariq al-Jamil (Swathmore College)
The Eastern Frontier: Limits of Empire in Late Antique and Early Medieval Central Asia, Robert Haug (University of Cincinnati)
Writing History in the Medieval Islamic World: The Value of Chronicles as Archives, Fozia Bora (University of Leeds)
Gypsies in the Medieval Islamic World: The History of a People, Kristina Richardson (City University, New York)
Narrating Muslim Sicily: War and Peace in the Medieval Mediterranean World, William Granara (Harvard University)
Gender and Succesion in Medieval Islam: Bilateral Descent and the Legacy of Fatima, Alyssa Gabbay (The University of North Carolina at Greensboro)

Music and Musicians in the Medieval Islamicate World

A Social History

Lisa Nielson

I.B.TAURIS

LONDON • NEW YORK • OXFORD • NEW DELHI • SYDNEY

I.B. TAURIS
Bloomsbury Publishing Plc
50 Bedford Square, London, WC1B 3DP, UK
1385 Broadway, New York, NY 10018, USA
29 Earlsfort Terrace, Dublin 2, Ireland

BLOOMSBURY, I.B. TAURIS and the I.B. Tauris logo are trademarks of
Bloomsbury Publishing Plc

First published in Great Britain 2021
This paperback edition published 2023

Series design by www.paulsmithdesign.com
Cover image: Bayâd et Riyâd, 13th century. (© The Yorck Project)

A catalogue record for this book is available from the British Library.

A catalog record for this book is available from the Library of Congress.

ISBN: HB: 978-1-7845-3954-2
PB: 978-0-7556-4181-9
ePDF: 978-0-7556-1789-0
eBook: 978-0-7556-1790-6

Series: The Early and Medieval Islamic World

Typeset by Newgen KnowledgeWorks Pvt. Ltd., Chennai, India

To find out more about our authors and books visit www.bloomsbury.com
and sign up for our newsletters.

To Amara, who got me started on this path.
Thank you, my friend.

Contents

Acknowledgments

The research for this project would not have been possible without a travel grant from the Baker Nord Center for the Humanities at Case Western Reserve University and a Balzan Fellowship from Towards a Global History of Music, led by Dr. Reinhard Strohm. Receiving the Balzan visitorship enabled me to spend the summer of 2016 in Israel for research, and I am grateful to Drs. Edwin Seroussi and Ruth Cohen for their sponsorship and support. I would not have been able to complete this book without the support of Peter Whiting, director of the Seminar Approach to General Education and Scholarship (SAGES) program at Case Western Reserve University, and Karen R. Long, manager of the Anisfield-Wolf Book Awards.

Endless gratitude is owed to Robert A. Green, Michael Grillo, Pernilla Myrne, Dwight Reynolds, Katherine Hain, Reinhard Strohm, Georgia Cowart, John Franklin, and Matthew Gordon for their enthusiasm, expertise, and encouragement to start, let alone finish, this project.

I am ever grateful for the wisdom and friendship of Gabrielle Parkin, Lance Parkin, Cara Byrne, Karen Long, Amara Simons, Mary Louise Hahn, Eric Dicken, Paul Putman, Jon Whitney, and Allison Morgan.

Last, my students have always been my best teachers. Although the list of people who have changed my life is extensive, the following remarkable individuals inspire me every day: Nusaiba Chowdhury, Anton Spencer, Cae Elizabeth Rosch, Zulaika Khan, Douglas Oswald, Douglas Hermes, and Jessica Yang.

Introduction

At the height of her career, the singer Jamīla (d. *c.* 720 CE/first century, *H*) set out from Medina to perform the hajj, or pilgrimage to Mecca. She brought an extensive entourage of musicians, servants, and companions, including fifty singing slave women and all the celebrated musicians of the day. The party was merry, stopping at oases, inns, and monasteries along the way to sing and drink wine. Jamīla was a *mawlā*, or freedwoman, who learned the rudiments of music by listening to the songs of her neighbor, the singer Sa'ib Khathir (d. 683 CE/mid-first century, *H*), who was himself the son of a Persian slave.[1] After she was freed, Jamīla married and achieved considerable wealth and fame as a musician, training many of the next generation of great musicians. As such, she became a link between pre-Islamic, polytheistic music traditions and the nascent Islamicate court culture. Jamīla's pilgrimage made a large enough impression on the social landscape that it is mentioned in a number of different sources.[2] What makes her story notable is not only that she was a woman of means and a former slave. It was her ability to use her musical skills to gain her freedom, acquire wealth, and rise in social status. Nor was she was the first or only woman during this time to do so.

For millennia, free and unfree women formed the backbone of what we today consider professional musicians.[3] The documentary and archeological records of the ancient cultures of Sumer (*c.* 3000 BCE), Egypt, Palestine, Babylon, and Assyria contain numerous textual and visual references to women musicians performing for public entertainments, intimate settings, and ritual and informal gatherings. Music performance was also gendered, with specific instruments and genres associated with women, others with men. With the advent of Islam in the seventh century, these perceptions and performance practices did not substantially change. As Islam spread during the seventh and eighth centuries, foreign musicians, new musical traditions, and instruments were brought into the heart of Islamicate urban centers. The resulting integration of outside musical influences with extant music traditions led to the development of a sophisticated musical culture.

Throughout the Islamicate states, singing women (Arabic, sing. *qayna*; pl. *qiyān*) and musical concubines (sing. *jāriya*; pl. *jawārī*) were integral to musical entertainments at all levels of the social order. Women musicians not only helped shape and define Islamicate musical culture, they remained a staple of musical life in Islamicate courts for centuries.[4] Along with singing women, male musicians (*mūsīkār, mughannūn*) and cross-gendered entertainers called *mukhannathūn* performed together at court, often competing for the same patrons. Yet, although musicians received accolades, remuneration, expensive gifts, and enhanced status, the fact of their profession placed them in a shared social space that continually wavered along a spectrum of acceptable to unacceptable. That liminal status enabled some to slip between social and physical boundaries, infiltrating and challenging the social hierarchy.

By the late eighth century, grumblings about the excesses of court entertainments and outright alarm at the embrace of music by some Ṣūfi raised questions as to whether *samāᶜ*, listening, was legal in Islam. Listening could include a number of auditory acts, ranging from poetic recitation and lectures to Ṣūfi *samāᶜ* and *dhikr* (remembrance of God), but of particular concern was listening to music. This discussion ranged (and raged) over an array of literary genres for centuries, with the most granular treatment appearing in philosophy and pietistic literature. Over the centuries, terminology related to music and a thick compendium of legal arguments related to listening were created, shared, and rigorously argued. As a result, terms used to describe music and listening were fluid, interrelated concepts that were in constant conversation with literature, politics, religion, and practice.

This book offers a social history of music in the early medieval Islamicate era (800–1400 CE). Using a sampling of literary discussions about music, musicians, and the legality of listening, I examine what the sources say about the shifting relationships among musician, patron, and society, and how these shaped a sophisticated and diverse musical culture. These relationships were not only defined through artistic and monetary exchange, but encompassed metaphysical considerations and the performing bodies of the musicians themselves. The physical and metaphysical were further intertwined with gender, sexuality, slavery, kinship, origin, and social status, providing additional kindling for discussions about the legality of music. To provide a nominal order to these intersections, this book is divided into two parts. The first is an overview of the social and cultural realities of what we know about music, musicians, and the patronate, while the second looks at the musician in the literary imaginary and development of the debate about *samāʿ*.

My focus on social history, rather than textual and performance history, is deliberate.[5] Music is fundamentally a social and cultural institution that imbues every layer of the human landscape. To remove it from that social context is to diminish the importance—and variety—of creative expression throughout history. More importantly, however, focusing on one aspect of music alone is anachronistic to how medieval people experienced musical expression. Regardless of whether one listened to or even thought about music, music and musical sound were enmeshed in the physical and metaphysical worlds medieval people inhabited.

In the medieval Islamicate world, the process of reflection and revision was intrinsic to constructing the linguistic apparatus needed to talk about music and write music history. Because such reflection operated over multiple intellectual and esoteric levels, I include musicological considerations such as instruments and performance practices but focus primarily on the social factors that affected music as a sociocultural practice. Following Michael Chamberlain in *Knowledge and Social Practice in Medieval Damascus, 1190–1350*, I define the social world as a set of practices, not a structure.[6] In essence, the social realm was a multifaceted, ever-changing organism.

Similarly, given the cultural diversity that existed within the Islamicate states, it is hard to find a universally satisfying term to denote the regions within Islamdom. "Islamic" is only partially accurate. Along with Marshall Hodgson, Michael Chamberlain comments that privileging Islam as the primary director of the culture has several pitfalls,[7] not least of which is that by placing Islam at the forefront, one can create a monolithic sense of sameness across divergent eras. Religion influenced the development of music but primarily in terms of practice—what instruments and song were appropriate or not—and how music influenced the practice of religion.

Part I, "Musical Culture in Early Islamicate Courts," gives an overview of music and performance in the early Islamicate states and terms commonly used to discuss and define music and classes of musicians. Since slavery, conquest, diplomatic gift exchange, and marriage brought different musicians and traditions into the early Islamicate courts, Chapter 1 considers what might have been borrowed from other cultures as well as those practices adopted from pre-Islamic traditions, such as singing slave women and *mukhannathūn* from pre-Islamic Arabia.

Chapters 2 and 3 look at musicianship, performance practices, and patrons in the early Islamicate courts. As in other cultures, the musical practices of the elite are easier to sketch due to there being more information about them. However, the rich trove of information in pietistic texts suggests there were shared musical practices and borrowings among social orders. That blend offers a tantalizing glimpse into uses of music in the middling and lower classes, along with diverse Ṣūfi practices and encroachment of song in religious cantillation.

Salons, gatherings related to music and poetry, including storytelling in public spaces, all operated within several dimensions: audience, patron, performer(s), word, and sound. Within this matrix, formal definition between song and poetic recitation was less important than the perspective of audience and performer on what they heard—or chose to hear. We continue to see analogues today, especially in popular and improvised musico-poetic events. Spoken word, rap, hip-hop, mash-ups, jazz, and so on all exist within the spectrum of sound-poetry while continuing to defy explicit definition.

Because expectations for both musical and extramusical performances were different for men and women, access to social mobility was tied to gender, kin, and origin, as well as legal and social status. Patrons and slave owners did not fully control social mobility. Musicians could and did manipulate the patronage system to their advantage. Relationships among patrons and musicians were asymmetrical dependencies, transactional, and rooted in gifting and obligation.[8] They were also laden with degrees of intimacy, especially in the case of enslaved women. Although patrons held power, patron and musician alike contributed to the construction and perpetuation of the patronage system.

Enslaved women musicians were an important community within Islamicate music cultures, so much so that references to them are ubiquitous in the literature. Chapter 4 goes into greater depth on the institutions of slavery and gender in the medieval Islamicate states. Articulating how perceptions of music and musicians in medieval Islamicate society were tied to gender, social status, and sexuality, however, is messy business. The fluidity of Arabic terminology and our tenuous understanding of the meaning of such concepts at the time fit uneasily within modern taxonomies. In addition to biological differences, some of the characteristics that contributed to gender identity included visible physical markers, such as length and style of hair, facial hair, dress, and mannerisms, as well as social/cultural categories, such as marriage and profession.[9]

Sexual practices reinforced gender identity; however, what we would define as sexual orientation and sexual acts were not necessarily tied to gender. Same-sex relations were technically illegal under Islamic law, but in practice, all sexual acts outside the bonds of marriage were illicit. Men who enjoyed same-sex partners in the dominant role were stepping out of bounds because they were having sex outside of marriage, not necessarily because they were having sex with other men.[10] Because women were penetrated and always passive partners, to penetrate was inherently masculine and to be penetrated was feminine. Therefore, men who preferred the passive role were unmasculine.[11]

Like the Greeks, age was another gender marker. Young boys were objects of desire because they were androgynous; having all the characteristics of women—smooth skin, shapely limbs—with the erotic allure of men. Passion for boys was included in categories of illicit love, not always because of the sex act, but because passion itself could be dangerous. The onset of puberty transformed boys from beardless youth to bearded adult, masculinizing them emotionally and physically. Thus, although there were distinctions between what constituted male and female, masculine and feminine, these were not strictly biological or binary structures in medieval Islamicate society.

Institutions of slavery in the medieval Islamicate world were similarly fluid and complicated, with a range of personal status along the spectrum of free to unfree. Recent scholarship into Islamicate slavery has provided keen insight into trade, economic, and social practices; however, with the exception of select studies of the harem (Arabic, *ḥarīm*), women in literature, and musical performance practice, the experiences of men have been privileged over those of women.[12] As in other slave systems, men and women in the Islamicate states experienced slavery differently. The work and expectations for men and women were divided by gender, and women's relegation to the broad category of domestic labor meant their work left little documentary evidence.[13] Chapter 4, "Slavery and Gender," is by no means as in-depth as it deserves to be. Rather, its purpose is to provide additional background on how music and the status of enslaved women musicians fit into the medieval Islamicate social order.

Part II, "Diversions of Pleasure: Representations of Musicianship and Identity," turns to the literary representation of music and musicians, especially conversations about *samāᶜ* and the politics of listening. In Chapter 5, I consider symbolic and rhetorical uses of music and the figure of the musician in literature, and what possible influence such uses may have had on the perception of music. Narratives involving musicians are found in a variety of Arabic literary genres and serve different symbolic purposes. Themes such as repentance, piety, and willful blasphemy were deployed as a means to support or undermine positive depictions of prominent musical figures and patrons, and therefore music itself.

Using the structure and content of these narratives as a frame, I discuss how the use of musician narratives enabled an author (or purported author) to enter the larger conversation about music and listening. Such narratives, and their familiarity to the reader, could offer a layered critique, praise the patronate, underline the purpose of a specific event, make a social or political point, and address moral implications of music audition. By way of example, I provide brief biographies of nine well-known musicians from the eighth, ninth, and tenth centuries to show some of the ways musicians were represented in medieval sources.

Chapter 6 focuses on the rise of discussions about the legality of listening to music, *samāᶜ*, in Islam. *Samāᶜ* was, and remains, a practice associated with Ṣūfism. As early as the eighth century, some Ṣūfi had begun to incorporate *samāᶜ* and movement into communal devotions. The purpose of *samāᶜ* was to induce an ecstatic state in the hearer, in order to bring them closer to the divine. Depending on the perspective of the order, *samāᶜ* and *dhikr* could be lengthy, emotionally intense, and drenched with music and recitation. Not unexpectedly, criticism of *samāᶜ* arose from religious, social, and political concerns about social and spiritual excesses. Although much has been written about Ṣūfism and *samāᶜ*, the development of *samāᶜ* as a broader philosophical-musical concept has not been fully explored.

The *Dhamm al-Malāhī* (*Censure of Instruments of Diversion*) of Ibn Abi'l Dūnya (823–94 CE/207–80 *H*) has been held up as the first extant treatise to focus specifically on *samāᶜ* as being chief among several unhealthy diversions.[14] However, discomfort around music is noted in earlier treatises. Two early treatises on music, the *Mukhtār (Kitāb) al-lahw wa'l malāhī* (Book of Play and Musical Instruments) by Ibn Khurdādhbih (*c.* 820–912 CE/203–99 *H*) and the *Kitāb al-malāhī* (Book of Musical Instruments) by Ibn Salama (*c.* 830 CE/214 *H*), allude to concerns about the appropriateness of music and singing.[15] What distinguished Ibn Abi'l Dūnya's treatise from the others was that it provoked heated discussion as to the value and legal standing of listening. Many of the scholars who advocated for *samāᶜ* (or allowed that music was acceptable under certain circumstances) were Ṣūfis, such as the first rebuttal to Ibn Abi'l Dūnya by 'Ubayd Ibn Surayj (fl. late seventh, early eighth centuries/first century, *H*) and later philosophers like Abū Hamid Muḥammad ibn Muḥammad al-Tusi al-Ghazālī (1058–1111 CE/450–505 *H*).[16] Not all Ṣūfis approved, however.

Within the Ṣūfi orders, opinions ranged from rulings firmly against all uses of *samāᶜ* to specifying that only those who had achieved age and wisdom should experience *samāᶜ* as they would have more immunity from earthly distractions. The issue for Ṣūfis who advocated for the use of *samāᶜ* was similar to that of those who preached against it; namely, how to divest the sensual pleasure of listening to music (especially when performed by a visually appealing musician) from its potential to act as a means to access the divine. It was too easy to transfer appreciation of the art to appreciation of the singer. For those who were skeptical as to whether such a divestment was possible, only avoiding music entirely would keep one safe.[17] Therefore, whether music was allowable or not centered on the emotional and social effect of audition, grounded in associations linked to gender, intimacy, and proximity.

Writers concerned about *samāᶜ* were essential to the development of music discourses. To show how concerns about *samāᶜ* shifted from the page to practice, Chapter 7 is dedicated to a selection of scholars who vehemently advocated against it. Although there were plenty of writers who wrote in defense of *samāᶜ*, I focus exclusively on the opposing view. The detail such authors brought to their standpoint sheds considerable light on contemporary performance practices, including elite and non-elite uses of music. They redefined music terminology and music history to bolster their position, soliciting ever more nuanced responses from those who supported *samāᶜ* and music audition. Because medieval scholars who argued against *samāᶜ* shared similar rhetorical language and writing conventions with those who were in favor, referring to different camps as "pro-" or "anti-"*samāᶜ* establishes a false binary when there was a range of opinion, often within the same juridical schools. Regardless of their standpoint, discussions about *samāᶜ* imbued general terminology for music, instruments, and musicians with moral and symbolic meanings and changed the social and conceptual framework for thinking about music. This change promoted the development of multivalent music discourses necessitating new vocabulary and symbolic language.

The final chapter attempts to bring these many threads together and propose some general conclusions about the politics of music. There are many questions left unanswered, and I consider further avenues of exploration needed to construct a fuller understanding of medieval Islamicate music history.

Reflections and Methodology

Writing a history of a musical culture that is distant in time is a process of reflection. Not only must one attempt to place themselves within the "foreign country" that is history, one must struggle to step outside the kaleidoscope of information that informs our own musico-cultural values. In the medieval Islamicate world, links among practical musicianship, music theory, and metaphysics were bound in the gaze of early Islamicate historians on their own past and present in conjunction with the personal and communal reflection inherent in the practice of Islam. How these intersections informed perceptions and uses for music is key to understanding the musical culture. Another reflective surface is the modern gaze. Because the European construction of the Orient is integral to understanding how we arrived at this history today, I note—albeit in broad strokes—aspects of the history of this scholarship as well.

As the Islamicate states expanded in the seventh and eighth centuries, the growing Muslim community needed to construct an identity that differentiated them from people of other religions. They also required a means to understand that identity as it unfolded. How sound genres functioned in an Islamicate frame, especially since music was intrinsic to polytheism and other monotheisms, was pondered by scholars of law, religion, and history. Early medieval Islamicate historians began by looking back on their history and that of the cultures that they conquered, admired, and established diplomatic relations with. Despite assertions by later religious scholars, music had always been part of the cultures of Arabic-speaking peoples. Folklore and poetry hinted at pre-Islamic practices, although the majority of that history was transmitted orally and therefore in constant motion. This motion was literal and figurative due to trade and travel of nomads and urbanites alike.

During the ninth century, translations of Greek, Roman, Indian, and Persian treatises on everything from science to literature, along with intellectuals from those regions, provided ample tools for the scholarly community. The importation of foreign slaves and skilled laborers into the urban centers was another conduit for new knowledge. Islamicate historians drew on all these sources, interpreting them within the context of Muslim identity and law. They reflected the past onto their present and tried to understand the present within their reading of the past. Often, those perceptions were wildly divergent, as we will see in constructions of music history.

The practice of Islam itself requires layers of reflection, radiating from the individual to community. In the West, Islam is translated as "to submit," with the basic understanding that Muslims submit to God. Although that is accurate on one level, this concept is far more complex. Submission was not a blind following of faith, but acknowledgment that there was a higher power guiding one's actions. Islam provided a process for constructing a balanced life and individual practice to serve God. Within that practice, one relinquished control to the greater good and continually reflected on one's individual relationship with God by studying the Qur'an and law and following the Pillars of Islam.[18]

Along with the influence of the Qur'an and *ḥadīth* on the development of literary conventions, the continuous cycle of reflection, introspection, and correction embedded in the practice of Islam is fundamental to understanding the role of music and conversations about listening in medieval Islamicate culture. When a caliph threw a drinking party with his singing women and beardless boys, a Ṣūfi order performed *dhikr* in a mosque, or a wedding party broke out instruments for impromptu music making, such actions had implications for the souls of the individual and community.

The study of medieval Islamicate music began in earnest in the nineteenth century and remains a tiny subset within the discipline of musicology. Much of what we know about music in the seventh to thirteenth centuries is still dependent on the work of a handful of late-nineteenth- and early-twentieth-century scholars.[19] A good portion of that work was excellent, with the caveat that there are additional layers to parse when examining nineteenth- and twentieth-century scholarship, such as why a text was chosen for translation, the intended audience, and the translator's discipline.[20]

Musicologists Henry George Farmer, the Baron D'erlanger, and Julian Ribera in the early twentieth century were among the first to present an outline of early Islamic music history, as well as theorize about the possibility of Arabian influence on the development of Western music. To this day, Henry George Farmer is among the most respected authorities, and his work, much of which was published in the 1920s and 1930s, continues to be invaluable. Although several of his theories have been disproven, Farmer's work did much to pave the way for a more nuanced understanding of global music history.[21]

Along with Farmer, the Arabist James Robson was responsible for several translations of music treatises. Musicologists are most familiar with Robson's 1937 English translation of Ibn Abi'l Dūnya's *Dhamm al-Malāhī* (*Censure of Instruments of Diversion*) as part of a series on non-Western music for the Royal Asiatic Society.[22] Robson also collaborated with Farmer on a translation of Ibn Salama's music treatise and commentary on Ibn Khurdādhbih's remarks on music, gleaned from an oration recorded by the historian al-Mas'ūdī and a manuscript fragment.[23]

Despite this important early body of work, the specter of Orientalism and the Eurocentric gaze cannot be banished, nor should it be. As Said and subsequent scholars have demonstrated, the work of dismantling Orientalism and decolonizing our understanding of non-Western histories is ongoing. Likewise, European fragmentation of history into epochs and modes of progress aided scholars in the construction of a framework for viewing history; however, that framework is also being reconstructed.

For example, the concept of a "middle" or "dark" age originated with the poet Petrarch in the fourteenth century when he compared the period between the Roman Empire and his own. As Michael Shank and David Lindberg explain, to intellectuals such as Petrarch

> the Middle Ages were a useful invention that contrasted the political fragmentation and barbarous degenerate Latin of the recent past with the lost glory and beautiful language of Rome, to which they aspired. To invoke the Middle Ages when discussing empire, language, or art, was implicitly to narrate history with the radical discontinuity of a sorry, if not necessarily vacuous, millennium.[24]

Although applying the term to other cultures, such as "medieval China" or "medieval Islam," gives this history a convenient reference point, "the price of calling everything between 400–1450 'medieval' is that the deeply entrenched unflattering connotations associated with the European Middle Ages automatically color other civilizations."[25] Therefore, my use of "medieval" is to signal the period, not the underlying implication (and judgment) of social and intellectual progress.

Similarly, Europeans scholars considered the shift from orality to literacy within a culture a sign of evolution and progress, which aligned neatly with Western renaissance and enlightenment principles. As recent studies have found, however, medieval cultures shared and stored knowledge on at least three levels: written, oral, and in memory. Orality was not limited to spoken transmission of texts, nor was "written" a word-for-word rendition. Both modes existed in tandem, with memory the connective tissue in between. This was certainly the case in the medieval Islamicate world.

Of course, ideologies of supremacy, revisionist histories, and creating intellectual hierarchies are by no means a modern, or even strictly Western, invention. Medieval people may have had a different perception of their relationship to the world and one another, but enslavement, colonization, patriarchy, and economic exploitation are nothing new. Yet, there are key differences. Although medieval cultures did establish sets of binaries—good/evil, man/woman, perfect/imperfect, enslaved/free, yin/yang—these were not necessarily firm categories or opposites. Rather, they could be complements, formulated along the lines of "this and," rather than "either/or." To reflect these connections, I position familiar terms as being on a spectrum of organizing principles: gender, sex, sexuality, slavery, orality-literacy-memory, religious-nonreligious, and song-recitation.[26] These concepts were woven into other social, religious, and philosophical categories as well as inhabited metaphysical realms, meaning the social and metaphysical were connected and reflective of one another as well. Although maddeningly elliptical, the shifts in how medieval Islamicate thinkers defined such concepts offer a means to attempt to hear the splendid cacophony of ideas, sounds, and practices that encompassed medieval Islamicate musical cultures.

The Sources

Using literature to speculate on history is always fraught. Medieval Islamicate literary conventions embraced the structure and form of the Qur'an, *ḥadīth*, and poetic meters. Authority was established through chains of authority, or *isnād*, as well as citation and commentary by previous authorities. Exaggeration and hyperbole were common, as was collaboration and outright plagiarism. Scholars constantly copied one another's works for their own libraries, dropping sections into their own. That does not mean that one must distrust all the information in these texts, but careful triangulation is necessary. Given that these texts resided within the interstices of oral, written, and memorized knowledge, my reading is less concerned with veracity than tone and image.

Another wrinkle is that although music and musicians are ubiquitous in Arabic literature, there are few texts that provide details about individual musicians. In addition, although a number of sources discuss women writing, reciting poetry, and publishing books of songs, none of these books are extant. Therefore, all the available sources for women's biographies, poetry collections, and songs attributed to women are filtered through male-authored literary works. That does not undercut their value; rather, it offers another point of reflection on the male gaze and female subject.

For this study, I examined texts devoted to music theory and philosophies of music (*mūsīqī*), but focus on nonspecialized texts, drawing primarily on literary sources (*adab*). These include poetry, essays, history, and biographies. In describing musicians, especially the *qiyān*, these texts not only purport to be making statements of fact about their lives and character, but make use of symbolic gestures that link music and audition to larger issues of morality, passionate love, music, and religious practice. Treatises intended for a wider or less specialized readership might use terminology and associated meanings from specialized texts, but often inflect that language towards a general audience. This language became integral to discourses regarding religious and legal positions on *samāᶜ*, as well as formed the underpinnings of social commentary in a range of literary genres.[27] Thus, nonspecialist texts provide a historical perspective on the literal performance of musicians as well as *literary* performance within a system of musical semiotics.

The sources that provide the most information about music and musicians are the *Kitāb al-Aghānī* (*Great Book of Songs*) of Abū'l faraj al-Iṣbahānī (897–969 CE/283–356 H), the *Risālat al-Qiyān* (*Epistle on Singing Girls*) by al-Jāḥiẓ (776/7–868/9 CE/159/60–253/4 H), the *Histories* of al-Ṭabarī (839–923 CE/224–310 H), and the *Murūj al-Dhahab* (*Meadows of Gold*) by al-Mas'ūdī (d. 956 CE/344 H).[28] I also draw on the eighth- and ninth-century music treatises by Ibn Khurdādhbih and Ibn Salama, the *Kitāb al-Muwashshā'* (*Book of Brocades*) of Ibn al-Washsha (d. 937 CE/325 H), the *Fihrist* of al-Nadīm (935–90/1 CE/322–79/380 H), *Music: The Precious Jewel* of the tenth-century Andalusi writer al-Rabbih (860–940 CE/245–328 H), and the memoirs of the *qāḍī* (judge) al-Tanūkhi (940–94 CE/324–84 H).

Although mention of music and performance is found in literature after the tenth century, there are fewer texts from the eleventh to the fourteenth century that focus exclusively on music. Philosophy, poetry, biography, and other literary genres continued to include commentary on music and descriptions of performance, with pietistic and theological treatises devoting more space to music and listening. As we will see, however, the question of music began to shift away from music as a practice to the effects of listening. That shift pushed listening further into the metaphysical, with discussion focused less on what melodic sounding constituted music to what vocal forms were musically exempt.

Because of our own sensibilities, Western scholars have tended to study only music-positive texts, with the consequence of dismissing those who advocated against music as fanatics.[29] Although there were authors who were decidedly on the lunatic fringe, their interpretation still has value. In addition, despite the rich and diverse musical traditions that flourish throughout cultures influenced by Islam today, the belief that music is not allowed in Islam continues to be based on a handful of texts condemning music.[30] To give a snapshot of the variety of opinion, I spotlight eight treatises from the ninth to fifteenth centuries that were collected in the mid-fifteenth century by Ibn Burayd Burhān al-Dīn Ibrāhīm al-Qāḍirī (1413–75 CE/815–79 H). According to his notations, Ibn Burayd copied the treatises between 1451 and 1456 CE, using texts from his personal collection and older extant versions. Although they are all strongly against listening, aside from the juridical elements, these treatises offer a glimpse into the development of and changes to the definitions for—and therefore uses of—music in early medieval Islamicate musical culture.

Now held at the National Library of Israel (NLI), this collection (*majmū*ᶜ) includes one of the four extant versions of the *Censure of Instruments of Diversion* by Ibn Abi'l Dūnya. The copy in the NLI is one of two that is nearly twice as long as the abridged version held at the Staatsbibliotek in Berlin. The order of the texts and authors is as follows:[31]

1. Abū Bakr al-Ājurrī (d. 971 CE/360 *H*): Ap. Ar. 158/1, f. 1a–10a. *Al-jawāb* *ᶜan mas'alat al-samā*ᶜ (Response to the question regarding listening)
2. Ibn Jamāᶜa (Burhān al-Dīn) (1325–88 CE/725–90 *H*): Ap. Ar. 158/2, f. 11a–20a. *Suwwāl sālahu shakhṣ min al-fuqarā'* (Response to a *faqīr*)
3. Diya al-Dīn al-Maqdisī (1173–1245 CE/569–643 *H*): Ap. Ar. 158/3, f. 21a–37b. *Al-amr bi-itbā*ᶜ *al-sunan wa ijtināb al-bida*ᶜ (The command to follow established laws and avoid heresy)
4. Abū Bakr al-Khallāl (848–923 CE/234–311 *H*): Ap. Ar. 158/4, f. 38a–58a. *Al-amr bi'l ma*ᶜ*rūf wa'l-nahy* ᶜ*an al-munkar* (Commanding the proper and condemnation of the improper)
5. Al-Khallāl: Ap. Ar. 158/5, f. 58b–61b. *Kitāb al-qirā* ᶜ*an al-qabūr*
6. Al-Wāsiṭī (1259–1311 CE/657–711 *H*): Ap. Ar. 158/6, f. 62a–63b. *Mas'alat fi al-samā*ᶜ (Question regarding *samā*ᶜ)
7. Al-Wāsiṭī: Ap. Ar. 158/7, f. 64a–72b. *Al-bulghat wa'l iqna*ᶜ *fi ḥill shubhat mas'alat al-samā*ᶜ (The exaggeration and persuasion of those who declare *samā*ᶜ is permitted)
8. Ibn Abi'l Dūnya (823–94 CE/208–81 *H*): Ap. Ar. 158/8, f. 73a–84b. *Dhamm al-Malāhī* (Censure of instruments of diversion)
9. Al-Ṭabarī (Abū'l Ṭayyib) (959/60–1058 CE/d. 450 *H*): Ap. Ar. 158/9, f. 85a–91b. *Kitāb fihi mas'alat fi'l radd* ᶜ*alā man yaqūl bi-jawāz al-samā*ᶜ *al-ghinā' wa'l raqṣ wa'l taghbīr* (Book refuting the opinions of those who allow listening to music, dance, and the *taghbīr*)[32]
10. Ibn Rajab (d. 1393/795 *H*): Ap. Ar. 158/1, f. 92a–155b. *Fū'ayn min Kalām Ibn Rajab* (A collection of teachings by Ibn Rajab)[33]

The second text by al-Khallāl and the final, longest text by Ibn Rajab are not concerned with *samā*ᶜ; therefore, I have left them out.[34] Why Ibn Burayd chose these particular texts for his *majmū*ᶜ is not specified; however, some conclusions can be drawn based on what is known of his background and that of the authors. First, these authors were all well-known scholars from Damascus, Jerusalem, and Cairo who ascribed to the Ḥanbali and Shāfiʿī schools of jurisprudence. Some shared a scholarly lineage, and since a few are contemporaries, it is possible they knew one another personally. The later texts reference the earlier scholars, nuancing their arguments as they incorporated them into their own. Although each text grew out of a distinct era, that they were brought together in the fifteenth century means the collection reflects, in part, Mamlūk Damascus and Jerusalem.[35] Thus, the challenge is to find a balance between the historical contexts of the collection and that of the individual texts.[36]

On Translation

Anyone accustomed to working with historical texts knows the difficulty of parsing a translation from a language we do not know (or are not comfortable in) and creating an accessible, reasonably accurate translation. Although the original author remains "authoritative," authority shifts to the translator and, by extension, the intended audience for the translation. As a result, the translator has to decide what words to use when translating certain concepts, some of which might not have a satisfactory equivalent in the receiving language.

Given the era in which it flourished, Orientalist scholarship was dominated by male scholars, and the documentary record has been read from the standpoint of European men.[37] In most Western languages (except perhaps French), there are few unbiased terms for women who are not married but have an intimate and artistic connection to men and live a public life. This lack makes it difficult to translate other relationships women had with men in a way that the Western reader would not subconsciously link to Western moral codes.[38]

More often than not, scholars relegated the roles of women musicians in the temples and courts of pre-Islamic Arabia, Mesopotamia, and Mediterranean cultures to prostitution, and therefore such women were assumed to have low status and little power. Reexamination of extant source material for ancient and medieval cultures has shown women musicians fulfilled a more complex social role. Women, free and unfree, filled the ranks of professional mourners, poets, musicians, and priestesses, often playing several roles simultaneously.[39] In the medieval Islamicate states, singing slave women ran the gamut of being companions, concubines, prostitutes, bawds, entrepreneurs, power brokers, and deeply pious. Some were members of the ruling families, legitimate and otherwise.

Despite their many roles in society, the term *qiyān* frequently is rendered as "singing girl" or "singing slave girl." In describing their role in medieval society, *qiyān* have been called "lady-like prostitutes" and well-trained concubines—designations that are not untrue, but carry moral judgment in a specifically Western context.[40] Referring to them as "girls" further relegates this diverse group of free and unfree professionals to a single, subordinate category. Thus, it is vital to avoid labels that diminish their importance and relegate them to sexual objects, disengaged from the events of their time. In that light, I refer to them as *qiyān*, *jawārī*, and singing women. I use singing slave women when speaking expressly of enslaved women musicians. Likewise, although the term *mukhannathūn* can be translated as "effeminate," this designation carries pejorative connotations. My preference is to use the Arabic and refer to this unique group of entertainers as being cross-gendered.[41]

To keep things as tidy as possible, all key terms are given in Arabic, with transliteration and translation for non-Arabic readers. Transliteration follows the conventions established by the *International Journal of Middle East Studies* (*IJMES*).

A Brief Comment on Geography

Medieval people traveled, fought, intermarried, and traded constantly, so to continue to divide the global medieval world of approximately the sixth to the fifteenth century into "East" and "West" is insufficient. Furthermore, the shifting borders of the Islamicate states covered a vast geographic area reaching from Spain to China well into the late nineteenth century, spanning "East" and "West." I try to avoid those divisions except when pinpointing geographic location. When I refer to the West, I mean the region that includes modern Europe, Scandinavia, and the Balkans, as well as the British Isles. By necessity, my geographic focus is limited to the urban centers and courts of Damascus, Jerusalem, and Baghdad from 661 to 1400 CE. For the purposes of this study, the regions referred to as Mesopotamia, Arabia, and the Ancient Near East include the Arabian Peninsula (the Gulf States), what are now Syria, Iraq, Palestine, and Israel (The Levant) and, peripherally, Egypt—the regions specified in antiquity as Arabia *felix* and Arabia *deserta* or upper and lower Arabia.

Part One

Musical Culture in Early Islamicate Courts

1

Music in the Near East before Islam

Since antiquity, ritual sounding and the act of audition resonated within the physical and metaphysical. Voiced sound grounded sacred tests, manifesting the words in the physical world. Sound-text passed though the body of the performer to that of the hearer, helping both retain the import of the message. In addition to being reflected in the body, ritual sounding needed to fit into the spaces built to contain and amplify it. The matrices in which sound existed in the metaphysical included not just concepts of celestial music but also language necessary to articulate the dimensions of what happened between sounding (performance) and hearing: giving, intent, reception, listening, hearing, and perception.

Voiced sound could be melodic without being music. Nor did one need to see the source of sound, which helped to blur the lines between the physical and metaphysical. For example, in the medieval Islamicate world, the tones and flavors of the *adhān* were woven into the soundscape in which everyone lived, serving to call the faithful by word and sound. The muezzin who called the faithful was an unseen voice (or many) whose call overlapped with others and echoed throughout urban centers, creating layers of sound which was (and is) beautifully melodic, but not considered music. What constituted song over recitation was predicated less on the purpose of the sound act than on the perception of the hearer. Intrinsic to that perception was the space in which sounding and listening happened. The technologies used to enhance sacred sounding were essential to preserving the sanctity of ritual. Key among those technologies was space.

The means to see and hear ritual sound forms was curated, with spaces designed to channel, enhance, and blend sound. Acoustic properties of ritual spaces required careful engineering to ensure sound carried legibly. Legibility was important, but so was the familiar sound keyed to recitation. Put another way, one did not need to hear (or understand) the words to know what they signified. Therefore, the question of how to wrap sacred sounding within the built environment was tied to social, architectural, and religious conversations about listening. Was it possible to capture the metaphysics of sounding? Should one? And in so doing, how did one control them?

In the Ancient Near East and into the Islamicate era, music and performance were similarly complex, layered practices that took place in physical and metaphysical realms. Because music and sound were a constant, they were considered real, tangible forces that could affect the body and emotional state of the hearer. Ancient philosophers and physicians knew music could heal, drive one mad, connect the hearer to the divine, and inspire dangerous passions. As a result, the act of playing music was differentiated from listening and hearing, subdivided into active listening and passive hearing. This relationship went in both directions, in which someone made sound and another heard, regardless as to whether or not they chose to hear.

Those individuals who interpreted, captured, and channeled sound were tapping into the unknown, and the form of capture could be sonic and textual. A musician was not necessarily someone who played; rather, a musician was a philosopher. Skilled players were appreciated, but were fundamentally technicians who brought to life the raw music of the cosmos. Since players were subject to the gaze of the audience, their visual impact contributed to the effect of their performance. Court and temple players could be sexually available and selected to be visually pleasing as well. When the visual aspect of performance was combined with the metaphysical forces of hearing, players could potentially inspire madness and passion in the unwary listener. Therefore, philosophers interpreted and theorized about sound not only to develop a basis for practical performance, but to render it safe for the player to relay to the hearer.

The impact of music on tangible and intangible realms necessitated the creation of several musical dialects. One enabled the player to speak of technical matters and construct sound (improvise, compose), while another gave the audience a means to articulate the experience of hearing. Yet another provided language to enable nonmusicians to discuss aesthetics and tools for philosophers to ruminate on the nature of music itself and for scholars to theorize on the broader social and moral implications of listening.

Based on the documentary evidence, the sound palette of the Ancient Near East and early Islamicate states was broad and the borders between music and other soundings tended to drift. To maintain this flexibility, I differentiate music from performative sound. Music included song, instruments, and ensembles, while performative sound consisted of a confederation of vocal and instrumental sound genres used for the purpose of focusing attention for a specific purpose, be it entertainment, ritual, or ceremony. Performative sounds could incorporate melody, modes, and other musical signposts, as well as recitation, sighs, groans, cries, ululation, body percussion (clapping, slapping one's chest), and dance. Similarly, although many ancient and medieval cultures had what we would consider "composed" genres, performance practices generally privileged improvisation and memory.

Playing and singing were gendered. Along with the profession of playing music, certain instruments and vocal genres were associated exclusively with women. This division was due in part to the use of enslaved women as court musicians in ancient Egypt, Sumer, and other cultures of the Ancient Near East; however, not all feminine musicians were enslaved and biologically women. Gender existed along a spectrum in the ancient world, and that spectrum included the outward performance of gender, such as clothing, gesture, and hairstyle, along with physical extremes like castration. Cultural acceptance of eunuchs and individuals who crossed genders ranged from considering them sacred and valued members of society, to their being reviled and relegated to the margins. In most cases, the status of cross-gendered and what we would now call gender fluid individuals was linked to their profession, and a common thread included performance, whether for entertainment or ritual.

As a result, players were defined according to their profession and visibility, and they navigated socially imposed strictures, boundaries, and expectations for extramusical performance.[1] Extramusical performance is that subjective realm of societal expectations for how a musician should behave, on and off-stage, dress, and interact with patrons.[2] The relationship between musician and patronate consisted of an expectation for improvisation, bounded within a complex modal, rhythmic, and textual framework for realizing new material, coupled with performance etiquette. Only truly exceptional musicians could transgress or innovate beyond established expectations. Their innovation could lead to censure, but just as often inspired the establishment of new sets of codes for behavior, expectations, and imitation.

Religion and Culture in the Ancient Near East

In the Ancient Near East and Mesopotamia, diverse systems of polytheism formed the basis of religious thinking cross-culturally. Cultural exchanges were effected not only through trade, warfare, and conquest, but with movements of people due to natural disasters, traditional nomadism, slavery, and exile. As people moved, so did their gods, rituals, stories, and arts. New religions came and went, including several monotheisms. The gradual infiltration of the Abrahamic religions took centuries, and communities of Jews, various Christian sects, Muslims, Zoroastrians, and polytheists lived side by side in the urban trade centers of Arabia and Mesopotamia. There was an equally broad range of belief systems in the rural areas and among nomadic peoples.[3]

Within a polytheistic worldview, gods represented facets of the human experience and natural world. Like humans, gods were not perfect. They competed with one another for adoration; loved, fought, and sought revenge; and frequently got into messy emotional entanglements with humans and human affairs. The majority of gods reflected the agricultural cycle, which in turn echoed human life spans—planting, harvest, birth, death, and so forth. Gods also were territorial and portable. They could travel with their chosen people, adopt new places, and oversee special, sacred locations. Crossing the borders of one god's demesne into another meant one had to be wary of unfamiliar rules and rituals expected by the local gods.

Monotheism did away with the fluidity of polytheism, although the concept of a singular deity was not new in the Ancient Near East. What was new was the melding of all aspects of previous gods into one, in combination with the belief that the one God was universal and timeless. The new, one God had no creation story, human characteristics, gender, or face; manifesting fully formed out of the unknowable darkness. Within the Abrahamic religions, belief in one, universal God required a new set of criteria for establishing rules that gave the community a clear identity and structure, as well as set them apart from polytheistic neighbors.

This isolation also reinforced the universality of monotheism. Unlike polytheism, the concept of a singular deity implied a singular, unmoving, immanent truth that could not be carried from place to place. Among the rules were prohibitions on rendering God artistically, and attempts to do so were made taboo. Without a face or image, the one God was distanced from humanity and human flaws, moving ritual practices from being centered on physical, symbolic representatives of deity to abstraction. Making images of God taboo also meant they could not be harmed symbolically, as was often the case with local gods, whose images could be captured, ransomed, or destroyed in warfare.[4]

In those regions where monotheism took hold, religious and physical borders became less permeable. Yet, when a community shifted to a monotheistic religion, the rich history of cultural practices, folktales and folk wisdom, and aspects of ritual were never fully eradicated or replaced. As monotheism slowly, and often violently, overcame extant polytheisms, traditions of coexistence and exchange among different groups, which had been on the cultural landscape for millennia, continued uneasily under the new, dominant religions.

One of the biggest issues shared among the Abrahamic religions was the perception and use of music, especially how to channel and contain music and ritual sound within a monotheistic worldview. Much like a good marketing campaign today, promoters of the new religions needed a means to entice new converts. Most importantly, monotheism had to be clearly differentiated from polytheism. To do so, religious leaders needed a means to encourage people to cast off unsavory practices (usually related to sensuous pleasures) and incorporate others acceptable to the new religion. Decisions also had to be made about what to ignore, as too many changes could serve to push possible converts away or be impossible to eradicate.

Retaining certain sacred and agricultural celebrations was one compromise; however, rules about food, drink, dress, and ritual purity needed to be set to ensure such celebrations did not edge into forms associated with polytheistic ritual. Because music, song, and sound were so deeply embedded in Ancient Near Eastern and Mediterranean cultures, how to control and regulate physical and metaphysical sounds properly in an Abrahamic framework was necessarily tied to bodily purity and forms of devotion.

Music and Musicians in the Ancient Near East and Mediterranean World

In nearly every culture in the Ancient Near East, instruments, song forms, and performance practices were associated with and allocated according to gender, social status, and the worship of specific gods.[5] Literary descriptions of performances emphasize the importance of memory and improvisation in performance and provide insight into the possible curricula of ancient music schools. In addition to modes, rhythm, declamation, singing, and playing instruments, theories of music and performance styles were taught by rote, with limited notation used by novices to aid in memory retrieval.[6]

Vocal music was considered the highest form of musical expression by many Ancient Near Eastern societies. Singers would sing solo and in chorus, with emphasis on improvisation in the lead voice. Groups of singers would also chant, hold a drone, and expand into intervals.[7] Although there may have been some purely instrumental music, instrumental accompaniment was used primarily to embellish and augment the text. Women sang and composed laments, while men sang and composed epic poetry, panegyrics, and odes.[8] With the exception of major religious and court events, when accompaniment was used for recitation (epics, poetry) and song, the use of instruments would be minimal. Music and recitation were also used for work to mark the passage of time, set a rhythm for work crews, and provide a means to stave off boredom in repetitious tasks, such as weaving and spinning.[9]

Music was most associated with entertainment and available at all levels of the social order. From ancient Sumer to the end of the Roman Empire, musicians, poets, storytellers, and dancers performed in courts and taverns alike. Images of musicians, music performance, musical instruments, and dancing are found throughout the Ancient Near East, including ancient Egypt and Persia, from 3000 BCE to well into the nineteenth century. At the top of the professional hierarchy were carefully trained elite musicians who were usually dedicated to a specific function. For example, in Sumer, the rank of chief musician was achieved only through a long, arduous apprenticeship.[10] These specialists performed rituals, laments, and recitation, and their status allowed them to play instruments reserved for special occasions.

Many of the professional ranks of musicians in the Ancient Near East were composed of women. Depictions of women playing flutes, small drums, and tambourines, some dated from 3000 BCE and earlier, can be found all over the Ancient Near East in temple paintings, statuary, stele, and archeological sites.[11] In addition, there are textual references to women playing these types of instruments, often differentiated from the instruments played by men. The small tambourine, called *duff* in modern Arabic and *tof* in Hebrew, is one of the oldest known Near Eastern instruments and is still viewed primarily as a women's instrument in areas of the modern Middle East today.[12]

The documentary evidence suggests that women musicians were generally employed for entertainment and select rituals and were available for hire as professional mourners. They were often enslaved, particularly women purchased by brothels and taverns, and residents of the women's quarters. Enslaved women were also sexually available, and several cultures associated enslaved women musicians with sexuality.[13] Yet, although a number of high-level musicians and women court entertainers were enslaved, the movement of musicians throughout the Ancient Near East indicates that some were free. In Sumer and ancient Egypt, noble and free women performed as priestesses.[14]

Women musicians played reeds, flutes, the aulos or double flute, large and small harps, and different types of small, handheld drums in Egypt and Sumer. These instruments were further differentiated according to social class and ritual. In ancient Egypt, for example, only noblewomen played the sistrum, whereas lyres, harps, and wind instruments—primarily double reeds and flutes—were played by court musicians.[15] The lute, which possibly originated in Persia, developed later and eventually was associated with women entertainers in pre-Islamic Arabia.[16] Such associations of instruments with gender, in conjunction with the status of their players, are referenced symbolically in literature and poetry. For example, there are several Sumerian proverbs related to the *gala* as well as Egyptian images linking women musicians and sex, often graphically.[17]

In addition to women, men, cross-gendered, and gender-fluid individuals held important musical roles in several cultures. Male musicians played in the temple, in groups, and for courtly entertainment; however, their expectations for performance and modes of advancement followed a different path. Male musicians could be enslaved, but many were not. Disability was also a separate social category and was interpreted in some cultures as being touched by and in service to the gods. For example, based on depictions of musicians in select dynasties, it seems that ancient Egyptians prized blind, male musicians.[18] Greek myth also refers to disabled musicians and punishment by the gods due to their musical prowess.[19]

Those individuals who performed as women and incorporated aspects of male and female gender performance were in a separate gender category. For example, Sumerian *gala* possibly were cross-gendered men, eunuchs, or intersex, but their gender performance was tied more to their musicianship. *Gala* dressed and wore their hair in women's styles, sang lamentations, and could hold the position of chief musician.[20] Some priests dedicated to certain goddesses were also eunuchs and castrated as children or adolescents by temple functionaries who might themselves be eunuchs. In some cases, they castrated themselves. This was the case in the cult of Cybele, where men who wished to dedicate themselves to the goddess would emulate her first priest by castrating themselves in a religious frenzy, literally sacrificing their sexuality to their deity.[21] In India, the *hijra* were, and are, individuals who might be biologically male but are spiritually male + female.[22]

Since there is little extant notation of ancient music beyond a few scraps, reconstructing how music was composed and performed is purely speculative.[23] What indications exist regarding performance practices suggest that the majority of popular and entertainment music was improvised based on a system of melodic and rhythmic modes. Details as to what pitches were used in melodic modes, rhythms, playing techniques, and singing styles are limited. Yet, iconographic sources and literary documents, in addition to contemporary practice, provide some possible scenarios.[24]

Based on how musicians are grouped in temple paintings from Egypt and Sumer, they apparently played in both large and small ensembles for courtly and ritual gatherings.[25] The gods were also patrons of music and art, in addition to being musicians themselves, and musicians likewise appear in myth and sacred texts.[26] The instruments that are depicted give clues to the event, with the dress and placement of the musicians suggesting their status. Inclusion of musicians in such images and their prominence implied the significance of the event, regardless of whether the musicians were symbolic gestures.[27] Even if relegated to the margins, musicians and dancers informed the viewer of the scale of the event, and possibly duration and types of music used, and demonstrated the wealth and power of the patron.

In those cultures where women played an important role in temple functions and as musicians, such as dynastic Egypt, Ur III Sumer, and Babylon, depictions of groups of women musicians are common. As we do not have the cultural keys to decode these images, one cannot read too much into them; however, similar scenes are found in other cultures of the region with groupings of related instruments.[28] This consistency suggests a shared symbolic meaning and use of specific instruments for particular events, in part due to trade, conquest, and other forms of cultural mixing among the civilizations of the Ancient Near East.[29] From the same evidence, it appears that single instrumentalists were used in intimate settings, probably to accompany poetry and ritual dance. That a majority of the singular musicians in these groups tend to be women suggests women provided much of the music content in social entertainments.

Larger ensembles likely were used for courtly events and community rituals that included dance or some type of scripted movement. This custom was practical, as a larger group can be heard over a large crowd, but it also could lend more prestige to the event as a display of power and wealth. The number of musicians could have ritual significance as well.[30] Based on the fragments of ancient notation and commentary about such performances, these ensembles would have performed in unison, possibly with minimal vertical harmony at the octave, fourth or fifth.[31]

Depending on the event, mood of the audience, and topic of poetry, songs and poems may have been sung, chanted, or declaimed, and possibly a combination of all three.[32] Recitation and chant could have fallen under the heading of singing, but other vocalizations, such as ululations, wails, moans, and beating the chest, might have been included as well, depending on genre and context.[33] Musicians improvised using combinations of modes, in addition to committing established or "composed" melodies to memory.[34]

According to extant records, melodic modes could have three to four notes and a variety of available transpositions.[35] Rhythm was likely modal and capable of transposition as well. Poetic meter may have informed or served as the basis for rhythmic modes, and there also may have been room for free rhythm.[36] Since there are no rhythmic indications to accompany notation fragments for the most ancient samples of Ancient Near Eastern music, it is unclear how rhythms were realized in performance. The only rhythmic indications for song fragments lie in the rhythm and syllabication of the texts themselves.[37]

The horizontal, improvised nature of melodic mode and rhythm in Ancient Near Eastern cultures is one reason why large ensembles played in unison with a limited range of intervallic options. For large-scale social and ritual events, there may also have been a repertoire of set melodies and modal formulas. The ensemble would play as one, with rhythm providing contrast underneath, leaving room for vocal or solo instrumental improvisation. This type of ensemble lends a certain amount of flexibility to a group in that everyone could hear the melody and respond according to their role in the ritual, chant, song, or movement, and the musicians could vary or improvise as needed.[38]

The spaces in which performances took place likely influenced performance practices as well. The extant ruins of ancient palaces, temples, and public spaces where performances and entertainments took place cover a broad footprint, even today. Given the commonly used building materials in the ancient world—stone, clay bricks, and wood—certain performance practices might have been a practical as well as aesthetic choice. Buildings in Mesopotamia, Egypt, and Arabia were constructed out of a combination of mud and stone, with various woods and reeds used to reinforce roofs and provide decoration. Temples and palaces had wall hangings, rugs, mats, and possibly used reeds on the floor, which, in conjunction with the people in the room, would diminish, but not eliminate, reverberation.

In conjunction with the materials, courts and centers of religious worship are crowded places, so musicians competed with a substantial amount of collateral noise. Large ensembles playing in unison made sense given the modal and improvisatory nature of the musical system, but were also practical. The documentary and iconographic record suggests that indoor (which could also take place in enclosed areas outside, as in a garden) solo performances were frequently accompanied by plucked or struck instruments (harps, lyres, small drums) while outdoor events used louder instruments, such as large drums, reeds, and brass. Brass instruments, drums, and woodwinds would be easily heard, but stringed instruments would need to be reinforced by more strings or the addition of woodwinds and percussion to be heard in such a live space.[39] Stringed instruments are softer and easily lost in large, resonant areas. However, a solo performer could make use of the reverberation, especially if playing a plucked or struck instrument.

Music in Arabia and Transition to the Early Islamicate States

As with the rest of the Ancient Near East, women musicians were prevalent in pre-Islamic Arabia. They appear in poetry and *ḥadīth*, with occasional distinctions made between their being free and those designated as singing slave women.[40] Women musicians were associated predominately with taverns and public houses, suggesting the majority were likely enslaved. The "first" singing slave women are referred to in several sources as belonging to ᶜAbdullāh ibn Juʼdān of the legendary tribe of ᶜĀd. They are called "the Two Crickets" or "Grasshoppers," known for their beauty, virtuosity on the lute, and singing ability.[41] Although this is a small body of evidence, these references indicate that prior to Islam, women musicians were kept as entertainers for private use, attached to public houses (they appear in poetic depictions of taverns and drinking parties), and hired for social events, such as weddings and festivals.[42]

Pre-Islamic Arabian societies also had a class of cross-gendered musician-entertainers. Referred to as *mukhannathūn* (the bent or effeminate ones; sing. *mukhannath*), they existed on the margins of society. Although they are visible as entertainers in the early Islamicate courts, little is known about their role prior to Islam. Based on what can be gleaned from references in the *ḥadīth* and Islamic historical sources, it is possible *mukhannathūn* acted as marriage brokers and entertainers for women's gatherings.[43] They dressed in feminine robes, were clean-shaven, and painted their hands with henna.[44] In addition to their feminine appearance, they also played "women's" instruments and provided entertainment similar to that of women, meaning light entertainment songs laced with bawdy humor and themes of passionate love. Although *mukhannathūn* were unmasculine, they were still male. This perception enabled them to maintain their status as men, if subordinate because of their gender performance and assumptions about their sexuality.

Despite their gender-bending and assumed orientation toward same-sex relationships, *mukhannathūn* cannot be categorized according to contemporary gender labels. The term *mukhannathūn* derives from the root خنث (*khanith*), which means to be soft, languid, and effeminate. It also means to be bent or doubled as in a reed or the flap of a wineskin.[45] With the addition of the participle *mim*, the word implies not a lack of manhood per se, but sexual passivity.[46] One form of this root, خنثى (*khuntā*), also means hermaphrodite, or what we now call intersex.[47] Some *mukhannathūn* may have been intersex, given the statistical possibilities for human differences we know to exist today, but to translate this term as such is limiting and inaccurate.

To call an artist a *mukhannath* included a reference to their physical bodies and sexual preferences, but was related more to their gender performance as entertainers. Therefore, the label can be understood to indicate a lack or diminishment of masculinity, but also queerness. Queerness refers to the odd and eccentric, or "bent," in the medieval Islamicate context. Applying "queer" to *mukhannathūn* wobbles on the boundary of anachronism, yet the references in the literature to an artist being "bent" in more ways than one suggest the connection is not too far-fetched. Therefore, because this category of musicians is not easily labeled transgender, nor can they all be considered effeminate, they are best framed as unmasculine, cross-gendered, and, possibly, queer.

Although music was an acceptable masculine profession in other cultures, such as those of the Ancient Near East and Mediterranean, this was not the case in pre-Islamic Arabia. Free men were discouraged socially from making their living as musicians. Informal music making was fine, but men who chose music were viewed with suspicion and ran the risk of social ostracism. Some scholars of medieval Islamicate history have theorized that the *mukhannathūn* represented a transition from female-dominated to male-dominated musical performance in the Islamicate courts but others assert that was not the case.[48] The existence of cross-gendered priests and entertainers in other cultures around the Ancient Near East and Asia supports the fact that, like singing slave women, *mukhannathūn* were a continuation of older practices.

Ambivalence about music and gender is hinted at in pre-Islamic sources, but derived primarily from early Islamicate perceptions of pre-Islamic nomadic cultures. Based on observations by outsiders and early Islamicate historians, pre-Islamic Arabic-speaking peoples were nomadic warriors who were highly regarded for their ability to compose heroic poetry and odes. As in other oral cultures, the ability to recite and compose poetry equated to power. Poetry was (and is) not alive unless spoken and heard. In an oral tradition, words can be shifted and changed, but the fundamental meaning of myth and stories cannot. Words themselves were powerful, especially those in religious texts, yet they were only as potent as the speaker's ability to perform them. More so than meaning, their power lay in the emotional effect of cadence, stress, and intonation.

Pre-Islamic poets functioned as tribal memory, interpreters of events, and politicians. To be accepted as a poet bestowed status on an individual, and a respected poet would in turn confer status to the tribe. Poetry was considered so important, in fact, there are accounts of battles being fought and won between tribes through poets, allowing the groups to resolve conflict without bloodshed and loss of honor. Recitation and improvisation were keyed to memory, and the ability to create a new image out of familiar symbols was a valued skill. Like musicians, poets had to have the repertoire of established epics and stories committed to memory and know the meters, structures, and formulas for improvising new poems.[49] Their audience would be familiar with the oral canon, forms, and conventions of performance and appreciate nuances in the recitation of a familiar or newly improvised poem.

Nomadic life was also a powerful metaphor. It consisted of a structured progression of stop and go, with the border between the two represented by the path taken from one place to another. The starting and stopping of everyday life was a metaphor for human mortality. This sense of movement is reflected in pre-Islamic poetry through meter, language, and the progression and placement of specific metaphors. An audience would listen for new uses for known symbols, such as the camel, wind, and water, which were metaphors for sedentary life versus movement. Poetry and music could be performed on the move—singing on camelback, for example—but most often was associated with stopping.[50]

An example of this distinction between stationary (i.e., written) words and the fluidity of the spoken word can be felt in the following extract from the *Muᶜallaqa* of Labīd (*c.* 560–661 CE, c 41. *H*):

The torrents have exposed the ruins,
As if they were
Writings whose texts pens have
Inscribed anew
Or like the tattooer sprinkling lampblack
Again and yet again

> Over hands on which tattoos appear.
> Then I stopped and questioned them,
> But how do we question
> Mute Immortals whose speech is indistinct?[51]

Another ancient reference to the generative power of spoken words is:

> In the beginning God created the heavens and the earth. The earth was a vast waste, darkness covered the deep, and the spirit of God hovered on the surface of the water. God said, "Let there be light," and there was light.[52]

This association of life and the word was restated as a new tradition grew out of the older, to describe the nature of the new religion's prophet:

> In the beginning the Word already was. The Word was in God's presence, and what God was, the Word was.[53]

Early Islamicate historians stated that many texts from the pre-Islamic period were lost. Given the transmission of poetry, folktales, songs, and epics via a hybrid of written and oral texts, how much was actually written down is not easily determined. Some texts were not written for several centuries, and some were copied and embedded within so many other texts, their original author was obscured. As in the Western medieval tradition, cultures in the Ancient Near East and Mediterranean placed more value on oral rather than written transmission of texts. Being able to read and write was primarily the province of the merchant and aristocratic classes. Yet, memory was not only flexible and portable, it was considered a more reliable means of storage and used to verify written documents. Even when literacy suffused the Islamicate world, the ability to memorize, recite, and improvise based on texts stored in memory remained a vital skill.[54]

Along with being carried in memory, documents from Arabia in the five hundred years prior to Islam were written and carved on whatever was at hand—rocks, bone, palm leaves, papyri—the variability of which resulted in few surviving except in fragments. The Qur'an similarly was recorded on a variety of materials, including leaves and papyrus. Along with a few extant texts and poetic fragments, there is a small trove of graffiti in various scripts from around Arabia. Some of these fragments were the casual notation of a bored shepherd, while others offered prayers to local gods or pointed to significant events and battles.[55]

Among the extant fragments are a collection of odes (sing. *qaṣīda*; pl. *qaṣa'īd*) called the *Muᶜallaqāt*, or Hanged Poems.[56] According to legend, they hung in the *kaᶜba* in Mecca and the Prophet Muḥammad allowed them to remain because of their cultural importance. Because they originated as oral literature, the written form in which these poems were preserved is a snapshot of that moment in time. As a result, although the *Muʿallaqāt* are attributed to specific poets and contexts, their origin cannot be ascertained with any certainty. This ambiguity has inspired studies into their relative "authenticity"; however, such questions are only relevant to a culture that relies on what is written.

A romantic vision of pre-Islamic nomads developed as early Islamicate society became sedentary and infused with people from around the world. Islamic historians would later insist that poetry, not music, was of highest importance in pre-Islamic Arabic cultures, with some going so far as to assert that the nomadic Arabs did not have music. The evidence, however, suggests otherwise. Accounts of performances are scattered throughout the writings of outsiders and early Islamic histories and are embedded in the poetry itself. The *Muʿallaqāt* contain references to music and singing women, and there are anecdotes about music, performances, and instruments in the *ḥadīth*. Other than these scraps, however, virtually nothing is known about pre-Islamic Arabian musical culture, let alone what sound genres included music.[57] It is evident there was song, yet both recitation and song might take the form of chant, employ instrumental accompaniment, and contain melodic inflections. Whether or not these were categorized as music is also unclear. The few references to music in the sources suggest performance of a poem or cycle of epics during the pre-Islamic era took place along a musical continuum, incorporating melodic cantillation, instrumental accompaniment, percussion, sighs, exclamations, and gestures.

Based on music treatises of the ninth and tenth centuries, the earliest genres of song grew from the camel traders (*ḥudā'*), who timed their songs to the pacing of the camel itself. Laments (*nasb*) are among the oldest song forms; as noted earlier, laments and epics appear in ancient Sumer and throughout other Near Eastern cultures. Some scholars have suggested that the development of odes (*qaṣīda*) and strophic song forms (such as *muwashshaḥ*) were derived from these earlier forms.[58]

Accompaniment of song and poetry was in service to the text, improvised, and minimal. Before the lute came into regular use, pre-Islamic musicians played a variety of small stringed instruments, such as lap harps, zithers, and other types of plucked instruments of one to three strings, as well as flutes and hand percussion.[59] When more than one instrument was used, the ensemble would likely play in unison and take turns supporting the performer. Purely instrumental music was likely heard in taverns, played by singing women and shepherds, typically on species of flute (*nāy* and possibly a type of aulos).

Impromptu music making for gatherings and weddings used simple, portable, and hardy instruments, particularly small drums, tambourines with and without metal jingles, heavy sticks, and clapping. Delicate instruments, such as plucked strings and large, specialized drums, were not easily transported and were difficult to maintain within a nomadic lifestyle. Such instruments were generally found in urban centers.

Music, poetry, and consumption of wine were a part of most occasions, including feasts for special occasions and business transactions.[60] Based on pre-Islamic poems and fragments, poetry recited at these events would include odes, panegyrics, and newly composed poems. The form and structure of the *qaṣīda* reflects this practice, in that the final section is often devoted to images of the group at rest and praise for the tribe or strength of a particular leader/warrior.[61]

Another common image is the singing woman with her lute.[62] Her allure is intrinsic to her representation as a musician, further emphasized by metaphors of the wine she serves (often in a tavern) and sensual pleasure. She appears in the praise section of the *Muᶜallaqa* of Labīd:

> I paid a dear price for a wine in an aged and darkened wineskin,
> Or in a pitch-lined jug, ladled into cups,
> Its seal broken.
> And many a morning draught of a pure wine
> And a slave girl with a lute,
> Plucking with her thumb on its taut strings.[63]

Likewise in a poem by Aᶜshā:

> 'Twas as though the harp waked the lute's responsive note,
> When the loose-robed chantress touched it, singing shrill
> With a quavering throat.
> Here and there, among the party, damsels fair superbly
> Glide: each her long white skirt lets trail and swings a
> Wineskin at her side.[64]

And again in the *Muᶜallaqa* of Ṭarafah:

> A singing-girl comes to us in her striped gown or her saffron robe,
> wide the opening of her collar,
> delicate her skin to my companions' fingers,
> tender her nakedness.
> When we say 'let us hear from you,' she advances to us,
> chanting fluently,
> her glance languid, in effortless song.[65]

As it was likely that enslaved women sang, served wine, and provided sexual services to patrons, these representations could be read literally. However, the image of the singing woman and wine were part of the repertoire of poetic gestures and expected to appear to represent stopping, feasting, and repose. How these images were worked into the narrative arc of the poem depended on the poet. The singing woman could be a sensual reminder of pleasure or a warning against dissipation and sometimes both.

Although the majority of extant pre-Islamic poetry is by men, there are fragments attributed to women.[66] A number of pre-Islamic women poets were noted for their skill during their time and in later histories. Similar to practices in ancient Mesopotamia, women in pre-Islamic Arabian society were expected to mourn the dead, so much of the extant poetry by women are laments for the loss of a loved one (brother, father, or husband) or tribal hero.[67] These poets do not simply express grief; they remind the tribe of the need for revenge and consequences to tribal honor if appropriate revenge is not taken.[68] Names could be euphemisms and nicknames, yet referenced in such a way as to leave no doubt about their identity. Although authorship of some poems by women is not always clear, references to family members, tribes, and enemies provide clues about the identity of the poet.[69]

Like the odes and epics of men, women's poetry was oral and formulaic, with a rich vocabulary of images and emphasis on improvisation. Based on references by men about women's poetry, laments were performed publically. Professional mourners provided emotional release by performing their grief, keening for hours over the body and grave. One of the *ḥadīth* used to argue against music states that the Prophet banned public mourning and lamentation due to the loud, excessive wailing of the women.[70] In addition to lamentation, the sources indicate women were hired to sing at festive events, religious celebrations, and funerals. There are also references to other musicians going to see public performances of elegies by women.[71]

Lamentation poetry could exhort the family and kin to revenge:

> You waste your time on the bottle and pleasuring about, oblivious to what goes on.
> You're not aware treacherous Jassās and ᶜAmr had killed Kulaib and dared to do the uncommitable.
> To hell with Jassās and ᶜAmr who lunged your brother with scorpioned spears.
> Get up and pull the spears out of your brother's corpse, for no one defies us and gets away with it.[72]

Or sorrow:

> The rising and setting of the sun keep turning on my memory of Sakhr's death.
> And only the host of mourners crying for their brothers saves me from myself.[73]

There are also references to women accompanying men into battle. They would surround the field and shout at the warriors, providing a constant reminder that if the men lost, all the women would be enslaved by the victor. Although later Islamic histories paint the status of women prior to Islam as being degraded, this visibility and their importance as poets suggest otherwise. That is not to say that women were socially and legally equal to men; rather, their significance as poets and accepted participation in social functions meant women held several important roles in pre-Islamic nomadic cultures.

As the early Islamicate states developed in the late seventh and early eighth centuries, pre-Islamic uses of musicians, instruments, and performance practices continued with little change. Patronage of women musicians in taverns and brothels likewise continued without pause. What did change was the uses to which music was put and how music and listening were perceived as a result. Social and diplomatic uses of music were an important part of other court cultures and were likewise adopted by the caliphate. Starting with the Umayyads, musico-poetic entertainments and a growing corps of musicians attached to the caliph and upper classes became intrinsic to court culture.

At the same time, foreign scholars, texts, slaves, and musical technologies were circulating throughout the urban centers of the Islamicate states. New styles of singing, songs, and melodic and rhythmic modes were adopted and incorporated into existing music practices. Song and instrumental potential were expanded, yet the porous boundaries between recitation of poetry and song made it difficult to determine what constituted song-music from poetry. Often the distinction was based on intent of the performer, audience perception, and type of accompaniment, if any.[74] The lavish entertainments of the court, complete with wine, singing slave women, and song, quickly became contested territory, giving rise to discussions about the place of music—and musical sounding—in Islam.

2

Musicianship and Performance

After the tumultuous reign of the four *Rashīdūn*, or Rightly Guided caliphs, following the death of the Prophet Muḥammed, the Umayyads (661–750 CE) held power for nearly one hundred years. They established their capital in Damascus along with an ambitious program of conquest and building projects.[1] Despite the fact that a number of courtly pastimes enjoyed by other cultures were not allowed within Islam, the Umayyads recognized that having a strong, wealthy court culture was essential to being a world power. Music and having a corps of elite musicians dedicated to court entertainments were intrinsic to other court cultures and the Umayyads followed suit. Beginning in the early eighth century, women musicians, free and unfree, and *mukhannathūn* were performing at the Umayyad court.

In order to consolidate power and solidify their right to rule the growing Islamicate states, the Umayyads needed to establish a royal family dynasty. They attempted to keep their bloodline "Arab" by allowing only the children by legal wives of the caliph, all of whom were purportedly of pure blood, to inherit the throne. That, however, did not prohibit Umayyad caliphs from keeping enslaved concubines in the women's quarters. The Qur'an states that concubines are sexually available in the same way as wives and specifies that they receive fair treatment.[2] Yet, although concubines did not share the same legal and social status as wives, they were not simply for sexual pleasure and bearing heirs. Concubines sometimes originated as war captives and slaves but were often educated in music and poetry.

In addition to being effective displays of wealth and status, concubines were useful political and diplomatic tools. They were employed as diplomatic gifts, given by foreign powers and wealthy courtiers to the caliph in hopes of winning favor. Concubines who were especially desirable were also purchased outright. By the time of the Abbasids (750–1258 CE), which I discuss in more detail in this chapter, the women's quarters grew to include thousands of residents. Within what later came to be called the *ḥarīm*, elite women musicians were among the most visible members of the court, ranked to a hierarchy of musical concubines to courtesan.

The growth of the Islamicate states during the ninth and tenth centuries added to the physical and intellectual wealth of the already cosmopolitan urban centers of Damascus, Jerusalem, and Alexandria. After the Abbasids usurped power in 750 CE, they shifted the capital to the city of Baghdad, built in 762 CE. Baghdad became the intellectual center of the Islamicate states and remained so until Abbasid power weakened in the tenth century. The continual flow of artisans, scholars, religious leaders, slaves, and books among urban centers provided additional vernaculars for written and oral expression, manifesting in a flowering of literature, art, and music.[3]

Although the intellectual riches of other cultures provided fresh tools for Islamic scholars, with these tools came customs and ideologies either expressly forbidden by the Qur'an or, more worrying, open to interpretation. Shaping the legacy of the Prophet and Islam into a comprehensive and sustainable way of life for a diverse population was a serious challenge. The religion was still developing in the seventh and eighth centuries and enmeshed with the ancient traditions of Arabia and the other Abrahamic religions. To establish some semblance of order on the rapid growth of Islam and the regions under its influence, a vast compendium of authority slowly accrued for every possible opinion on every possible subject. By the ninth century, the major canonical schools of Islamic law were forming, using philosophical and exegetical tools from Judaism, Greece, Persia, and India to develop a complex theological system of verification and analysis.

As the Islamicate states continued their expansion in the ninth, tenth, and eleventh centuries, so did the expansion of musical practices. Higher standards for performance and musicianship developed in the ninth and tenth centuries as demand for technical prowess increased for elite musicians. Court entertainments became more lavish, and mimicry by the upper and middling classes established a robust music patronate.

The saturation of music throughout the social orders, however, inspired concerns as early as the eighth century. Musical salons at court, private residences, taverns, and travel stops were often lengthy, wine-soaked affairs. Use of music by some Ṣūfi orders involved instruments and melodic sounding, both of which could be heard in major mosques such as the Umayyad Mosque in Damascus and the Al-Aqsa Mosque in Jerusalem. Similarly, poetic recitation remained theoretically distinct from song, but in practice, the distinction could be negligible. This porous boundary meant that suspiciously song-like performances of the *adhān* and melodic recitation of the Qur'an—sometimes set to known tunes—were sneaking into devotional practices. It is little wonder that concerns about music intensified.

How to fit music into an Islamic framework was a difficult proposition for medieval scholars. There is no music in communal Islamic worship, which was a deliberate choice by the Prophet and his followers. One reason for this choice is that they sought to distance themselves from pre-Islamic and foreign polytheistic religious practices; another was to differentiate Islam from the other monotheistic traditions. Reading the Qur'an beautifully was an adaptation of Jewish cantillation, although it remained firmly defined as recitation, not singing. The recitation of sacred poetry, or *nashīd*s, was also a form of cantillation, yet similarly framed as recitation and not song. We will later encounter rising concerns about *taghbīr*, a form of sacred recitation-singing, and stern condemnation of its use.

As a result, the line between religious and nonreligious sound genres was wobbly and often subjective, and scholars argued continually over where the line should be drawn. What was more troubling was that musical sounding was sensual and evoked emotions in the hearer. It was agreed that some emotions, such as love for God, were to be pursued, but hearing not only could distract a listener from prayer, it could be a catalyst for illicit behavior.

Within Islam, the laws related to purity, community, and practice give the individual a means to create the sacred on a daily basis, shifting the burden of preserving sanctity away from places and objects (with the exception of the Qur'an itself) onto the believer. For the uneducated and simple masses that is a heavy burden, and it fell to the religious leadership to provide guidance on proper living. What developed was a detailed framework for what constituted religious and nonreligious to help the individual decide what actions were proper. A helpful way to understand where music fit into this calculation is to place it within actions and practices cataloged according to what was allowable or forbidden, and degrees of reward and punishment associated with each.

What was allowable and what was not existed along a spectrum ranging from *ḥarām*—absolutely forbidden—to *halāl*—acceptable. Some acts were unequivocally *ḥarām*, such as drinking alcohol and sex outside of marriage. Yet, even these acts were parsed and debated, such as what degree of fermentation might be allowed before a beverage became unallowable and what substances constituted an intoxicant. When eighth- and ninth-century authors such as Ibn al-Washsha, al-Jāḥiẓ, and Ibn Abi'l Dūnya invoked the dangers of passion as *ḥarām*, they were entering the discussion about what constituted illicit sex (and with whom) and bodily excess. Injunctions to avoid excess were not intrinsic to Islam; the ancient Greeks were similarly concerned with overindulgence and passion, and Islamicate philosophers ruminated on Greek metaphysics. Like the Greeks, some Islamicate scholars considered excess a form of hubris, and passion was believed to have serious medical implications.[4]

Even after the science of Islamic law was developed, there were enough loopholes in interpretation that one could either justify certain acts or change their definition to shift them into a stronger moral footing. In order to address the proliferation of music and growing conversation about the role of music in Islam, the boundaries of what constituted music were adjusted, rendering some sound genres ambiguous. This kind of semantic shuffling took place several times. For example, when criticism about melodic recitation and certain forms of instrumental music arose, definitions for "music" shifted. Select melodic forms were strictly relegated to the category of "not music," such as melodic soundings of the *adhān* and religious recitation, while others were unavoidably music and relegated to entertainment.[5] Such restructuring still placed instrumental music within the realm of diversion, but an element of propriety could be achieved by keeping the subject matter and tone of the musical gathering high. No one was fooled, of course, and the differentiation between music for entertainment and music for religious purpose in the medieval Islamicate world remained murky and contested.

The social codes for performers and patrons were a sticky hodge-podge of laws, customs, and outside influences, involving everything from courtly etiquette, treatment of enslaved women singers, and how best to write a love letter. Treatises were written to articulate and explain these rules. Having the ability to write well, with the proper forms of address, use of euphemisms, and polite language, was a requirement for the educated man. Those texts intended for the refined courtier and those aspiring to be, such as Ibn al-Washsha's *Book of Brocade*, provided a tutorial on etiquette, dress, comportment, and behavior. They also provided guidelines for the pious on how to deal with different situations regarding potentially harmful influences. Although the upper classes established the majority of such rules, the middling classes adopted them as well. At root, the main purposes for written and unwritten social rules were to preserve individual piety and attempt to regulate consumption of alcohol and illicit sex. Music was considered a primary culprit in leading to both, whether in seemingly harmless events such as singing at a wedding or the drinking parties enjoyed by the upper classes. These attempts to regulate music—and accompanying illicit behavior—were rarely successful.

Starting in the eighth century, scholars began to examine the history of music in pre-Islamic cultures in order to construct effective arguments about listening. Regardless of their standpoint, their intent was to make an historical connection to contemporary practices. Drawing on texts from Greece, Rome, India, and Persia, scholars examined the past and interpreted what pre-Islamic authorities said about music practices through the lens of religious law. Others used the same body of work to construct music history through a combination of law, philosophy, science, and the dialectic process. Not surprisingly, some scholars used this history to justify the use of music, others used alternative readings to repudiate and erase it from Islamicate history altogether.[6]

More so than law, practice, and history, however, what became fundamental to discussions about music was the relationship between speaker-performer and listener, and emphasis on listening as a creative and interactive act. The rich corpus of symbolic imagery and poetic language from pre-Islamic cultures supplied a basic vocabulary, although as the conversation became more nuanced, there was a need for new vocabulary. Discourse related to music, even tangentially, examined and reconstructed familiar terms for music and listening, slowly developing terminology and a compendium of symbols associated with music performance.

Such flexibility in language and interpretation was related to the hybridization of written and oral culture taking place from the eighth to tenth centuries. Although the written word was vital to Islamicate knowledge, that did not mean memory and orality were on the wane. Much like the pre-Islamic poets, early Islamicate scholars viewed writing as secondary to and as a companion to memorization. In addition to memorizing the Qur'an, an educated person was expected to memorize entire books. Doing so was not only a means to internalize the information and pass it on to others, but provided a foundation for new works.[7]

The continuum of memory, to written word, back to memory was fundamental to the process of learning, as it not only provided students with the technical knowledge they needed but the exercise incorporated the text into their physical being. Mary Carruthers elegantly defined this continuum as follows:

> A work is not truly read until one has made it a part of oneself—that process constitutes a necessary stage of its "textualization." Merely running one's eyes over the written pages is not reading at all, for the writing must be transferred

into memory, from graphemes on parchment or papyrus or paper to images written in one's brain by emotion and sense.[8]

Because of the emphasis on memory, the book was beautiful and durable. Paper was introduced into the Islamicate world in the late eighth century, leading to a boom in writing and bookselling. The earliest extant book fragments date from the tenth to eleventh century.[9] Books were works of art, embellished with calligraphy, decoration, gilding, and illumination.[10] Those books intended for regular use might be plainer, but were made with quality ink and materials, copied with a clear hand, and bound with care. As a result, there is a body of iconography available for the study of instruments and performance practices, with most of the earliest surviving images dating from the eleventh century.[11]

People seeking to learn acquired knowledge through listening (*samāt*), making copies of books and lectures held in libraries, and purchasing from booksellers. Lectures were held at schools (*madrasas*) and mosques and were frequently open to the public; even slaves, women, and the poor could listen. In public spaces and private schools, scholarly treatises, lectures, bureaucratic letters, poetry, stories, and folktales were read aloud and memorized.[12]

Islamic scholars regularly copied entire books or lengthy extracts of other texts into their own work, preserving many texts that would otherwise have been lost.[13] The integration of extensive quotations and entire texts into new works was how an author established their credibility. Using religious texts and exegesis as a model, an author's authority was manufactured by layering texts and previous authorities. This process held true for extemporaneous performances of poetry and music. The citation of authorities and ancillary commentary provides additional insight into why or how an imbedded text was selected for quotation, as well as the intellectual lineage of the author.[14]

Exaggeration and hyperbole were also expected forms of literary expression, and satire could add yet another facet. During the eighth and ninth centuries, new genres and stylistic conventions developed that allowed room for individual expression and opinion. These included the *risāla*, *maqāma*, and *maqāla*, whose structures did not require extensive quotation or *isnād* to validate the author's position.[15] Similar to other medieval literary traditions, details such as the location of a familiar place, name of a popular writer, or local type of food were generally understood to the degree that authors did not feel it necessary to mention them, unless in reference to another text or collection of texts to aid in memory retrieval. Likewise, the majority of new texts were generated through patronage. As a result, few, if any, literary endeavors (including libraries, collections, and treatises) lacked baggage. Regardless of veracity, the wealth of available commentary and injection of new genres shed light on acceptable and unacceptable social practices from the ninth well into the fourteenth century.[16]

Because of the importance of books, the accumulation of a library, no matter the size, reflected the life of a person. Therefore, a personal library was not merely a collection of books; it reflected the history and legacy of the scholar themselves. Upon their retirement or death, the disposition of a scholar's library was a serious matter. Libraries were gifted to a protégé or school, and there are a number of stories about the fate of libraries. In one famous story, al-Jāḥiẓ is said to have died when his library collapsed on him.[17]

The building blocks of music—rhythmic modes, melodic modes, instrumental tutelage, and melody—were also transmitted orally and held in the memory and supplemented and commented upon through written philosophical and practical tutors.[18] The intersections among oral-aural learning, memory, and written texts is more fluid in musical cultures based on improvisation. Frustratingly, it makes firm identification of authorship nearly impossible, because improvisation is inherently collaborative. And Islamicate musicians collaborated constantly. Hearing poetry and song in performance settings was an important dimension for composition as well as educating novices. Musicians composed in groups, borrowed and shared melodic and textual fragments, and blatantly plagiarized one another. The sources are full of references to collaboration and accusations of theft, often with hastily convened juries of patrons or the caliph to help adjudicate the claims of authorship.

Referencing Musicians

Labels and nicknames for musicians could refer to their origin, status, gender, appearance, personality, and even preferred instruments. Broadly speaking, singers were *mughanniyat/ūn* (pl.), meaning those who sang (*ghināʾ*), or *mūsīkār* (generally to refer to men only), those who make music. Later, the feminine *mughanniyat* referred primarily to musical concubines. Singing slave women were *qiyān* and *jawārī*, labels indicating their relative status within the musician hierarchy.[19] Even as musical culture was becoming firmly entrenched in the medieval Islamicate courts, associations of music with women continued to prohibit men socially from becoming musicians. Such prohibitions did not stop men from working as entertainers, however. During the eighth and ninth centuries, some Arab men risked (and met) social displeasure to study music, but the majority of *mukhannathūn* and male-identified musicians were *mawālī* (sing. *mawlā*) or formerly enslaved, and of foreign extraction.[20]

Mukhannathūn remained debased for their gender performance and reputation as party animals, although they flourished in some urban centers, notably Medina, which had a vibrant musical culture.[21] Much like the castrati of seventeenth- and eighteenth-century Europe, not all *mukhannathūn* were hopeless Lotharios, and some were married with children. There were, however, several who flirted and enticed lovers of all genders openly. As a result, there were periodic exiles and purges of *mukhannathūn*, particularly when illicit (and politically unwise) liaisons were discovered.[22] Male musicians and *mukhannathūn* did have their champions, and several of their key patrons were elite women musicians.[23] Throughout the early Islamicate era, *mukhannathūn* continued to be visible as performers; however, eventually, male-identified musicians displaced them, relegating them to theatrical entertainments.[24]

Establishing Musicianship

Definitions for musicianship vary cross-culturally and historically. Who is considered a musician, as opposed to being musical, is grounded in a combination of biology and socially constructed expectations. These include both an inherent biologic component to explain talent and aptitude, as well as sociocultural markers such as genre choices, legal status, and gender performance. In addition, there is often a distinction between technical mastery of an instrument and comprehensive mastery of the discipline, both of which are established through collaboration and mediation with the patronate.

To legitimize music and musicianship, one needs a social and theoretical structure enfolding the components of the body of music itself: that is, mode, rhythm, genre, and instrumentation. This framework serves to shape audience expectations and performance contexts, recognize and standardize the skills of performers, and establish a hierarchy of listening from elite to amateur. These structures in turn lead to a musical canon, theories of music, and methodology for assessing what should or should not be included. Legitimization of music in the medieval Islamicate world also meant that what happened to a listener under the influence of music needed to be monitored and regulated.[25] Demands from an increasingly sophisticated patronate soon required clear standards for mastery.

What constituted musicianship and separated an amateur from a professional in the medieval Islamicate world? Talented amateurs might be true masters of their craft, but a professional was visible and made a living as a performer. Given that a substantial portion of musicians in the medieval Islamicate courts were unfree, their visibility, and therefore their mantle of professionalism, was controlled by the patronate and individual owners. Similar to today, comprehensive mastery included a thorough understanding of music theory and history of the repertoire in conjunction with the ability to interpret familiar and new music flawlessly. Memory was essential, and the musician needed to memorize all the possible combinations of mode and rhythm, as well as set songs, well-known ancient and contemporary poems, and the formulaic tools required for new compositions. Having technical facility could be enough to earn a skilled instrumentalist or singer a place in the musician corps and patronage, but often such professionals were perceived as technicians, not musicians.[26]

Comprehensive mastery further required the ability to meet established conventions for extramusical performances, such as stage presence, nonverbal communication with audience-patrons, and having an intriguing persona. These extramusical components are intangible and subjective, but essentially can be boiled down to social virtuosity or simply, charisma. Therefore, the combination of social, technical, and intellectual mastery was key to gaining access to patronage, and the patronate in turn affirmed achievement of the highest standards of musicianship.

Standards for musicianship and differentiation between elite music performance and genres from non-elite levels of society developed during the eighth and ninth centuries with the establishment of music schools. Music schools were not necessarily brick-and-mortar institutions but were associated with specific teachers. Most musicians learned by apprenticing themselves to a teacher, and free and unfree musicians were identified as members of their teacher's tradition and lineage.

At first, the establishment of music schools was predominately to train singing slave women. The famous musician Ibrāhīm al-Mawṣilī (742–804 CE/125–88 *H*), father of Isḥāq al-Mawṣilī and friend of the Abbasid caliph Hārūn al-Rashīd (763 or 768–809 CE/148–193 *H*), was among the first to found a music school and handpicked prospective singers (i.e., enslaved women) for training. According to al-Iṣbahānī, al-Mawṣilī started his school partially as a means to standardize music training, but he also made a tidy profit from selling the women he trained.[27] Music schools also loosened social strictures around men working as musicians, enabling them to study music and earn patronage.[28]

Although performance and listening were important features of courtly life, music, as in the West, was divided into two aspects: the contemplation and study of music as a science and those who considered it a performing art. A person who played music was not a musician. Rather, a musician was a theorist, philosopher, and scientist.[29] Not all Islamicate music theorists held this view, however, and practical musicianship came to be valued as much as theoretical scholarship in some circles.[30] Yet, being an instrumentalist remained beneath that of a musician-singer-poet, so no matter how appreciated for their skill, performing musicians held lower status.[31] Separating musicianship into theory and performance added more layers to what constituted performance and further served to distance, and potentially sanitize, music for those on the fence as to its legal status.

Despite being considered technicians, performing musicians were troubling. Patrons valued their ability to elicit heightened emotion in the hearer, yet that skill also made musicians dangerous. A listener could become dependent on—perhaps even addicted to—the emotional high of listening. More concerning was that a listener might transfer that need to the figure of the musician themselves. This transference was at the heart of rising discomfort around music. Music could distract the hearer from proper contemplation of God, but musicians themselves—men, women, and cross-gendered entertainers—were often sexual, ambiguously gendered objects of desire. Their instruments, performance practices, and songs were integral to that image, taking on symbolic importance in the literature. I address these entanglements in the next section.

Instruments, Song, Music

Along with the evocation of the senses associated with listening and pleasure, medieval Islamicate terminology for music and musicians included several layers of meaning. Terms that have a certain resonance within the context of conversations about *samāᶜ* could have a different meaning in philosophical and theoretical texts. Within *adab* and poetry, the same terms could be used referentially or symbolically to evoke a literary soundscape, moral judgment, naughty story, erotic euphemism, and social commentary. Sometimes, all of the above.

During the seventh and early eighth centuries, terms such as *malāhī, maᶜāzif, ālat al-lahw, samāᶜ*, *ṣawt*, and *ālat al-ṭarab* were generic references for music, song, and musical instruments. These terms appear in a variety of literary genres, not just those concerned with music. Although the conversation about music in Islam remained under the surface until the ninth century, earlier treatises indicate that the question of listening was already under discussion. As discussed earlier, the earliest extant medieval treatises on music are the *Mukhtār al-lahw wa'l malāhī* (Book of Play and Musical Instruments) by Ibn Khurdādhbih (*c.* 820–912 CE/203–99 *H*) and the *Kitāb al-malāhī* (Book of Musical Instruments) by Ibn Salama (*c.* 830 CE/214 *H*), both of which note concerns about music and singing.[32]

Not only do these treatises foreshadow later discussions, they share a similar pattern and tone. Both treatises provide a brief history of music, including the origins of a variety of drums, stringed instruments, and woodwinds, many of which are theorized to have foreign or mythic roots. In addition, they comment on prevailing opinions about whether singing was morally acceptable, hinting that instrumental music was even more suspicious. Last, both treatises point to the allure of listening. Although Ibn Khurdādhbih and Ibn Salama are careful not to give their opinions about music in general, they don't see harm in song and listening. Their commentary suggests that the assignment of layered meanings to musical concepts was under discussion before the ninth century and possibly carried over from other cultures and pre-Islamic music traditions.

This jumble of possibility allowed scholars to nuance, interpret, and manipulate increasingly thick musical concepts to suit their purposes. Except in texts primarily devoted to practical musicianship, music terminology remained fluid, later deepening to associate music and song with intimacy and emotion. For example, on one level, *maʿāzif* refers to sounds from nature, on another, to abstain, be adverse.[33] It appears most often as a reference to stringed instruments and later came to mean instruments specific to singing women, particularly plucked strings such as the lute and *ṭunbūr*.

Likewise, *malāhī* included formal and informal music making. It was used to refer to the concept of music overall and the act of listening to music. *Malāhī* derives from the root *lahw*, meaning diversion and play, as does *ālat al-lahw*. *Ālat al-lahw* can be translated as "diverting things" and "instruments that divert."[34] With the addition of the mim, *lahw* is transformed into a passive construction; thus, *malāhī* literally means "that which diverts" or more simply "diverting." Concubines, sexual amusements, and games could be—and were—included in this category, stretching the metaphor of play to include music, song, listening, and sex.

The invocation of play and pleasure aroused by *lahw* is shared in part by the concept of *ṭarab*. *Ṭarab* is difficult to translate, as there is no adequate equivalent in English. The verb *ṭariba* means to achieve or come to ecstasy, but it is more akin to metaphysical transcendence.[35] Although it can have an earthier undertone, *ṭarab* describes the emotional and spiritual transportation of hearing. There might be a physical reaction as well, such as crying out in joy, weeping, fainting, and even rending garments. Such acts signified the depth of emotion. *Ālat al-ṭarab* means, variously, that which causes ecstasy or delight, diverts, and to sing. As such, it was another general referent for music, though it could also be expanded to encompass the body of the musician. Another reference to a musician is *muṭrib*.[36] Because poetic and musical performances were intended to inspire the audience to experience *ṭarab*, those musicians who provoked that moment of transcendence were valuable and dangerous.[37] We see similar complications in the use of music in Ṣūfi *samāᶜ*.

Along with *malāhī*, the terms *ṣawt*, *ghināʾ*, and *samāᶜ* were general references to music, particularly song and song-like genres. *Ṣawt* most often indicated accompanied and solo song, although the difference between lyric composed with and for music and accompanied poetry was not distinct. Both were *ṣawt* if there was a melodic component to performance. *Ṣawt* also referred to extemporaneous composition and improvisation, as well as set, composed songs. For example, in the *Aghānī*, al-Iṣbahānī indicates song texts by using the heading *ṣawt*. When known, he includes performances notes such as rhythmic and melodic mode used. The most common term for song was *ghināʾ*, which specifically means to sing, and therefore singers were *mughanniyat/ūn*.

The primary difference between *ṣawt* and *ghināʾ* was that *ṣawt* could mean music in general and accompanied song. *Ghināʾ* could be accompanied or solo song, but also was an action. To sing, be a singer, render a song, and perform *ṣawt* fit under the umbrella of *ghināʾ*. Last, *samāᶜ* referred to listening to melodic sounding, religious and nonreligious, which could include song and instrumental performance. It included nonmusical listening as well, and treatises make a distinction between listening to music, *samāᶜ al-malāhī*, and other forms of listening. It was (and still is) a devotional practice in some Ṣūfi orders, which I discuss in more detail later.

According to eighth- and ninth-century music treatises and broader literary discussion, there was considerable variety in the instruments available for both professional and amateur music making. As in the medieval West, "loud" and "soft" instruments had specific purposes and were not used together often.[38] Loud instruments included reeds, horns, large drums, different sizes of bells, clappers, and cymbals. Not surprisingly, they were generally used outdoors and for special occasions. Most of the instruments used in formal and informal music making were "soft" and employed in intimate settings, such as taverns, private houses, and court entertainments. They could also be used outside for private entertainments and salons. Soft instruments included plucked strings, flutes, and smaller percussion instruments such as hand drums and tambourines.

Instrumental ensembles were not regularly used, as performance practice of songs emphasized minimal accompaniment, if any. When used, instrumental ensembles were small and might use a mix of strings, percussion, and woodwind, though only one of each. When large groups were used, which was rare, the musicians generally played in unison. For example, al-Iṣbahānī relates a story of a musical event in which two thousand singing women played in unison. Even in such grand events, accompaniment of songs remained simple, using a single drum, wand, or plucked instrument.[39]

As in the Ancient Near East, unison performances with large groups of musicians were a practical solution, though with some variation. While caliphal palaces were primarily constructed out of stone, marble, and wood, with huge rooms and ceilings, intimate settings, such as private quarters, were softened with rugs, cloth, pillows, and drapery. The intimacy of the setting would favor plucked instruments and have less reverberation. In addition, other musicians could be hidden or secluded in the room, awaiting their turn, enjoying the show, and being held in reserve for later. Outdoor performances could be similarly intimate by holding them in gardens and groves and using gazebos to house musicians and party. When large groups are mentioned, they are clearly special occasions, as in the visit of a foreign dignitary, celebration, or particularly epic party. Therefore, unison playing was both a necessary aural solution for a large space (receiving rooms of the caliphal palace) and a display of wealth (the visual impact of two thousand singing women).

Court musicians specialized in plucked strings, small drums, and an assortment of woodwinds. The most common plucked stringed instruments were members of the lute family, or *ᶜūd* (oud),[40] and included the *ṭunbūr* (also transliterated as *ṭambūr/pandore*)[41] and *barbaṭ*,[42] lyres, such as the *kīthāra* and *lūra*, and the harp, or *ṣanj*.[43] The name *ᶜūd* derives from materials used for its construction and musical properties; among the meanings derived from the root are wand, reed, or aloe wood, from which the *ᶜūd* was made.[44] Early lutes had many variations but generally had a pear-shaped, elongated body and flat neck and were played with a plectrum made of wood, bone, or quills. Medieval Islamicate music historians asserted these instruments had Persian or Greek origins, and were introduced to the Arabs later, which may well have been the case. Early lutes had four single-course strings and al-Kindī notes that a fifth course was added later. Ibn Salama states that the lute also had frets, and other treatises discussed use of fretted and unfretted lutes.[45]

According to Ibn Salama and Ibn Khurdādhbih, the origin of the lute had several possibilities, including being adopted from Persia to a more colorful history of its invention by the ancient prophet Lamech (also transliterated as Lamek).[46] Of the variations on the story of Lamech, Ibn Salama's is delightfully vivid. According to the authority of Hishām ibn al-Kalbī, he relates that Lamech had an extraordinary number of wives and concubines, but only three children—two girls and one boy. When his son died, Lamech hung himself in grief. As his flesh dried, he fashioned an instrument from wood representing the bones and sinews of his own leg. The neck represented his leg bone, the peg box his foot and the pegs his toes. He played only lamentations and eventually went blind.[47] Following the family tradition, one of his daughters was responsible for the invention of stringed instruments and drums.

The *barbaṭ* and *ṭunbūr* were long-necked lutes that originated in Persia, although the terms *ᶜūd* and *barbaṭ* are frequently used interchangeably to reference the same instrument. In addition to the *barbaṭ* possibly having a longer, thinner neck, the main difference between the two was their construction. The *barbaṭ* purportedly was made of one piece of wood and the *ᶜūd* made of two.[48] *Ṭunbūr* was a generic reference for the *pandore* and long-necked instruments in general.[49] It was fretted and could have two to four strings.[50] According to Ibn Salama, *pandore*s were invented by Lot's children and played by beardless youths (*ghilmān*). This connection implied they had a sensual, homoerotic connotation.[51] *Ghilmān*, like Greek ephebes, were desirable for their gender ambiguity and sexual appeal.[52] Although *ᶜūd*, *barbaṭ*, and *ṭunbūr* appear in some texts as generic references to the lute family, based on how they are discussed in conversations about music it is evident they were different instruments.

The *kīthāra*, or *kītāra*, was a type of lyre likely adapted from the Greeks.[53] It had twelve strings, in contrast to the *lūra* with five.[54] Ibn Salama also mentions an instrument called the *kinnāra*, which he ascribes to being a type of lute, but Farmer suggests it was a form of cithara or lyre, possibly related to the Hebrew *kinnor*.[55] Ibn Salama also refers to singing girls as *karina*, calling the lute a *kirān*, and mentions other instruments called *muwattar* and *mizhar*.[56] Of bowed strings, Ibn Khurdādhbih mentions the *rabāb*, which is a small bowed instrument and possible ancestor of the Western violin.

The most common percussion instruments were small wood drums, *ṭabl* (pl. *ṭabūl*), and tambourines, *duff* (pl. *dufūf*).[57] There were several species of *dufūf*, including rectangular and round shapes, with or without snares, plates, or rings. Both men and women played *dufūf*, and there was possibly a particular type of *duff* played by *mukhannathūn* called the *duff murabba*ᶜ.[58] In addition to *ṭabl* and *duff*, there were cymbals, *sonaj*, and bells, *jarasu*.[59] Ibn Salama makes the case that music existed in Arabia prior to Islam and points to the use of certain instruments as proof. Among these are the *duff*, which he suggests were an Arab invention. His evidence is use of *duff* by the "first" singing women, the Two Grasshoppers, whose story appears in several other sources.[60]

Ṭabūl could be hourglass-shaped with two membranes or vase-shaped with one; the latter are also referred to as *darabukka*. Ibn Salama refers to the *kabar* and *kūba*, as well as an instrument called the *dirridj*, which he likens to a *ṭunbūr*, though again Farmer suggests it is a *darabukka*.[61] The *kūba* was possibly associated with *mukhannathūn*, although how it might be differentiated from other percussion instruments is unclear.[62] The family of *ṭabl* included larger drums called *naqqāra* or *dabdāb/dabbada* (pl. *dabādib*), which were used in war and are the origin of the Western kettledrum (naker).[63] In his notes on Ibn Salama's text, Farmer comments that certain drums were forbidden, like the *ṭabl al-mukhannath*. As the name implies, it was purportedly a type of drum played by *mukhannathūn*, although, yet again, what made it different is unclear. As with the *duff murabba*ᶜ, it was likely the shape or another aspect of its construction that distinguished it from other instruments in conjunction with association with *mukhannathūn*.

Another percussive instrument that was used to accompany song and recitation was the *qaḍib*, or wand.[64] The *qaḍib* was thumped on the ground and used in entertainments and Ṣūfi *dhikr*. It did not require a great deal of expertise to play other than steady rhythm, although there are accounts of musicians, such as Ṭuways, who used it expertly to support a song. The *qaḍib* also appears to have been used primarily by men, although women could have used it when no other percussion was handy. There were likely local variations, such as different sized wands, simple branches, and some adorned with rings. Al-Ṭabarī's treatise on *samā*ᶜ mentions something called a *sayeer*, which in one possible translation of the term means a thong fashioned out of leather or fabric strung with rings and affixed to a branch.[65]

Woodwinds included the flute (*nāy*),[66] reeds (*mizmār*), shepherd's pipes (*kawal*), the *quṣaba*,[67] and *zammāra*.[68] The *zammāra* was a small type of bagpipe.[69] Other woodwinds included the *surnāy* or *surnā* (or *zurnā*), which was a smaller reed pipe, and the *shabbāba*, a type of flute.[70] *Nāy* and *mizmār* appear to reference woodwinds generically in the treatises, though the *mizmār* was understood to be a reed instrument. *Mizmār* included single and double pipes, or aulos. According to Ibn Khurdādhbih, the *nāy* was invented by the Persians and derived from an instrument called the *diyānāy*.[71] Ibn Salama suggested that with the exception of certain "whistling flutes," woodwind instruments were invented by the Jews and modeled on the throat of King David.[72] He also includes a list of other woodwinds, several of which are obscure or uncertain, such as *ᶜirān*,[73] *mishtaq*, *yarāᶜ* (also listed by Ibn Khurdādhbih), *hanbaqa*, and *zanbaq*.[74]

Brass instruments such as trumpets/horns were called *būq* and generally used outside for military processions. They were made out of horn or metal, and some could be fitted with a reed. The *urghan* was apparently another stringed instrument, whereas the *urghanūn* was an artificial woodwind or organ. Ibn Khurdādhbih notes that the organ came from the Byzantines.[75] The organ never gained the status of virtuosic instrument in the way the *ᶜūd* and other court instruments did; rather, it was more a mechanical curiosity.[76]

The verb most commonly used to describe the act of playing an instrument is *ḍaraba*, to strike. *Ḍaraba* could also carry several meanings, as in the musician striking the heart of the hearer or, more ominously, implying emotional manipulation.[77] Lutes were (and are) played with a plectrum made of bone, wood, or quill, and playing technique includes striking the string from above and below. Bowed instruments are similarly struck with the bow.[78] Drums—*duff* and *ṭabl*—are struck with the hand and fingers. The sources may indicate what kind of instrument is being struck, such as "*ḍaraba al-ᶜūd*" and "*ḍaraba al-duff*," but *ḍaraba* could be used without reference to a specific instrument. When *ḍaraba* is used alone, it generally was shorthand for instruments being played, especially lutes.

For woodwinds, the most common verb for play was *zammāra*, which meant to blow on a *mizmār* and extended to other woodwinds.[79] Occasionally, *laᶜiba* was used, however often with a secondary meaning. *Laᶜiba* refers to playing games, such as chess and backgammon, two common and questionable diversions that appear with music in texts concerned with *samāᶜ*. When used to reference playing instruments, *laᶜiba* reinforces the frivolity of play and places the instrument (or musician, as will be seen later) into the category of useless diversion. In some cases, *laᶜiba* is paired with diversion (*lahw*) to delineate the connection between play and music.[80] When verbs for play—*ḍaraba*, *zammāra*—are accompanied with *samāᶜ* and *ṣawt*, the implication is that the song-musical sounding was performed with instrumental accompaniment. Because *samāᶜ* could also relate to other kinds of listening, it is often paired with *ṣawt* to specify listening to song or music: *samāᶜ al-ṣawt*. Likewise, *malāhī* could imply other forms of diversion and so would be qualified as playing (or diverting oneself) with musical instruments.

Performance Practices

Medieval Islamicate cultures heard and read a wide array of sound genres that do not blend comfortably into Western categories. The medieval construction of sound and ritual were rooted in set word forms—poetry, holy text—which were carried by improvised music-sound. As such, song cannot be divorced from poetry. Within the sources, the demarcation between song and poetry was rarely firm. Like poetry, song and instrumental performances were improvised, and older tunes could be applied to new poems. Since song could be chanted or declaimed and poetry accompanied, the distinction between the two was often vague and dependent on the whim of the performer and patron.[81] The philosopher al-Fārābī defined melody as inhabiting two purposes, in that it could be a series of notes composed for the purpose of being pleasing, or a series of notes wedded to poetry. In his definition, both were music and sound genres.[82]

Despite descriptions of performances in the sources, we are missing extramusical soundings and other elements of performance. Gesture, sighs, and body movements are integral to spoken performance and song; without those visual cues, we can only speculate on what was heard. That being said, there were boundaries, often unspoken, and the subjectivity of those boundaries is seen in the literature. Such boundaries were not set in stone, but provided a snapshot of events and perspectives which in turn reflect the prevailing aesthetics of the time.[83]

Musico-poetic gatherings were called *majlis* (pl. *majālis*) and held by rulers, courtiers, and members of the wealthier classes.[84] Much like a Greek symposium, *majālis* could be bibulous and included entertainers with a variety of talents (music, sex, serving wine, all of the above). The format of a *majlis* was highly ritualized and organized, with standing conventions of behavior, appearance, and subject matter.[85] Despite the rigors of the format, *majālis* could be painstakingly planned or completely spontaneous. They could also last for several days. Although there were rules for etiquette, things could certainly get out of hand. There are many stories scattered across the sources detailing epic drinking parties and impromptu musical events, rife with social disasters, questionable assignations, battles of wit, and impressively crude poetry.

Majālis were mostly held by men; however, women did organize them, including former singing slave women and free women with wealth. Formerly enslaved singing women held salons in their houses, while free women of the merchant and upper classes held them in the women's quarters. Like the European salons of the eighteenth century, which were also predominately held by women, *majālis* organized by women patrons could include wine, music, romantic assignations, and gift exchanges.[86] Women who held *majālis* often patronized the same poets and artists, inviting men and *mukhannathūn* into spaces that men did not ordinarily have access to.

A *majlis* could be formal, summoned by a caliph or high-ranking official, or an informal gathering of peers. The formal *majlis* could be indoor or outdoor, though outdoor performances were focused on musical entertainment and by nature more informal. Vocal and instrumental improvisation was expected at both in- and outdoor events, though the mood and scenery of the *majlis* dictated how the performance would unfold. Sometimes a *majlis* would have a theme, such as pre-Islamic poetry, or devoted to the work of a specific poet and school of poetry.

When an event took place outdoors, the singers could choose their songs and subjects, while at an indoor event, songs were requested by the patrons and could be repeated many times. Outdoor events were also less likely to have improvisation, as they were less serious and scripted.[87] The visual element of a *majlis* was also important, and a great amount of effort and expense went into setting the right environment.[88] In one famous story, the color scheme was yellow, which was carried to such an extreme that saffron was sprinkled into the water.[89]

Based on depictions of musical gatherings in the literature, whether a performance was musical or poetic might be initially established by the patron or theme of the event, but often shifted depending on the mood of the audience. The only obvious distinction made between song and recitation was instrumental support, and accounts of song performances often include a reference to a musician taking up an instrument.[90] The difference related more to the intent behind the composition. Intent included whether the text was organized around rhythmic or melodic accompaniment and how interrelated music was with the text. Starting in the tenth into the eleventh centuries, music and song began to disentangle from poetic recitation and gain traction as an art in its own right. The upside was the development of instrumental music somewhat independent from vocal. On the other hand, instrumental music was "gradually becoming the best accompaniment to drinking."[91]

Current theories about the development of medieval Islamic modal systems suggest that they began in the ninth and tenth centuries. They likely derived from existing modal systems from Persia and Mesopotamia and were later influenced by Greek music theory.[92] By the tenth century, a complex system of intervallic relations and theories of improvisation was being codified.[93] There was possibly a form of notation by the tenth or eleventh century, although few examples remain.[94] As with early notation in the West, notation was likely a mnemonic device to aid in swift retrieval of composed melodies-poems.[95] Modes were associated with mood and affect, and a musician needed to know which mode was appropriate for use with what themes and poems.[96] This feat of memory is considerable, particularly when one considers that contemporary performance practice includes more than thirty individual melodic modes, over forty rhythmic modes, and infinite possibilities in combining the two.[97] Given the interchange of musical styles within the Islamicate states, the number of possible melodic and rhythmic modes available in the eighth, ninth, and tenth centuries was much higher.[98]

The ability to perform *murtajilan*, or extemporaneous solo, was the highest standard for a musician.[99] During a performance, singers played their own compositions and performed works of others at the request of patrons. The ability of a musician to accompany themselves, especially on the *ᶜūd*, was considered important to composition. Instrumental accompaniment of song was the next level of required skill, with pure instrumental music the third. Musicians gave solo instrumental performances; however, the primary role of instruments was to accompany song and poetic recitation. Instrumental music served mostly as preludes and postludes to a solo song performance.[100]

Beautiful vocal expression was the highest standard for any sounding performance, including sacred recitation and the *adhān*. What voices sounded like is hard to say, however. Women's voices are regularly described as high, sweet, and soft; however, there are plenty of references to men singing in high voice. Range was also important, as was the ability to embellish tastefully in such a way as to not obscure the text. Some singers had a limited range but knew how to exploit it to their advantage. Men, women, and *mukhannathūn* may have shared a sound palette and performance practices, yet their genres and topics varied. Singing women had the freedom to sing songs on bawdy topics, comment on their lovers, and even tease the host. Men might employ humor in their songs, but few could go as far as singing women without being impertinent.

Mukhannathūn incorporated aspects of each gender into their performance. They could be bold and coy like a singing woman and noble and reverent like a male singer.

Due to emphasis on improvisation and memory, the use of a broad sound palette and limited written notation mean that often the only performance practice indications we have are what rhythmic and melodic mode(s) were used. For example, al-Iṣbahānī frequently notes melodic and rhythmic modes, but these are essentially performance shorthand.

Hilary Kilpatrick comments:

> It is important to realise that the indications of rhythmic and melodic mode were not enough to enable a singer to perform a song. They are more informative than an expression such as "Minuet in G," which simply gives the rhythm and tonality of a piece of music, since they prescribe certain patterns of tone, accent and measure. But they cannot convey how the song sounds. In the absence of a widely used system of notation, as song could be transmitted only through performance. This means that when Abū l-Faraj mentions rhythmic and melodic information derived from a third/ninth century source, particularly a written one, that does not prove that he himself heard the song, or that it was still part of the repertoire. For when the melody was forgotten, the musical indications could still be preserved in writing or, perhaps with less probability, orally … And the standard information about song settings does not give any hint as to whether the transmission of the modes was accompanied by performance.[101]

Even when the patron established strict rules for performance, musicians had a certain amount of creative control based on their reputation. In order to step outside the boundaries of the event, however, all aspects of their performance—music, poetry, and presentation—needed to be virtuosic. If a musician's performance exceeded expectations, they could reap considerable monetary rewards and assurance of continued patronage. It was imperative a musician learned to read the room during a performance and adjust quickly if necessary. Those who skillfully adapted to the mood—and politics—of the audience reaped the most rewards, and there are numerous gossipy stories about singers failing spectacularly. Musicians who put on a lackluster or politically tone-deaf performance would, at best, be ridiculed and humiliated. At worst, they would be beaten, kicked out of the party, and lose favor. Testing the boundaries of a musician's knowledge was common, and there are many anecdotes about singers having their memory tested, being tricked, and sent away in shame when unable to perform a requested song.[102]

Although the majority of musicians were poets, they might lean more on one skill than the other. Some artists were primarily musicians, such as Maᶜbad (*d. c.* 743 CE /125 H) and Ibrāhīm al-Mawṣilī, while others were more notable (or portrayed as such) as poets. Singing women could be noted for their poetry but were always considered musicians. Therefore, references to those musicians who emphasized their musicianship imply the use of instruments and song. For those musicians who were equally known as poets, descriptions of their performances drift constantly along the hazy spectrum of song and poetry.

To compose poetry well required taste and clever uses of language, as well as knowledge of complex poetic meters and classical forms like the *qaṣīda*. Religious poetry focused on symbols of love and reverence for God and pious themes, while nonreligious poems and song could vary from the profound to the profane. Some poets specialized in bawdy and humorous poetry, but the rules of appropriateness, even when strained to limits, had to be observed.[103] In order to keep things on the up and up, as well as help audiences decode certain turns of speech, books of euphemisms were written that explained the meanings of certain terms or phrases. These were helpful to the writer of chaste love letters as well as the reader and writer of love poetry.[104]

Love songs were oriented toward abstraction and metaphor rather than directly naming an individual, but the setting in which they were performed nearly always gave the intended away. The stricture on naming women in poetry continued into the Islamicate era, although enslaved singing women were not afforded such protection. Since their names were often metaphoric or euphemistic, there was plenty of room for word play, especially double and triple entendres.

Despite the importance of music in the early Islamicate courts in the ninth and tenth centuries, musicians remained socially marginal figures. Their marginality revolved around a number of factors, including the (not without basis) association of music and sound with polytheistic ritual, femininity, drinking alcohol, and sensuality. Musicians, especially enslaved women musicians, were found everywhere, from court to brothel. In addition, music and varieties of sound expression could be heard everywhere. As melody and vocal embellishment began creeping even into recitation of the Qur'an, it became imperative to establish a distinction between song and recitation.

Of particular concern was the temptation posed by the body of the musician themselves and the moral foundation of the patrons who enthusiastically supported them.[105] Philosophical and legal discussions concerning music increasingly focused on the emotional effect of music and consequences of listening, drawing on religious law, medicine, and tradition to build their cases. Those who advocated for listening stressed the ability of music to heal, calm, and bring one closer to God. Others casually dismissed music as harmless entertainment, while ardent connoisseurs argued that music was a sign of refinement. Those who were against listening were similarly varied, with arguments ranging from grumpy assertions that enjoying music was stupid to breathless rants that listening would lead to apostasy and global destruction. In the midst of these discussions, musical culture, and the musicians who sustained it, expanded into every corner of the Islamicate states.

3

Patrons, Singing Women, *Mukhannathūn*, and Men

The story of music patronage in the medieval Islamicate world encircles women, *mukhannathūn*, and men but is especially vivid in the many stories about singing slave women. Among the more familiar figures in medieval Arabic literature, singing women appear in the background to major court events in history, tempt (or swindle) the unwary in treatises and memoirs, and stroll seductively through poetry. Although male musicians and *mukhannathūn* were subject to praise and vilification alike, singing slave women were the focus of the majority of discussions about listening to music. Singing women were not just passive actors, however. In addition to their influence on the development of Islamicate music and court culture, singing women were visible as poets, advisors, and what we now call "social influencers."

Like courtiers in other sophisticated cultures, musicians in the medieval Islamicate world, especially those at the elite levels, operated within an intricate web of patronage, obligation, and reward. The most powerful members of the patronate were the caliph and his courtiers, the latter of which included religious scholars, merchants, belletrists, judges, poets, and military leaders. The patronate shaped the social and financial framework for interactions with artists, but artists were also engaged in defining their relationships with patrons. In the case of singing slave women, their ability to manipulate others for gifts and status and to seek new patrons was part of their allure and therefore integral to their patronage.

Patrons operated within several layers of the economy. The exchange of gift and favors that comprised the patronage system moved such interactions from being a purely monetary one, as with the purchase of sex, to a relationship. Despite the pressure of competition and high standards of performance, patrons and musicians were brokering intimacy, regardless of their intentions and expected outcome.[1] Patronage also included religious uses for music and sound. To give a sense of how music patronage functioned and was perceived, I place it in two loosely defined categories of active and passive. These categories reflect degrees of listening, with active patrons being those who sought musical entertainments while passive listeners were bystanders. The active role entailed planning and summoning/hiring/inviting musicians for an event; for example, a caliph holding a *majlis* and patrons going to taverns and private houses to hear singing women perform. Active patronage could also include informal and impromptu music making, as well as purchase, trade, lending, and borrowing of musical slaves. An active listener might even pause to listen to music heard casually on the street.

Passive patronage included those patrons who might attend musical entertainments and reward musicians, but as members of the audience rather than as engaged participants. This category also included those who tried to avoid music. Passing a group of musicians in a public place, hearing music through a window or in the market, and seeing instruments for sale or in a house were among the ways someone—patron or not—could be exposed to music-sound genres. Both active and passive listening in nonreligious and religious circumstances are scrutinized in discussions about the legality of listening to music.

The wealthiest patrons, including the caliph and his courtiers, provided venues for private entertainments along with owning and employing elite musicians. Those patrons with enough wealth to own singing slave women could loan and barter her services to other patrons; however, there are plenty of stories of jealous patrons guarding their favorites from poachers. Music lovers who did not have the wealth to own singing women (or wanted to appear pious) could visit them at private houses, brothels, and taverns. Singing slave women could also be borrowed for an evening's entertainment, albeit with the expectation of a fee, gift, or favors extended to both owner and singing woman.[2]

A patron could dictate subject matter, poetic forms and genres, instrumentation, if any, codes of etiquette, physical appearance of the performance space, and the food served. In turn, entertainers, regardless of whether they were enslaved or free, expected compensation commensurate with their skill. Such compensation could be monetary, but patrons also were expected to give gifts and favors. Favors were currency, and the social network was built upon the exchange of favors and obligation in order to move up the social ladder. If a person was invited to an event, at minimum, they needed to provide costly gifts to the host. Guests likewise expected gifts, wine, and food and were obligated to reciprocate at some point in the future. As a result, even a mild gathering of friends could become quite expensive, and a status-seeker could quickly find themselves in financial trouble, if not complete ruin.

Hosting *majālis* was expected of men who held even minor bureaucratic office, even if it stretched their means. Due to the expectations for gifts, a host could potentially acquire enough gifts and favors so that if they did not turn a profit, he might at least break even. Those patrons and status-seekers who did not fulfill their obligations, however, could swiftly lose status or be labeled stingy. There are plenty of stories about freeloaders and drunks taking advantage of a host's generosity, as well as criticisms about lackluster offerings. Musicians could aid in a patron's success just as easily as their downfall. By shifting loyalties to a new patron, scorning or refusing their offer to perform, and spreading rumors about their poor taste, highly regarded musicians could undermine a patron's standing. Singing women were especially notorious for spurning patrons and lovers and even publically shifting their loyalties to a rival and casting hopeful young swains aside.[3]

The symbiotic relationship among performers and patrons was mediated by expectations for behavior on both sides, which either party could circumvent if they had enough power or wealth. Court and private entertainments frequently involved drinking large amounts of wine, which, in addition to being prohibited by religion, broke down emotional barriers and rendered listeners more vulnerable. Thus, the balance of power between musician and patron was constantly in flux, a fact that was not lost on many belletrists, including al-Iṣbahānī, al-Jāḥiẓ, and al-Mas'ūdī.

Men, women, and *mukhannathūn* competed for patronage in a number of ways and frequently in mixed company. The social and legal status of musicians remained important to how they came to be recognized by the patronate, and a well-placed patron could help smooth the way. For enslaved women musicians, patronage equated to ownership, which carried an expectation of sexual intimacy, yet also the potential for freedom if an enslaved woman bore a child to their owner. Because of the high costs of singing women, their patrons held financial power over the slave trade. They also had political power through the trade in favors, which in turn had an impact on musical training.

Musicians who wished to be regarded with respect managed their fame through a careful performance of propriety, piety, and refined behavior. Those associated with or aspiring to perform at court needed to be well schooled in court etiquette. Courtiers were expected to have good grooming and educated in courtly behavior, which included having good musical tastes.[4] Etiquette manuals were available detailing everything from how to enter the chamber of the caliph to writing a proper letter.[5] Minding the rules was important for all courtiers, but women musicians and *mukhannathūn* could periodically get away with outrageous behavior.[6] Men had to be more cautious. Regardless of their fame or status, a male musician had to be careful not to flaunt his profession in the way a singing woman or *mukhannath* could. Visible reference to their musicianship could diminish their overall status as well as their performance of masculinity, and positive descriptions of their performance were often framed within the context of their good behavior.

Yet, while having a respectful, moral persona was to be commended, it was by no means necessary for success. Even a musician who had a poor reputation could still win patronage, as there was always an audience for the outrageous and talented.[7] Those who gained fame through notoriety (or simply did not care) may have enhanced their questionable origins and behavior in order to provide a reason for their excesses. Patrons who dared to engage such musicians were either wealthy enough to ignore their critics or too important to be subject to open condemnation, such as the caliph and his boon companions. Other patrons who skirted the line were already on the edges of society, like former *qiyān*.

If there was a shift in political perspectives regarding music and listening that annoyed powerful music patrons, corrective action could be taken. One darkly funny yet likely apocryphal example of the system asserting itself is the case of the caliph al-Muhtadī (reigned 869–70 CE/255–6 *H*). According to an account by al-Mas'ūdī, al-Muhtadī was very pious and cracked down on music for entertainment, singing women, and wine, eventually banning all such entertainments from his court. In addition, he advocated a simple and abstemious life for himself and his courtiers and made everyone pray five times a day. His reign lasted for about eleven months, until the people got bored with his piety and killed him.[8]

Negotiating—and justifying—relationships among musician, patron, and performance expectations was slippery. Because of traditional gender roles within music performance, music was associated with sensuality and intimacy. Due to the visibility of singing women, music continued to be perceived as a feminine, private, and fundamentally domestic art. Those men who chose to pursue it as musicians and patrons ran the risk of being considered unmasculine and debased, despite their gender performance and other virtues.

Regardless of their standpoint on listening, scholars theorized about the transformative nature of sound and its ability to forge intimate connections between performer and audience. As mentioned earlier, medieval Islamicate audiences sought performances that brought them to a heightened emotional state (*ṭarab*), and those musicians who invoked this reaction in their patron reaped the highest rewards.[9] This ecstatic state was differentiated by the means and purpose for getting there. *Ṭarab* appears in the sources to indicate the state of emotional vulnerability generally for nonreligious uses of music, such as music in the court. *Wajd* is a form of spiritual-emotional engagement to refer to this state in Ṣūfism. It is the ecstasy one reaches when connecting closely with God, induced through *samāᶜ* and *dhikr*.[10] Unfortunately, emotional intimacy and transformative power of listening could turn to obsession and addiction just as easily as transcendence.

This peril was heightened when listening was combined with physical beauty. An audience was subjected to a barrage on their senses as music penetrated the subconscious through the act of listening, while the beauty of the singer stimulated the heart and emotions. Singing women and preadolescent boys commonly appear in poetry as lovely objects, with vivid details extolling their charms, aesthetic virtues, and pitfalls.[11] For the unwary aesthete, innocent appreciation of beauty could become obsession for the body and company of the singer, leading to lust, drink, and apostasy.[12]

The perception that musicians were dangerous and listening was an infectious agent relates to the third problem with music patronage: it was transactional. In practice, musicians functioned within three levels of intimacy and exchange: (1) purchase of the song, (2) purchase of the performance, and (3) purchase of the performer. Intimacy was a problem because religious laws forbade adultery and illicit sex, and these transactions were complicated further by the gender of the parties involved. As the primary source for all three levels of exchange, it is no surprise singing women were singled out by patrons and detractors alike.

Singing Slave Women: Elite Courtesans and Musical Concubines

According to the documentary record, singing slave women were valuable commodities and their trade was incredibly lucrative. As a result, only the very wealthy could afford to own one. Not all singing women were created equal, however. The generic, Arabic term for a female slave and concubine was *jāriya* (pl. *jawārī*), which translates as "runner."[13] This term indicated a woman's role as a concubine and a slave in Arabic sources, though there are other Arabic words that specifically mean concubine.[14] The highest ranks of women musicians were the *qiyān*, and they could wield more power than legal wives and administrators.[15] Although *qiyān* and *jawārī* are used interchangeably in the sources to discuss women musicians, to call a woman a *qayna* indicated elite musicianship and status. *Qiyān* could also refer to free women, whereas *jawārī* were always enslaved.

When the term *qiyān* appears, it is to distinguish between singing women and other categories of female slaves, though all enslaved musicians could be referred to as *jawārī*. For example, al-Mas'ūdī makes a distinction between slaves and *qiyān* in the Abbasid history section of the *Murūj al-Dhahab*, as does al-Iṣbahānī in the *Aghānī*. Though the latter refers interchangeably to singing slave women as *qiyān* and *jawārī*, his descriptions of their performances and patronage demonstrate that there were different classes of singing women. This distinction is also seen in the writings of al-Jāḥiẓ, who in one satirical essay calls women musicians *jawārī*, while specifically focusing on *qiyān* in the *Risālat al-Qiyan*.[16] Therefore, the word *qiyān* is more in line with the ambiguity of the meaning of the Chinese *ji* and the Japanese geisha in that it implies status and technical skill as well as a function.[17] Simply put, not all musical concubines were *qiyān*, and not all *qiyān* were concubines.

In trying to untangle these distinctions, the problem becomes how best to translate these terms. The English language has only three categories to classify women whose profession includes sex and intimacy: prostitute, concubine, and courtesan. These terms contain moral and social implications; therefore, it is essential to choose a translation that does not imbue the role of singing women with implied judgment. Given the lifestyle, training, social reaction to, and patronage of the singing slave women, the closest label for them is courtesan.

Courtesans are frequently classified merely as upscale prostitutes, with marginal attention paid to their artistic abilities and training.[18] That connection is understandable as the word "courtesan" derives from the feminine of "courtier" or "woman of the court" in French, and means "prostitute" in Italian.[19] The profession of a prostitute involves sex, with an emphasis on monetary payment for services rendered. In contrast, courtesans trafficked in intimacy and could be paid for sex, but that was only one aspect of their role, nor was it always the most important. The roles could blur, as some courtesans made most of their living from sex while some prostitutes also were artists, but it is the mode of transaction and social expectations that mark the distinction between the two.

Definition of what constitutes a courtesan is not clear-cut and takes many forms cross-culturally, but there are some general similarities. Essentially, a courtesan is a female companion, with varying degrees of musical skill, literacy, and education, whose clientele were men from the aristocratic classes and those aspiring to upward mobility. A courtesan could be a musician, poet, social companion, and entertainer, often chosen and trained specifically for that purpose. They could be free and unfree, came from all levels of the social order, and some were neither young nor beautiful. Courtesans dealt in intimacy, not just sex, and their education in the arts was what drew their patrons.

High-level courtesans were members of the court as entertainers and mistresses to the powerful, with their most distinctive trait being independence. Although courtesans were dependent on the largesse of a wealthy patron or enslaved, they had freedom of movement and access to men's social circles that most married women did not. Courtesans performed at court, at public entertainments, by invitation of the ruler or member of the nobility, and in her own home. Most courtesans were based in urban environments, though some had a residence—or a patron—in the countryside. They appear when cultures begin to shift from a tribal or feudal structure to a society where social mobility is becoming available to the middle classes and the "marriage system separates love and sexual passion from the institution of matrimony."[20]

This last distinction is key. In those cultures where wives are given legal and social status in exchange for domestic labor and expectations of heirs, the emotional component of intimacy is outsourced. From antiquity well into the modern era, marriage was primarily a legal institution, solemnized by religion to ensure fidelity (at least of the wife), and matches were prearranged. Spouses may come to love one another, but they lived in different social worlds. Sex between husband and wife was to be for procreation only; pleasure was to be found elsewhere. Men might never see their wife naked, and certain sex acts were only performed by prostitutes and courtesans. Therefore, courtesans fulfilled the need for conversation, sexual exploration, and loving companionship wives were not expected—or allowed—to fulfill. In many cultures (but not all), there was no equivalent outlet for women, as their domestic duties and children were expected to meet their emotional needs.

With the exception of courtesan-like women devoted to sacred places, the music and poetry of courtesans focused on themes of profane love.[21] In addition, courtesans often had specific instruments associated with their art, and these instruments additionally become symbols of courtesanship. This association tainted certain instruments with the illicit, and performers who chose to study these instruments risked their reputation and social position.[22] As a result, the courtesan's identity was bound with musical and poetic performance. Part of her mystique also lay in her origins. Frequently, courtesans were women with no legal connection or kinship ties. They could be orphans, the progeny of other courtesans, illegitimate daughters, widows, and trafficked by slavers. Their separation from patriarchal structure enhanced their mystery and enabled them to create their own history and image to accompany their persona.

Although courtesans could be sexually available, they chose their lovers by offering the illusion of availability, fantasy, and seduction. Along with skill in music and poetry, a courtesan was prized for her ability to converse on different subjects, flirt, act coy, and other vital trappings of seduction, all of which were woven into her performance. The extrasensory performance of seduction incorporated those signifiers of desire that her culture held, such as scanty, seductive dress, expensive fabrics, jewelry, dance, gestures, scents, and trappings of comfort in her home.

Seduction also required a keen ability to read people, so a courtesan needed to be adept at evaluating and manipulating the emotions and moods of her patrons. The most successful courtesans were not always considered the most beautiful or accomplished of their peers; often, they were the most intelligent, astute, and ruthless. Therefore, although a courtesan's performance used all the expectations of an artistic performance because she often was in the position of actually *performing*, she also had to meet audience expectations of her bodily performance, and implied intimacy, through dress, gesture, and extrasensory props.

Due to their unique cultural roles, courtesans were especially visible through their social and literary reception. There are similarities cross-culturally in the type of arguments used by supporters and detractors of courtesans based on moral, religious, and artistic concerns. The focus of such arguments is not always the fact of the courtesan's existence, but the effect of their art. Frequently, these arguments center on music. Patrons of courtesans laud their skill, beauty, and wit, while their detractors point to their use of music, poetry, and seduction to distract, even destroy, men. Critics are concerned with the intimacy of her performance, in conjunction with the subject matter of her songs and poetry and the mixed company in which she performs.

Bound in these issues was the influence of music on the emotions. The latter was intrinsic to discussions about medical uses of music along with the kinds of music best suited for religious contemplation. This criticism was not without evidence. Courtesans were linked to larger social issues such as the reality that men were leaving their wives and families for them, and the enslavement and trafficking of women into prostitution. Unfortunately, courtesans (and prostitutes) also bore the brunt of fear during epidemics and religious movements and were accused of spreading disease as well as causing it through witchcraft and sinful living.[23]

A last key aspect of courtesans is they subverted patriarchal structures by being matrilineal and created a community within a, usually, unfree group of women. Courtesans did not form families in the sense of loving, close bonds, although that was possible. Rather, they formed communities similar to kin and clan structures, with the assumption of a basic level of care to be given to new members and the potential to be "adopted" by an important teacher. In some cultures, courtesans became a distinct social group or caste, as in India and Japan. They passed their knowledge on to daughters and girls brought (and bought) into the house and community, which could be part of a broader community of courtesan families. Male children born to courtesans were less valuable. They would be given away or sold, and on rare occasion, taken by their fathers. Generally, they were trained to serve the courtesan community by becoming clerks, hairdressers, handymen, and accompanists.[24]

Based on these markers and their role in medieval Islamicate culture, *qiyān* and *jawārī* were courtesans. Enslaved Islamicate courtesans experienced sexual assault and bondage as did other enslaved women, yet they inhabited a specialized subclass. They had the ability to penetrate social borders, such as going out in public unveiled and performing publically in mixed company. As they lived in the women's quarters, they shared physical space with all the other free and unfree women and young children of the household. Based on references in the literature, singing slave women, like other courtesans, created spheres of influence and supporters in the patronate as well as within the women's community. Last, singing women not only trained other courtesans and profited from their labor, but they had the opportunity to do something ordinarily available only to men: construct a lineage.

Lineage in the medieval Islamicate world—as in many other patriarchal cultures—derived from the male line. Property and status likewise passed through the paternal line; however, according to Islamic law, women could inherit and hold property. Nor was slave status inherited. By law, if an enslaved woman bore a child to her owner, she was supposed to be freed and given the status of *umm walad*.[25] If the father had wealth and station, he could elevate children born to his concubines and bestow them with his rank and lineage. *Qiyān* and *jawārī* who were born to notable fathers drew on that status for professional gain. Whether that lineage was manufactured was not always verifiable, nor did it really matter. For women, notoriety or exoticism was a benefit and the only slim advantage they had over men of similar circumstances. Sometimes, freed women owned their own singing women, training them for prospective patrons. A number of famous singing slave women were trained in this fashion and traced their musical lineage to specific *qiyān* and *jawārī*. Therefore, like other courtesans, *qiyān* and *jawārī* were not only a distinct community, they co-opted the family dynamic.

Training and Trade

The primary function of singing women was to provide musical entertainment. Enslaved women with potential to become *jawārī* and *qiyān* were trained by professionals hired for that purpose or by an in-house music specialist who could also be one of the advanced students. Although music was their primary skill, singing women also were trained in courtly etiquette, Arabic, recitation of the Qur'an, and, it was suspected, techniques for seduction and emotional manipulation.[26] As enslaved women, they were sexually available, and that trainees had sexual training is suggested in several sources. Patrons and connoisseurs ostensibly visited taverns, schools, and houses of singing women in order to be entertained, though some schools were in reality thinly disguised brothels.[27]

The main instrument of singing women was the lute, though they also played zithers and flutes, sang, and recited poetry. Their songs were about love, but they also used song for satire, political propaganda, and sending secret messages to lovers. Singing women were required to memorize huge numbers of songs, perhaps more than other musicians, and essentially functioned as living archives.

Al-Jāḥiẓ summarizes their repertoire thusly:

> An accomplished singing girl has a repertoire of upwards of four thousand songs, each of them two to four verses long, so that the total amount of poetry contained in it, if one multiplies one figure by the other, comes to ten thousand verses, in which there is not one mention of God (except by inadvertence) or of the terrors of future punishment or the attractions of future reward. They are all founded on references to fornication, pimping, passion, yearning, desire and lust. Later on she continues to study her profession assiduously, learning from music teachers whose lessons are all flirting and whose directives are a seduction.[28]

In the *Book of Brocade*, Ibn al-Washsha does not mention their musical skill so much as their ability to manipulate potential lovers. He corroborates al-Jāḥiẓ's assessment of their tactics:

> It is evident that they (singing women) have malignant intentions by one glance: at a gathering (*majlis*) if she saw a young man of wealth and great fortune, of good cheer and handsome, she thus inclined herself to mislead him. This brought destruction upon him.[29]

Singing women also taught music. Their pupils included men, women (generally enslaved, but not always), and *mukhannathūn*. Formerly enslaved singing women often had their own enslaved pupils who performed their songs as part of their training. Some singing women may have taught out of the house they were associated with, and it is possible they gave lessons at the houses of patrons as well. The fact that they taught music in mixed company was not unusual; women were allowed into libraries and schools to study, although they were separated from men.

At large-scale musical gatherings at court, singing women performed and competed with other musicians. During the early Abbasid era, they played behind a curtain, but later caliphs placed them in full view. Childbirth conferred status on an enslaved woman. When a singing woman bore a child to the caliph, she became an *umm walad* and was entitled to sit behind the curtain. As a slave, she was not allowed to veil, but could at least be shielded from sight while performing.

In addition to being freed by their owners for marriage or childbirth, singing women could purchase their freedom. They had the option of staying with their patron as a *mawlā*, unless their freedom was granted for marriage. Once freed, singing women could open schools to train singers, while others held musical gatherings at their houses for mixed company. Wealthy singing women enhanced their reputation by endowing charities and social works, while others quietly supported up and coming musicians.

Attractiveness of both face and voice was important for male musicians, but essential for singing women. Men did not have the same standards of beauty as women, nor did they have the same expectations for extramusical performance. For men and women, however, the use of gesture, facial expression, and carriage were just as important as technical skill, though men could rely on skill alone if not blessed with physical attractiveness. Additional courtly graces and accomplishments only heightened the value of a given artist. The *Kitāb al-Aghānī* says of the singing slave woman Bas-Bas (Caress):

> Bas-Bas had a beautiful face, and was an excellent singer, in the top class of singers. She was first owned by Yaḥyā ibn Naffs, but when al-Mahdī saw her, he had to have her. He paid 10,000 dirhams for her.[30]

If the figures in the *Aghānī* are even remotely accurate, ownership of singing slave women was prohibitively expensive for everyone except the caliph and the very wealthy. A caliph might own thousands of singing women, but a wealthy merchant could only aspire to one or two. In addition, although ownership might save the owner some of the cost of visiting singing women at their houses, owning a singing women was a costly investment. Not unlike a geisha, singing women needed to keep up with their training by learning new songs, which required regular lessons with a music master, in addition to the cost of lute strings, plectra, and writing implements.[31] This additional cost had to be underwritten by their owner, as was their expected upkeep in good clothes, household comforts, and gifts.

Some of the cost could be defrayed by loaning or, more crudely, pimping her to friends for sexual and musical services. In the *Risālat al-Qiyān*, al-Jāḥiẓ comments pointedly on how patrons circumvented the law:

> Furthermore, people send along to her owner's house presents of all sorts in the way of food and drink, but if they come to visit, they just get a sight [of the woman] and go away frustrated, while her master reaps the fruit of what they have sown, so that he, not they, has the enjoyment of it and is amply provided against the expense of maintaining his [other] slave women.[32]

While on the road, men made use of taverns and houses of singing women, the reason being that men were believed to have strong sexual urges and therefore allowed access to sexual services if they were traveling without their wives and slaves.[33] One solution, and possible holdover from polytheistic practice, was that men could retain the services of a temporary wife while traveling.[34] Yet, despite these loopholes, sex outside of marriage and accepted forms of concubinage were still fornication and therefore illegal.[35] The houses where singing women lived and worked were not, strictly speaking, brothels, but the problem of how to get around the issue of purchasing the services of a prostitute remained.

One means was through gift exchange, rather than payment for services.[36] That could include the trade in singing women. Enslaved women were subject to the same standards of decency as married, free women, but if a slave continued to commit fornication (i.e., taking lovers who were not her owner), she could be sold or returned to her former owner. There are a few cases of singing women being returned or sold in this fashion, but not many. This suggests that a brothel stood as an "owner" and that the owner's rights over her body, with the monetary aspects being hidden through lending and gifting, superseded laws about adultery.[37] Therefore, the practice of gifting, rather than strict monetary exchange, made patronage of houses where singing women could be heard marginally legal.

This lack of direct monetary exchange further served to elevate, and rationalize, the relationship between patron and singer.[38] High-ranking singing slave women demanded costly gifts, threatening to abandon their lovers if they did not receive them. According to Ibn al-Washsha, singing slave women provided a list of desired items to their lover and used them as emotional leverage.[39] Lower-ranking concubines and novices were generally not paid themselves, but gifts were given to their owners on their behalf. As a result, the owner of a single, talented singing woman could earn considerable wealth in the form of gifts and favors. Al-Jāḥiẓ states:

> Among the advantages enjoyed by each man among us is that other men seek him out eagerly in his abode, just as one eagerly seeks out caliphs and great folk; is visited without having the trouble of visiting; receives gifts and is not compelled to give; has presents made to him and none required from him.[40]

Traders and those who managed the training houses also stood to gain financially and politically, though they ran the risk of losing a lucrative property if a patron decided to purchase a favorite. According to al-Jāḥiẓ:

> He (the trader) reckons up each victim's income separately, and knows how much money he is good for ... When he has an influential customer, he takes advantage of his influence and makes requests of him; if the customer is rich but not influential, he borrows money from him without interest. If he is a person connected with the authorities, such a one can be used as a shield against the unfriendly attentions of the police.[41]

Though singing women are lumped into one group by detractors, there was a substantial difference between the artistry of a singer at court and one in the town. There are references about the fees of singing women (and their houses), although what services the fees covered is not clear. The sources state fees were paid to hear songs, but in the cases of music schools and the private salons of sole practitioners (who would also have trainees and slaves available for their clients), other services were available.[42] These services were not necessarily sexual; sometimes patrons wanted companionship. A visit to singing women included the purchase of food, drink, and, sometimes, accommodation, if the party went on too late. Just one evening could quickly rack up high bills, and there are many stories of men nearly bankrupting and outright ruining themselves by visiting singing women.

Despite their economic and social value, and religious injunctions against prostitution and mistreatment of slaves, enslaved *qiyān* and *jawārī* were subject to sexual and physical violence. The sources are coy about sexual assault, although there are enough references, including in satire, pointing to the vulnerability of enslaved women. Because singing slave women were both property and concubines, rape was likely common.[43] Another complication is that much of the information available about the private lives of singing slave women revolves around love stories. These stories commonly reference enslaved women being kept in seclusion in the women's quarters or guarded by a jealous lover-patron to prevent them from sneaking off to visit a secret lover. Sometimes the patron is the secret lover. There are anecdotes about singing women being murdered by lovers and committing suicide.[44] Singing women could also be murdered by rivals in the women's quarters. Al-Iṣbahānī and al-Jāḥiẓ unabashedly tell stories of women being beaten, chained, and raped, including abuse endured by the well-known singing woman ᶜArīb.

In some cultures, a rise in moral policing translated into additional violence against courtesans in the form of physical and psychological abuse.[45] Because singing women were synonymous with entertainment and leisure, they were easy to blame when a party got out of control. Patrons might also bear some of the brunt of censure for their consorting with singing women, but those who were against music and singing altogether pointed to the allure of singing women as leading their patrons into vice. The combination of wine, women, and song led to illicit behavior, they argued, and (not unjustly) this combination is featured in many moral tales about the dangers of overindulgence.[46] The peril of singing women and music was potentially so great that, more than wine, gambling, and rich foods, their patronage was painted as a straight line to moral bankruptcy.

Mukhannathūn and Men

Singing slave women were loved and loathed, but they were women and therefore understood within the patriarchal fabric of society. Male singers, on the other hand, were a problem. Professional male singers not only transgressed socially inscribed expectations of masculinity, but their stepping into an unmasculine role was a transgression of family. This was especially true if they were *mukhannathūn*, passive sexual partners, and made a living as musicians.

The Qur'an allows for concubinage in addition to four legal wives—a rule many caliphs and wealthy men enthusiastically embraced. Love of men, however, had also been a part of pre-Islamic life. This love could be sexual, but that might be just one aspect of the relationship. The love of one's brother, tribesman, and companion was considered among the deepest bonds a human could achieve. Even as the social code was being rewritten to privilege heterosexual marriage as the proper, normative form of love and relationships for Muslims, several loopholes remained.

According to Islamic law, same-sex relations were technically illegal, but in practice, the sexual mores of the Abbasid court were flexible. During the ninth and tenth centuries, debating the sexual merits of women versus men was the topic of much poetry, satire, and song. Both were considered acceptable sexual partners, though several poets, and caliphs, clearly favored one over the other.[47] Men took male and female lovers, as evidenced by wine poetry lauding the beauty of *ghilmān* (beardless boys) and *sāqī* (wine-pourers).[48] Women also took other women as lovers.[49] Nor were the *mukhannathūn* the only ones bending gender. At one point, there was a fad for dressing singing women as boys, referred to as *ghilmāniyāt* (feminine plural of *ghulām*), and boys as singing women.[50] Al-Jāḥiẓ penned a delightfully raunchy essay called *Kitāb Moufākharat al-jawārī wa'l ghilmān*, which, given the context, translates rudely as *The Debate between the Concubines and Catamites*.[51] In this highly theatrical piece, two men—one a lover of women, the other of men—debate the sexual charms of women versus men (and girls and boys), including granular detail on the mechanics of intercourse. (Spoiler alert: By the end, the women emerge victorious.)[52] Objections to such affairs could condemn same-sex relations, but they would also frame the objection within the overall sin of adultery and fornication, not necessarily the gender of the partner.

As Kecia Ali demonstrates in her study of the foundations of early Islamic law, men held certain rights and privileges because they were men, regardless of their legal or social status. Enslaved men might be commodities, but they remained men in the eyes of the law. Likewise, *mukhannathūn* retained their rights as men, despite their gender performance. Although women did have some legal rights, these rights similarly were tied to their biological sex, which shaped what roles were considered socially appropriate.[53] Interestingly, these roles differed based on whether they were free or unfree, such as prices paid for crimes against enslaved women, who was allowed to veil, and, in the case of enslaved women, whether they could be legally condemned for sex outside of marriage.

Inclusion of men, *mukhannathūn*, and boys in debates about music reflect an ongoing social conversation about sexuality and gender roles. Overt celebration of male love ranged from frank lust to the same arena as chaste love for women, with similar warnings about passion. Passion was dangerous and considered an illness. Loss of restraint, indulgence, and subsequent addiction to one's physical passions represented a loss of control and transfer of power. In early Islamicate society, free and unfree women were transacted upon, whereas men were the ones who effected the transactions. This dynamic meant that the purchase of sex, music, and poetry from singing slave women was problematic, but within cultural and legal boundaries. The purchase of music, and therefore intimacy, from a free or unfree man, however, put him in a feminized social position, compounding his already complicated gender role as a musician.[54]

As discussed earlier, *mukhannathūn* existed prior to Islam, along with singing slave women. According to the sources, they were singers and raconteurs, known for their bawdy entertainments and penchant for being party animals. The songs and performances of *mukhannathūn*, like those of some singing slave women, were often bawdy, funny, and either skirted the line of propriety or leaped gleefully over it. The increased sophistication of musical entertainments and standards for musicianship, fed in large part by the market for singing slave women, created demand for musicians at all levels of the social order. Although *mukhannathūn* appear in narratives about court entertainments, there is evidence in the *ḥadīth* and treatises on *samāᶜ* indicating they were also available to the middling classes.

Mukhannathūn were troubling due to their biological status as men who openly expressed submission or passivity through their feminine gender performance and sexual encounters. Their association with sex was firmly linked to their feminine performance and status as musicians. Women were always passive partners due to their penetrability, and it was believed they had strong sexual urges. They could lure men, even without thinking, and men were particularly susceptible to losing control. As a result, women needed to be protected and guarded from men, and men needed to be careful around women. Unmasculine men were tempting and potential tempters for other men, while also lampooning aspects of culturally inscribed masculinity. In other words, the ability of *mukhannathūn* to make wealthy, elite men submissive to them through music had the potential to upset the masculine-dominant power structure.

Being "bent" was part of their identity, although several *mukhannathūn* were married with children. Some were beardless, aligning them with boys and women, while some *mukhannathūn* had beards and brought masculine and feminine traits into their music and gender performance. Whether or not *mukhannathūn* also provided sexual services is difficult to determine, but it is heavily implied in some cases and stated outright in others.[55]

Needless to say, these social strictures did not prevent men from working as entertainers. The sources credit Ṭuways (632–710 CE/first century, H) as the first male musician in Islam. His teacher and patron was the singing woman Jamīla, and he was known for his beautiful singing and wit. Ṭuways was referred to as a *mukhannath* due to his gender performance and choice of repertoire. He was married and had children, although it is possible he had male lovers as well. Ṭuways lived in Medina where a number of *mukhannathūn*, some more infamous than others, made their living. They were not popular with everyone, however. In the early eighth century, the governor of Medina, for reasons that are not entirely clear, ordered that all *mukhannathūn* were to be rounded up, castrated, and exiled.[56] Ṭuways and several of his students were caught, but he continued with his career.[57]

Male and cross-gendered musicians had champions, and some of their key patrons were elite women musicians who were former *qiyān*.[58] It is their support, as well as the patronage and visible musicianship of a few key noblemen that contributed to making professional musicianship more accessible for men.[59] The majority of the first celebrity male musicians were non-Arabs and *mawālī* who came from different regions of the Islamicate states. Their being considered foreign is one possible reason why they were nominally accepted as entertainers.

It is important to note that although some of the first generation of known male musicians were labeled *mukhannathūn* and questions raised about their sexual preferences, acceptance of free and foreign male musicians did not replace women and *mukhannathūn*. Men never edged out women as musicians; quite the contrary. The use of women musicians, especially unfree courtesans and concubines, continued throughout the Islamicate states and were adopted by other Islamicate regimes, such as Mughal India. Eventually, *mukhannathūn* became less prominent, although they were featured in entertainments as buffoons, actors in plays, and singers.[60]

Like *mukhannathūn*, male musicians struggled to overcome the stigma of their profession, managing to carve out an uneasy niche in the social order. That a number of the most famous were boon companions (*nadīm*) to the caliph, celebrated for their piety, and members of the nobility gave them status. Yet, no matter how spotless their reputation, to be a musician remained a dubious profession and male musicians had less social status than poets and belletrists.[61] The reason was that by virtue of being men, male musicians had more freedom of choice. Even if they were born into a family of musicians, their choosing a similar path was questionable. How some male musicians not only differentiated themselves from their colleagues and earned a modicum of respect is difficult to pinpoint. Generally, the primary difference between the performance of male musicians, *qiyān*, and *mukhannathūn* lay in their social persona.

Men avoided being classified as *mukhannathūn* by creating a masculine identity separate from music to counterbalance their role as musician. They did so by emphasizing their familial and regional origins, downplaying their visibility as musicians, dressing in male fashions, and engaging in masculine pursuits, such as hunting and the study of jurisprudence, all of which gave them a social presence outside music. Some of the origin stories of male musicians may also have been changed or exaggerated, as the rules of propriety demanded a respectable background in addition to appropriate behavior.

Origin was important, as it was more acceptable for a male musician to be of foreign extraction, such as the Persian musician family of Ibrāhīm and Isḥāq al-Mawṣilī. If a musician was Arab, they faced more difficulty, though a number of Arabs, including nobility, were musicians. For example, the half brother of Hārūn al-Rashīd, Ibrāhīm ibn al-Mahdī (779–839 CE/162–224 *H*), was an accomplished musician and rival of Isḥāq al-Mawṣilī.[62] Although Arab nobles could receive censure for their choice, their rank offered protection. In addition to their emphasis on noble pursuits outside music, male musicians reinforced their performance of masculinity through their relationships with women. Sexual preference could play into their persona, but generally in relation to their dominance in the sex act. Marriage was an essential state, so most were (or had been) married. A male musician was either known for his loyalty and attention to his wife and children or admired for his conquests. For the rowdier set, the ability to hold their wine and stamina were masculine traits—though many singing women could do the same—and all men strictly adhered to male fashion, including wearing a beard.

Given the combination of listening, sensuality, and intimacy between musician and patronate, it is hardly surprising that ascertaining the moral impact of music was tricky. In times of confusion about where the moral and legal line should be drawn regarding music and musical entertainments, accounts by patrons (and trenchant commentary by scholars and satirists) were masterful examples of spin. By attesting to the high tone of the poetry read and songs sung, patrons attempted to demonstrate that listening was harmless, even edifying for the refined gentleman. Whether or not such gatherings were as lofty as claimed was not important. Rather, it was the performance of propriety and recognition of the boundaries between acceptable and not acceptable that helped patrons downplay transgressions against religious opinion. Regardless of gender and sexuality, however, the primary distinction among musicians was their legal status. Male musicians were predominately free and freedmen, while the majority of women musicians were enslaved. Because the experience of slavery differed for men and women, considering the intersection of gender and enslavement is essential to unraveling the roles and statuses of enslaved people, particularly women.

4

Slavery and Gender

When they first began studying cultures in what we now call the Middle East, eighteenth- and nineteenth-century Orientalists and travelers were unsurprised by the prevalence of slavery; however, they judged Islamicate slavery as more humane than slavery in the Americas.[1] Given the atrocities of the transatlantic slave trade and dehumanization of enslaved Africans under American plantation slavery, this assumption is not surprising. Entrenched ideologies of white supremacy led some scholars to conclude that Islamicate slavery was benign, even beneficial, to Black Africans.[2] Until recently, this comparative perspective has been echoed in studies of slavery outside the Americas, which has continued to mask the reality that Islamicate slave trades, like all institutions of slavery, were corrupt and destructive to entire cultures.[3] Despite opportunities for some elite slaves to gain power, availability of manumission, and those few laws that protected the limited rights of slaves, slavery, even when the chains were luxurious, was always an act of violence and upheaval.[4]

Another challenge to understanding institutions of slavery in the region has been the shifting landscape of enslaved-slaver status in primary sources and translated material. In the Ancient Near East and cultures of the Mediterranean, women were both property and political tools. Many terms in the Ancient Near East and other ancient cultures equate "slave" with "slave/servant/wife/woman" or "child."[5] Such terms could also be associated with the tasks they performed. Up until the modern era (and for some time after), unfree and enslaved women were acquired through conquest and diplomatic exchange, while free women of the upper and middling classes were used to cement political and economic alliances through marriage. Free women rarely had a say in such alliances.

One key difference between early modern slavery and that of the ancient and medieval world is that enslaved people were also humans. The simple reason being that during antiquity and well into the medieval era, to be enslaved was a possibility for anyone. It is difficult for us today to wrap our heads around how an individual can be both human and property, especially those of us in

Western cultures that are steeped in Enlightenment principles of citizenship, individuality, and freedom. Islamicate slavery was not a monolithic institution but rather a constantly changing and overlapping series of Islamicate slaveries. In order to attempt to understand what constituted unfreedom, one needs to consider each Islamicate court and government within the boundaries of its own definition and context of slavery, manumission, and conquest.[6] Within these overlapping systems and terms is the clear fact that experiences of slavery differed for men and women, complete with different sets of laws.

What constituted enslavement in the medieval Islamicate world? As in other slave systems, slavery in the medieval Islamicate world was comprised of asymmetrical dependencies.[7] The role and status of enslaved people in the medieval Islamicate states is difficult to pinpoint, in part because their roles ranged along a long spectrum of responsibility, including holding positions of power at the highest levels of governance and military service to providing back-breaking physical labor. Nor can one arrive at a clear understanding of unfreedom by looking at what constituted freedom. Like unfreedom, freedom was relative and existed along a spectrum.

Slavery in the early medieval Islamicate world was not only intrinsic to broader cultural, political, and economic developments, it was fundamental to the development of social units, such as marriage, family, and kinship. At the state level, the primary modes of slavery were military and civil service, with everything else falling under the loose grab bag of domestic slavery. Although chattel slavery existed, it was not as prevalent in the Islamicate states, nor as long-lived. Families were composed of enslaved and free members, and all were expected to contribute to the wealth and status of the family. All women's labor was relegated to the domestic realm, which included sexual access. Enslaved men were teachers, companions, soldiers, and civil servants. In short, slavery shaped and informed the family unit, which in turn echoed the larger social order.

Though we have little in the way of a documentary record from the medieval era containing the voices of enslaved people (particularly of women), enslaved people in the Islamicate world were not voiceless victims. The sources, even those written by and for male authority, indicate that there were a number of areas of resistance available to them. These included open revolt, political intrigue, silence, sex, conspiracy, music, and poetry.[8] Islamicate history is filled with slave revolts, many of which were successful.[9] Violence was not the only means of resistance, either. As in all slave systems, enslaved people in the medieval Islamicate world had an internal and external hierarchy, complex culture, and community. Enslaved people were fundamental to the development of civilization and empire; bluntly put, their labor made intellectual, social, and political advances possible. Therefore, although individual voices might have been diminished or lost, there is no mistaking that enslaved people had significant influence on politics, literature, music, and religious thought.

One of the hardest truths is that enslaved people and their slavers could love one another.[10] Romantic relationships and loving friendships are found even in the worst forms of chattel slavery. In the medieval Islamicate world, these ties were murkier as slaves, even when emancipated, often remained part of the family unit. By remaining with the family, slavers could provide a means for the enslaved to gain status. Medieval Islamicate sources contain many stories of the enslaved and slavers loving one another, marrying, fighting, and even dying for one another. Yet, when one takes a clear look at what lay beneath, these asymmetrical dependencies remained enmeshed in coercion and power; a fact that was not lost on ancient and medieval people. Such juxtapositions of an enslaved person with agency-access, loving their masters, masters loving their slaves, and messy interpersonal, asymmetrical, dynamics are difficult for us to grasp today. In the medieval cultural perspective, however, this messiness was understood and accepted as intrinsic to the system itself.[11]

The final complexity one encounters when studying institutions of slavery in the medieval Islamicate world (or any context) is what constituted emancipation and manumission. In Islam, manumission was a legal, financial, and spiritual act, encouraged by the Qur'an and *ḥadīth*. For example, Sura 24:33 (al-Nūr) states that a slave can ask for a contract to purchase their freedom.[12] Numerous *ḥadīth* also discuss manumission and its virtues, as well as proper treatment of slaves. Former slaves in the Islamicate world had the chance to become citizens and earn wealth and status, a practice that had ancient roots and connections to Rome and other sophisticated cultures. It is important to note, however, that manumission and emancipation were individual acts, not a prelude to widespread abolition. Nor did being freed from slavery guarantee equality. Equality was not a concern, especially in a cultural milieu organized around concentric circles of dependency. As a result, the degrees of status along the spectrum of "enslaved," "unfree," and "free" were nebulous and fluid.

Slavery in the Medieval Islamicate World

Medieval Arabic terms for slavery, different degrees of being unfree, and the concepts of freedom and emancipation are rooted in metaphor and ambiguous. As in other cultures, general terms for slaves reflected profession, origin, appearance, gender, and social status, not to mention the whimsy of the slaver. This ambiguity has contributed to the difficulty in finding a definition and translation of slavery within early Islam, particularly in how best to render varying degrees of servile status.[13] Similarly, finding a definition for "free," and what that meant, is complicated by the same factors as being unfree. Having been enslaved was not necessarily an impediment to social movement. The stigma lingered, however, placing formerly enslaved people into the category of being "other," along with individuals with non-Islamic and foreign origins. These markers became part of one's social lineage, and, occasionally, leveraged for social mobility.

In the Qur'an, there are only three terms used to reference unfree status: *ᶜabd*, the phrase "that which your right hand possesses," and *raqabah*. Of these, the most unambiguous term for "slave" is *ᶜabd*. In addition to indicating enslavement and servitude, *ᶜabd* could also include the concept of submission. Prior to Islam, Arabic names included *ᶜabd* to indicate allegiance to a deity, and that convention continued into Islam. For example, the common name ᶜAbdullāh is ᶜAbd Allah or "servant of Allah." Parsing the phrase "that which your right hand possesses" is more complicated. It implies slave status, but also war captive. As such, it could refer to men and women, though it appears more often in the Qur'an in regards to women who are enslaved concubines.[14] Last, *raqabah* denotes status, indicating a low or ignoble person, servant, slave, or bondsman. An additional meaning implies one who is supervised.[15]

Terms related to patronage and fealty could point to enslaved or formerly enslaved status as well. Two of the most common were *wala'*, from which *mawlā* is derived, and *mukātaba*.[16] These states were different than *mawālī*, however. A *mukātaba* was a contract between a slaver and an enslaved outlining the terms of freedom; in essence, a form of indenture. Such contracts predated Islam, and the mechanism through which people entered into these contracts is not entirely clear. Over time, the term came to represent a broader discussion of the nature of the concepts tied to legal enslavement.

As slavery became more entrenched in the Islamicate social order, there was a need to clarify laws delineating enslavement and the legal and financial rights of enslaved people. Such laws were broken into smaller parts, primarily to articulate status within the growing enslaved population and divisions of labor.[17] Thus, the increasingly complex legal structure, as well as religious commentary on the moral and spiritual consequences of slavery, met a growing institutional need to justify the stratigraphy of the enslaved population along professional lines and origin.

Other Arabic terms employed to depict asymmetrical dependencies use terminology that elides gender and work. For those tasks grounded in gender, such as *qiyān* and *jawārī*, there was no equivalent in the other gender. For example, *fata* (fem. *fatāt*) references a manservant/maidservant, along with *ghulām*, *wasif* (fem. *wasīfa*), and *khādim*. *Ghulām* referred specifically to a domestic boy servant, usually prepubescent. The term *khādim* referred to eunuchs and later came to reference a woman slave of some status in the *ḥarīm*. As the meanings of the majority of these terms evolved and changed, a word that meant "slave" at one point later became associated with a specific type of slave, indicated race, origin, or referred to a legally free individual who owed service to a family for a specific period. By the seventeenth century, terms such as ᶜ*abd* and *ḥabshī* came to mean specifically Black Africans.[18]

The word in Arabic for "free" is *ḥurr*, and like ᶜ*abd* and related terms, it did not contain the same associations with individual choice and citizenship that we attach to the concept of freedom today. *Ḥurr* could include spiritual as well as social liberation. It also referred to someone who was born free or noble.[19] Manumitted slaves became *ḥurr*, so the term encompassed the act of freeing one from bondage, such as in Sura 5:89 (al-Mā'idah) where the freeing of slaves is a means to gain favor with God.[20] The term that is closest to our understanding of freedom as citizenship, *ḥilūn*, also appears in the Qur'an. Like *ḥurr*, it means status, indicating someone who is a free man and citizen.[21]

Enslaved people had a means, albeit slim, to work, earn money, and protest poor treatment. Laws protecting the enslaved might be meager in comparison to free-born people, yet they existed. The oldest laws on record, such as the laws of Ur Namma and the more familiar Code of Hammurabi, contain separate punishments for free and unfree people, but there are also laws protecting their basic personhood that discourage violence and abuse. Therefore, the laws of the Ancient Near East and later Mediterranean cultures are a mixture of legal protection for the enslaved while preserving the social dominance of the owner.

For women, freedom was complicated because they were the property of men. At all levels of the social order, free and enslaved women worked and lived together with young children in the women's quarters. Women of the nobility could be educated, but they were bound by rules of propriety and by sumptuary laws and were frequently prohibited from going out in public without a male escort. Nor did they choose their husbands. The veil was the mark of a free woman, and as such imposed some nominal protection to a free woman's body as she moved in public. Enslaved women were denied the veil, further demarcating the visible boundaries of free and unfree. As a result, enslaved women had more freedom to move in public spaces, but their uncovered heads rendered them vulnerable to predation.

Marriage and enslavement differed by degree. Women were enslaved as the result of war and conquest, but faced additional peril in being sold by their family and community. When slavers raided small villages and nomadic enclaves, families could offer a selection of women and children to avoid capture themselves or as a means to persuade the slavers to spare the whole community. The sale of women to brothels to stave off starvation or pay debts was common. For the desperately poor, selling children could be the difference between life and death. The funds acquired by selling a child could temporarily keep the rest of the family from starving and offer the child sold a chance at survival as enslaved people generally received basic food and shelter.[22] Although it is difficult for us to suppress our outrage at the idea of people selling members of their family into slavery, such transactions were the norm for centuries.[23]

Enslaved people in the medieval Islamicate states were outsiders, although what constituted an outsider was not based solely on geographic origin. The slave trade, including market preferences, and laws pertaining to slaves and slave status were influenced by gender, origin, and *ethnos*. Slaves were acquired through four basic means: (1) Capture in warfare, (2) gifting and trade for diplomatic purposes, (3) birth to enslaved parents, though primarily only in rural areas and, (4) selling oneself into slavery to avoid bankruptcy, poverty, and criminal persecution.[24]

The majority of enslaved people in the Islamicate states were obtained through warfare and diplomatic gifting which meant that most slaves were, at least in the first one hundred years of Islamic expansion, non-Muslims.[25] Although there are several verses in the Qur'an mandating reasonable treatment of slaves and *ḥadīth* advocating manumission, slavery and the slave trade were not abolished. One reason is practical: slavery had been part of every culture since antiquity and contained in the other two Abrahamic religions, therefore eliminating slavery outright would have been radical, if not impossible. Slavery was embedded in family and kin structures, tied intimately with conquest, expectations for labor, domestic work, and politics. Moreover, slavery was highly profitable. Enslaved people were human tools, and therefore property, appearing in trade records listed with other luxury goods such as gems and textiles. As more territories were brought under control of the Islamicate states, trade routes reaching from what is now Brittany into China channeled new and exotic trade goods into the center of the Empire, including people.

In Greece, the law of Pericles mandated that Athenian citizenship or "Greekness" passed through the mother, as did culture, meaning that slavery was inherited. The medieval Islamicate states were similar to the Romans in that status or origin could pass through the mother, but a child fathered by a slaver was free. A slaver had complete control over a slave's body, labor, and upkeep, allowing them to sell, gift, and free enslaved people at will. Yet, there was no question enslaved people were human beings and had basic legal rights for fair treatment.[26] The Qur'an specified that enslaved people could marry, have a trade, and acquire wealth. In addition, since enslaved people were also part of the family unit, breaking up families by selling children and spouses was discouraged legally and socially.

Enslaved people with specialized skills could be loaned to others and given commissions through an arrangement with their owner. In some cases, they brokered their own contracts. Technically, a slave's owner could take their all their earnings and some did, but enslaved people were able to acquire the means to buy their freedom. However, despite the nominal legal protections put in place and emphasis on good treatment in the Qur'an, access to legal recourse and social movement varied for enslaved people and depended on their relationship with their slavers.

As in other cultures of late antiquity and the medieval era, having been enslaved was not necessarily a social impediment. In some cases, former slaves were able to achieve political rank and wealth.[27] The permeability of free and unfree statuses was due in part to Islamic law and fundamentals of the religion, but these were integrated into long-standing traditions of intertribal mixing through adoption and conquest. There were several means of integrating non-Arabs and formerly enslaved people into the community. They could be connected to kin networks by blood through war and oaths, adoption, sharing mother's milk, and clientage. These practices were common in antiquity and provided a means by which to forge diplomatic relationships with other tribes and kin groups. *Mawālī* could be manumitted slaves, non-Arab Muslims, and other relationships that were not delineated strictly by blood relations. They were not necessarily marginalized due to their non-Arab or outsider status but were designated as *mawālī* to differentiate them from other members of the community.

Enslavement and purity could be interrelated in religious commentary, with enslavement implying a less than pure moral status.[28] Within Islam, an individual's fate is predetermined. Therefore, whether one was free or unfree was determined by God, not humanity. To have been enslaved and then freed suggested a moral cleansing in the sense of moving from an impure state to achieving purification through freedom. Being freed was also part of one's fate, as it was likewise determined by God. Owning people, particularly for pleasure, could also imply moral impurity, and there is plenty of commentary on use of manumission to remove moral stains. Therefore, having gone from unfree to free did not prohibit social movement because only God could judge.

Slavers were, in theory, prohibited from enslaving Muslims and other "People of the Book"; that is, fellow monotheists such as Jews and Christians. Common practice was frequently the opposite. Because it was technically not allowable to enslave Muslim Arab women, acceptable women to enslave were—again, in theory—not Arab. According to the sources, that was not always the case. Many enslaved women, including singing women, were from Arabic-speaking regions.[29] The Qur'an was mined for verses related to conversion and conquest, subjugation, and religious superiority to use as justification for enslavement of others. Included among the justifications to conduct slave raids was the concept of *jihād*, which can include actual battle in defense of religion, but also represents inner struggle. Like other philosophical ideas, it became corrupted and was used to justify the slave trade and conquest.

Vulnerable communities on the fringes of the ever-expanding Islamic states, especially nomadic and pastoralist groups, were easy targets for slavers. Even when much of Africa had converted to Islam, the *Bilād al-sūdān* (Region of the Blacks) remained an important resource for slave traders.[30] Men, women, children, and entire communities were captured and transported to urban centers around the Mediterranean and North Africa. The journey from point of capture to a trading center could be several hundred miles by foot over harsh terrain, and many captives died on the trip.

All major urban centers, including what is now Western Europe, had a slave market.[31] Upon arrival at the market, slaves were assessed for health, age, and overall marketability. Although health and attractiveness were important, a slave's origin and gender determined their value. Similar to the Greeks, medieval Islamicate traders and scholars deemed people from certain regions to be more civilized based on cultural achievements and the environment that nurtured them. Civilized peoples—generally urban and sedentary—had more value. Nomadic peoples, such as the northern tribes of what are now Europe, Russia, and the pastoralists of Africa, were not considered civilized and therefore judged incapable of more complicated tasks.

People selected for training as soldiers and civil servants—and in the case of women, musicians and concubines—were separated from those considered best suited for labor. Certain duties required skill, such as cooking, teaching, administration, and entertainment, whereas minding children, wet-nursing, and cleaning were relegated to basic labor. Slave traders were notorious for covering and hiding flaws with artful draping of clothing, cosmetics, and lighting, and early slave manuals gave tips to the buyer on how to spot such tricks.[32] Depending on their prospective market, men and boys might be castrated prior to sale, necessitating that they remain at the trading center to recover if they survived.[33]

Once sold, enslaved people were given Arabic names. These names could be religious, affiliated with the slaver, descriptive of function, country of origin, and reference their appearance.[34] Name changes also emphasized the status of enslaved people as noncitizens and property, stripping them of their identity and culture while reattaching them to the new culture and "kin" of the master.[35] Singing slave women likewise were subjected to this form of social erasure. Their names were a reference to their role and origin but were frequently tied to their appearance: Jamīla (beautiful), Danānir (shower of gold), Dhāt al Khāl (lady with the mole), Maḥbūba (beloved), and so on. When freed, formerly enslaved women kept their name and sometimes added the name of their patron.[36] Yet even if their basic geographical origins were known, some enslaved women had—or were allowed to construct—a form of lineage that served to legitimize their connections to powerful men, and in turn rationalize their patron's perceived addiction to them. Such maneuverings also provided a more acceptable pedigree for their children, especially those who stood to inherit.

In contrast, free women would be referred to by euphemism and honorific. To publically state and write the name of a woman was a breach of privacy, and the only men allowed to do so were her husband and close male relatives. For example, the free mother of a son would be referred to as "Umm Jaᶜfar," meaning mother of Jaᶜfar, as opposed to her given name. Similarly, she might be referenced as the "queen mother," "wife of the caliph," or in more salacious material, "his lover." Few of these designations tell us a woman's true name, let alone if they were real people.[37] Records noting religious donations (*waqf*, pl. *awqāf*) and endowments may be similarly vague, giving only an honorific.

Although all enslaved women were potentially sexually available, there were legal and social rules that gave them nominal protection. According to religious law, men were not supposed to marry a slave woman unless they freed them first. If a concubine became an *umm walad*, she and her child were supposed to be freed either once the child was born or upon the death of the master, depending on the family and legal arrangements. Like freedmen, freedwomen joined the ranks of *mawālī* and were referred to as such. When they became part of the family, they acquired the rights of inheritance and protection that implied, including taking the name of their former owner or patron to indicate they shared the same social circle and broader kin group. Because free women were not independent from men, freedwomen were associated with the male head of the family.

Enslaved men, with their owner's permission, were allowed to marry, have children, and profit from a profession. The children of a marriage between enslaved people were not to be sold away from their parents; rather, the whole family had to be sold or freed as a group. Enslaved men could also buy their freedom and became part of the family or kin group as *mawālī* following their manumission. Male children fathered by a slaver were also allowed to inherit or share in the inheritance with the children of his legal wife.[38] Free women, however, could not marry their male slaves, nor were they allowed sex with them. Based on the legal injunctions against women having sex with their slaves, however, it is probable women did have sex with male and female slaves.

Enslaved women were put to work in the household and performed all tasks that fell under domestic labor. What constituted "domestic" is a frustratingly vast, unsatisfying category for the many roles women undertook. Enslaved and free women shared what we still recognize as "domestic" tasks such as cleaning, gathering food, child-rearing, and cooking, in addition to managing finances, overseeing charitable donations, and providing business advice. Today, our concept of domestic is limited, which in turn limits how we see these roles. During the medieval era, to care for the home, bear children, and cater to the needs of men—however defined—was the only possible role for women. Their role was further justified through law and religion. That is not to say that women did not own businesses and engage in trade; rather their primary function was grounded in the family.

Like the Greeks, Romans, Persians, and Chinese, medieval Islamicate cultures created a physical and psychological separation between the domestic realm of women and visible spaces of men. Gender segregation existed prior to Islam in nomadic and urban environments throughout Arabia and the Mediterranean; however, the segregation of women from public life did not happen until later in the medieval era. The enforcement of the veil and the development of the *ḥarīm* as a specific location for women were institutionalized by the Abbasid caliphs, and armies of scholars worked to justify and legalize these practices. Their interpretation of the *ḥarīm* and veil were borrowed from Byzantine and Persian cultures, with rules relating to women's sexuality, marriage rights, and requirements for veiling becoming increasingly more Draconian over time. As married and free women began to lose their visibility, singing women became more visible and increasingly integral to social life at court.

Giving enslaved women access to the highest levels of court, including the caliph, it was later argued, increased the potential for religious and social corruption. Fear of influence from the women's quarters is attested to in other sources in the form of warnings and the narration of historical fact. Several caliphs were controlled by the women's quarters and criticized severely as a result.[39] Some openly choose the counsel of their wives and slaves, while others were believed to be manipulated by politicking from the women's quarters.

The reasoning for gender segregation was rooted in social and moral philosophy in that the balance and well-being of each sphere contributed to a balanced society. Christian Europe and the medieval Islamicate world relegated much of the public spaces to men and unfree people, although there were public places where there could be a mix of gender and social classes, such as marketplaces and the public areas of mosques and schools. The domestic sphere may have been the domain of women, but it also was where members of the family could go to relax from the rigors of public life. There were rules for proper conduct within each sphere, and they were physically connected and monitored. Yet, men and women had distinct ways of living.[40]

Because free and unfree women lived in the women's quarters together, they had exclusive control of the domestic realm. Despite their seclusion and protection falling under the supervision of men, the women's quarters had their own staff and a strict hierarchy, including control over who entered their spaces. Free women maneuvered within and manipulated the system, exerting power in the form of wit, wisdom, selective contributions of funds and time, and politicking. Starting in the eighth century, the enthusiasm of the Abbasid caliphate for having a large women's quarters necessitated a shift away from insistence on "pure" Arab leadership, meaning perceptions of what constituted an acceptable lineage for men had to be adjusted. This shift also changed the status of women in that they became less important to lineage—a change that transferred power out of the hands of free, noble Arab women and redistributed it among enslaved and formerly enslaved women and their children.[41]

Such reliance on enslaved women concubines complicated bodily and moral purity. As discussed earlier, fornication and adultery are unequivocally against the law, yet enslaved women, including musical concubines, were sexually available outside of marriage. Sura 4:25 states that enslaved women cannot be held to the same legal standard as free women. Even lewd slave women are to receive half the punishment if caught, as being enslaved, they are not responsible for their actions.[42] This rule was key for singing slave women, otherwise, they—and their patrons—would have constantly been vulnerable to charges of adultery.

Because singing slave women were expected to behave differently due to their profession and status, there was understanding that they did not have a choice. Al-Jāḥiẓ riffs on these points in the *Risālat al-Qiyān*, by noting that singing slave women were notorious flirts (and free women can be boring), yet grudgingly admits that given their place as enslaved singers, they really could not help it. Despite this understanding, enslaved women musicians are represented consistently in opposition to "good" women, meaning women of Arab descent, converts by marriage, and those noblewomen from high-status tribes and families.[43]

Although marriage and bearing children were among the primary means by which women were manumitted, women did purchase their freedom. Music remained the primary tool enslaved women had to co-opt masculine language and power. Singing women subverted the power dynamic in that they were perceived as being in control of their male patrons. They existed in a dual liminal space: as musicians and as unfree residents of the household. As enslaved concubines, singing women were not allowed to veil, yet they were able to move in public spaces without a male escort. This visibility placed enslaved women into masculine territory, whereas free singing women were constrained from performing in public unless under specific circumstances.

The *Aghānī* provides vivid detail concerning the ability of enslaved women musicians to slip under the rules. Not only does al-Iṣbahānī give helpful information regarding transactions involving enslaved people, there is variety in how he indicates enslaved, unfree, and foreign status. Through his descriptions of patrons, singers, and notable performances, we can see preferences for trafficking in women from a variety of ethnic and mixed backgrounds, and the enormous fees paid for their services. Such preferences are filtered through the voices of the narrator(s), including those individuals who did not mesh with social norms and prevailing market trends.[44]

What is evident, however, is that the combination of gender, status, and musicianship created a legal grey area that enabled singing women a means to avoid the harshest punishments for their intimacies, musical and otherwise, and provided tools for negotiation within the patronate. This ability of enslaved singing women to hold a modicum of power over men, reinforced by tangible points of law, would prove to be quite vexing to those scholars who advocated against listening.

Part Two

Diversions of Pleasure: Representations of Musicianship and Identity

5

Literary Performance of Music and Reading Musical Identity

Narratives about and featuring musicians in early Abbasid sources provide information about music performance as well as vital clues as to social uses of music at different levels of early Islamicate society. That said, it is difficult to claim with any certainty how much of the information in biographies and anecdotes is factual. Because musicians were familiar symbols of the court and court culture, whether stories about an individual, performance, party, and so forth were true was not essential. Much like our internet celebrity culture today, to the medieval reader, those narrative elements that articulated a musician's role, character, and social image were just as relevant (and perhaps more) as the facts surrounding their lives.

Musicians appear as political actors, satirical figures, and ornamentation in a diverse cross-section of literature. Their exploits, virtuosity (musically and in love), and patronage were employed purposefully in depictions of performances and discussions about listening. As a result, literary representations of musicians in medieval Islamicate literature reflect a variety of opinion about the visibility of their profession, participation at court, and, most vividly, how sound genres permeated Islamicate cultures. In this chapter, I discuss some of the forms biographies and stories about musicians can take, followed by a look at symbolic uses of musicians and sampling of ways these symbols were employed in the literature. This view is by no means definitive. Rather, it is a set of observations culled from a variety of literary genres, including histories, poetry, essay, and satire, all of which give a backdrop to the concerns about listening I discuss in the following two chapters.

To illustrate the form and content of biographies about musicians, I include short biographies of nine musicians from the seventh through tenth centuries. The musicians featured are well known and appear in a variety of sources. Their fame continued into later generations as well, and their stories are frequently entangled in political intrigue, social commentary, and musical rivalries. Some of these musicians knew one another intimately, to the point of sharing kinship and patronage. It's more than possible some were lovers.

The accuracy of these connections cannot be ascertained, although it is clear these musicians were connected via interpersonal networks and musical styles. They also represent the initial waves of musical development in the early Islamicate era. To show how they overlap, I present them in a rough chronological order. Some we have met before. They are: Ṭuways, Ibn Jāmiᶜ, Ibrāhīm al-Mawṣilī, Isḥāq al-Mawṣilī, the musician prince Ibrāhīm ibn al-Mahdī, the celebrated courtesan ᶜArīb al-Ma'mūniyya, Isḥāq's famous pupil, the singing woman Badhl (Gift), the noblewoman ᶜUlayya bint al-Mahdī, and the singing woman Khunth, called Dhāt al-Khāl (the lady with the mole).

As noted earlier, Ṭuways was a *mukhannath* and *mawlā*, meaning he was a vassal to a specific tribe. In contrast, Ibn Jāmiᶜ was an Arab of the prestigious Quraysh tribe, the tribe of the Prophet Muḥammad, and he had a lengthy rivalry with Ibrāhīm al-Mawṣilī, a musician of Persian origin. Ibrāhīm al-Mawṣilī was one of the boon companions of the Abbasid caliph Hārūn al-Rashīd, both of whom appear in many stories, including the *1001 Nights*. Isḥāq al-Mawṣilī was Ibrāhīm's son, and, possibly because of his colorful father, lived a moral and pious life. His musical rival was al-Rashīd's half brother, Ibrāhīm ibn al-Mahdī, a rather dashing figure who briefly became caliph through a series of political intrigues.

Although she was a free woman and also half sister to al-Rashīd, ᶜUlayya bint al-Mahdī was a *qiyān*. She died young, much to the sorrow of her family, leaving a small legacy of her poetry and music. ᶜArīb, Badhl and Dhāt al-Khāl were contemporaries of ᶜUlayya bint al-Mahdī and were *qiyān* as well. As slaves, however, they were also *jawārī*, with ᶜArīb becoming a *mawlā* when she was freed. ᶜArīb was one of the most revered musicians of her generation. Badhl was a pupil of Isḥāq al-Mawṣilī, who in turn trained many other famous musicians, including the singing woman Danānir (shower of gold). Dhāt al-Khāl was renowned for her beauty (and cunning), but she was also an accomplished musician. The narratives for these four women provide glimpses into the hierarchy within the ranks of women musicians, free and unfree.

Narratives and Identity

Narratives from the ninth to eleventh century that involve or use musicians share a number of commonalities. Because of their complicated status, musicians could slip between or circumvent cultural boundaries related to social status, physical space, gender, and sexuality. Whereas all musicians were subject to the literal and figurative gaze, *qiyān*, and to a lesser degree *mukhannathūn*, were popular literary subjects through their promise of intimacy, beauty, and gender ambiguity. Since gender play was intertwined with sexuality in musico-poetic entertainments, some musicians appear to have emphasized their gender performance as a component of their musicianship to capture the attention of the patronate.

What constituted musical identity? And how, if they even had a hand in it, did musicians construct a socially responsible—or titillating—identity? Did it make a difference if one was virtuous or not? Since many known musicians were courtiers (including *qiyān*), their identity needed to reflect their level of skill, legal status, gender identity, and, for want of a better term, moral compass. The caliph was the leader of the people as well as the Islamic community; therefore, his companions needed to be (or appear to be) of good character and genteel. Courtiers also needed to be physically compelling in some way, understand the intricacies of courtly etiquette, and skilled in the courtly arts.[1] Musicians were already debased by their choice of profession (or non-choice, as with enslaved women), making the distinction between a musician of good character and one who was not dependent on the tastes of the patronate. How well an individual crafted a persona to suit those tastes required social dexterity, skill, luck, and keen powers of observation.

Although these are not formal literary categories, I suggest there is a distinction between musician biographies and musician narratives based on their content and function. In biographies, such as those found in the *Aghānī* and *Fihrist*, the format is not unlike Western medieval *vida*s of troubadours.[2] The full name (if known) and nickname (their stage name) of the musician are given, followed by what is known of their origin, training, and career. An accounting of their works, instrumental and genre specialties, and any students of note may be included, as well as direct or euphemistic reference to important patrons, such as the caliph and nobility.[3] If remarkable, one will also find comments about the musician's personal habits, notable lovers, owners, and physical appearance. Such biographies can have additional information and context when they appear in literature, but when presented in texts about music and musicians and collections of biographies of notable persons and their works (like the *Fihrist*), they function primarily as encyclopedia references.

Because musicians appear in many different texts, the type of narrative I define as a musician narrative is one in which a musician is the protagonist, narrator, or otherwise central to the story in texts that are not expressly concerned with music. Such narratives may include biographical and anecdotal material about a specific musician, but with the exception of al-Iṣbahānī, biographical information is often included only if it has a direct bearing on the larger story and relates to the actions of the people involved.[4] Nor is this information presented in a linear fashion.

In accordance with the literary style, information about individuals could be spread over a series of reports (*akhbār*) that could jump among many volumes of a larger work, as in the *Aghānī* and the histories of al-Ṭabarī and al-Mas'ūdī. These anecdotes and references may be connected according to context of a performance, notable patron or shared transmitter.[5] Last, although a musical event is often the starting point, not all musician narratives are concerned with music and performance.[6]

Despite their different uses and trajectories, musician narratives share commonalities in what information is included and emphasized, centering on three interrelated factors: construction of identity, musicianship, and social position. Of these factors, construction of identity and social position are the most clearly articulated. Such narratives could offer details about performance practices and what types of music were performed but serve primarily to illustrate the social context. However, those musicians who reached the highest levels of their professions were assumed to be expert singers, instrumentalists, and composers, meaning that sometimes these details are omitted. Invocation of their name would have been sufficient to indicate the level of skill and, with some, types of music performed. Depending on the focus of the narrative, those accounts detailing how well individual artists performed and the number of songs they composed demonstrate how intrinsic musicianship was to their identity and social role.

Given the entanglements of music, gender, and social performance, how important was literary identity to performance practices and reception? Why did some musicians incorporate gender play into their performance and others not? What effect did their representation have on the perception of music within medieval Islamicate culture? Given that court and elite musical entertainments were not available to the middling and lower classes, such representations may well have been the only exposure scholars and people of the lower classes had to high-ranking musicians and courtesans.[7] As we know from our own celebrity culture, without direct access, such stories take on a life of their own, blurring facts until the story itself overtakes the reality of the event or individual.

Musicians who wanted to earn respect managed their fame through a careful performance of propriety. As noted previously, however, outrageous behavior was not a deterrent to obtaining patronage. The sources indicate a grudging respect for the "bad boys and girls" of music owing to their skill and sheer audacity. Maintaining an audacious identity also required skill and effort. Those musicians who had one (or had one imposed on them) did so through a balance of naughty behavior, good works, periodic demonstrations of piety, and acknowledgment of their debased status. The last could be a mix of gleeful, defiant, and repentant, depending on the context. Having a supportive patron was key, especially if the boundaries were pushed too far.[8]

Just as some musicians appeared to embrace a scandalous image, some enacted propriety by diminishing their visibility as a musician. For example, respected musicians such as Isḥāq al-Mawṣilī took pains to hide the tools of his trade. In order to avoid impropriety, women of the nobility and wealthy classes, such as ᶜUlayya bint al-Mahdī, could perform only under specific circumstances, generally only for close family. Although difficult to maintain, a reputation for piety was not limited to free women. There are accounts of singing slave women known for their piety and virtue, or connections to pious men, such as Sallāmat al-Qass. As slaves, their piety may not be expressed bodily; however, their ability to recite the Qur'an, strict adherence to prayer, and loyalty contributed to their reputation. Such representations were reserved for the most visible and notable *qiyān*; *jawārī* ordinarily had no choice in the role and image they were given.

Musicians might be able to manipulate perceptions of their moral and religious character, but their identity could not be divested fully from legal status (i.e., free and unfree), origin and family, and gender. In constructing identity, a musician's familial and cultural background pointed to the musical traditions that influenced them, as well as provided an explanation for their actions and choices. Having been enslaved, foreign-born, or a *mawlā* is a common theme in musician narratives. Those who were not of verifiable Arab descent were exotic, and therefore prone to forgivable limits of eccentricity and immorality. Musicians were aware of these assumptions, and just as sexuality could be exploited by singing women and *mukhannathūn*, exoticism could be emphasized by some men and downplayed by others.

Another notable aspect of a musician's identity was their history of patronage. Patronage constituted another kind of lineage, outlining both musical heritage and, in the case of enslaved singers and *mawālī*, actual lineage in the form of ownership and kin affiliations. Accounts of musicians and performances documented that lineage by noting who was in the audience, the political and social position of an individual musician, and their movement through the patronate. Because of the importance of this relationship, details as to the context of a performance, repertoire, and reception were part of the construction of a musician's image and a reflection of their ability.

Last, depending on the source and audience, narratives featuring musicians could have a subtext of repentance (or total lack thereof). A number of important musicians were reported to have renounced and repented their profession after enjoying a successful career. Patrons could make the same assertions as well, including former Ṣūfis who previously enjoyed *dhikr* and *samā*ᶜ, only to be shown the error of their ways.[9] To express regret or renounce their profession was not only a personal renunciation of impiety, but a subtle acknowledgment that providing musical diversions for oneself as well as one's patrons was, in essence, spreading corruption. In such stories of repentance, those musicians and patrons who chose to abjure music are represented as penitents, while the fate of those who engage in dangerous listening is made clear: transformation, damnation, and apostasy. The transition from musician to penitent is seen more often in narratives related to men of rank and singing women who earned enough wealth to purchase their freedom and retire.[10]

Narratives concerned with listening and piety also used musicians as a means to reflect on proper behavior. For example, narratives that include singing women might refer to qualities desirable for women of good character, using singing women as the counterbalance.[11] In some cases, however, a singing woman is noted as an example of piety and loyalty.[12] Other representations of famed singing women may present their career as a passage out of slavery, culminating in the ending of their professional career through a redemptive event such as retirement, marriage, going on pilgrimage, sponsoring other artists, and death. Male musicians make similar pronouncements about ending their career and devoting themselves to pious living. Such gestures did not prevent musicians from performing, however. Having retired—or asserting they had renounced their profession—allowed some musicians to step back into that role when asked by a highly ranked patron without fully donning the mantle of professionalism.

Singing women, free and unfree, sometimes retreated into religion, while others rejected it completely. In his comparison of ᶜArīb and ᶜUlayya, Matthew Gordon points to how the latter devoted herself to prayer to overcome her shortcomings (music and drinking wine), while ᶜArīb's narratives have little mention of religion.[13] ᶜArīb is even bold enough to say that observing religious ritual for her would be a lie. Such statements about religion are found in other narratives of enslaved women, and function as an acknowledgment of their role legally, socially, and spiritually. These echo al-Jāḥiẓ's assertion that singing women do not know better and possibly allude to the Qur'an's injunction that enslaved women have a different moral level than free women. At root is the question of how an enslaved woman who is pious can preserve her dignity before God. In essence, she may not be able to do so with her body but can with her soul. Therefore, having enslaved women protest their fate and speak boldly of their conquests in literature could constitute acknowledgment of that contradiction between law and practice.[14]

Based on the prevalence of these themes, individual musicians did establish a professional persona, even if that persona was or became embellished later. In addition, given the shared resonance of these personalities across diverse sources, their identities informed development of what it meant to be a musician. Their expertise, legacy of songs and performances, and sheer charisma pushed the standards of performance to the highest possible levels. They accrued a series of stories that provide insight into their context, patrons, and social environment, which informed the development of literary and actual musicianship. Last, whether the individuals had a hand in their own legends is unknown. To the reader and patron, the truth mattered less than the symbol. Regardless of whether their stories are true, the following musicians were powerful touchstones in the development of Islamicate musical practices.

Nine Musicians

Ṭuways: The seventh-century singer Abū ᶜAbd al-Munᶜim ᶜIsā ibn ᶜAbdullāh al-Dhaᶜib (632–711 CE/11–92 *H*) was best known by his nickname Ṭuways (the Little Peacock). He was a *mawlā* who was associated with the Banū Makhzūm.[15] Ṭuways was raised in Medina in the household of the mother of the caliph ᶜUthmān (644–56 CE/23–25 *H*), who was the third of the *Rashīdūn*.[16] According to the *Aghānī*, Ṭuways was a student of the famed singing girl Jamīla and was the first to employ what al-Iṣbahānī referred to as the "new style," meaning an integration of Arabian and Persian song melodies.

Ṭuways purportedly dressed and presented himself in a feminine manner and is described as having a soft, effeminate character. He further emphasized his gender ambiguity by accompanying himself with a small hand drum and singing light, entertainment songs—both of which were associated with singing women. Yet, Ṭuways was married with children, giving him a socially grounded mark of masculinity. Due to his gender performance, Ṭuways was suspected of engaging in affairs with men, and indeed many of his audiences and devotees were young men. When the governor of Medina rounded up the *mukhannathūn*, Ṭuways was caught, castrated, and exiled with everyone else. According to the

Aghānī, he continued his music career and trained many of the next generation of male musicians. The combination of his sexuality and gender performance are intrinsic to his representation in the literature, to the degree that phrases such as "more effeminate than Ṭuways" became euphemisms in later sources.

Of the named *mukhannathūn*, Ṭuways is among the few to receive praise, albeit tempered by references to his gender, sexuality, and social status. It is difficult to know whether he was termed a *mukhannath* due to his appearance or profession; his performance of femininity could certainly have been exaggerated to align with his image as a musician. Ṭuways also is a tragic figure who is given to melancholy and bitterness. In contrast, his colleague, the *mukhannath* al-Dalāl, is depicted as being an unrepentant deviant. Like Ṭuways, a feminized persona was intrinsic to his music performance, but he flaunted his gender bending, was sexually available to men and boys, and wrote scurrilous songs about his affairs.[17] Narratives related to the *mukhannathūn*, therefore, shared aspects of both male and female modes of description, and details about their choices of genre, instrument, and clothing are linked to their behavior and sexual and gender ambiguity. Unlike singing women and male musicians, *mukhannathūn* in literary sources do not often repent of their profession, or if they do, it is ironic and under duress.[18]

Ibn Jāmiᶜ: According to the biography and narratives about Abū'l Qasim Ismāᶜīl ibn Jāmiᶜ (fl. late eighth century CE/second century, *H*) he was an Arab born in Mecca into a branch of the noble Quraysh tribe.[19] In accordance with his origins, Ibn Jāmiᶜ was raised with the assumption that he would take a station appropriate to his birth and was well educated in law and religion. His father died when he was a child, and his mother married the well-known musician Siyāṭ (*c.* 739–85 CE/122–69 *H*).[20] The young Ibn Jāmiᶜ decided he would rather pursue music and began studying first with his stepfather, then later with other prominent musicians. Accompanied by Ibrāhīm al-Mawṣilī (742–804 CE/125–88 *H*), Ibn Jāmiᶜ traveled to the court of the third Abbasid caliph al-Mahdī (*c.*744/5–78 CE/126–69 *H*), catching the notice of and befriending the caliph's sons, the young Hārūn (later al-Rashīd) and Mūsā (al-Hādī) (*c.* 764–86 CE/145–70 *H*).

Fearing censure by the people because of his sons' love of music, al-Mahdī soon forbade the young musicians from visiting the princes. They broke the rule, and when caught, Ibrāhīm was sentenced to the lash, but Ibn Jāmiᶜ argued he should not be punished due to his noble, Arab heritage. The caliph apparently spared him a beating but castigated him for his unseemly choice of profession as a man of noble blood and threw him out of court. When al-Hādī ascended to the throne, he summoned Ibn Jāmiᶜ back and presented him with thirty thousand pieces of gold.

After enjoying the high life at court, Ibn Jāmiᶜ intended to retire to Mecca, but, despite his knowledge of the Qur'an and purportedly deep piety, his penchant for luxurious living soon reduced his savings so that he had to return to performing to support himself. He entered the court of Hārūn al-Rashīd and there found his former colleague, Ibrāhīm al-Mawṣilī. A tense rivalry grew between them to the extent that other musicians chose sides, creating divisive music factions at court that echoed through several generations of musicians.

The stories of this rivalry are played out over a broad range of musical and social events and are related according to many different perspectives.[21] Depending on one's point of view, Ibn Jāmiᶜ was an accomplished musician, pious believer, or hopeless rake, with similar traits (minus the piety) ascribed to Ibrāhīm al-Mawṣilī. Al-Iṣbahānī portrays them warts and all. Ibn Jāmiᶜ apparently continued to perform throughout his life without active retirement, possibly because of his family connections and prowess, but just as possibly out of necessity.

In the *Aghānī*, Ibn Jāmiᶜ voices some of the most concrete descriptions of performance and the role of instrumental music in the court. As with other court musicians, his primary instrument was the lute, and he was a virtuosic singer and prolific composter. Musically, Ibn Jāmiᶜ was more experimental than Ibrāhīm al-Mawṣilī, which was at the heart of their rivalry. Ibn Jāmiᶜ, along with others in his camp and musical lineage, advocated for individual interpretation and integration of foreign musical influences.

Throughout his narratives, his noble birth is both a benefit and a point of censure. As represented through the narrative of his punishment at the hands of al-Mahdī, although Ibn Jāmiᶜ is noted for his prowess, such acknowledgment is tempered by the ignobility of his profession. The financial struggles that continually dragged him back to performance hint that despite his piety, the lure of music and his enjoyment of luxury were too strong. It is hinted that if he were truly pious, he would have been able to resist; besides, his noble blood should have protected him. Ultimately, he could not resist and was enabled in his vices by the patrons who supported him. As such, Ibn Jāmiᶜ is a complex figure who provides information about performance practices and court entertainments, while serving as a symbol of the patron and musician classes through his masculinity and nobility.

Ibrāhīm al-Mawṣilī: According to every source that mentions him, Ibrāhīm ibn Māhān (Maymūn) al-Mawṣilī (742–804 CE/125–88 *H*) was among the most celebrated musicians of his time. Like his son Isḥāq, Ibrāhīm al-Mawṣilī is a constant presence in the *Aghānī*, and he appears in histories, poetry, and even the *1001 Nights* along with the caliph Hārūn al-Rashīd and other familiar Abbasid personages. Stories and songs attributed to him are referenced in nearly every volume of the *Aghānī*, and his main article is nearly one hundred pages long.[22]

According to the *Aghānī*, Ibrāhīm was born in Kufa to a noble Persian family.[23] His father and mother were from Arradjan, and moved to Iraq with their patrons.[24] Ibrāhīm's father died when he was young, and his mother undertook his care alone.[25] He was raised by a respected member of the Banū Tamīm, but he ran off to Mawṣil because he was not allowed to study music; hence his name despite his Persian origins. As he pursued his music studies, al-Mawṣilī studied poetry and the lute, later traveling to Rayy in Persia where he gained mastery in Persian and Arabian musical styles.[26] While in Persia, he met one of the representatives of the third Abbasid caliph, al-Mahdī, who gave him the means to go to Basra for further music studies. Eventually, al-Mawṣilī traveled to Baghdad and studied with Siyāṭ.[27]

Al-Mawṣilī gained a position in the court al-Mahdī and furthered his studies with the famous musician Fulayḥ ibn Abī'l ᶜArwā' (fl. late eighth century CE/late second, H).[28] He joined with Ibn Jāmiᶜ at the court and they befriended Al-Mahdī's sons, Mūsā and Hārūn. The princes invited both musicians to their banquets (i.e., drinking parties) which earned the wrath of their father. Ibrāhīm was beaten and imprisoned, while Ibn Jāmiᶜ was exiled. Later, al-Hādī welcomed both men back, paying Ibrāhīm one hundred and fifty gold pieces for his troubles according to one source, a monthly stipend of ten thousand dirhams according to another.[29]

When al-Rashīd became caliph, Ibrāhīm's close friendship with him earned him a place among his boon companions, and the nickname al-Nadīm. Ibrāhīm's lengthy article is filled with his exploits with women, other musicians, an astonishing capacity for wine, and impressive social virtuosity. Unlike Ibn Jāmiᶜ, Ibrāhīm was not particularly pious and did not renounce his profession (even when it got him into trouble). Along with composing at least nine hundred songs, Ibrāhīm is credited with inventing several new modes. He gained enormous wealth and status through the generosity of his patrons, income from his property, and giving music lessons.[30]

Ibrāhīm sang and played the lute, adhering to the "classic Hijazi" style. This designation meant he advocated keeping to tradition, discouraging foreign influences and individual innovation. Such a conservative choice is intriguing, given his own foreign roots, broad musical training, and freewheeling character. Many of his songs noted in the *Aghānī* include performance indications, such as rhythmic and melodic mode, as well as the effect on the audience. His rivalry with Ibn Jāmiᶜ was a constant thorn in the side of the court. It was also a source of entertainment, with a volley of stories related to the men's attempts to one-up each other. In one story, thirty singing women were playing lutes, apparently in unison, when Ibn Jāmiᶜ complained that one was out of tune. Ibrāhīm not only singled out who it was, he pointed out the offending string. Ibn Jāmiᶜ was abashed and everyone in court was impressed.

Despite their differences, as court companions, Ibrāhīm and Ibn Jāmiᶜ were integral to the hothouse environment of the court and collaborated out of necessity. Their most notable collaboration was ordered by Hārūn al-Rashīd, who requested they compile one hundred songs with their former teacher, Fulayḥ. This collection purportedly formed the backbone of al-Iṣbahānī's *Kitāb al-Aghānī*.

Al-Iṣbahānī credits Ibrāhīm as the first to start 'training beautiful women to sing'. One reason was to standardize musical training, but another was to train "handsome" singers because they fetched a higher price than "yellow" and "black" women.[31] These schools were the first formalized music schools, and eventually more were established in the urban centers. Ibrāhīm's pupils included men and woman, many of whom became famous in their own right. Along with his son, Isḥāq, Ibrāhīm trained Zalzal (*f.* late eighth, early ninth century CE/second century, *H*) and Mukhāriq (d. *c.* 845 CE/231 *H*), both of whom contributed numerous songs as well as developments in music theory.[32] When Ibrāhīm was on his deathbed, al-Rashīd himself was present to comfort him. Ibrāhīm died at the age of 63 from a stomach disease, and the caliph al-Ma'mūn (786–833 CE/170–218 *H*) recited the prayers at his funeral. Ibrāhīm's legend continued well beyond his death, with it said that his songs were so captivating, they were inspired by the devil himself.[33]

Like Ibn Jāmiᶜ, stories about Ibrāhīm include performance practices, but also demonstrate how musicianship was entangled in morality. As a foreigner, Ibrāhīm was allowed moral leeway, although it seems he manipulated people's expectations and had the charm to dodge censure. He was not particularly religious, nor was he repentant. Women are frequently noted as being his weakness, and he had a lifelong affection for wine, both of which were symptoms of his profession. His masculinity is never in question, reinforced not only by his exploits with and lucrative trade in singing women, but also his friendships with powerful, respected men.

Isḥāq ibn Ibrāhīm al-Mawṣilī: Abū Muḥammad Isḥāq ibn Ibrāhīm al-Mawṣilī (767–850 CE/150–235 H) was the son of Ibrāhīm al-Mawṣilī.[34] He was born in Persia in Rayy and had a long, distinguished musical career in the Abbasid court in Baghdad. In addition to music, Isḥāq received an excellent education in literature, law, the Qur'an, and religious sciences. His primary music teacher was his father, and he inherited his father's place in the rivalry with Ibn Jāmiᶜ's faction. Along with his father, Isḥāq studied with important musicians, including Zalzal and the singing woman ᶜĀtika bint Shuhda (*fl.* late eighth century CE/late second century, H).[35] Under his father's tutelage, Isḥāq also became a famous court companion.[36] Due to his father's origins and being raised in Persia and Iraq, Isḥāq was also considered foreign.

According to Hilary Kilpatrick, much of the *Aghānī* features Isḥāq al-Mawṣilī.[37] Just flipping through the many volumes, one finds constant references to Isḥāq, not only for his songs, but as a reporter on everything from events to information about individuals. Like his father, his fame continued for centuries, and he appears in histories and literature, including the *Maqāmāt* of al-Ḥarīrī (1054–1122 CE/ 446–516 H) and the *1001 Nights*. Because of his profession, and likely because his father was an unrepentant party animal, Isḥāq was extremely careful about his reputation. He hid the symbols of his trade and preferred not to be referred to as a musician, yet fiercely championed the older, traditional performance and compositional styles in which he was trained.[38] Isḥāq was similarly critical of poets who strayed from traditional styles, such as Abū Tammām (*c.* 805–45 CE/189–232 H) and Abū Nuwās (*c.* 755–813 CE/140–98 H), advocating strict adherence to the style and form of ancient poetry. Since musicians were of lesser status, however, Isḥāq was also not allowed to sit at the table with nobles of rank and hold certain titles. According to al-Iṣbahānī, the caliph al-Ma'mūn was said to remark that if Isḥāq were not a musician, he would make him a judge (*qāḍī*).[39] Al-Ma'mūn did allow him to wear the Abbasid black robes, reserved for legists, and Isḥāq was elevated to join the ᶜ*ulama'*.[40]

Known for his piety, Isḥāq died in Baghdad as a result of fasting at Ramadan. The *Fihrist* records that Isḥāq hoped for such an end, saying: "I do not want to die until the month of Ramadan has gone by, so that I can profit by observing its fast and it [my death] will be when my balance is favorable."[41] He purportedly received gifts for his excellent character and sagacity and wrote on a variety of subjects. In fact, Isḥāq regularly brought his books with him when he traveled and even paid Ibn al-Aᶜrābī a stipend.[42] Al-Nadīm lists over twenty books he authored, many on artists of the past such as Ṭuways, al-Dalāl, the famous singing woman ᶜAzza al-Maylā᾿ (*f.* late seventh century CE/late first century, *H*), and two books on *qiyān*.[43] Isḥāq is credited further with writing fifty leaves of poetry, which probably included songs, judging by the numbers of singers al-Nadīm includes in the list of poets.[44]

The sources uniformly paint Isḥāq as a man of honor, moral living, and poise, not to mention a polymath, revered poet, belletrist, and respected jurisconsult. Because of his reputation, his presence and authority is often used to lend legitimacy. The historian al-Ṭabari uses Isḥāq frequently as an authority and transmitter of important events, with no reference to his being a musician.[45] Similarly, Isḥāq al-Mawṣilī appears as a regular authority in the *Fihrist*. When his authority is invoked, he comes across as a somewhat dour, if thoughtful person. Similar to narratives about and including Ibrāhīm and Ibn Jāmiᶜ, stories about Isḥāq include actual as well as social performance. He is also masculine, with his performance of masculinity conveyed through his piety and knowledge.

Isḥāq's life as a musician touches equally on his skill as a singer, instrumentalist, and composer. Any sensuality is sublimated; Isḥāq might be present at drinking parties and spar with his colleagues on points of art, but he retains his cool throughout. He is the musician's musician, dedicated to promoting a sober art music scene where conversations are kept at a high order. Yet, the specter of his profession is always present. Like Ibn Jāmiᶜ, there are hints and asides about his status, with subtle implications that despite his foreign and musical origins, he might have made a better choice. By dying as the result of religious observance, he is afforded redemption.

Ibrāhīm ibn al-Mahdī: The musician prince Ibrāhīm ibn al-Mahdī (779–839 CE/162–224 *H*) was born in Baghdad to an enslaved woman and the caliph al-Mahdī, making him a half brother of Hārūn al-Rashīd. His mother was named Shikla, a *jāriya* from Dailam, and was rumored to be the daughter of the king of Tabaristan. Al-Nadīm describes Ibrāhīm ibn al-Mahdī as "the blackest of blacks, with a large body and lofty character," and other sources note he was handsome and had dark skin.[46] Ibrāhīm was only six years old when his father died, and he lived in the women's quarters with his mother until he came of age. He received the best education wealth could endow, studying poetry, science, jurisprudence, and philosophy. Although teaching royal children music was considered déclassé, as the older brother, Hārūn al-Rashīd insisted that Ibrāhīm—and his half sister ᶜUlayya—receive a musical education.

When al-Amīn (reigned 809–13 CE/193–98 *H*) became caliph after al-Rashīd's death, he summoned Ibrāhīm to the court to display his musical talents which had been acknowledged by both Ibrāhīm al-Mawṣilī and Ibn Jāmiᶜ. During the brief period of rebellion between al-Amīn and al-Ma'mūn in 817, Ibrāhīm ibn al-Mahdī was declared caliph. He had occupied this role uneasily for less than a year when al-Ma'mūn took power.[47] How complicit Ibrāhīm was in the coup is generally unknown, but his reluctance to be named caliph is noted repeatedly in the sources. Once al-Ma'mūn was confirmed as caliph, Ibrāhīm went into hiding for several years until he was discovered and put in prison.[48] He was freed after he begged al-Ma'mūn for forgiveness, and he lived out his life as a professional musician in Baghdad and later Samarra.

Ibrāhīm took up the standard for the other musical faction originally headed by Ibn Jāmiᶜ. Like Ibn Jāmiᶜ and his adherents, Ibrāhīm ibn al-Mahdī advocated for individual interpretation of older work and championed the newer style, one flavored by Persian and other foreign musical influences.[49] According to al-Iṣbahānī, Ibrāhīm was an expert in notes, rhythm, and modes and a virtuoso instrumentalist. In addition to the lute, he played the *mizmār* and *ṭabl*, and apparently had a huge voice encompassing a three-octave range.[50] Among his books, al-Nadīm notes Ibrāhīm wrote a book on singing, along with books on food and perfume.

Ibrāhīm is a fascinating contrast to the other musicians. He is masculine, handsome, and noble, yet also somewhat hapless. His lack of political acumen is a regular subtext in stories about him, and although he was briefly caliph and then had to flee for his life, he seemed to have accepted his fate and circumstances with aplomb. Ibrāhīm reads not unlike a nineteenth-century bon vivant, with his witty repartee, passion for music and women, and near untouchable status as a member of the ruling family. For all his passion, he walks a careful line: he is religious, but not too sober, he loves women, but is not cruel, and although he loved wine, he is not a sot. His social status padded him from much censure, yet at heart, like other male musicians, his profession couldn't help but mark him.

Badhl (Gift): The singing slave woman Badhl lived in the early ninth century CE/third century, H.[51] The *Aghānī* relates she was born in Medina and trained in Basra, making her a slave without foreign origin. Her teacher was Fulayḥ ibn Abī'l ᶜArwā', and therefore she shared a musical lineage with Ibrāhīm al-Mawṣilī and Ibn Jāmiᶜ. Badhl had a lengthy career and served in the courts of the Abbasid caliphs al-Hādī, Hārūn al-Rashīd, al-Amīn, al-Ma'mūn, and al-Muᶜtaṣim (reigned 833–42 CE/218–27 H).[52] Her talent and appeal were so strong that al-Amīn begged al-Hādī to sell her to him, to which al-Hādī replied: "Men of rank do not sell their slave women."[53] Eventually, however, he relented and al-Amīn was able to purchase her for himself.[54]

An excellent musician, Badhl was especially known for her incredible memory. In one story, she claimed to know thirty thousand songs, which she was forced to defend when a rumor spread, purportedly by ᶜAli ibn Hishām (d. 832 CE/217 H), that she knew merely four thousand. His challenge caused a rift, and when ᶜAli ibn Hishām was asked to apologize, Badhl wrote a *Kitāb al-Aghānī* for him containing twelve thousand songs.[55] According to al-Iṣbahānī, Badhl wrote the book not only to prove how many songs she knew, but as a peace offering. ᶜAli ibn Hishām thanked her graciously, and she received ten thousand dirhams as a reward.[56] In another story, when challenged by a young Isḥāq al-Mawṣilī about the composer of a song she just sang, she challenged him in turn by asking if he knew the composers of three different songs. He did not.[57] Given her wealth, she likely was able to purchase her freedom (though it is uncertain if she did), and when she died, she left a large fortune. The sources note that the singing woman Danānir was her pupil, although others list her as another student of Fulayḥ.[58]

Musically, Badhl was allied with Isḥāq al-Mawṣilī, meaning she defended the older, traditional styles and maintained performance traditions as they were passed down. Because of her association with Isḥāq, role as a teacher to several famous musicians, and prodigious memory, she appears in several sections of the *Aghānī*.[59] Most of those mentions relate specifically to her compositions and repertoire; few comment on her status and appearance. The emphasis on her memory, acquisition of wealth, and ability to openly challenge men point to her status as *qiyān*; however, she was clearly enslaved for at least half, if not all, her career. When her memory is criticized, she is allowed an apology, yet produces a book for her critic to prove her claim. It is a class act, to be sure, but one has the sense from the story that some kind of response or assertion was required. These intersections of her status as *qiyān* and *jawārī*, her deft handling of social and political situations, and musical skill serve to underscore the complexities of the relationship and asymmetrical power dynamics singing women negotiated with the patronate.

ᶜUlayya bint al-Mahdī: ᶜUlayya bint al-Mahdī (777–825 CE/160–210 H) was a half sister of caliph Hārūn al-Rashīd and the musician prince Ibrāhīm ibn al-Mahdī.[60] She was born in Medina and her mother, Maknūna, was a *jāriya* for the Marwanids. Maknūna was later sold to the Abbasids and installed in the women's quarters as a concubine for al-Mahdī.[61] According to the sources, ᶜUlayya was a talented poet and singer, known for her elegance, good taste, wit, and intelligence.[62] She was married to one of the Abbasid cousins, Mūsā ibn Isaʾ, but he died in 799, after three years of marriage. ᶜUlayya was much loved by her half brothers, especially Hārūn al-Rashīd, so much so that she trained women singers for his court. When al-Rashīd died in 809, ᶜUlayya became less visible as a musician, and is only noted a few times in accounts of the courts of al-Amīn and al-Ma'mūn.[63]

The *Aghānī* and *Fihrist* note that ᶜUlayya's songs were known by later generations of musicians, including ᶜArīb, who knew seventy-two of them. Two hundred songs attributed to ᶜUlayya were apparently preserved in different sources.[64] The topics of her songs centered on courtly love and wine, although as a woman of the aristocratic classes, ᶜUlayya could not perform in public unless chaperoned by one of her male relatives. When she did, the company needed to be proper and the tone lofty, in order to avoid any impropriety.

ᶜUlayya is called a *qiyān*, signifying her status as an elite woman musician, though her poetry is also emphasized in narratives about her talent. The borders between public and private music making, particularly between free and unfree women, is seen through representations of ᶜUlayya's performances in contrast to those of men and singing slave women. Because she always performed with a male relative present, many of the stories in which she is featured also reflect on her male relatives. They are passive and tender in her presence, encouraging her to perform and lauding her skill. As such, ᶜUlayya represents the genteel lady of the court who shares her talents, but does not seek attention as would a *jāriya*. Her piety and humility further exemplify the ideal for a noblewoman; many of the traits ascribed to her are noted by Ibn al-Washsha as being appropriate for the refined woman. Although her stories are possibly embellished and symbolic, ᶜUlayya's impact on her powerful family, early death, and her literary skills were strong enough that her contributions to musical culture became part of the literary landscape.

ᶜArīb al-Ma'mūniyya: The *akhbār* dedicated to the famous singing slave woman ᶜArīb al-Ma'mūniyya in the *Aghānī* runs to over sixty individual stories.[65] Narratives about her appear in other texts, commenting on her skill as a musician, wit, and occasional ability to shock. Even detractors of music and singing women treated ᶜArīb with grudging respect. The nickname "al-Ma'mūniyya" is something of a mystery, as it does not appear in earlier sources. Although ᶜArīb was purchased by the seventh Abbasid caliph, al-Ma'mūn, she was actually freed by al-Muᶜtaṣim and had stronger associations with later caliphs.[66] It is probable later historians added the appellation.[67]

The first paragraph of her biography in the *Aghānī* establishes her impressive credentials:

> ᶜArīb was an excellent singer and a poet with fine poetry. She had beautiful handwriting and diction. She was exceedingly charming, beautiful and elegant with a beautiful voice. Moreover, she was a talented *ᶜūd*-player with a superior command of composition, with knowledge of melodic modes and strings as well as the art of memorizing and reciting poetry and *adab*. None of her equals related to her, and no one like her has been seen among women after the old *qiyān* of Hijāz, such as Jamīla, ᶜAzza al-Maylā, Sallāma al-Zarqā and others who followed their path, though they are few. But they did not have some of the advantages that we have described, which belong to her equals among the caliphs *jawārī*; they who grew up in the caliphal palaces, and were nourished by a comfortable life, far from the life in Hijāz and growing up among common people [*al-ᶜāmma*], rude Arabs and rough characters. Authorities whose witnesses are enough have testified to this.[68]

ᶜArīb was born in 797/798 CE/181 *H* to a slave woman named Fatima, who was a *ḥarīm* inspector for the mother of Yāḥya ibn Khālid, Umm ᶜAbdullāh ibn Yāḥya ibn Khālid, of the powerful Barmakid family.[69] ᶜArīb's father was Jaᶜfar ibn Yaḥyā al-Barmaki (d. 803 CE/187 *H*), whose parentage lent more credence to ᶜArīb's poise and talent.[70] When the Barmakids were purged, ᶜArīb was a small child. She was stolen in the chaos of battle and sold to a slave trader.[71] The slave trader in turn sold her to the wealthy al-Marakibi, after which she was sold several more times, including to the caliphs al-Amīn and al-Ma'mūn. Her last purchase was by the caliph al-Muᶜtaṣim for one hundred thousand dirhams and he freed her. Once freed, ᶜArīb became his *mawlā*.

Along with her virtuosity as a singer and instrumentalist, ᶜArīb was a prolific composer and had a prodigious memory: Al-Iṣbahānī credits her with writing over one thousand songs and having over twenty thousand committed to memory.[72] She was also precocious. In one anecdote, she apparently began composing songs at age 14.[73] When criticized by Abū ᶜAbdullāh al-Hishāmi for having written the same song a thousand times, her admirers leapt to her defense. Their argument was that no musician could write one thousand perfect songs, so there necessarily will be some turkeys in the mix. Therefore, they asserted, denigrating ᶜArīb's output along these lines was churlish, and besides, she wrote more good quality songs than most.[74] To drive the point home, al-Iṣbahānī cites an impeachable authority to refute al-Hishāmi, none other than Isḥāq al-Mawṣilī:

> No one in any craft is exempted from situations in which he falls short of the intention. Perfection is only for the great God; imperfection is the nature He created in Adam's sons. If something is found in some of ᶜArīb's songs, this does not mean that the rest should be rejected and be labelled defective and feeble.[75]

When the issue of the value of her compositions came up again, a similar defense was launched, loaded with a sarcastic barb for good measure: "ᶜArīb did not leave behind any woman who was as able as she in singing, transmitting and composition. I said to him: 'No, and not many men either.' "[76]

The descriptions of her performances in the *Aghānī* include song titles, complete songs attributed to her, and notes as to what rhythmic and melodic modes she used.[77] ᶜArīb seems to have preferred the mode *wustā*, as it is noted several times.[78] As a *qayna*, many of her songs are on love, loss, and yearning. In addition to her own poems, she set poems she liked to music. The narratives state that she recited and sang, and in one case, danced and clapped as she sang.

ᶜArīb's singing is noted for its clarity, intonation, and her excellent diction. Her compositions were apparently distinctive and reflected her deep knowledge of music theory and the lute. In one story, when Isḥāq al-Mawṣilī arrives breathless at the court of the caliph al-Muᶜtaṣim, he is asked to identify a song:

> He (al-Muᶜtaṣim) commanded a *jāriya* behind a curtain and she sang, playing the *ᶜūd*, imitating the old singing. I said: "Add for me another lute; it would make me more certain." He added another lute and I said: "This is a new song by female lute player." He said: "What made you say that?" I said: "When I heard its softness, I knew it was new, from women's singing, and when I heard its excellent phrasing, I knew its composer was a lute player." I had memorized its phrasing and feet. Then I asked for another lute, and I did not have doubts. He said: "You are right; the song is by ᶜArīb."[79]

In all the stories about her and her interactions among patrons, ᶜArīb is a vivid figure. Like troubadour *vida*s, however, descriptions of ᶜArīb's performance and life are undoubtedly subject to exaggeration. Yet, the consistency in details across different sources about her origins, abuse at the hands of owners, and prowess give shape to who she might have been. ᶜArīb comes across as an intelligent, savvy woman, virtuous yet capable of ribald banter, especially on the subject of love and sex.

Along with memorable performances, ᶜArīb's biography contains stories about her rivals, colleagues, students, notable patrons, social influence, and many lovers. Over the course of her long life, ᶜArīb had numerous lovers which included caliphs, generals, and scholars, all of whom developed a searing passion for her. Al-Iṣbahānī has her stating that she had sex with eight caliphs, but the only one she desired was al-Muᶜtazz (reigned 866–69 CE/252–55 *H*). She would serve under two more, meaning she outlived ten caliphs.[80]

Despite the prestige of her lovers, ᶜArīb spurned several for some unknown swain, risking physical violence at the hands of her slaver, patron, and current lover. In one story, ᶜArīb has a daughter by a secret lover and sneaks off to marry him, much to the annoyance of the caliph and her slaver. When caught, her slaver beat her while she shouted in defiance, asserting she was free and if not, he should just sell her.[81] Although such stories depict her as admirable and strong, there is real peril at the heart of her actions. ᶜArīb was subject to the sexual whims of her slavers and patrons, and there is tacit understanding in the sources that her status might allow her to protest, but not refuse.

ᶜArīb's fame continued to grow after she was freed, and she acquired wealth and lands. After a long career, ᶜArīb retired to the country and transitioned into the role of patron. Her gradual retirement from public performance—if not public appearances—is positioned as an act of repentance. None of the stories paint her as being particularly pious, so her retirement cannot be read as an indictment of music, per se, but rather a personal desire to become a better Muslim.

According to the *Aghānī*, ᶜArīb bought and trained *jawārī* who became an extension of her by performing for her guests and at *majālis*. Having her singing slave women perform in her stead was also a means to train them, and they were offered as intimate companions for guests.[82] The sources name two of them—Bidᶜa and Tuhfa—and Bidᶜa became an established singer of some renown. ᶜArīb periodically came out of retirement when asked or when she wanted something. In his memoirs, al-Tanūkhi relates how ᶜArīb used a performance to manipulate a land deal so she could add a neighbor's parcel to her estate.[83] Until her death at age 96 (890 CE/277 *H*), ᶜArīb was respected for her skill, political acumen, and impact on the development of musical culture. Her influence in the form of the musicians she trained and powerful friendships she fostered resonated for generations.

Dhāt al-Khāl: The singing woman Dhāt al-Khāl (f. ninth century CE/third century, *H*) was a contemporary of ᶜArīb, Badhl, and ᶜUlayya bint al-Mahdī. Her name was Khunth, but she was called by her nickname because she had a mole or beauty mark, which, according to different sources, was either on her upper lip or on her cheek. Khunth first belonged to a slave trader who was in the employ of Hārūn al-Rashīd's sister, ᶜAbbasa. According to one story, she attracted the attention of Ibrāhīm al-Mawṣilī, and he then sang her praises to al-Rashīd who, upon hearing and seeing her, bought her for seventy thousand dirhams. Yet, when al-Rashīd interrogated Dhāt al-Khāl about the nature of her relationship with Ibrāhīm, al-Rashīd became incensed when she admitted she and Ibrāhīm had been intimate.

In a fit of pique, al-Rashīd married her to his favorite slave Hammawaih. (His slave was understandably quite grateful.) There are several stories related to this incident, but all point to how al-Rashīd eventually came to miss her songs and took her back. According to one, she returned to al-Rashīd only after the death of her husband. Others are vague on the status of her marriage when she returned. Once Dhāt al-Khāl was reinstated at court, she apparently trained her entire arsenal of beauty and musical skill to keeping the attention of the caliph.[84] As an elite *qayna* and concubine of the caliph, Dhāt al Khāl had access to power, enabling her to use the patronage system through her skill as a musician. Along with the singing women Sihr (charm) and Diya (splendor), Dhāt al-Khāl remained among al-Rashīd's favorites.[85]

The primary distinctions among these four *qiyān* lay in their legal status, which influenced how they were represented as musicians and women. Despite her numerous lovers, ᶜArīb was valued as a musician, and narratives about and including her consistently dwell on her skill as a poet and artist. Similarly, narratives about Badhl dwell on her musicianship and note her beauty, but, like ᶜArīb, she is an elite musician. In contrast, although Dhāt al-Khāl was also a fine musician, there is more emphasis on her role as a courtesan and intimate companion. She is depicted using her musical skill as an adjunct to her physical charms in order to move to the highest levels of the patronate. Even if a singing woman might declare her love for an individual patron, purchase her freedom, marry, or renounce her past, the fact that these women were courtesans could not be fully erased. Badhl may be lauded for her memory and savvy, ᶜArīb for her mastery and wit, while Dhāt al-Khāl is saucy and sexy, but both are still *qiyān* and *jawārī*.

Of the three, ᶜUlayya bint al-Mahdī is unique. She was a member of the royal family, pious, chaste, and yet a respected *qiyān*. Her modesty about her skill and reluctance to perform are themes among narratives about her; often, her male relatives had to coax her into performance. As a result, her musicianship is downplayed, and any moral burden is placed on the men who encouraged her. ᶜUlayya's propriety is thus served on two fronts: as a modest, pious woman who only performs under proper circumstances, and an obedient woman who listens to her male relatives.

The Musician as a Literary Symbol

Although it is tempting to speculate on how much is true in a given event or biography, medieval readers were less interested in facts. Details about the lives and loves of musicians conveyed the opulence of the court and added spice to events most people would never witness. Citing different authorities to confirm such details provided the reader an assertion of truth, but why those particular details were included and for what purpose often mattered more. As such, musicians functioned as participants and symbols within larger social, political, historical, and religious discussion. Their presence not only placed events in context for the reader, it served to demonstrate their influence on key political actors.

For example, the presence of musicians, even as a nameless group of singers, reflected the prestige and taste (or lack thereof) of their patrons. Name-dropping specific musicians gave additional authority and pungency to the anecdote. Who is invoked matters a great deal, as knowledge of and personal acquaintance with certain celebrities underscored the authority of the narrator and foregrounded the tone for the event. The musician may also be the vehicle of the narrative if the anecdote is related by them or on their authority. Having a musician as an authority, particularly a highly regarded one, lent veracity and framed the social context of the anecdote.

Due to their history prior to Islam and ubiquity as musical concubines, it is no surprise that singing slave women remained synonymous with entertainment music and sensual pleasures. As discussed earlier, during the pre-Islamic era, reference to a singing woman and her lute symbolized entertainment, a pause in a journey, and the promise of sex and wine. By the eighth and ninth century, this image became further invested with social status, passionate love, dissipation, frivolity, and, of course, sex and wine. The deliberateness and vehemence with which this image came to be used after the ninth century, particularly by those against *samāᶜ*, points not only to concerns about the excesses of the court and competing ideologies related to music, but the growing pains of the religion as it continually brushed against new cultures.

Archetypes of the saucy vixen, pious maid, worldly teacher, and lovelorn singing woman pepper the literature.[86] Each character would be familiar to the reader, representing different aspects of social concern and entertainment, depending on the source. Therefore, by establishing a universal set of characteristics for singing slave women and then referring to them collectively as "the singing women," the reader is given a clear mental picture. They become a collection of associations used for social commentary, most frequently to illuminate social issues. When a singing woman is named, it is to illustrate a point and, occasionally, to indicate repentance.[87] Singing women are the most real in the work of al-Iṣbahānī, but he was unique in his approach to music history.

Throughout the *Aghānī*, singing women are represented as authentic people and larger than life. Even when they are subject to brutality and exploitation, there is a distance between representation and reality.

By the tenth century, singing women increasingly were invoked as harbingers of vice and euphemisms for distraction. Regardless of the purpose behind their inclusion in a given text, the sources agreed that *qiyān* were undeniably fascinating. The combination of their visibility, along with their function as musicians and the dangers of passive audition, ultimately became the most common tropes in symbolic representation of the singing woman. Their individuality faded, transforming them into a means to convey opinions about the nature of music, diversion, politics, artistic sophistication, and the place of listening in Islam.

For example, in his account of the reign of the fourth Abbasid caliph al-Hādī, the historian al-Ṭabari includes several anecdotes involving famous musicians to illustrate al-Hādī's music preferences. During the year 787, he cites a story about the musician al-Wadī, and the story is told in the voice of al-Wadī himself. It describes an evening with Ibn Jāmiᶜ, Ibrāhīm al-Mawṣilī, Zubayr ibn Daḥmān (*fl.* end of eight century CE/end of second, *H*), and al-Ghanawī (*fl.* end of eight century CE/end of second, *H*), all important, well-established court musicians. A wager is set to see who can please the caliph, and ultimately al-Wadī wins because he intuitively sings the exact type of song that the caliph wanted. We are told: "al-Hādī used to like songs of medium length with a short chorus, and still never was able to be greatly enlivened by music."[88] Al-Wadī wins the money after his song and everyone drinks. Next, Ibn Jāmiᶜ steps forward to praise al-Wadī. Because of his generosity and praise for a colleague and rival, the caliph affirms al-Wadī as the winner. Everyone continues to drink and more songs are performed. After the party, al-Wadī thanks Ibn Jāmiᶜ and shares some of the money with him. We learn he doesn't share with Ibrāhīm al-Mawṣilī because he did nothing to improve the situation, meaning adding to the goodwill and inspiring more gifts.[89]

This story provides context for al-Hādī's character—and his courtiers—in several ways. First, we understand the opulence of al-Hādī's court and the skill of his companions through who was present and description of the informal *majlis*. Second, that the winner of the musical competition relates the story lends it gravitas and underscores the importance of al-Wadi's authority as an appropriate judge of music and musicians. Third, Ibn Jāmiᶜ's deft reading of the situation and flattery lends his approval to the caliph's choice, giving him a political edge over his rival Ibrāhīm al-Mawṣilī. Finally, despite al-Hādī's liking of music, we see that he is particular and his taste is not very sophisticated.

This last detail could also be commentary on the rivalry between Ibn Jāmiᶜ and Ibrāhīm al-Mawṣilī, both of whom were brought back to court and remunerated handsomely by al-Hādī when he became caliph. Al-Hādī might prefer Ibn Jāmiᶜ's innovations, or perhaps lack the sophistication to appreciate Ibrāhīm ibn al-Mahdī's traditional approach. Therefore, although al-Wadi's skill is not questioned, the subtle manipulation of the event by his companions—Ibn Jāmiᶜ's praise, Ibrāhīm al-Mawṣilī's apparent indifference—and the details provided by this one narrative suggest that al-Hādī's character might not be very strong after all.

Uses of musicians in social commentary could also be blatant. Narratives describing an outrageous or failed performance could reflect badly upon the performer and patron, along with evidence for the dangers of music and wine. Similarly, a successful performance, regardless of the content of the song texts, might highlight the generosity of the patron, skill of the musician, and sophistication of the audience in order to provide an argument for the innate harmlessness of listening.

For example, the *Risālat al-Qiyān* by al-Jāḥiẓ and the *Kitāb al-Muwashshā*ʾ by Ibn al-Washsha highlight the patronage of singing women as a reflection of a larger social problem. Not only do al-Jāḥiẓ and Ibn al-Washsha point to the corruption of the slave trade and how patronage of singing women leads to neglect of one's social duties, singing women themselves are simultaneously agents and victims of corruption. Al-Jāḥiẓ and Ibn al-Washsha do not go so far as to suggest that music is at issue, although they each outline the potential moral and financial consequences of the patronage system. The judge al-Tanūkhi, who was himself a respected patron of the arts, likewise relates pointed stories of dissipation related to music and musicians, though generally from the standpoint of being critical of the patron, rather than singer.

The use of musicians to outline moral consequences and place subtle judgment is found in larger historical and encyclopedic works as well. In this example from the *Histories* of al-Ṭabarī, he places two brief narratives concerning the famous musician Ashᶜab (*fl.* early eighth century CE/early second, *H*) within the lengthy events of the year 774–5 CE at the end of the reign of the second Abbasid caliph Al-Manṣūr (reigned 754–75 CE/136–58 *H*). The first reads:

> According to Aṣmaᶜi, Ashᶜab came to Baghdad in the days of Abū Jaᶜfar and he was surrounded by the young men of Banū Hashim and he sang to them and, when his songs were moving and his voice was (as good) as ever, Jaᶜfar said to him, "Who composed this poem? Whose are the traces of the camp at Dhat al-Jaysh, which became obliterated and worn out?

> They (the women on the riding camels) were out in the open desert, and the grief-stricken passed a sleepless night"
>
> He replied, "I took the song from Maᶜbad, I used to take melodies from him and if he was asked for it he would say 'Go to Ashᶜab, for he has a better rendering of it than I.' "[90]

This anecdote is lent weight by the authority of al-Asmaᶜi (740–*c.* 828 CE/122–*c.* 213 H), who was an important grammarian and scholar, as well as places Ashᶜab within masculine society. Here, Ashᶜab demonstrates his prowess in epic poetry, a masculine genre, through the focus on an important Arab tribe, the Banū Hashim, warfare, and evocation of the pre-Islamic *qaṣīda* in the song text. Immediately following this anecdote is a funny aside about him and his son, which further underscores Ashᶜab's status.[91] These stories are inserted into a bigger series of tales related to morality and events that took place around the city and are bracketed by scenes of violence.

Throughout the *Histories*, Al-Ṭabarī frequently (and not always favorably) includes anecdotes concerned with the morality of wine and music. Given how he references music and musicians, I read these particular anecdotes as contributing to his broader portrayal of the power struggles and resulting ethical concerns in different courts. In the eighth century, the Abbasids were still consolidating their power, so the figure of Ashᶜab, a "good" musician who has not forgotten his roots as an Arab or his place in society likewise underscores the "Arabness" of the Abbasids and their connection to tradition.[92]

The consistency of the musician narrative across literary genres suggests several layers of meaning. First, there is the context of the story, including setting, time of day, and its placement in relation to the other anecdotes. This scene setting is important, as it reveals much about the wealth, profession and piety of those involved. Second, there is the purpose of the story itself, who is relating it, and on what authority. Musicians served as a backdrop to important events and real players were included to underline the action and purpose of the narrative. Last, there is the record of the performance context, including the songs sung and reception, serving to illustrate the wealth, taste, and skill of musician and members of the audience.

Singly, these aspects provide insight into the complexities of the hierarchy of musicians at court as well as the developments of musical style. Taken together, one can see how the uses of music at court filtered into the broader culture through the growing prevalence of descriptions of musical gatherings in the middle and upper classes during the ninth and tenth centuries.[93] As a result, narratives concerned with musicians and court life contributed to the development not only of musicianship, but also musical identity, so that the symbol of the musician, real or imagined, became as canonical as the musical system or tradition they represented. This transformation became particularly useful to arguments against *samā*[c], as listening, musicianship, and the body of the musician became abstracted further in pietistic literature.

6

Politics of Listening

What were the catalysts for arguments about *samāc*? Although it is difficult to pinpoint when and why the discussion began in earnest, it undoubtedly was present at the beginning of Islamicate rule. Differentiating the new religion from others required that un-Islamic practices be identified and, ideally, pruned from social life. Given the number of practices, musical and otherwise, that continued, such pruning was haphazard. We see hints of the conversation in the *ḥadīth*, with references to incidences where music is being made and judgments about specific instruments, but many are merely anecdotal. Questions about the history of musical instruments and effect of listening are noted by Ibn Khurdādhbih and Ibn Salama; however, although both scholars suggest singing is harmless, their commentary indicates singing was clearly a topic of conversation.

The most obvious catalyst for concerns about listening were excesses of the court, which were perceived as wine-soaked bacchanals, rife with music, scandalous behavior, and dancing. Whether these gatherings were really taking place at the level of debauchery attributed to them cannot be verified, but the perception that they were wild was enough.[1] Few outside the wealthy classes and status climbers had access to them, so the majority of people only had rumor to go by.

Another catalyst was the use of music and dance by some Ṣūfi orders. Although *dhikr* and *samāc* might be as sparse as repeated recitation of a line from the Qur'an, some Ṣūfi embraced music and dance with sensual ecstasy. Last, there is what we might term "nativist tension." The influx of foreign people and ideas to the urban centers created fears that Islam would be corrupted. This tension is seen in the *shucūbiyya* movement, as well as early injunctions to return to the "original" practice of religion as outlined by the Prophet and *Rashīdūn*. Music was perceived as a foreign and corrupting influence; therefore, rooting it out would preserve Islam.

Lurking under such social, religious, and political concerns was the metaphysical. In the medieval world, boundaries between mind, body, and spirit were thin, and corruption of one led to corruption of the others. As the leader of the people as well as the faith, excesses by the caliph could have apocalyptic consequences for the community. Likewise, although each individual was responsible for their own practice of religion, that practice needed to be correct. Lapses and mistakes in individual practice could be corrected through education and, under desperate circumstances, intervention by others. This need for the pious to remain vigilant, including protection against the transgressions of others, is fundamental to discussions about listening.

The question of music came into stronger focus during the eighth and ninth centuries with the development of the four major schools of Islamic jurisprudence, in tandem with that of several schools of theology and philosophy.[2] Each school of thought established a position on music, and depending on which way the political pendulum swung had influence on the opinions of the caliph and general populace. The Muᶜtazilite doctrine had lost popularity by the middle of the ninth century, and a conservative backlash to its perceived liberality was on the rise. In addition, the overall political climate was tense, compounded by palace intrigues, slave revolts, and frequent warfare both within and without the empire. It is in that thick atmosphere that the first compilations of rulings about music appear in pietistic texts.

Pietistic texts are especially fertile soil for commentary about listening. Not only do they provide guidance on practice, they give concrete examples of where and how music took place in Islamicate society. Functioning similarly to books in our self-help aisles today, these texts devoted much scrutiny to what defined good practice, including prayer, cleanliness, fasting, improper and proper behavior, acceptable foods and moderation in eating, and what to do if one's neighbors and family were not behaving properly. Pietistic texts were geared toward the middling and educated classes. As a result, they were populist and instructional, providing examples in the form of quotations from the Qur'an, *ḥadīth*, important scholars and legal authorities, and stories related to famous people.[3]

Texts on piety were subject to interpretation and wrapped in the politics of endowments, leadership, and other tensions at the time.[4] Understanding what constituted excess was important, as even the practice of piety could become extreme. Therefore, there was discussion as to moderation as well as examples of extremes to give people clearer guidance. Maintaining purity and avoiding excess, also referred to as commanding the right and forbidding the illicit, remained the fundamental purpose of these treatises, with ever more granular examinations of what purity and excess meant.

As Matthew Gordon points out, the clashes between caliph and *ᶜulama'* regarding legal and moral issues were constant.[5] In piety texts, the *ᶜulama'* enter a conversation with the institution of music and singing, primarily singling out singing women and their patrons. Other religious scholars were meatier targets, especially in debates circling music in Ṣūfism, and there are many direct criticisms and refutations of the opinions of different scholars in such texts.

What makes these texts excellent sources is that even the most virulent screed against *samāᶜ* shows the medieval Islamicate world had a rich soundscape. That soundscape not only continued unabated, it metastasized throughout the Islamicate states for centuries. Music was consumed at all levels of the social order, as instruments, songs, itinerant troupes of entertainers, rogue Ṣūfi, traders, and singing slave women flowed constantly through the urban centers of the Islamicate states. Similarly, *samāᶜ* as a devotional practice was taking place in Ṣūfi cloisters and the streets of the major cities. Major mosques, including the Umayyad mosque in Damascus and the al-Aqsa mosque in Jerusalem, were filled with music. Melodic sound was everywhere.

Responding to the Question about Music

Although there are plenty of available critiques of performances, discussions about listening were not concerned with "good" and "bad" music in the artistic sense. Instead, conversations about listening focused on the cycle of distraction, indulgence, and the potential for addiction. The fundamental argument about listening to music was that it was distracting and diverted one from proper practice of religion. To those who advocated against listening, melodic and instrumental soundings were a catalyst for all manner of naughtiness. Once one was diverted by sound, even inadvertently, the emotional effect could lead to worse vices. From there, one's acceptance of different distractions expanded and priorities might shift towards worldly matters, such as illicit sex, drink, and greed. The ultimate result was apostasy, and therefore damnation.

Of especial concern was there was no control over what happened when a hearer was brought to a heightened emotional state. The problem was essentially this: a musician, poet, skilled reciter, and singer might initiate a performance with the purest intent, and the audience might similarly be prepared to receive the sound as intended. These could be a folk song at a wedding, or recitation of the Qur'an during Ṣūfi *samā*ᶜ and *dhikr*. What happened in the middle, however, was unknowable. A pure, innocent spirit could be seduced and driven mad.[6] That state could take place unwittingly, and when one was overwhelmed by emotion—love, anger, sorrow, passion—they might act out involuntarily. Once in the throes of emotional extremes, a listener might rend and toss their clothes, clap their hands, consume wine, fall in love, laugh, cry, and dance.[7] In Ṣūfi and pietistic texts, one reads an array of advice on how to avoid weird behavior and excess, as well as signs to watch out for when in thrall to something beautiful. If one must listen at all, some cautioned, it must be done quietly and reverently. To others, only the sounds of nature, non-melodic cantillation of the Qur'an, and recitation of noble poetry are to be heard, and only from a restrained, attentive position.

Scholars advocating against *samā*ᶜ expanded on their argument by asserting that although physical indulgences might feed the senses and inspire immediate pleasure, these pleasures were transitory and shallow in comparison to leading a pious, temperate life. That is not to say all medieval scholars who disapproved of *samā*ᶜ were rigid fundamentalists. Some do read as dour puritans, but a number of scholars concerned about listening were also members of the literati, Ṣūfis, and philosophers.

Those who advocated for *samā*ᶜ were also members of the same social and economic classes: literati, Ṣūfis, philosophers, and scholars. In addition, they shared concerns about the uncontrollable effect of listening, although with caveats. Some philosophers and physicians pointed out that feeding the senses could cure disease, especially melancholy and other mental illnesses. There was speculation that music could aid in curing physical disorders as well. Humoral medicine and astrology were linked to music, with strict guidelines for the practitioner lest a prescribed course of listening might make the patient worse. For their part, the bon vivants of the upper and middling classes insisted their pursuit of singing slave women (and pretty boys) and enjoyment of musical entertainments were perfectly harmless. Some went further by arguing that music patronage was a mark of educated sophistication. Certain Ṣūfi orders asserted that listening was indeed a catalyst, but one that could lead one to an intimate relationship with God.

How scholars on all sides of the conversation developed their arguments required considerable legal tap dancing, as there is meager evidence about listening in the Qur'an and *ḥadīth*. The Qur'an is the only unimpeachable authority, yet there is no opinion—or even mention—of music in the Qur'an. This lack meant scholars needed to study the potential of verses that referenced listening and pore through thousands of *ḥadīth*. Of the hundreds of thousands of *ḥadīth*, there are fewer than fifty that mention music, singing women, *mukhannathūn*, and instruments, and render a moral judgment on these issues.[8] Most have several variants and many are weak (*ḍaif*), meaning their lineage (*isnād*) is dodgy and hard to authenticate. To complicate matters further, several *ḥadīth* pertaining to listening are specific to a given incident or person, and many are so vague that their interpretation could go in any direction.

Those *ḥadīth* that are clearly in the "no" column include variations on a *ḥadīth* relating that bells are the "instruments of Satan." Another is a selection of situations featuring important historical personages advocating one is to cover their ears when accidentally hearing musical instruments. Singing women are singled out as leading patrons not only to drink, but global apostasy, transformation into "apes and swine," and the end of the world. Another frequently cited *ḥadīth* is that listening causes hypocrisy to grow in the heart.[9]

There are fewer *ḥadīth* suggesting listening is acceptable, and they are less in the form of pronouncements than relating stories. In one of two favorable to listening, we are given a vignette in which the Prophet and his favorite wife, ᶜĀ'isha, are listening to a group of Abyssinians sing and dance. ᶜĀ'isha is still a child, and the Prophet puts her on his shoulders so she can see above the crowd. When Abū Bakr criticizes the Abyssinians for making music (and the Prophet for allowing it), the Prophet asserts that everyone is allowed music for ᶜId. The second is another vignette of the Prophet and ᶜĀ'isha, this time being entertained in their home by two women singers. The *ḥadīth* is careful to note, "They were not, however, singing slave women." Again, there is criticism by Abū Bakr, and again the Prophet dismisses his concerns because ᶜĀ'isha is clearly enjoying the music and the singers are not singing women.

Early pietistic writings concerned with listening are essentially lists of *ḥadīth* and *responsa* by legal and religious scholars.[10] Given the paucity of evidence in the *ḥadīth* and the weakness of the most strident traditions, a connection to the Qur'an was vital. That was accomplished by widening the definition of diverting speech as expressed in Sura Luqmān 31:6 to include music: "Some men there are who buy diverting talk to lead astray from the way of God without knowledge, and to take it in mockery; those, there awaits them a humbling chastisement."[11] Having established this connection, scholars could include other diversions (games and wagering being chief among them), undesirable foreign influences (mostly Persian), hypocrisy, and the power of women (primarily singing slave women) to cause disruption, or *fitna*. Making these connections to listening offered social critique and guidelines for improving one's personal practice, in addition to clarifying non-Islamic practices.[12]

Later treatises expand on previous arguments using the same *ḥadīth* and connections to the Qur'an, but shift to a lecture format. In the opinion of some, listening to music was a distraction to be sure, but it was really just a stupid waste of time and for that reason alone should be avoided. Several texts literally say, "Listening to music is stupid and foolish."[13] That argument might be expanded to include other activities deemed unacceptable and stupid, such as chess, backgammon, gambling, and wagering. Such activities could lead to drinking and illicit sex, but the basic point was to avoid frivolous behavior.

Others had a more ominous interpretation of listening and diversion. Listening was an act of submission because the hearer physically absorbed sound into the body. It was pleasurable, to be sure, but the ecstasy one felt in listening could be dangerously close to the ecstasy of submitting to God. Or another human. An ecstatic union with God and passion for the flesh could be indistinguishable, awakening sexual urges. This confusion was especially likely when desire for God was transferred to the body of the musician.

Some took this line of reasoning further by stating that when a listener surrendered their emotional state to the sexual ecstasy of music, it was akin to being the passive sexual partner. Put crudely, listening to music was a form of spiritual penetration, and those who chose to listen were effectively emasculating themselves. The tenth-century scholar al-Ājurrī takes this position in the *Response to the Question about Listening*. He asserts that listening to *mughanniyat, mukhannathūn*, and therefore music itself is not only a diversion; it has a feminizing effect. Other authors agreed, emphasizing the feminine influence of music, regardless of the gender of the musician. Although *mūsīkār* (i.e., male musicians) are mentioned occasionally, singing women and all they represented are singled out as the primary culprits, with additional invective against *mukhannathūn* and their assumed sexual orientation. Interestingly, none of the arguments against singing women speaks against the practice of keeping enslaved concubines except in regard to maintaining individual sexual purity. Only concubines who were purchased to provide music are at issue. This hypocrisy was not missed by satirical writers such as al-Jāḥiẓ.

The first gauntlet thrown against listening was the *Dhamm al-Malāhī (Censure of Instruments of Diversion)* by Ibn Abi'l Dūnya. Although considered the first treatise concerned with *samā*ᶜ, Ibn Abi'l Dūnya was not presenting an original opinion, nor was he an especially skilled legalist. Written in the ninth century, the *Censure* reflects the political and cultural shift from the Umayyad to the far more opulent Abbasid court and the questionable diversions to be found there. In addition to censure against music, individual instruments, and singing slave women, Ibn Abi'l Dūnya includes wine, *mukhannathūn*, various forms of gambling and illicit sex (i.e., adultery). Illicit sex included dallying with women and *mukhannathūn*.

The *Censure* remains one of a few primary texts on medieval Islamicate music available in translation.[14] Yet, it has received minimal critical and literary study by Western scholars other than to discuss its content and note its opinions within the broader context of Islamicate music history. This lack is partially due to Ibn Abi'l Dūnya being viewed in his time as a minor writer, but also because to the Western reader, his writing style and position on music are extreme.[15] In his introduction to the *Censure*, Robson describes Ibn Abi'l Dūnya's position as "puritan," and others have used similar terminology to describe the tone of Ibn Abi'l Dūnya's writing.[16] As we shall see later, however, Ibn Abi'l Dūnya is quite mild when compared with other treatises.

Ibn Abi'l Dūnya's treatise inspired responses from other scholars, and a lively debate and subgenre within pietistic literature focused on listening emerged in the ninth and into the tenth centuries.[17] As these conversations unfolded, translations of Greek, Roman, Persian, and Indian approaches to music and music theory helped scholars and belletrists place music and other sound genres within an Islamic framework. Specialist texts on music theory and philosophy (*mūsīqī*) by giants such as al-Kindī and al-Fārābī provided the foundations for practical musicianship and theoretical thinking.

Therefore, within the context of his culture and readership, Ibn Abi'l Dūnya and those who shared his point of view were not just writing from a one-dimensional position of condemnation, but within a complicated legal, social, and political environment. The resulting profusion of literature related to listening and *samā*ᶜ demonstrates a shift from a conversation on the margins concerned with where music fit into religious and nonreligious daily life, to a flowering of standpoints taking place in the center.

Defining *Samā*ᶜ

Because *samā*ᶜ was and still is associated with Ṣūfism, it is a practice and a form of devotion. Yet, we cannot assume that *samā*ᶜ was used and defined the same in the medieval world. As with other medieval Arabic terms, the root سمع (*sami*ᶜ*a*) carried additional meanings that changed over time. The constant was that *samā*ᶜ required two elements: the one who created the sound-message and the one who heard it. Again, the uneasy variable was what happened in the netherworld between intent and reception, the latter of which could not be controlled by the performer.

During the medieval period, *samā*ᶜ included acts of listening and hearing. Treatises clarified the distinction between accidental hearing, which could be forgiven, to actively seeking out and listening to music, which could not.[18] Both fell under *samā*ᶜ. This relationship echoed the mind-body-spirit connection and addressed the spectrum of possible sound experiences, from amateur music making in the streets to the highest levels of professional performance at court. Along with sound genres associated with music, *samā*ᶜ referred to listening to poetry, a lecture, and recitation of the Qur'an.[19] *Samā*ᶜ was a means to learn, as well as certification of what one learned (*samā*ᶜ*at*).[20] For the hearer, sound was a conduit for information in the form of words-plus-sound, and what they heard—song, lecture, recitation—could cause an emotional-spiritual response.

This combination had a variety of effects on the person who experienced it.[21] For some, sound facilitated memorization, as in the case of a new song or lecture. To others, the sound itself was an enticement, as in listening to a song and recitation of poetry. Listening could also be accidental. Walking past a house where someone was playing the lute, listening to a public lecture in the mosque, and being entertained by singing slave women in the court—each of these actions encompassed *samā*ᶜ. As a result, *samā*ᶜ is not a stable concept in medieval texts.[22]

Ṣūfism

Like the *samā*ᶜ some orders embraced, Ṣūfism was a varied and fluid practice during the medieval era. Ṣūfism has suffered from being relegated in one monolithic block to the nebulous region of mysticism. Although it is a mystic tradition, the concept of mysticism, and therefore interpretation of diverse Ṣūfi practices, has been inhered with a Eurocentric understanding of the term.[23] In addition, Ṣūfism has been placed in opposition to "orthodoxy," "dry legalism," and the "elite" as a populist movement in positivist, Eurocentric ways—definitions which recently have been recast by studies into piety and non-elite culture in medieval Islamicate society.[24]

In his book on popular Ṣūfism in medieval Cairo, Nathan Hofer provides a helpful framework for understanding Ṣūfism in medieval urban centers. He suggests that

> "Ṣūfism" might refer to certain Ṣūfi practices that drew the ire and suspicion of *some* jurists and Ṣūfi masters. Such practices might include the performance of *samāᶜ* (audition), the veneration of Ṣūfi saints and the visitation of saint's tombs. In this construction, historians often artificially isolate the popular "Ṣūfism" of the masses from the "Ṣūfism" of the elites who wrote sophisticated theoretical treatments.[25]

Hofer continues by pointing out that the term "Ṣūfi" referred less to a stable identity and group than a shared set of values and practical traditions. These traditions were grounded in "very specific historical, social and political contexts … What all the individuals I examine here had in common was recourse to and contestation of a shared discursive and practical tradition transmitted through the institutions of Ṣūfism. But the nature of this engagement—its specific valance and substance in any given instance—was entirely contingent."[26]

Given the fluidity of Ṣūfism in the medieval era, how it interacted with and was understood at different levels of the social hierarchy is similarly broad. Hofer states:

> The popularization of Ṣūfism is fundamentally linked to the social and cultural production of Ṣūfism on a wide scale. By production, I mean the discursive and practical effects of people who call themselves Ṣūfis doing "Ṣūfi" things: dressing in certain ways, dancing, chanting, writing treatises, teaching disciples, parading in the streets and so on. By popularization, I mean the reception and consumption of those products by large numbers of people, regardless of social status … Third, and most importantly, the production of Ṣūfism involves the interplay of multiple strata of society and thus cannot be represented as either and elite or a non-elite phenomenon. Despite socio-economic divisions that might obtain in other ways, Ṣūfism was a cultural sphere in which these divisions often came together, even in conflict.[27]

This framework is useful for several reasons. First, the reflection and interpretation intrinsic to the development of conversations about listening and sound genres operated similarly within different levels of the social order. Second, this process gives insight into different reactions to the use of music within Ṣūfism, especially as expressed in treatises concerned with *samāᶜ*. Third, it reassesses how music consumption in the medieval Islamicate urban centers has been studied by challenging the Ṣūfi versus Traditionalist binary.[28] Last, it lends insight into how to look at social uses for music outside the urban centers.

Although the record is scarce regarding popular, non-elite musical expression, focusing solely on the use of music by the elite and establishing boundaries between high and low culture imply that non-elite art (however broadly defined) is of lesser value. That there were differences was indeed the case, but the primary sources and secondary studies indicate there were shared practices among different social groups.[29] Ṣūfism, along with *samāᶜ* and different types of entertainment music, may have become more popular and populist, but that led to a further blurring and extension of what was included in these categories.[30] Addressing the intersection of Ṣūfism and its impact on popular culture is essential to understanding how Ṣūfis—and by extension, uses of *samāᶜ*—were perceived by medieval scholars and studied by modern historians.

Samāᶜ as a specific devotional practice grew out of early Ṣūfism, although there is no firm consensus on how and why it began. Ṣūfism itself developed in the eighth and ninth centuries, first as an ascetic movement, and later shifted to mysticism.[31] The early Ṣūfis were peripatetic, lived simply, and abjured personal possessions. They believed love was the path to God, and it was possible to have a personal, loving relationship with God. Referred to as "friends of God," Ṣūfi poets not only wrote passionately about their love affair with God, some advocated that music and poetry could inspire a state of ecstatic oneness with God.

As Ṣūfism moved from asceticism towards mysticism, the quest for a personal relationship with God continued, but each community developed how best to establish that relationship. In the eleventh century, the previous composition of individualistic, ascetic communities of Ṣūfis composed of a loose confederation of teacher and students shifted into regulated and formal communities. From the eleventh century onward, Ṣūfis from the eastern and western reaches of the Islamicate states settled in the intellectual centers of Damascus, Jerusalem, Baghdad, and Cairo. At first, their communities lived on the fringes, but later different Ṣūfi communities received government support in the forms of endowments and building projects.[32] During the Ayyubid period (1171–1250 CE) in Damascus, a great number of building projects were undertaken, including schools, mosques, and libraries.[33] By the fifteenth century, Ṣūfi *madrasas*, *ribāṭ*, and other communal spaces were woven into the fabric of the city to the degree that delineating what location was used for what is difficult.

Schools and communal spaces were used for study and ritual, merging the juristic and mystic sides of Ṣūfism within one physical space.[34] Royal endowments, such as the *khanqah* (a Ṣūfi convent), would be built in proximity to the major mosques, such as the Umayyad Mosque in Damascus and the al-Aqsa Mosque in Jerusalem. Other communal spaces, like the less formal *zāwiya*, arose throughout the city, on the hills leading to Jabal Qaysūn, and for the poor, on the walls of the city itself.[35]

Listening sessions (*dhikr* and *samāᶜ*) took place in schools, madrasas, convents, and mosques. They could use recitation of specific syllables and passages from the Qur'an, as well as song, instrumental music, and dance.[36] *Dhikr* and *samāᶜ* might intersect, but were different practices.[37] As various Ṣūfi groups became established in urban centers, several developed fixed rules, often codified into written manuals. These manuals outlined essential details such as their affiliation and lineage to important teachers, conditions and rituals for admission, and instructions about *samāᶜ* and formulas for *dhikr*. In those orders where music was important to *dhikr* and *samāᶜ*, these instructions might specify the correct rhythm for recitation, where to breathe in so as not to disrupt the verse cycle, and tempi for performance.[38]

The sources imply that musicians could be hired for *samāᶜ* and an order might also use talent from within. Some orders purportedly used singing slave women and attractive young men, with the idea that their beauty acted as a stand-in for the beauty of God.[39] A flower or other beautiful object could also be used to inspire the viewer with love for the divine. This practice was called *naẓar*, to gaze. Gazing could include looking on a beautiful face to seek the face of God as well as the power of the gaze of the learned sheik on his followers.[40] *Naẓar* was dangerous territory, however. Love for a beautiful object could easily halt at the object, rather than act as a conduit for love of the divine. Furthermore, the promise of sensual love wrapped in the economics of the gaze was among the expectations for secular musical gatherings (despite nominal protestations otherwise), with the promise of intimacy being one aspect of the overall experience.

Not surprisingly, warnings about beautiful singers (generally young men) begin to appear in *samāᶜ* treatises for the Ṣūfi as well as broader discussions about music.[41] Concerns about the effect of *samāᶜ* are found not only in Ṣūfi manuals, but in ruminations of Ṣūfi philosophers such as al-Ghazālī.[42] They note who is most vulnerable to being ensnared by beauty—namely young, virile novices—and prescribe that *samāᶜ* be available only to those with the most spiritual strength and wisdom.[43]

Although many Ṣūfi orders sought stability in urban centers, antinomian orders remained itinerant and continued to live on the fringes of society, drifting throughout the boundaries of the Islamicate world and occasionally disrupting communities with their presence. These groups contrasted sharply from "sober" communities. They not only openly carried instruments to make music, but they played them in public, danced, and might use intoxicants to inspire an ecstatic state. Some also lived roughly, flouted rules about proper clothing—sometimes scandalously minimal—gazed on beautiful young people, and shaved their beards. In the thirteenth century, Damascus was one of the centers of what Ahmet Karamustafa defines as "new asceticism," and both the Qalandars and Haydaris had communities there. Although it is suspected these groups were composed of ethnic Iranians, there were also groups, like the Rifāʿī, who were from the Levant and given to similar performances of asceticism.[44]

Their exploits inspired awe and horror in the populace, and Qalandars and Haydaris appear as tricksters and agent provocateurs in popular literature.[45] Such eccentricity was tolerated when perceived as a manifestation of spirituality; therefore, the weird and compelling behavior of itinerant Ṣūfis could be the will of God.[46] People wondered: were they mad? Touched by God? A bit of both? These questions appear in pietistic treatises as well as other genres of Arabic literature, including biographical accounts, legal commentaries, *bidᶜa*, and *ḥisba*.[47]

Although it has been theorized the Ḥanbali were the harshest critics of Ṣūfism, this was not the case in the medieval era.[48] In fact, several important Ṣūfi scholars were Ḥanbalis.[49] Ḥanbalism and Ṣūfism developed at the same time and have similarities, such as a focus on piety, meditation on the Qur'an, and being *ahl al-ḥadīth* (people of the *ḥadīth*, sometimes called Traditionalists).[50] As Christopher Melchert points out in his article on the parallel growth of Ḥanbalism and Ṣūfism, this representation is due to their mission (and that of all pious believers) to "order the good and prohibit evil"; in Arabic, *al-amr bi'l maᶜrūf wa'l-nahy ᶜan al-munkar*.[51]

In his fascinating study of what this injunction meant and how it was enacted in different medieval religious circles, Michael Cook traces it from its wiggly origins in the Qur'an through different legal and social interpretations.[52] Cook frames different approaches to how one persuaded others to command right as the "three modes"—deed, word, and heart. These modes are present in texts concerned with *samāᶜ*, as evidenced by some either explicitly having the title *al-amr bi'l maᶜrūf wa'l-nahy ᶜan al-munkar* or some near variation that includes *samāᶜ* or *malāhī* to indicate the treatise is concerned with listening.[53]

Given that different Ṣūfi orders, itinerant preachers, traveling scholars, and common people mixed constantly on the streets and in the mosque, musical and religious practices were jumbled together. How did one decide what was proper?[54] To help the reader maintain spiritual and physical purity, pietistic texts began to proliferate on a variety of topics. How to avoid metaphysical impurity was essential to the physical embodiment of pietistic devotion (fasting, abstinence, etc.), and musical diversions fell handily into that formulation.[55] Inclusion of *samāᶜ* provided a dual function as guide to piety and legal argument.

Like fad diets and self-help manuals today, these texts exist along a spectrum of sensationalism. Some are simple tracts on how to pray and what to do when confronted by possible spiritual pollutants. Others are extreme, with virulent screeds against specific practices, sensationalized descriptions of licentious behavior, and dire warnings of consequences. These texts are social commentary as well as a conversation with one another, including references to and subtle (and not-so-subtle) digs at other scholars. Given the hyperbole and complex web of references, pietistic texts were reacting to what was going on around them. As such, they may be extreme—even bizarrely so as we will see in the next chapter—but give considerable detail as to contemporary practices. As one sees over the five hundred years covered by these treatises, efforts to control *samāᶜ* had little effect.

7

Discomfort and Censure: The Case against *Samā*ᶜ

Given the need for an accessible means to convey their standpoint to different audiences, how did medieval writers concerned with *samā*ᶜ develop a shared critical apparatus? To give a taste of how these arguments developed, I turn to eight texts spanning the ninth to the fifteenth century from a collection held at the National Library of Israel, catalogued as Ap. Ar. 158. The collection provides a useful compendium of arguments against *samā*ᶜ, including development of vocabulary, symbolic gestures, legal points, and shared rhetorical devices that are echoed in later *samā*ᶜ discussions. Through these developments, we see an ongoing ideological and metaphysical conversation related to what defined music, how it affected the body and spirit, and best practices in avoiding listening. Most tellingly, the collection gives a snapshot of contemporary practices across several urban centers, from instrument sales in the market to people brazenly drinking (and singing) in the streets, all suggesting music was part of daily life. In addition to *samā*ᶜ, the treatises offer advice on other distractions, ruminate on music history, and have interesting digressions. Therefore, although *samā*ᶜ is the organizing principle, the collection is fundamentally concerned with maintaining piety, with each text not only offering instruction as to what to avoid, but also specifying actions one might take to prevent others from transgressing.

In the treatises, the term *samā*ᶜ serves several purposes: to invoke Ṣūfi practice, nonreligious music, singing, and, more broadly, listening to music. Not surprisingly, the instruments mentioned in the treatises were used by singing women, for entertainments, and Ṣūfi *samā*ᶜ. Of the lute family, the *ᶜūd*, *ṭunbūr*, and *barbaṭ* are mentioned the most, while other plucked strings, such as the harp, are barely noted. The next most frequent mentions go to drums of all types, singly and in ensembles called *ṭablkhane*.[1] Based on anecdotes related to the *duff* and *ṭabl*, large and small instruments were used in special events as well as impromptu music making. Different varieties of tambourines are listed, with the most criticism levied at those with bells and jingles. Some scholars grudgingly allow use of tambourines at weddings, others explicitly not. Bells are singled out because they are mentioned in an oft-cited *ḥadīth* that states unequivocally, "Bells are the instruments of Satan."[2] Other percussion instruments that appear are the *qaḍib* and *kūba*, both apparently specific to Ṣūfi *samāᶜ* and *mukhannathūn*.

Among woodwinds, the worst offender is the *mizmār*, although no wind instruments are innocent. The *nāy*, *quṣaba*, *shabbāba*, and *zammāra* are not allowed, although instruments associated with shepherds, such as the *zammāra*, are not as bad. Opinion on singing also varies. According to some scholars, lullabies, work songs, and informal singing for special occasions are allowable, as long as there was no instrumental accompaniment. The addition of tambourines, bells, *qaḍib*, drums, and flutes was polluting, and to be avoided. Professional musicians and singers are identified generically as *mughanniyat/ūn*, *mūsīkār*, and *muṭrib*, with the most common group to avoid being *jawārī*. *Qiyān* are rarely mentioned.

Along with specific references to instruments, musicians, and singing, the treatises signify making music with the verbs associated with play and hearing. Most common are to strike, as in a lute or drum (*ḍaraba*), to blow into a pipe (*zammāra*), and to sing (*ghinā'*). Instruments used for entertainment, primarily stringed instruments, fall under the umbrella term *maᶜāzif*. Clapping (*qasf*) and dancing (*raqṣ*) are included in lists of diversions related to music and listening. Seeking and playing music is consistently a diversion (*lahw*) and frivolity (*laᶜiba*). Music itself is referred to as *ṣawt*, with *samāᶜ* functioning as a catchall inclusive of music and listening. The consensus among all the treatises is that those who seek singers and entertainments are in the wrong; therefore, active listening is worse than accidentally hearing.

Along with Ṣūfi *samāᶜ* and music entertainments, the treatises are critical of melodic soundings, particularly melodic recitation of sacred poems, *taghbīr*, and the Qur'an. Although there is a distinction among these sound forms, how *taghbīr* differed from the other two is hard to say. *Nashīd*s and melodic recitation of poetry in general—specified by the use of the word for melody, *nagham*—are generally condemned by all the authors, with the sternest criticism levied at *taghbīr* and melodic recitation of the Qur'an. *Taghbīr* is religious cantillation, but whether the term is keyed to a specific genre, practice, or even group that used it most is unclear. Based on these descriptions of practice and vehemence of condemnation, it was evident that melody was creeping into sacred recitation. Most alarmingly, people were singing the Qur'an.

The Compiler: Ibn Burayd Burhān al-Dīn Ibrāhīm al-Qādirī (1413–75 CE/816–80 H)

Little is known about Ibn Burayd. According to his contemporary al-Sakhāwī, he was born Dir al-Ashᶜarī and studied and read the Qur'an with Ibrāhīm al-Maqrizi. He was a Shāfiᶜī follower of the Qādiriyya order and lived in Cairo and Damascus.[3] Founded by famous Ḥanbalite theologian, preacher, and Ṣūfi ᶜAbd al-Qāḍir al-Jilānī (1077–1166 CE/469–560 *H*), the Qādiriyya were among the most prominent religious orders in Damascus and greater Syria. Some sources indicate they used music in their practices.[4] As with other religious orders, the teachings of the Qādiriyya expanded as al-Jilānī's followers traveled to study with him first in Baghdad and then in Syria.[5] Ibn Burayd is credited with writing a biography of al-Jilānī, but it has not been found.[6] Brockelmann lists at least two other treatises attributed to him that are also lost.[7] Among Ibn Burayd's lost works is a treatise excoriating the musical practices of the Sumadiyya, who were a subgroup of the Qādiriyya based in Damascus. They purportedly played a special type of drum in their *samāᶜ*, which, much to the horror of some, they held in the Umayyad Mosque.[8]

The social milieu in which Ibn Burayd lived was diverse and cosmopolitan. During the fifteenth century, mosques—particularly the major Friday mosques of Damascus and Jerusalem—were busy places, with near constant movement and opportunities for education in all possible subjects.[9] Mosques were where the poor, indigent, drunk, and the mad were sheltered and fed, surrounded by the sound of daily recitations of the Qur'an, lectures, and study in the libraries. Ṣūfis and ascetics also lived in the mosque and in cloisters nearby. They would meet to read, hold *dhikr* and *samāᶜ*, and pray.[10] Music was not only heard around the major mosques, it was being played in the mosques themselves. The entertainment industry was going strong and attempts to control the music-plus-sex trade, as represented by the market in singing slave women, had little to no effect.

Although the details about Ibn Burayd's life are meager, the treatises he collected shed some light on who he was. He was clearly well educated, established in his order, and had the means to acquire and copy books. Whether that meant he had wealth is unclear, although the quality of his materials and the time put into creating the collection suggest he had, at minimum, a solid scholarly network. Although his other books are presumed lost, the topics he undertook are revealing. He knew the history of his order and founder well enough to write a biography that was noted by others. The use of *samāᶜ* by other Ṣūfi orders, particularly the Sumadiyya, was vexing, especially those orders that shared a lineage with his. As other treatises in the collection consistently address uses of drums and the *ṭablkhane*, one wonders if that focus was intentional. Last, where and why did Ibn Burayd compile these treatises in the first place? Could this collection have been a study guide and source material for his treatise against the Sumadiyya? Was he working on a more comprehensive treatise of *samāᶜ*, which was lost or not completed? These questions are tantalizing, but the evidence is too thin to speculate.

Regarding where they were compiled, given what is known about Ibn Burayd, a case could be made for Damascus. First, he spent much of his life there, and in addition to being an important intellectual center, Damascus was home to several Ṣūfi communities. As a Ṣūfi of an established order, Ibn Burayd would have known and been known by roving, rowdier sects as well as those settled into *khanqahs* and *ribāṭs*. Second, the majority of the authors he chose had a connection to Damascus and discussed musical practices taking place there at the time. Finally, another argument for an origin of Damascus is that copies of several of the texts in the collection were also held in the al-Ẓāhiriyya library.[11] The al-Ẓāhiriyya library and school was established in 1277 CE and situated in the heart of the city close to the Umayyad Mosque.[12]

Ibn Burayd's notes indicate he compiled the collection (*majmūᶜ*) over a five year span from 1451 to 1456 CE (855–61 *H*). He gives a short overview of each author and when it was copied in either the introduction or final commentary of each text. Some of the notes indicate where he got his copy, such as from an older copy or a lecture. Other than his notes and marginal comments, there is no separate text by him.[13] The collection begins with the title page and *Response to the Question Regarding Listening* by Abū Bakr al-Ājurrī (d. 971 CE/360 *H*).[14] This choice could imply a thematic introduction, as all the treatises are responses to the question of audition. Of course, it is just as possible Ibn Burayd simply liked al-Ājurrī's treatise or it was closest to hand when he began copying.

Following al-Ājurrī, the order jumps chronologically:

1. Ibn Jamā'a (Burhān al-Dīn) (1325–88 CE/725–90 *H*): *Suwwāl sālahu shakhṣ min al-fuqarā'* (Response to a *faqīr*)
2. Diya al-Dīn al-Maqdisī (1173–1245 CE/569–643 *H*): *Al-amr bi-itbāᶜ al-sunan wa ijtināb al-bidaᶜ* (The command to follow established laws and avoid heresy)

3. Abū Bakr al-Khallāl (848–923 CE/234–311 H): *Al-amr bi'l maᶜrūf wa'l-nahy ᶜan al-munkar* (Commanding the proper and condemnation of the improper)
4. Al-Wāsiṭī (1259–1311 CE/657–711 H): *Mas'alat fi al-samāᶜ* (Question regarding *samāᶜ*)
5. Al-Wāsiṭī: *Al-bulghat wa'l iqnaᶜ fi ḥill shubhat mas'alat al-samāᶜ* (The exaggeration and persuasion of those who declare *samāᶜ* is permitted)
6. Ibn Abi'l Dunya (823–94 CE/208–81 H): *Dhamm al-Malāhī* (Censure of instruments of diversion)
7. Al-Ṭabarī (Abū'l Ṭayyib) (959/60–1058 CE/d. 450 H): *Kitāb fihi mas'alat fi'l radd ᶜalā man yaqūl bi-jawāz al-samāᶜ al-ghinā' wa'l raqṣ wa'l taghbīr* (Book refuting the opinions of those who allow listening to music, dance, and the *taghbīr*)

The earliest treatises in the collection by Ibn Abi'l Dūnya, al-Khallāl, and al-Ājurrī are compilations of *ḥadīth* and *responsa*, including variations, grouped into chapters and thematic sections. Among the range of diversions included with listening are games, dancing, gambling, sex, and consorting with *mukhannathūn*. By the eleventh century, arguments concerned with *samāᶜ* had moved away from listing *ḥadīth* and *responsa* to a more narrative format. *Ḥadīth*, the Qur'an, and legal authorities remained the legal backbone, but presented in the form of a lecture sparked by specific questions.

Although the later treatises by Abū'l Ṭayyib al-Ṭabarī, Ibn Jamāᶜa, al-Maqdisī, and al-Wāsiṭī remain concerned with entertainment music and the dangers of wine, women, and song, they focus more on Ṣūfi *samāᶜ*. They criticize the use of instruments and ensembles in Ṣūfi devotions, comment on dance and hand clapping, and offer opinions about recitation of poetry and accompaniment. Such arguments against Ṣūfi practices are interleaved with a careful revision of music history. Whereas there is a tacit acknowledgment in the treatises from the ninth and tenth centuries that music existed on the margins in pre-Islamic cultures as evidenced in the poetry, the later treatises assert music was not indigenous to pre-Islamic Arabs. Because of the influence of Persian music and musicians, the Persians are generally blamed for the introduction of *samāᶜ* and *ghinā'* to the Arabs.[15]

Due to their emphasis on contemporary Ṣūfi practices, redrawing music history to deny pre-Islamic uses for music is more prevalent in the later treatises. For example, several treatises have an interlocutor asking if *samāᶜ*, *ṣawt*, and *ghinā'* originated in the time of the Prophet and his Companions, wanting to know if past practice was the same as present. The answer is usually no, with only occasionally a cautious yes. When a yes is given, it is tempered by the fact that such practices were marginally acceptable only when related to travel songs and work songs. According to some traditions, Persian workers sang songs while restoring the Kaᶜba, which Ṭuways then passed on to the Arabs.[16] Since the origin of Persia sometimes was linked to Lot (a point mentioned by Ibn Salama and Ibn Khurdādhbih as well), a tenuous connection to emasculation could be aligned with *samāᶜ* and the consequences of listening.[17]

The progression of language, terminology, and rhetorical shifts found in the treatises from the eleventh to fourteenth centuries highlight two key aspects of medieval Islamicate musical culture. First, *samāᶜ* remained a fluid concept and an important social concern, necessitating that all sides clarify, refine, and strengthen their position. The second is that music, dance, and melodic soundings continued unabated at all levels of the social order in religious and nonreligious contexts.

Rather than follow the order of the treatises in the collection, my tour here organizes them in chronological order to make it easier to follow the progression of arguments about *samāᶜ*. Before going into an overview of the key points of each text, I give a short biography of each author to place them in context.

The Instigator: Abū Bakr ᶜAbdullāh ibn Muḥammad ibn Sufyān Ibn Abi'l Dūnya (823–94 CE)

Ibn Abi'l Dūnya was from a family of *mawālī* under the Umayyads, although whether this label meant his family was foreign or previously enslaved is unclear. He was a tutor to the Abbasid caliph al-Muᶜtaḍid (reigned 892–902 CE/278–89 *H*) and his son al-Muktāfi (reigned 902–8 CE/289–95 *H*) in Baghdad.[18] Al-Muwaffaq (842–91 CE/227–77 *H*), the brother of the caliph al-Muᶜtamid (reigned 870–92 CE/256–79 *H*), was his patron later in life.[19] According to accounts by those who knew him, Ibn Abi'l Dūnya was educated, well read, enjoyed writing poetry as well as prose, and apparently had an excellent sense of humor.[20] He was a respected religious authority, and credited with writing at least 102 books, of which approximately 33 survive. Of these, 7 were dedicated to piety comprising a morality series. In addition to the *Censure of Instruments of Diversion*, there are two other texts in this series known to be extant: the *Censure of the World* and *Censure of Intoxicants*, along with a treatise on *Al-amr bi'l maᶜrūf wa'l-nahy ᶜan al-munkar*.[21]

Ibn Abi'l Dūnya subscribed to the Ḥanafi school of jurisprudence, and held conservative views regarding consumption of luxury items, including music. Though respected for his religious knowledge, his peers did not consider him a legal authority. Rather, Ibn Abi'l Dūnya was a populist who wrote pietistic treatises for a broader audience.[22] As a result, his choices in which *ḥadīth* to use and their authentication often fall short of the standards set by legal scholars, and so his work is not a legal argument within the context of Islamic legal science.[23]

Dhamm al-Malāhī (Censure of Instruments of Diversion)

Why Ibn Abi'l Dūnya chose to dedicate a treatise specifically to listening and diversion is not difficult to guess. Despite having had Ibn Abi'l Dūnya as their tutor, al-Muᶜtaḍid and al-Muktāfi both enjoyed a luxurious lifestyle. Al-Muᶜtaḍid was more pious than his son, though his piety did not prevent him from employing singers and enjoying music. Al-Muktāfi was his son by an enslaved Persian concubine, and during his short reign, he openly indulged in sensual pleasures. In addition, several of the instruments Ibn Abi'l Dūnya references were used in Ṣūfi *samāᶜ* and *dhikr*. Even if his readers did not have direct experience with Ṣūfi *samāᶜ* and court music, the reputations of singing women and antinomian Ṣūfi would be familiar. Thus, it is likely Ibn Abi'l Dūnya's *Censure* was composed as a reaction to excesses of court culture and select groups of Sufis.[24]

Given the subject matter and methodology, one could say that there was both an audience and a target for the *Censure*. The popularity of the book and subsequent literature it inspired suggests it took root in the rising middling classes. Those striving for upward mobility emulated the upper classes and what they perceived as noble pursuits. The lower classes never saw the pomp of the courts directly, with their only experience limited to reports and witnessing the excesses of the middling classes above them. Imagining the worst made some retreat into religious conservatism.[25]

The title can be translated several ways, such as *Censure of Instruments of Pleasure* or Henry George Farmer's colorful *Disapprobation of Musical Instruments*. Although listening to music takes up nearly half the treatise, the *Censure* is concerned with diversion overall. As such, it falls under the categories of *zuhd* and *raqā'iq*, both of which are genres of pietistic literature.[26] *Zuhd* has a moralizing and religious intent; advocating moderation and functioning as an ethical guide.[27] *Raqā'iq* refers to the heart and is a genre intended to supply edifying reading.[28] The *Censure* includes diversions such as playing chess, backgammon, gambling, and adultery and ends with condemnation of the patronage of *mukhannathūn*. In so doing, Ibn Abi'l Dūnya broadened the range of diverting and impious activities and pointed to how they connected.[29] Therefore, Robson's translation of *Censure of instruments of diversion* conveys this intent best.

There are four extant copies of the *Censure*, fortuitously balanced between two longer versions and two abridged. The longer versions are in the NLI collection and another formerly in the al-Ẓāhiriyya library in Damascus, Syria, with the two abridged versions held in the Berlin Staatsbibilotek and Istanbul.[30] Both versions share the same chapters and content, with the longer versions containing nearly twice the *ḥadīth* as the abridged versions—about 158 compared to about 70. The longer versions contain additional *ḥadīth*, the majority of which are variations, and fuller chains of authority (*isnād*). Although the longer version is more thorough, it is a bit of a slog in comparison to the abridged, which prunes the variations.[31] The abridged *Censure* uses brief, descriptive, and, occasionally, lurid examples from *ḥadīth* (albeit few are *ṣaḥīḥ* or strong), with abbreviated authentication. The abridged version may not adhere to the stringent legal process of the time, but it was authoritative enough for his audience.

The *Censure* begins with immediate condemnation of all music. No form of musical sounding is innocent. Among unacceptable forms of sound are wailing at funerals and all social music making. To give his argument more weight, he references Sura Luqmān, although al-Ājurrī is the first to make the connection to Luqmān explicit by citing the relevant verse at the beginning of his treatise. Ibn Abi'l Dūnya implies that unless society changes its ways, the entire community could fall into apostasy and destruction. The only solution for the pious was to return to the simpler pursuits from the time of the Prophet and *Rashīdūn* and cast off foreign and impious influences.

This concern is evident from the incipit, in which Ibn Abi'l Dūnya conflates *qiyān* with apocalyptic consequences of their patronage:

> On the authority of Sahl ibn Saᶜad (Allah be pleased with them both), Allah's Apostle (Peace be Upon Him) said, "Among the last of my people there will be swallowing up, pelting, and metamorphosis." It was said, "O, apostle of Allah, when?" He said. "When the *maᶜāzif* and the *qaināt* appear, and wine is considered lawful." The *maᶜāzif* are musical instruments (*'ālāt al-ṭarab*), and the *qaināt* are the singing girls.[32]

This first *ḥadīth* is on the authority of al-Bukhārī, making it one of the strongest (*ṣaḥīḥ*) traditions in the treatise. He follows this passage by describing the impending loss of humanity by transformation into "apes and swine," as well as violent natural disasters.[33] Ibn Abi'l Dūnya heightens the peril by providing guidance for the individual to retain their piety, namely, avoiding listening, but it might not be enough. There are regular reminders that regardless of how careful an individual might be to avoid music and diversion, the consequences are severe for the entire community unless everyone changes their ways.

Having established the metaphysical dangers of listening, Ibn Abi'l Dūnya turns to singing and specific instruments. Because of their association with singing women and nonreligious entertainments, the *ᶜūd*, *ṭunbūr*, *duff*, *ṭabl*, and *mizmār* receive especial attention. Ibn Abi'l Dūnya uses *malāhī* as a pejorative and categorizes other terms previously used to designate musical instruments as *ḥarām*, such as *maᶜāzif* and *ālat al-ṭarab*. Within the section on instruments, he includes a brief digression into the unlawfulness of cross-dressing in the transition from music to games.[34] Here, he is pointing to the fad at court for dressing young slave girls as boys and writing poems to the beauty of young boys, sometimes dressed as girls.

Following music, Ibn Abi'l Dūnya turns to gambling and other diversions, placing condemnation of *mukhannathūn* at the end. Citing the fate of Lot's people, the last two sentences of the treatise are an indictment of sodomy, stating, bluntly, that men are not to have anal sex with women or men and that seeking anal penetration (*liwāṭ*) is *ḥarām*.[35] Robson delicately translates the last statement into Latin, a common move at the time to shield the tender sensibilities of the Western reader: "Tāwus (Allah have mercy on him!) was asked *de eo qui feminam per clunes ineat* (is it allowable to penetrate a woman via the buttocks) and said, 'That is unbelief. Lot's people perished simply for that. *Ad hunc modum viri cum viris, feminae cum feminis coierunt* (in this way men fornicated with men, women with women)."[36]

This reference to *mukhannathūn* at the end is intriguing. Ibn Abi'l Dūnya includes them after a frightening parable of adultery, pointing out that consorting with them is wrong not only for their place as unmasculine men, but as a specific type of performer. In so doing, Ibn Abi'l Dūnya comes full circle by linking *mukhannathūn*, singing women, and, by extension, their patrons, with music and unlawful sex. Ibn Abi'l Dūnya leaves it to the reader to infer that active listening to music was, in effect, a form of unwelcome spiritual penetration. Starting with al-Ājurrī, later treatises develop arguments about the emasculating effects of music, general perils of listening to women singers, and spiritual dangers of listening to instruments, although all remain entwined with diversions such as gambling, chess, and backgammon.

The Jurist: Abū Bakr Aḥmad ibn Hārūn al-Khallāl (848–923 CE)

Al-Khallāl was a major Ḥanbali jurisprudence expert who was instrumental in the compilation of the collected sayings of Ibn Ḥanbal.[37] Despite his key role in the development of early Ḥanbalism, little is known about his life. He was a student of Abū Bakr al-Marwadhi (d. 889 CE/275 H), who was one of Ibn Ḥanbal's favorite pupils. Al-Khallāl followed ᶜAbdullāh (d. 903 CE/289 H), the younger son of Ibn Ḥanbal, who transmitted almost all of his father's teachings. Later, al-Khallāl taught in Baghdad at the mosque of al-Mahdī, which was one of the most important mosques in the city.

Of al-Khallāl's extant work, the massive *Kitāb al-jamīᶜ* is the best known, noted as the "first great juristic corpus of Ḥanbalism."[38] It was completed by his main disciple, Abū Bakr ᶜAbd al-ᶜAziz, and scholars such as Ibn Taymiyya referenced it well into the fourteenth century.[39] Along with the *Kitāb al-jamīᶜ*, al-Khallāl is said to have written a history of Ḥanbalism, of which a few leaves purportedly survive in the al-Ẓāhiriyya library. Much of the work is contained in two histories of Ḥanbalism, one of which is the *Dhayl* of Ibn Rajab (d. 1392/3 CE/785 H). In addition, al-Khallāl apparently transmitted a text by Ibn Ḥanbal on music, although it has not been located.[40]

Al-amr bi'l maᶜrūf wa'l-nahy ᶜan al-munkar (Commanding the Proper and Condemnation of the Improper)

With the exception of Ibn Abi'l Dūnya's *Censure*, *Commanding the Proper* is the only other well-known text in the NLI collection. At least two modern editions exist, and there are two additional manuscripts in Syria and Egypt.[41] Like Ibn Abi'l Dūnya's *Censure*, *Commanding the Proper* is not a narrative, but a series of forty-two scenarios or case studies, as Shiloah terms them.[42] The *responsa* are divided into thematic sections and cover a broad array of contexts in which the reader might encounter improper behavior. Not everything in the treatise is concerned with listening. Other diversions and ethical situations are included, particularly luxury activities enjoyed by the caliph and wealthy courtiers.[43] The inclusion of other diversions gives additional insight to the social structure of the time and provides a *vademecum* for those studying different aspects of Ḥanbalite opinion on social mores.

In his study of the injunction to "command the proper," Michael Cook provides a detailed analysis of how al-Khallāl's text fits within the literary subgenres of *samāᶜ* and pietistic guidebooks.[44] Cook emphasizes there were limits to how far one can go in "forbidding wrong" in order to avoid breaking the law or angering the wrong person. For example, depending on the situation and nature of intervention, one could invite negative political attention and risk judgment for butting in where one is not welcome. Politely asking a neighbor to stop making music and taking the drastic step of moving out if they won't stop is one thing; tramping about looking for people to lecture and invading their homes to smash instruments is quite another. An instrument needed to be visible in a person's home, nor may one snoop even if there is a suspiciously lute-shaped form concealed under a curtain. Regardless of the infraction, infringing upon the privacy of another is not acceptable.

To help the reader make the right decisions regarding listening, *Commanding the Proper* covers an array of situations, including instruments to avoid, avoiding use of melody in recitation, and the contexts in which the unwary might encounter music in day-to-day activities. There is also commentary on Ṣūfi *dhikr*, particularly inclusion of singing, dance, and instruments. In addition to the expected citation of relevant *ḥadīth*, al-Khallāl includes examples of situations one might encounter and how they were dealt with. These case studies give fascinating insight into uses for music in elite and non-elite spheres.

Instruments to avoid are, predictably, those used for entertainment: *ᶜūd*, *ṭunbūr*, *ṭabl*, *duff*, and *mizmār*. The *qaḍib* and *quṣaba* are mentioned in passing. Playing woodwinds is right out. For the physical act of playing an instrument, al-Khallāl uses *ḍaraba* when talking about striking lutes and drums, *zammāra* for woodwinds. These verbs also stand alone to indicate the playing of instruments in general. When referring to music and listening, he uses *ṣawt* and *samāᶜ*, drawing both terms together to include listening to music in *samāᶜ*. Invoking the authority of the Prophet, al-Khallāl uses *laᶜiba* in reference to playing *ṭabl* and *zammāra*, commenting that both are frivolous and not allowed. There is passing mention of musicians in the form of *jawārī*, *mughanniyat*, two references to *qiyān*, and one to *mukhannathūn*.[45] His examination of instruments is detailed, noting distinctions that some *duff* have skin coverings, and, along with the *ṭunbūr*, he comments on their use in different social events.

In addition to giving advice about what musical instruments are allowable and under what circumstances (not much and not often), the reader is advised about what to do if one sees instruments in the market, hears music coming from a neighbor's house, and encounters different types of singing and lamentation. An important question is what action to take, especially with those who insist on making music after one has asked them to stop. Breaking instruments is allowed under extreme circumstances, and al-Khallāl offers advice on when one might break instruments, supported by notable authorities.

Among the scenarios is a story of a sheik who hears music coming from the house of a woman as he passes by. He knocks on the door, intending to ask her to stop. When her servant girl answers the door, the sheik tells her to ask her mistress to stop playing and destroy her lute. After receiving the message from her servant, the mistress refuses and continues to play. The sheik next tries a new tactic and begins to lament, cry, and recite the Qur'an outside her house. A large crowd soon gathers (no doubt enjoying the spectacle), and the woman has no choice but to surrender the instrument.[46]

Al-Khallāl comments on melodic vocal soundings, including a detailed discussion of *taghbīr* and melodic recitation of the Qur'an.[47] Both are forbidden in the strongest terms, and he uses *ṣawt* and *ghinā'* to clarify that these are song-like and therefore musical genres. Between the discussion of *taghbīr* and melodic recitation, al-Khallāl makes an interesting passing reference via a discussion of *ᶜajab* to Qur'an 37 (Al-Ṣaffāt: The Ranks), verses 12-13:

> Nay, but thou dost marvel when they mock
> And heed not when they are reminded.[48]

These verses present another interpretation for the offence of *taghbīr* and melodic recitation of the Qur'an. The verb *ᶜajiba* means to wonder, especially at the strange or improbable.[49] This complex passage offers a conundrum. On the one hand, it can be read that people discount the reality that God places before them as extraordinary and ridicule that which they do not understand regardless of being reminded of the truth. Yet another reading is that people believe improbable (and stupid) things without proper evidence. In this context, it is possible al-Khallāl is making a statement as to why people persist in these practices that are clearly not supported by exegesis (he cites *tafsīr* explicitly), thus allowing themselves to be bamboozled by those who assure them it is fine. At the end of the treatise, al-Khallāl abandons music to comment on poetry and sober (i.e., non-melodic) recitation, both of which he deems okay.

Strengthening the Case: Abū Bakr Muḥammad ibn Husayn ibn ᶜAbdullāh al-Ājurrī (d. 971 CE)

Al-Ājurrī was a respected Shāfiᶜī jurist whose legal and religious works were important sources for the development of Shāfiᶜī jurisprudence.[50] Like al-Khallāl, little is known about his life. Ibn Khallikan (1211–82 CE/608–681 *H*) includes an entry on al-Ājurrī, corroborating that in addition to memorizing the Qur'an, he was a respected Shāfiᶜī and *ḥadīth* scholar.[51] The *Fihrist* gives the same biography and states al-Ājurrī was a righteous and consecrated jurist who wrote about piety.[52] According to both sources, al-Ājurrī was born in the western part of Baghdad in the area called Durr al-Ājurr, from which he takes his name. Al-Ājurrī apparently received an excellent education, and his teachers included Abū Dāwūd, the author of the *Sunan*. He lived and taught in Baghdad for many years before moving to Mecca. According to one story, he fell in love with the city after a visit and decided to move there, living in Mecca for thirty years where he served as the imām of the Grand Mosque. The *Fihrist* corroborates this fact by stating al-Ājurrī lived in Mecca and had "died recently."

Like his scholarly contemporaries, al-Ājurrī was a prolific author and did not range far outside his areas of expertise. Few of his works remain, however. The *Response* exists only in manuscript, and other than Amnon Shiloah's entry in RISM and a few references in the footnotes of a handful of articles, it has not been studied in detail.[53] Interestingly, although the *Fihrist* notes his books have been "mentioned in their proper place," there is no such mention elsewhere. Only three books are listed: "Abridgement of the Law"; "Judicial Decisions concerning Women"; and "Advice" (which included a number of chapters about the law).

Al-jawāb ᶜan mas'alat al-samāᶜ (Response to the Question Regarding Listening)

Given that music was music was increasingly a hot topic, it is not surprising al-Ājurrī weighed in to provide a Shāfiᶜī perspective. As an expert in jurisprudence, al-Ājurrī's argument is more legally sound than that of Ibn Abi'l Dūnya. Although he follows a similar format as Ibn Abi'l Dūnya and al-Khallāl by listing *ḥadīth*, al-Ājurrī enters the text himself to add the occasional comment or interpretation. The treatise has a clear structure, and he leads the reader smoothly through each component of his position. Throughout the treatise, al-Ājurrī uses the strongest possible language, referring to people who assert listening to music is fine as dissolute, deluded, and stupid.

As stated in the title, his purpose is to answer the question about listening, and he opens by reiterating the question and giving the answer, which is an unequivocal no. He then establishes the evidence he will use to argue his case.[54] Al-Ājurrī first makes a direct link between listening to music and diversion by directly citing Sura Luqmān 31:6, connecting the patronage of singers to the purchase of idle tales. He strengthens his interpretation by noting he is not the first or only one to do so and supports this claim by including several variations on a *ḥadīth* on the authority of Abū Muḥammad ᶜAbdullāh ibn Muḥammad ibn Najīya, reaching back to ᶜAbdullāh al-Wāsiṭī who said, essentially: "When people purchase idle tales, that, he says, is song." There follows a number of authorities to support this claim and variants that include song and singers. He includes many of the same *ḥadīth* as Ibn Abi'l Dūnya, such as the one asserting that "song causes hypocrisy to grow in the heart."

Next, al-Ājurrī extends the definition of idle diversion to encompass all aspects of musical soundings. He cites the major legal scholars, including Abū Ḥanifa, Abū Mālik, Abū Dāwūd, and al-Shāfiᶜī. As he was a student of Abū Dāwūd, Abū Dāwūd is among his key authorities. Having established his evidence, al-Ājurrī proceeds with his own arguments, carefully documenting each set of *ḥadīth* and staying within each point of discussion until it is exhausted.

The definition of music and singing gets more specific as al-Ājurrī moves from music in general to musicians in particular. He uses *mughanniyat* and *jawārī* interchangeably, implying they are synonymous.[55] The *mukhannathūn* are noted, with condemnation of their performance as unmasculine men and musicians.[56] Furthermore, he connects the purchase of enslaved women singers to the purchase of idle tales,[57] along with those who purchase songs, listen to songs, and composers of songs. Therefore, musicians (in the feminine) are the root of the problem, not poets, along with those who make (train, trade) them. Of course, he says, there are some who disagree song alone constitutes idle tales, but they are incorrect and he states at the close of this section that "the Qur'an says this is true."[58]

In addition to kinds of listening to avoid, al-Ājurrī addresses the act of playing itself. He uses *laᶜiba* to enhance his opinion of playing music as well as the pursuit of hearing.[59] Like the other early treatises, al-Ājurrī links playing music (and by extension, singing) with childish behavior, marking it as an unlawful diversion. He backs this point up unequivocally with the statement that play brings one close to Satan.[60] He continues with commentary on musical instruments, specifically stringed instruments which are *maᶜāzif*. What makes al-Ājurrī's argument particularly interesting here is that he makes a distinction between song and poetry. Al-Ājurrī again clarifies that singers, not poets, are at issue.[61] He comments that although there are some who assert that poets and poetry fall into the same category of diversion as singers and song, he does not agree.

This clarification allows him to step back to comment more broadly on why diversion and the purchase of idle tales in the form of music is wrong. He reiterates that the Qur'an states that purchase of idle tales removes one of the path to knowledge of God.[62] Al-Ājurrī uses the term *ṣawt* to refer to musical sound and notes music is inherently distracting.[63] Because of this quality, the average person seeking to live a pious life needs good examples in order to take steps to avoid music. Since powerful, influential people, like the caliph and his governors, are listening to music, al-Ājurrī recommends that those seeking to be pious instead follow the teachings of religion and advice of the learned authorities on such things.[64]

Interestingly, he ends the treatise with a discussion of circumcision, folk music, and other cultural practices. Among the anecdotes about different folkways, al-Ājurrī includes a discussion of the problems between men and women.[65] Not surprisingly, passion and wine are among these problems. The treatise ends with a benign exhortation for piety, the implication he hopes he has presented a persuasive argument, and closes with gratitude for the wisdom of God and the Prophet.

The Teacher: Abū'l Ṭayyib Ṭahir ibn ᶜAbdullāh ibn ᶜUmar ibn Tahir al-Ṭabarī (959/60–1058 CE)

Abū'l Ṭayyib, as he was commonly known, was a beloved, respected, and long-lived teacher of the Shāfiᶜī school. He was born in Amol, Tabaristan, where he purportedly began his studies at the tender age of 14. Among his first teachers was Abū ᶜAli al-Zajājī whose academic lineage included Ibn Surayj. Students regularly traveled among the urban centers in pursuit of an education, and Abū'l Ṭayyib did the same. He went first to Gorgan and Nishapur, then finished his studies in Baghdad. Abū'l Ṭayyib remained and taught in Baghdad for many years, becoming one of the leading Shāfiᶜī jurisconsults and scholars, earning him the position of judge (*qāḍī*). He also founded an important school (*madrasa*) where he attracted a large student following.[66] Abū'l Ṭayyib's fame was such that Shāfiᶜī scholars in Iraq referred to him simply as "The Qāḍī."[67]

In 1045, Abū'l Ṭayyib retired to take a position as chief *qāḍī* in Karkh and left the school to his students. Many of his students became famous legists and scholars, including al-Khātib al-Baghdādī and the Ḥanbali scholar Ibn ᶜAkīl.[68] Abū'l Ṭayyib's successor at the madrasa was none other than the great Ṣūfi scholar al-Ghazālī, who later addressed the question of *samāᶜ* in his own work. Although he was cautiously in support of *samāᶜ*, al-Ghazālī shared Abū'l Ṭayyib's opinion of what constituted inappropriate uses of music and recitation.[69] Accounts of Abū'l Ṭayyib present him as a gentle, humorous man who enjoyed verse (apparently once giving a fatwa in verse) and retained his faculties well into advanced age, only beginning to fade before his death at the age of 102.[70]

As would be expected of an important teacher and jurist of the time, Abū'l Ṭayyib wrote many works on the legal sciences, although only a few are extant.[71] In addition to the *Kitāb fīhi mas'alat fi'l radd ᶜalā man yaqūl bi-jawāz al-samāᶜ al-ghināʾ wa'l raqṣ wa'l taghbīr* (Book refuting the opinions of those who allow listening to music, dance, and the *taghbīr*), Shiloah notes that Abū'l Ṭayyib wrote another text on *samāᶜ* called *Jawāb fi samāᶜ al-ghināʾ*, the manuscript of which he located in Morocco.

Kitāb fīhi mas'alat fi'l radd ᶜalā man yaqūl bi-jawāz al-samāᶜ al-ghināʾ wa'l raqṣ wa'l taghbīr (Book Refuting the Opinions of Those Who Allow Listening to Music, Dance, and the *Taghbīr*)

Abū'l Ṭayyib's treatise is the only text without a title page in the NLI collection.[72] It begins immediately following the conclusion of the *Censure*, with no additional information preceding its introduction. The only indication it is a new author and text is the title in red ink, followed by a short introduction to the author of the treatise and his importance as a *qāḍī* and scholar.[73]

As with the other texts, Abū'l Ṭayyib's discussion of listening is a dialogue between a questioner and respondent. He uses a mixture of questions, responses, anecdotes, and lecture, making his treatise an intermediary step between the list of *responsa* and *ḥadīth* format used by Ibn Abi'l Dūnya, al-Khallāl, and al-Ājurrī and the more narrative forms of the later treatises. He marks the individual sections by topic, generally with a question—"it was asked (*sa'lat*)"—and response—"it was responded (*jawāb*)."[74]

Abū'l Ṭayyib begins with a complex and detailed introduction to the question of listening. He breaks the question into several parts, asking if listening to singing is allowed (*samāᶜ al-ghināʾ*), what the possible origins of listening might be, and whether it goes back to the *Rashīdūn*, the Prophet, and his companions. Related questions are: what about those who advocate music as a mild entertainment? Doesn't music inspire love and liven up a gathering?

Using the Shāfiᶜīte perspective, the response (*jawāb*) examines active and passive diversion, intertwining gender with morality and ethical conduct. The answer is unequivocal in that singing is a diversion and not allowable (*ghinā' lahw al-makrūh*). Abū'l Ṭayyib hammers it home by stating those people who do so are foolish.[75] He comments that although there are some who insist music is harmless and singing can lead one to a state of joyous ecstasy, they are sadly mistaken. Using descriptive language, Abū'l Ṭayyib asserts that those who insist listening is harmless are pigheaded, and their smooth arguments hide a cozy lie. When asked if such practices existed during the time of the Prophet and companions, the answer is simply no.

Abū'l Ṭayyib is concerned with entertainment music but focuses more on melodic recitation of holy texts and Ṣūfi *samāᶜ*. That Abū'l Ṭayyib was reacting to *samāᶜ* in Ṣūfi *dhikr* as well as entertainment music is clear. By focusing on the relationship between the performer (including reciter) and hearer, he implies that *samāᶜ* is active and passive, and the choices made by the reciter can and will have an effect on the audience. He foregrounds the relationship between intention and effect more than the earlier treatises, and the narrative format of his treatise gives him rhetorical breathing room. Like the other texts, however, there is considerable repetition. He repeats the key points to his argument throughout the treatise by employing different authorities and circumstances.

In the same vein as the previous scholars, Abū'l Ṭayyib singles out specific instruments for the pious to avoid and different social situations in which they might be encountered. The instruments he focuses on most are the *ᶜūd*, *duff*, and *qaḍib* for their use in entertainment and Ṣūfi *samāᶜ*. He uses *laᶜiba*, *ḍaraba*, *ṭarab*, and *lahw* to indicate the act of play, reception, and effect. Abū'l Ṭayyib also makes a connection to *liwāṭ*, adding his opinion that music is emasculating. His choices in what instruments and practices to use in his examples point to the often elaborate uses of music throughout the social structure. Furthermore, Abū'l Ṭayyib's descriptions indicate that people were also confused about the difference between song and recitation, and subjective interpretation, whether deliberate or not, made bending the rules easy. That people enjoyed listening to beautiful recitation—particularly the much-criticized *taghbīr*—was evident. Yet was it recitation or singing? How did one determine what was singing and what was not?

Abū'l Ṭayyib focuses especial attention on listening to women. Listening to all women, veiled, unveiled, enslaved, or free, is not allowed according to Shāfiᶜī interpretation of the law.[76] Therefore, wine, women, and song are a dangerous trifecta, and Abū'l Ṭayyib supports his position through corroboration from other schools of jurisprudence, citing the opinion of Mālik Ibn Anas and Abū Ḥanifa. According to Abū Ḥanifa, listening is associated with drinking *nabīdh*, that is, fermented beverages, and because such activities were popular among polytheists before Islam (the *Jāhiliyya*), they are to be avoided. Along with associating song with drink and women, Abū'l Ṭayyib follows previous scholars by citing Sura 31:6. Other forms of play, such as chess and backgammon, also fall into the category of unallowable diversion.

Needless to say, listening to and the purchase of musical entertainment (and sex) from singing slave women (referred to as *jawārī* and *mughanniyat*) are forbidden. Abū'l Ṭayyib condemns *qiyān* and their instruments, the latter of which are included under the umbrella of *ma*ᶜ*āzif*. When he refers to *qiyān*, he is pointing directly to entertainments enjoyed by the upper classes. For reinforcement, Abū'l Ṭayyib cites the same authority that Ibn Abi'l Dūnya uses at the opening of the *Censure*, Sahl ibn Saᶜad, followed by additional *ḥadīth* related to *ma*ᶜ*āzif* and *qiyān*. Unlike Ibn Abi'l Dūnya, however, he does not define these terms.[77] This lack probably is based on the assumption his reader knew what these terms meant; therefore, the moral, social, and symbolic implications they invoked did not require further clarification.

Abū'l Ṭayyib helpfully provides direction as to what constitutes illegal music-sounding, using the term *ṣawt* to encompass music. He states that music and singing were sent by Satan to deflect the unwary from the proper path. His use of *ṣawt* along with *ghinā*' implies a difference; possibly accompanied as opposed to unaccompanied song. Whether he was deliberately making a distinction between recitation and song is uncertain, but what is clear is that all song is illegal. To reinforce his position, Abū'l Ṭayyib invokes the Prophet himself, who, according to one *ḥadīth*, said Iblis (Satan) invented the flute and singing. Then, he brings in a lengthy series of authorities concerned with how singing and playing instruments affect performer and hearer. Abū'l Ṭayyib firmly refutes those who might be soft on certain aspects of music. He comments that although some authorities might rule that the *duff* and *zammāra* (bagpipe) are fine when used for work or weddings, they are, in fact, *ḥarām*. He includes several variations of the *ḥadīth* that state listening causes hypocrisy to grow in the heart and how it leads to fornication and deceitfulness.[78]

Although the distinction between song and melodic soundings is not entirely clear, Abū'l Ṭayyib is unequivocal that recitation of epic poems (*qaṣīda*) and sacred poetry (*nashīd*) may not be infused with song and melody.[79]

Since poetry, like song, is tied to metric organization, recitation naturally has melodic and rhythmic structure. Yet, he notes that some reciters take liberties by incorporating melody in the recitation of poetry. As the Qur'an is a poetic text, if one allows recitation of poetry to become melodic and veer into singing, this practice can infect recitation of the Qur'an, leading one to effectively sing the holy text.

In a similar vein, the *taghbīr* and the rattling of the wand (*taqtaq bi'l qaḍib*) are right out. Abū'l Ṭayyib criticizes those freethinkers who assert these activities are allowable, promising that such fabrications will turn people away from the Qur'an.[80] According to al-Shāfiᶜī and other authorities, the only acceptable form of listening is to the Qur'an, but only when done with pious intent and reverence. He reiterates that listening to the Qur'an is not the same as listening to poetry, and therefore it should not be recited in the same way. To do so is absolutely forbidden. Turning to the role of the reciter, Abū'l Ṭayyib comments that although it is important to recite the Qur'an beautifully, it must be done without melody and with proper intention. Those who believe such embellished recitation is harmless are deceiving themselves and others. His argument is understandable in that a sonically compelling recitation will divert the listener to focus on the voice, not the message. (And that people enjoyed listening to poetry more was common knowledge.)[81]

Abū'l Ṭayyib closes by stating that avoiding music, like other carnal pleasures, is the key to good health. By way of example, he insists he never indulged in music and that was why he remained healthy into his sixties. Based on this statement, the treatise was written in the late tenth century, and he had another forty-two years to live.

The Ethnographer: Diya al-Dīn Abū ᶜAbdullāh ibn Manṣūr al-Saᶜdi al-Ḥanbalī al-Maqdisī (1173–1245 CE)

Called Diya al-Dīn, he was from a long line of scholars and among the most respected traditionalists of the Ayyubid era. He adhered to the Shāfiᶜī school of jurisprudence and studied religious sciences and jurisprudence in Damascus. After completing his initial education, he left Damascus and traveled widely, continuing his studies in Egypt and Baghdad.[82] Diya al-Dīn was an early ethnographer who interviewed his relatives, neighbors, and émigrés from other cities about their life and experiences. These anecdotes formed the basis of "The Cited Tales of the Wondrous Doings of the Shaykhs of the Holy Land," a "hagiographical dictionary" that has been translated and studied by Daniella Talmon-Heller.[83]

The anecdotes provide a detailed look at life in the local villages and contain several references to local musical practices as well as Ṣūfi *samā*ᶜ and dance. Of particular interest are the variety of opinions about what constituted proper use of music among the merchant and lower classes. These vary from acceptance of casual music making at social events to total condemnation, showing that concerns about piety and what was proper were also part of the conversation among the middling classes. Based on some of the stories, it seems traveling preachers and itinerant scholars periodically stoked people's concerns about listening and piety.

In her book-length study of piety in Damascus, *Islamic Piety*, Talmon-Heller includes a revealing story demonstrating how concerns about piety could be manipulated by a good con man. According to an anecdote related by al-Jawbarī, a charlatan arrived in a village one day, hoping to gain a following and gifts of money. Posing as a preacher, he planted a confederate with a tambourine in the audience. The false preacher began to fulminate against different diversions, and at the right moment, his collaborator handed him the tambourine, ostensibly moved by the preacher's orations. The preacher dramatically smashed the tambourine, the "musician" had his hair clipped in penance, and the crowd went wild at the performance.[84]

As a scholar and observer of humanity, Diya al-Dīn uses anecdotes as instructions for maintaining piety and what to do in certain situations. In her analysis of "The Cited Tales," Talmon-Heller discusses an anecdote about music and dance that purportedly formed the basis of Diya al-Dīn's personal opinion:

> Diya al-Dīn al-Maqdisī recalls the impression that a Ṣūfi shaykh, ᶜAbd Allah b. ᶜAbd al-Jabbar Abū Muḥammad al-Ta'i, known as al-Badawi, made on him when he was a little boy. Having seen him on Fridays in the great mosque of Damascus, he was sure that the man prayed for the entire day "so as not to miss the hour of the public prayer." Moreover, al-Badawi used to preach against dancing and against the company of dancers, of whom he said: "These people who neglect the Qur'an and busy themselves with nonsense."[85]

Another anecdote concerns music at social events. In this story, a local man invites a sheik to a wedding, but the sheik hesitates to accept in case there is "something loathsome there." The man assures him it will be fine, yet on the way, the sheik first hears a tambourine, which gives him pause, followed by the piping of a flute, which makes him stop. He emits a cry that makes stones roll off the mountain, scaring the villagers and musicians alike. Everyone flees, stopping the music.[86]

Al-amr bi-itbāᶜ al-sunan wa ijtināb al-bidaᶜ (The Command to Follow Established Laws and Avoid Heresy)

Although the title does not include a reference to *samāᶜ*, it is clear from the outset that the purpose of the treatise is to address listening within the context of "commanding the proper."[87] Similar to Abū'l Ṭayyib, Diya al-Dīn integrates intention and the gaze with music and listening, building a dual case against entertainment music and Ṣūfi *samāᶜ*. The tone and content reflect Diya al-Dīn's expertise as a jurisconsult, and as such, it is on the pedantic side. As expected, he cites key *ḥadīth* and supporting authorities containing substantive chains of transmission. Among the authorities he cites are al-Khallāl, Ibn Ḥanbal, and al-Shāfiᶜī. Despite its legal fussiness, the treatise is written in the style of a lecture, showing a further departure from the previous *ḥadīth*-centered compilations to a more conversational, narrative structure.

Following the title, there is a brief introduction to the author and a statement that the treatise was "compiled by the learned sheik and Imām, the enlightened man of religion and *hafiẓ*, Abi ᶜAbdullāh Muḥammad ibn ᶜAbd al-Rahman al-Maqdisī. Spiritual crumbs gathered to aid in good practices for Muslims."[88] His position is unequivocal from the first chapter—entitled "On Heresy"—in which *samāᶜ* is specified as a path to heresy. Diya al-Dīn asserts *samāᶜ* has never been allowable, even in the times of the *Rashīdūn*. He refers to *ghinā'* and music generally as *ṣawt* and *samāᶜ*, formulating melodic sound genres as diversional play: *al-lahw laᶜiba*. Therefore, listening is doubly prohibited because its very nature is diversion and as such it is frivolous and childish.[89]

Unlike the other treatises, Diya al-Dīn takes a broader, more philosophical approach. He notes specific instruments and musicians, however primarily as a means to illustrate intention and effect. Among the instruments, he includes the usual culprits: *ṭabl*, *duff*, and *mizmār*, and *ḍaraba* to reference lutes and drums. The *qiyān* and stringed instruments (*maᶜāzif*) merit passing mention, but most of his discussion addresses music in Ṣūfi *samāᶜ* and *dhikr*, commenting at length on song, tambourines, and "striking the *qaḍib*."

Fundamental to avoiding diversion and heresy, Diya al-Dīn asserts, is avoiding gazing at women. Listening and looking are not discrete actions but work in combination to undermine the spiritual will of the listener. Diya al-Dīn includes a chapter on avoiding singing women, but comments that looking at all women is a bad idea. To add weight to this point, he notes that the Prophet himself said it is harmful for men to look at women, and he includes a number of opinions related to the gaze.

The section about proper behavior by men around women is lengthy and transitions into several side discussions of *zinā*. Following his discussion of the perils of looking, he dedicates a chapter just to singing (*ghinā'*). In this chapter, Diya al-Dīn includes singing in entertainments and *samā^c*, moving the reader through different authorities to arrive at the conclusion that singing is not allowable. To connect back to previous injunctions against gazing at women, he focuses on patronage of women singers.[90] Similar to the previous treatises, he restates that, regardless of one's intention, purchasing singers (bodily as slaves and for musical services) is purchasing diverting speech.

Along with dangers inherent in the gaze and emotional transference, Diya al-Dīn takes the issue of intent and reception further than Abū'l Ṭayyib. Such emphasis on intent is a deliberate move to counter advocates of music and *samā^c*. Those in favor of *samā^c* argued that intent on the part of listener and performer were what determined the quality of the experience. Without proper intent, even recitation of the Qur'an could have a sensuous tone, amplified by a beautiful voice and face. Therefore, if a performance were given with careful attention and pure intent, it would be harmless. For those who believed, as Diya al-Dīn did, intent did not matter, no one could control what the hearer heard. What happened in the uncontrolled space between performer and reception was the issue, so better to be safe than sorry.

Diya al-Dīn turns to individual instruments later in the treatise, primarily drums and woodwinds. To emphasize their immoral nature, particularly the evil origins of the *mizmār*, he references a dialogue between God and Satan about the role of Satan on earth. Satan exists to tempt humanity, which leads to the question of the history of music and instruments prior to Islam. The question of whether *ma^cāzif* and *qiyān* existed in the time of the Prophet appears more frequently in later treatises, demonstrating a shift in how music history was being written. According to Diya al-Dīn, *ma^cāzif* and *qiyān* did not exist prior to Islam, and he supports the argument music was introduced by the Persians. Furthermore, he states, those who assert Ṣūfi masters such as Junayd approved of *samā^c* and use that assertion to justify their use of music are simply wrong.[91]

His next volley against Ṣūfi *dhikr* and *samā^c* comes in a section on dance. Unsurprisingly, dance is not allowed. To illustrate the connection between illegal instruments and the illegality of dance, he points to instruments used to accompany Ṣūfi *samā^c*, particularly the wand (*qaḍib*). He states the *qaḍib* has pre-Islamic roots, and because it is from the *Jāhiliyya*, it has no place in Islam. Diya al-Dīn cites al-Shāfiᶜī, who stated that the *qaḍib* was invented by nonbelievers for the sole purpose of diverting people from religion. Included is a colorful morality tale about Iblis and a Ṣūfi who enjoyed music. In this story, Diya al-Dīn relates how a Ṣūfi leader used to love *samāᶜ* and dance, finding ecstasy as he danced. One night, he dreamed Iblis invited him to dance! Terrified, he refused. When he woke up the next morning, his taste for *samāᶜ* and dance were completely gone.[92] The treatise closes with condemnation of other Ṣūfi practices, such as hand clapping and shouting, commenting sourly that the Ṣūfi sheiks are leading their followers into vice.

Disciple of Ibn Taymiyya: ᶜImād al-Dīn Aḥmad al-Wāsiṭī (1259–1311 CE)

Although al-Wāsiṭī appears in the sources as a favored disciple of Ibn Taymiyya, until recently, very little was available about his life.[93] Al-Wāsiṭī was born near Wāsiṭ in what is now Iraq.[94] He grew up in the Rifāʿī Ṣūfi order, in which his father was a sheik, but as a young man decided it was not the path for him. His quest for the right path led him to travel extensively, immersing himself in different theological traditions and engaging the scholarly community of several key intellectual centers. Al-Wāsiṭī first traveled to Baghdad, where he studied Shāfiᶜīte law, and then went to Alexandria where he encountered the Shādhilīyya order.[95] Soon, however, he became disaffected with them and left for Cairo.

While in Cairo, al-Wāsiṭī lived in a *khanqah* and was introduced to the Akbarian school based on the works of Muhyi al-Dīn Ibn ᶜArabi. Al-Wāsiṭī became skeptical of their practices after spending time with the *faqīrs* of this community and studying their doctrine. He was especially dubious of their innovations in *samāᶜ* whereby, if the *faqīrs* were aligned with antinomian orders roaming Cairo and Damascus, they might have incorporated music and dance in their practice of *dhikr* and *samāᶜ*. Disappointed again, al-Wāsiṭī left Cairo to see what he could learn in Damascus. It is there he met Ibn Taymiyya and found his intellectual and doctrinal home. Al-Wāsiṭī became one of Ibn Taymiyya's disciples, switched to the Ḥanbalite school, and became a Ṣūfi sheik. His experience with different Ṣūfi orders helped him craft his own practice of Ṣūfism within a Ḥanbalite frame, and he tutored several important students of Ibn Taymiyya, including Shams al-Dīn al-Dhahabī and Zayn al-Dīn al-Baᶜlabakkī.[96]

Al-Wāsiṭī is credited with writing a number of works in the Ḥanbali tradition, several of which are extant.[97] In *Sources for Arabian Music*, Farmer mentions a book presumed lost called *Kitāb al-bulgha*, commenting it was "apparently a Ḥanbalite condemnation of music."[98] Although the title is different in the NLI collection, *Al-bulghat wa'l iqna*ᶜ *fi ḥill shubhat mas'alat al-samā*ᶜ may be that lost book.

*Mas'alat fi al-samā*ᶜ (Question regarding *Samā*ᶜ) and *Al-bulghat wa'l iqna*ᶜ *fi ḥill shubhat mas'alat al-samā*ᶜ *(The Exaggeration and Persuasion of Those Who Declare Samā*ᶜ *Is Permitted)*

Although the *Question* does not have a formal answer, in his summary of both texts in RISM, Shiloah notes that the fullness of the discussion in the longer treatise gives a good idea of what the answers would have been.[99] The *Question* has a separate title page, with the title indicated in red ink, and the outline of the question takes up the next page.[100] There is a blank page between the *Question* and *Exaggeration*, but whether that was intentional or there was supposed to be more to the *Question* is unknown.[101] It is possible there is nothing missing, and that the question was intended to stand alone to clarify the complexity of the issues examined in the following treatise. Among the components to the question are legal positions regarding *samā*ᶜ, whether it was practiced during the time of the Prophet and his Companions, its use in attaining religious ecstasy (*wajd*), and the effect of repeated exposure. Would experiencing *samā*ᶜ lead to illumination or cause one to turn from the proper path? The question ends at the bottom of the page, with the phrase indicating the hopes of the interlocutor to receive a clear "response in agreement with what is proper."

The *Exaggeration* likewise has a separate title page with a short introduction to the qualifications and titles of al-Wāsiṭī.[102] Ibn Burayd further states he copied it in 1455, from the author's autograph dated 1303.[103] The focus of the *Exaggeration* is almost exclusively on Ṣūfi *samā*ᶜ, albeit with some commentary on entertainment music. It is in twelve detailed chapters, each dealing with unacceptable practices associated with audition.[104] Of all the treatises, it is the most complex and sophisticated, weaving *ḥadīth*, key authorities, and commentary together in the register of a philosophical lecture. The lack of folksy meandering and digression that some of the other treatises have suggests the *Exaggeration* was a pietistic text for the intellectual set.

At issue is the "new" *samā*ᶜ being used and promoted by select Ṣūfi orders. Al-Wāsiṭī defines what acts comprise *samā*ᶜ, presents evidence against their use, and then gives counterarguments to those legists who have ruled in its favor. Those acts that fall within *samā*ᶜ include dancing, clapping, shouting, and instrumental accompaniment. Al-Wāsiṭī sternly refutes those who assert that dancing and shouting will bring one closer to God. His main point is that if using music, dance, and other expression in *dhikr* and *samā*ᶜ were considered allowable and good, the Prophet and his Companions would have explicitly said so. Because they did not, he argues, they did not take place. The only allowable practices involving sound and music are those that have support from authorities attesting to their use or approval by the Prophet and Companions. These include "natural" forms of expression, such as recitation and, unexpectedly, some uses of drumming at weddings.

Like Diya al-Dīn, al-Wāsiṭī makes scant mention of specific instruments, focusing instead on specific musical practices and their effect. Tellingly, he refers to those who cause and those who seek emotional ecstasy as *muṭrib* and *ṭarab*. He establishes that melody (*nagham*) encompasses all sound genres, making a distinction between music (*ṣawt*) and singing (*ghinā*ʾ) by implying the difference lies in performance practices (i.e., accompanied by instruments) and context.

The first chapter starts by refuting the assertion of some Ṣūfis that music helps bring out what is in the heart to connect one with God. Yet, what if there is nothing in the heart? Or what lies in the heart is rotten? Al-Wāsiṭī agrees music can indeed bring out what is in the heart, such as lustful thoughts of an adulterer as they look upon an object of desire. Music can easily draw out sensuous feelings if they already exist. He concedes that *samā*ᶜ is powerful for those who are spiritually pure, but that is not enough of an argument for its widespread use. In any gathering, the same music that feeds the spiritual ecstasy of the adept can fuel lust in those around them.

The next chapter challenges those justifications for *samā*ᶜ grounded in assumed past practices. Like Diya al-Dīn, he states some assert *samā*ᶜ was used by important Ṣūfis of the past, such as Junayd, therefore, they argue it ought to be allowed in current practice. Clearly, al-Wāsiṭī says, this is false. He follows this chapter with one on how the new *samā*ᶜ negatively affects the natural world, people, and animals alike, and then devotes several chapters to issues such as proper recitation of the Qur'an, poetry and song, and select instruments. The only instruments he mentions by name are the *zammāra*, *shabbāba* (pan-flute), and *duff*. Although flutes are generally not allowed, the *zammāra* (in this case a kind of *mizmār*, not the bagpipe) and the panpipe are acceptable because they are shepherd's instruments. There are also times when playing *duff* is allowed, such as at weddings.

Following his condemnation of instruments and the excited state music can inspire in the listener, he returns to the theme of sexual excitement. Listening to singing women is naturally a bad idea, but so is gazing upon beautiful young men (*amrād*) and the practice of *naẓar*. To show how the gaze and listening are dangerous, he describes a *samā*ᶜ session in detail, particularly how singing, looking, and instruments (specifically *duff*) inspire confusing levels of passion.[105] Like Diya al-Dīn, al-Wāsiṭī reiterates how the combination of listening and the gaze inspire sexual interest, leading inevitably to illicit sex, impurity, and, ultimately, apostasy.

The Intellectual Scion: Burhān al-Dīn Abū Isḥāq Ibrāhīm ibn ᶜAbd al-Raḥīm Ibn Jamāʿa (1325–88 CE)

The last treatise chronologically is by the fourteenth-century scholar Abū Isḥāq Ibrāhīm ibn ᶜAbd al-Raḥīm Ibn Jamāʿa, called Burhān al-Dīn, who was a member of the prestigious Banū Jamāʿa family of Shāfiᶜī jurists during the Mamlūk era.[106] The intellectual influence of the Banū Jamāʿa was felt in Damascus, Jerusalem, and Cairo, and the Jerusalem branch of the family remained notable until the Ottoman conquest in 1517. Among the most distinguished members of the family were Burhān al-Dīn's grandfather, Badr al-Dīn Abū ᶜAbdullāh Muḥammad (1241–1333 CE/639–733 H), and uncle, ᶜIzz al-Dīn ᶜAbd al-Aziz (1294–1366 CE/694–767 H). Badr al-Dīn was the *kātib* of the al-Aqsa mosque in Jerusalem, a position he held until becoming chief *qāḍī* of Egypt in 1291 CE.

Burhān al-Dīn was born in Cairo, where he received an excellent education and later furthered his studies in Damascus. He lived up to his illustrious family name. Like his grandfather and uncle, he taught in Cairo, preached in Jerusalem, and was the chief *qāḍī* of Egypt twice. After his death, the Jerusalem branch of the family went into a decline, although their legacy remained important in intellectual circles.[107] The influence of the Banū Jamāʿa in Jerusalem is still visible today. They oversaw the restoration of the "Summer Pulpit" (*minbar*) on the platform of the Dome of the Rock, which is also called the Burhān al-Dīn Minbar.[108]

In addition to the *Response*, Burhān al-Dīn is the author of several other treatises, including two others concerned with music and *samā*ᶜ.[109] In *The*

Sources of Arabian Music, Farmer listed a treatise by Burhān al-Dīn called *Nasiha fi Dhamm al-malāhī* held in Berlin, but he apparently did not know about the treatise in NLI.[110]

Suwwāl sālahu shakhṣ min al-fuqarā' (Response to a *Faqīr*)

In his brief introduction of the author and text, Ibn Burayd states he copied the *Response* in 1456 from a lecture,[111] the inspiration for which were a series of questions Burhān al-Dīn received from a *faqīr* while he was lecturing in Jerusalem in 1370.[112] As the questions come from a Ṣūfi from an ascetic sect (i.e., poor) much of the lecture relates to Ṣūfi practices, although Burhān al-Dīn includes entertainment music and public performances.

Burhān al-Dīn begins by "aligning the questions" of which there are many. The questions range from generalities, such as what the legal opinions are regarding *samāᶜ* and different musical instruments, to singing and singers, specific uses of *samāᶜ*, whether music and singing originated during the time of the Prophet and his Companions, and if music and drumming are allowed in the mosque. Since all these practices were taking place in Damascus and Jerusalem, including *samāᶜ* sessions in the Umayyad Mosque, it is not surprising that Burhān al-Dīn focused on these specific issues.[113]

The answer to all the questions is a decisive no.[114] Burhān al-Dīn states that with the exception of beautiful recitation of noble poetry, all sound genres and listening fall under what is improper. Only recitation of the Qur'an using proper practice is acceptable. Similar to Diya al-Dīn and al-Wāsiṭī, Burhān al-Dīn focuses on intent, specific practices, and effect of listening, especially in Ṣūfi *samāᶜ*. To strengthen his position, Burhān al-Dīn invokes weighty legal authorities, including Abū Ḥanifa, al-Shāfiᶜī, and al-Mālik, along with *ḥadīth* and select verses from the Qur'an. Burhān al-Dīn states there is a difference between recitation and melodic chanting, asserting that melodic soundings and accompaniment with drums are absolutely forbidden. He uses *samāᶜ* and *ṣawt* to reference both Ṣūfi *samāᶜ* and sound genres that use instruments. Among the top activities to avoid are singing, patronage of women singers (referred to generically as *mughanniyat*), those who inspire *ṭarab* (*muṭrib*), and playing musical instruments. He highlights the *qaḍib*, *mizmār*, and *ṭabl*, using *maᶜāzif* to refer to stringed instruments and *ḍaraba* to indicate instruments that are struck.

Like the other treatises, Burhān al-Dīn makes the connection to frivolous play (*laᶜiba*) and positions music as a form of diverting speech. By play, he implies not just playing musical instruments, but joking and goofing around. Musicians and poets actively engaged their audiences by jesting with them, reading their mood and interests in order to tailor their performances to suit. Burhān al-Dīn asserts such goofiness has no place in solemn contemplation of God. He also makes a sweeping connection between secular entertainments and Ṣūfi *samāᶜ* by stating one should beware of Ṣūfi who are deluded by Satan into thinking such practices are acceptable, as well as women and effeminate men who are drawn to music and dance.

Following his definition of what constitutes song and types of entertainment music, Burhān al-Dīn addresses accompanied song, formulated literally as singers striking music.[115] Here, he offers a pointed refutation of those who insist listening to and patronage of song and poetry are marks of refinement, echoing the standpoints of Abū'l Ṭayyib and Diya al-Dīn al-Maqdisī. Burhān al-Dīn calls out those who insist "good music" (*ṣawt latif*) is fine for the salon (*majlis*), stating that since neither *ṣawt* nor *samāᶜ* are in the Qur'an, one should not be persuaded by those who insist music is allowed. As with the distinction between recitation and singing, Burhān al-Dīn clarifies the difference between *samāᶜ* and entertainment music as being melodic and using instruments. Neither is allowed, yet frustratingly they continue to be used—and justified—in different contexts and social classes.

Burhān al-Dīn reiterates that although the only permissible form of vocal expression is recitation, it must not become melodic. Doing so can slide dangerously close to song. He underscores his point by stating that those who insist that melody (and by extension, all music and melodic recitation) is fine in certain cases are deluded by Satan and have a poor understanding of religion. The vehemence of his argument suggests that people were taking unacceptable melodic liberties with recitation frequently enough to merit concern.

Burhān al-Dīn next turns to complex legal maneuvering to outline why *samāᶜ* is a form of *fitna* and distraction, taking several pages to develop his standpoint.[116] Earlier in the treatise, he established that *samāᶜ* was not an indigenous practice, pointing to *ṭabl*, singing, and *taghbīr* as evidence. In addition, he is the third author in the collection to reject the argument that earlier Ṣūfis, like Junayd, used *samāᶜ*.[117] Not only are these practices against religion, he argues they were not in use during the time of the Prophet and his Companions. To support this reading of history, he includes a complex lineage of authorities as evidence that such amusements were not used by the Prophet or his Companions.

In the section on *fitna*, Burhān al-Dīn returns to history and provides supporting evidence that singing and playing of music did not originate with the

Arabs. Instead, they are foreign practices introduced by Ṭuways the *mukhannath* who Burhān al-Dīn states was of Persian origin.[118] Before Ṭuways, there was no *samā*ᶜ and entertainment music, but when he played for the Arabs, they fell in love with it. *Samā*ᶜ has been around since. To emphasize this point further, the next section is offset by a lengthy comment in red ink that states: "And which response as to whether it has been around since the time of the Prophet and his companions."[119] This heading leads into a compendium of evidence against those who assert *samā*ᶜ existed prior to Islam. Burhān al-Dīn includes a section on the *ṭablkhane*, but it is brief, because he comments he does not have enough resources to make a clear ruling.[120]

The final question concerns the use of *samā*ᶜ in the mosque. Based on similar concerns in the other treatises about melodic recitation of the Qur'an, use of drums and the *taghbīr*, and the practice of *samā*ᶜ in sacred, communal spaces, it is apparent that music was common enough in the mosque to be of significant concern. Not unexpectedly, Burhān al-Dīn says absolutely not, adding the statement that even the Jews and Christians do not allow such things in their temples and churches, so why should Muslims? The treatise closes with his hope that by following these guidelines, those aspiring to follow what is proper will avoid Satan and follow (stay on) the proper path.

Summations

The story these treatises tell illuminate the increasingly sophisticated battle for the souls of music-loving aristocracy, scholars, Ṣūfis, and rising middling classes. Their focus on defining music, singing and recitation, and origins of different practices make it evident that, despite best efforts, musical expression was pervasive. From the perspective of the "sober" schools of Ṣūfism and broader conservative thinking, these were grave concerns. If music, drinking wine, and ogling attractive musicians were allowed, then not only were the caliph, nobility, and religious leaders enabling others to do the same, the broader community was opened to potential chaos and apostasy by their actions. Likewise, the enthusiasm of certain Ṣūfi orders for incorporating movement and sound into *dhikr* and *samā*ᶜ had the same potential for corruption. They might indeed be on the path to the divine, however where love for the divine ended and sexual excitement for another began was difficult to know and impossible to control, especially for young novitiates.

Because there was no equivocal statement in the Qur'an on music, dance, and *samāᶜ*, scholars had to rely on those verses that could be stretched to include listening, *ḥadīth*, and pre-Islamic poetry. References in *ḥadīth* and pre-Islamic poetry hint at tambourines used for weddings, singing women in taverns, and instruments used for work and celebration (shepherd's pipes, singing to animals, dancing in celebration of feast days). Yet, many of the *ḥadīth* that pass firm judgment on select instruments are weak and exist in many variations and possible interpretations. Those scholars against *samāᶜ* had to be nimble in how they employed these authorities, which suggests why the format for such refutations needed to develop away from a *responsa* format.

Among the *ḥadīth* cited the most was that hearing music causes hypocrisy to grow in the heart. In the earlier treatises, this linked not only to the idea that listening could lead to apostasy but also to the conflict with the Hypocrites.[121] Like hubris in the Greek world, hypocrisy was anathema to the believer. Later, this *ḥadīth* was used more subtly to counter the arguments for *samāᶜ* as a means to reveal what is hidden. Those advocating against it note that dangerous emotions lurk in the heart as well and that in the untested heart, lust or love for someone other than God could just as easily be grown.

The subtext of spiritual metastasis was linked to intent and maintaining bodily piety. Listening, even when innocent or unwitting, could invite spiritual pollution. However, just as ablution, fasting, and prayer did not automatically impart piety, neither did complete abstention from listening. The pious needed to understand the purpose for their actions, as well as the modes of observing what was proper to better instruct others. Therefore, people were concerned with deeper questions. Was music inherently a source of filth? How could one know? What about accidental contamination? When such nuances of intent and effect were understood, then complete abstention from music and listening was considered an intelligent step in bodily practice of daily piety.[122]

Along with broader social concerns, these treatises offer a wealth of information about performance practices and diversity of sound genres permeating the culture. It is clear that melodic recitation of poetry and the Qur'an, religious poetry, and *adhān* were commonplace, and a variety of music entertainments could be had at all levels of society. Because of the association of instrumental music with bad behavior, authors concerned with piety—including those in favor of *samāᶜ*—were specific about what instruments were the most harmful. Instruments associated with singing women, taverns, brothels, *mukhannathūn* and casual drinking, specifically tambourines with jingles, bells, stringed instruments and reeds, were to be avoided, even destroyed if necessary.

Even among those who advocated against *samā*ᶜ, however, there were differences of opinion on when music might be appropriate. Although some condemned all song by women and instruments, there were rare occasions when a woman might be heard and certain instruments allowed. To some, a tambourine was acceptable for weddings, and other uses of drums and rhythm were fine if controlled carefully. This latter was possibly a sop for the military. The Abbasid caliph and later different sultans had a dedicated military band, and large drums were used on the battlefield to signal and inspire the troops.

At the heart of these concerns was the effect of music on emotions. Instrumental sounds were by their nature and purpose intended to distract. People were predisposed to associate such sounds with celebration, ritual, and distraction. Bells, jingles, tambourines, drums, and wands were portable and easily made by objects on hand, such as a hollow pot for a drum and stick to thump on the ground to keep rhythm. Although reed instruments and flutes could be used for work, they, like lutes, were generally for one purpose: to inspire a response in the hearer.

Interestingly, the treatises in the NLI collection do not explicitly address rhythm, but its emotional impact is everywhere. Rhythm was the backbone of poetry as well as dance and song, with some rhythms used purposefully for emotional impact. Al-Fārābī, among others, devoted an exhaustive study to the different possible rhythms, along with their combinations and uses.[123] Scholars of poetry wrote similarly detailed studies of metrics, and musicians were expected to know metrics as well as rhythm. It is not surprising instruments used to keep rhythm were singled out, and, as we see in the treatises, the body could also be a percussion instrument.

More than the sound, the manner in which instruments were deployed was what drew and caught the hearer's attention. Use of the term *ḍaraba* indicated all struck instruments, although a singer could also strike the ear. Melody might twist the will of the unwary, but the power of words—driven by rhythm or accompaniment—led people to dance and ecstatic responses. Rhythm as an organizing and inspirational power was recognized by different Ṣūfi orders, as with the Sumadiyya and their special drum, the *ṭablkhane*, and melodic cantillation of sacred poetry. Such diversity not only illustrates the variety of sound and complexity of rhythms being used but hints at the status and wealth of certain groups.

For example, descriptions of *ṭablkhane* suggest they ranged in size and instrumentation. Some were an ensemble of the same kind of drum while others an assortment. The sonic and rhythmic possibilities would have been driven by the space as well as the skill of individual musicians. The acoustics of the large mosques would necessitate a different performance practice for *samāᶜ* than a more intimate space. In a more acoustically live space, musicians would need to play in unison, using shorter, sharper strikes and deeper (i.e., larger) sounding instruments in order to reach larger groups of listeners and keep the rhythm cohesive. Hence, the special drum of the Sumadiyya, although ceremonial due to its age and history, would fit acoustically in a large space far better than a smaller instrument with high timbre.

Although the rhythmic thumping of a stick on the ground does not seem like much of a musical threat, its versatility, simplicity, and roots in pre-Islamic practices made it worth singling out. Not only can a stick be used as a musical instrument, it can be played while one is dancing. There are several examples of skilled dancers using sticks and wands to punctuate their dance and interact with accompanying musicians.[124] The wand also served as a rhetorical marker in storytelling. A storyteller could punctuate recitation by thumping the stick on the ground, enact scenes of battle through pantomime, and simply wave it for emphasis.[125]

There were plenty of scholars and bon vivants who asserted music and listening were allowed, but even they advocated caution. Young, impressionable men were particularly at risk. Concerns about the activities of free women seldom are referenced, although we know from anecdotes in the treatises and broader documentary record that they were playing music in their homes. This silence may have to do with the greater access men had to public spaces, along with different rules for piety for men and women. Women were exempt from certain religious duties owing to their domestic responsibilities. They could pray, fast, and undertake a life of asceticism, but it was unusual.[126] And, much of this life took place in the women's quarters, out of public view.

What everyone could agree on was that entertainment music, especially instrumental music, was risky. Along with the sound capabilities of the instruments and their effect on the hearer, the text itself was carried and modulated if sung, declaimed, and accompanied. The eye was drawn inevitably to the musician, and if that musician were attractive, the eye lingered. A compelling voice only enhanced visual appeal. Noble poetry and the Qur'an itself could become a sensual feast when declaimed by an attractive person with a beautiful voice. How did one know the love they felt was purely for God and not the reciter? As seen through the development of arguments in the treatises, concerns about intent, effect, and the gaze became more urgent. Given the choice of a dry recitation of religion over a wildly beautiful one, an audience would seek the latter every time. The evidence was everywhere: streets, taverns, courts, and, most concerning, the mosques.

8

Reflections

The story of music in the medieval Islamicate world is essentially a conversation about the boundaries of liberation and constraint. Musical soundings were not confined to performance practices, but infused with religious, social, and metaphysical practice. Medieval scholars may have considered each of these elements separately in their own musings on music, but the broader constellation of influences remained present. As a praxis, musicians, instruments, compositional styles, and genres were subject to detailed examination in practical tutors, with additional commentary in philosophy and works on the natural sciences.

The court, intelligentsia, and middling classes were the bedrock of the patronate for entertainment music, although those same audiences—and performers—bled into religious uses as well. Along with the excesses of the wealthier classes, the insinuation of melody into religious spaces initiated the conversation about the place of music in Islam. Central to all discussion was the physical and metaphysical effects on the hearer. Music was a living, unpredictable force that permeated the seen and unseen. Musical soundings did not happen in isolation either; regardless of how private a musical event, quiet song on the road, and lonely shepherd's pipe might be. Making sound triggered hearing. And not only could one hear at the subliminal level in the physical world, but one was subject to the subluminal in the metaphysical realm as well.

Music practices in the Islamicate world germinated from extant traditions and external borrowings. Poetry was important to pre-Islamic Arabs, as was poetic improvisation and a tradition of emotional recitation. Song existed alongside poetry in the form of travel, work, wedding, funeral, and tavern songs. It would not be out of bounds to suggest there were other types of song, including set songs, although there are no concrete references (that I have found, that is) to say for certain. Pre-Islamic Arabic-speaking groups lived throughout what is now the Middle East as nomads, urban merchants, mercenaries, and pastoralists. As such, poetry and song were the most portable forms of entertainment and cultural exchange. Instruments needed to be portable and durable as well, often fashioned out of whatever was at hand.

Given references in *ḥadīth* and early sources, percussion instruments such as the *duff*, *qaḍib*, and *ṭabl* were in use, along with woodwinds, well before Islam. There were varieties within each species of instrument as well, such as round and square tambourines, tambourines with metal jingles, bells, and drums of different shapes and materials. Larger drums were for special occasions and used by warriors, later organized military. Although of Persian origin, the lute was also used by Arabic-speaking peoples prior to Islam, based on references in pre-Islamic poetry. Plucked strings were best suited for private entertainments and had likewise been part of the cultural landscape since antiquity. They were more delicate and required more maintenance, so such instruments were often the province of the wealthier classes.

Softer instruments could be overwhelmed in a large, resonating space, so performance practice would include larger numbers playing in unison or a few instrumentalists playing in intimate settings. Along with plucked strings, flutes were used in smaller performance environments, with the more strident reeds and brass relegated to ceremonial events held outdoors. Regardless of the performance context, the sound and performance space would require unrelated people to sit closely in order to hear.

Distinct classes of musicians existed prior to Islam as well, particularly singing women and *mukhannathūn*. Given that men were discouraged socially from earning a living as musicians, there are few pre-Islamic references to men making music and singing except in social settings. However, the line between song and poetry was often thin, so it is probable men sang and played, albeit under the rubric of poetic recitation. Enslaved women musicians performed in taverns and for private entertainments, and enslaved and free women served as professional mourners. Lamentation was the specialty of women reaching back to the Ancient Near Eastern and Mediterranean cultures. The existence of cross-gendered musicians such as the *mukhannathūn* also had ancient roots, with varying degrees of acceptance.

As Islam spread and intermingled with other cultures through conquest and trade, the rapid influx of people, knowledge, and ideas into the nascent Islamicate states precipitated several social reactions. Pre-Islamic practices continued, melding with aspects of the new religion and practices from other cultures. These influences were examined for social, religious, and educational value, with different interpretations of what fit best into the shape of developing Islamicate cultures. Fear of losing the purity of the religion and, by extension, the purity of the people from which it sprang created different ideological factions along with scholarly attempts to codify the law and new social rules grounded in Islam. Mystic and heretical sects sprang up, some radical and disruptive, others merely strange. Conservative opinions struggled to prune un-Islamic practices and provide guidance for proper observance of religion. Because of its association with polytheism, sensuality, and ritual, music was an obvious target, but a complete purge of musical soundings from devotional and nonreligious practices proved impossible.

The actual practice of music flowered and spilled into every aspect of social life, particularly in urban centers. Middling classes adopted elite forms of music, and some non-elite forms trickled upward. These borrowings were enabled by a shared pool of musicians, schools, and commerce. Music schools developed initially to train singing women, but also provided a means for men to study and perpetuate their own musical styles. Practical tutors and lengthy philosophical studies on theory and composition were written, along with commentary on the uses of music in medicine and metaphysical roots of music by natural philosophers. As different strands of musical practice and genres developed, so did a vocabulary of musicianship. The most enthusiastic patrons of entertainment music remained the court and wealthy classes, although singing women, *mukhannathūn*, and itinerant male musicians could be heard and hired by the middling classes in houses and taverns.

In the court, the corps of skilled musicians swelled during the Abbasid era, augmented by foreign artists and singing slave women. A hierarchy based on musical, social, and political skills developed by the ninth and tenth centuries, led, in part, by prominent singing slave women. At the top were *qiyān* and court companions (*nadīm*), musical concubines (*jawārī*), select free and noblewomen, *mukhannathūn*, and male musicians. Skill and charisma contributed to one's visibility and reputation as a musician, and identities were guarded, hidden, or manufactured to facilitate navigation of the patronate.

Concerns about the effect of listening on the individual and broader social order were voiced starting in the late eighth century, and first given shape by Ibn Abi'l Dūnya in the ninth. The battle for *samā*ᶜ within Ṣūfism began in earnest during the ninth century as well. Although the format for conversations about music and listening changed from the ninth to the fourteenth century, the key arguments and *ḥadīth* remained the same. The link to the Qur'an was tenuous and limited to a handful of tangential references to diversion. Similarly, *ḥadīth* concerned with music were few and either open to interpretation or legally weak.

Central to arguments surrounding *samāᶜ* was the question of intent. Like *samāᶜ* itself, intent existed outside the bounds of control and could be active and passive. The intersection of the gaze and visual impact of the reciter, melody, and accompaniment, as well as the mood of the audience, could conspire to change an innocent *samāᶜ* session and musical entertainment into something darker. Even if one had the noblest intent in reciting a religious text, their performance might still inspire lust in the hearer.

Because of this unknown, to some, music had no place in religious contemplation for its ability to distract and inspire complex emotions. Others argued that this very quality is what brought one in closer contact with God. Furthermore, God had created a sounding world, and humans had the ability to expand on that world; therefore, it stood to reason that music, and listening, were acceptable. Indeed, hearing a powerful message or recitation could convert one from a life of hedonism to devout worship. Where the different opinions linked on this front was the potential for social disorder if listeners were led astray, and, tainted by earthly passion, abandoned or bankrupted their families and souls in pursuit of pleasure.

Another aspect of intent in these arguments was justification for using sensorial accompaniments to embellish a gathering. Because there was such a fragile thread between what the performer did and the listener heard, those who asserted *samāᶜ* helped guide one to a closer relationship with God were considered brokers of vice just as much as those who insisted music was an accomplishment for the nobility. The expansion on such arguments in literature concerned with *samāᶜ* and narratives about music and musicians point to the persuasiveness of counterarguments as well as actual practice.

One useful side effect of the conversation about music and *samāᶜ* was that it inspired scholars to construct a history of music. Starting in the ninth century, Islamicate scholars and writers began to ask if pre-Islamic Arabs used music and practiced *samāᶜ*. The only evidence lay in outsider reports, pre-Islamic poetry, folklore, and what could be gleaned from *ḥadīth*. Some concluded musical expression was part of Arab culture prior to Islam, although it was difficult to determine how important it was. Opinion ranged from speculation that music was not as valued as poetry and therefore limited to simple instruments and song to those who insisted that song and playing instruments were common. However, where and when *samāᶜ* as a devotional practice originated could not be determined to anyone's satisfaction.

As a history of music developed, the origin of select instruments and practices became more detailed, with musicians increasingly referred to in the abstract.

Those refuting an indigenous origin for music and *samāᶜ* claimed both were not part of Arab culture before Islam, as attested to by a lack of mention in the *ḥadīth* and Qur'an. They concluded music was introduced by foreigners and singled out the Persians. Depending on the author, the Persians brought music and song into the newborn Islamicate states either actively, as in the case of Ṭuways and foreign workers, or through a slow infiltration of outsiders as Islamicate influence expanded. If music was a foreign practice, it was argued, *samāᶜ* did not have a legal and cultural precedent. Despite *ḥadīth* and pre-Islamic poetry implying otherwise, those who insisted *samāᶜ* was not indigenous neatly sidestepped this evidence by leaning on condemnation of instruments, rather than the fact of their existence.

Throughout the progression of these conversations, terminology for music and distinctions between song and recitation changed. *Ṣawt* and *ghinā'* are music, melody, and song, later joined by *samāᶜ* and *mūsīqī*. Over time, *samāᶜ* breaks into components. In one aspect, it is a practice, used in and with *dhikr*, and employing a wide variety of modalities among those Ṣūfi orders that use them. The other aspect was accompanied *samāᶜ*, which had a rhythmic or melodic backbone. Herein lay a major point of contention. Those who advocated purging *samāᶜ* specified the difference between *samāᶜ* as a form of religious recitation, including *taghbīr*, and that which is accompanied. This distinction was made linguistically: *samāᶜ al-ṣawt* and *samāᶜ al-ghinā'*. To those concerned with *samāᶜ*, both were to be avoided.

Similarly, *ṣawt* and *ghinā'* diverged, possibly to make a cleaner distinction between song and recitation. *Ṣawt* generally meant accompanied song, while *ghinā'* is song, not recitation. Where it gets sticky is how melodic and songlike recitation had to get before it was song, and how speech-like a lyric needed to be before turning into recitation. No one had a definitive answer, except in debates over epic poetry versus religious cantillation. This comparison in itself implies that epics were more declamatory, but the line between song and recitation remained tied to intent and perception. Basically, no one knew the answer. What everyone could agree on was melody plus rhythm—through textual and instrumental emphasis—had unpredictable effects on people.

The names for instruments and musicians did not change, except in moral and symbolic registers. Certain instruments represented entertainment and specific groups of musicians, such as associations of the lute with *qiyān*, *jawārī*, and the more generic *mughanniyat*. Their instruments were referred to as *maᶜāzif*, which went from being a reference to instruments in general to specifically stringed instruments used by singing women. *Maᶜāzif* later included all instruments that were struck for entertainment, whether physically or not. Except in histories and unique works like the *Aghānī*, singers are rarely individuals but conduits for sound; their role as physical, often beautiful and tempting, objects for the gaze is bound up with their being musicians.

As the Islamicate world expanded through the rise of new dynasties, the institutions of music, art, literature, and slavery followed. Tighter controls over marriage, gender segregation, and the veil for women developed during the thirteenth century, although gender roles and increased control over women were already being established in the ninth and tenth centuries.[1] Conquest and enslavement continued unabated as different dynasties pushed their borders outward. Increasingly, the majority of enslaved people came from Africa and what is now central and Eastern Europe, with the trade in women remaining the most lucrative. Therefore, slavery, gender, and origin continued to be linked to social status.

Throughout the expansion and contractions of Islamicate societies, music and listening continued to be robust cultural staples. The flow of ideas and musicians from what is now Europe to China continued unabated throughout the medieval and early modern eras. Singing women, courtesans, and musical concubines are found in the Ottoman sultanates, Mughal courts in India, and Islamic kingdoms in Africa. Their adoption was not an innovation but shared among every sophisticated culture, from ancient Greece and Rome, China, Korea, and Europe. Although some Ṣūfi orders took a hard stance against *samāᶜ*, several orders continued to use *samāᶜ* and *dhikr*, accompanied by instruments, clapping, and dancing. Over time, *samāᶜ* became increasingly associated with Ṣūfism, which is the primary association today.

The purpose of this study is to bring a tiny slice of medieval Islamicate music history into better focus. It is my hope that others will fill in the many gaps I have left, especially the tantalizing intersections and borrowings among cultures from the eleventh to the fifteenth centuries. There is a great need to understand how medieval Islamicate music developed within different regions of the Islamicate states, and the impact of these histories on global musical cultures. Although tracing the threads of specific genres, melody, instruments, and rhythm across such vast stretches of time and geography is difficult, it is safe to say that medieval cultures borrowed and shared music directly and indirectly. For those threads we can pinpoint, further inquiry into how they might have traveled would be valuable supplements to studies that have been done to date.

Those more elusive borrowings may require a different approach, necessitating a wider range of inquiry. Of those, we need more study of the influences of enslaved people on medieval cultures overall, as well as how gender, *ethnos*, and geographic origin contributed to the justification of the slave trade through the nineteenth century. The impact of enslaved peoples and institutions of slavery on family structure, rules about gender segregation, and other asymmetrical dependencies also deserve more attention. Uncovering these histories will lead inexorably to a broader understanding of intersections of music histories, cultural borrowing, and, importantly, the influence of enslaved people to the development of global music cultures.

Medieval people understood social, physical, and metaphysical connections and contradictions in ways that, I argue, would be fruitful to recapture. Our currently narrow edifice of "medieval," "history," and "music" will be richer for it. That is not to say medieval thinkers were correct and more accurate; rather, their purpose in seeking knowledge was based on the journey, not the end. Taking a medieval approach to musico-social history is one means to insert music back into the world. Not our world, but the world—and continuum of cultural influences—in which this rich serving of music grew and flourished.

Last, how we think about music and its reach merits challenge. Music is too complex to be confined to the page, and doing so robs it of vitality. Throughout this book, I have taken the stance that music is fundamentally a social institution and relationship, driven by other physical and metaphysical institutions. That does not diminish its power as a creative, evocative, and elusive medium, however. Quite the contrary. Reinserting music into the muddy waters of experience, cognition, history, and text requires a different approach to how we think about creativity, fact, and truth. In so doing, we have the potential to construct different histories and therefore deeper understanding of how those histories continue to influence us today.

Appendix I

A Selection of *Ḥadīth* on Music and Listening

To put together a comprehensive document of all extant *ḥadīth* related to music and listening would be an extensive (if fascinating) project requiring a book in itself. Therefore, this list is just a sampling of the most commonly found *ḥadīth* used in discussions of *samāᶜ*.[1] Several of these *ḥadīth* appear in the *samāᶜ* treatises from the NLI collection in multiple variations. In the case of those *ḥadīth* with many versions, I have included only one or two variations here. If it is in one of the *ṣaḥīḥ* collections of al-Bukhārī and Abū Muslim, I have chosen that version.[2] The source where the version I used is found follows the quotation in parentheses, for example, "(al-Bukhārī)."

Ḥadīth have a specific format. They begin with the authority who recited the tradition, followed by the text (*matn*), and close with the source and chain of transmission called *isnād*. The *isnād* can be quite long, so there are shortcuts used, such as noting the scholarly lineage and key source. Those *ḥadīth* considered reliable are authentic, *ṣaḥīḥ*, and therefore give firmer support to a legal-religious argument. *Ṣaḥīḥ* traditions have a chain of transmission reaching back to the Prophet or his Companions, with verifiable scholars and transmitters carrying it forward. Weak or *ḍaif ḥadīth* have a tentative provenance, meaning there are breaks in the chain of transmission or they cannot be reliably verified. Those that cannot be authenticated are considered inauthentic. Some reciters were considered unreliable and outright fabricators; however, that does not necessarily mean the traditions under their authority were culled.

Although many of the *ḥadīth* on this list are not *ṣaḥīḥ*, I have omitted that assessment primarily because I am not a *ḥadīth* scholar and there are ample, expert resources for assessing the authenticity of *ḥadīth*. There are several online sources for the major *ḥadīth* collections that provide authenticity and commentary. For this list, I consulted the collaborative efforts of *Ḥadīth* Collection (http://hadithcollection.com/) and *Muflihun* (https://muflihun.

com/). The latter provides both the Arabic and English versions and indicates whether the tradition is authentic.

When the source is the Prophet Muḥammad, he is referred to by name, as well as "Messenger of God" (*Rasulullāh*), "Apostle of God," and Nabi (Prophet). The Arabic phrase *ṣallā llāhu ᶜalayhī wa-sallam* (Peace be upon him) is always said when the Prophet is invoked. The phrase *raḍiyallāhu ᶜanhu* (God be pleased with him) is used after the name of a Companion or respected reciter of *ḥadīth*. Women transmitted *ḥadīth* as well, so when used with a woman, as in the Prophet's favorite wife ᶜĀ'isha, the phrase uses the feminine ending, becoming *raḍiyallāhu ᶜanhā* (God be pleased with her). I have kept these formulas as they appear in the *ḥadīth*, but rendered them in English.

On Singing Women

Abū Amir or Abū Mālik al-Ashᶜarī (God be pleased with him) says that he heard the Messenger of God (Peace be upon him) saying: "From among my followers there will be some people who will consider illegal sexual intercourse, the wearing of silk, the drinking of alcoholic drinks and the use of musical instruments, as lawful. And there will be some people who will stay near the side of a mountain and in the evening their shepherd will come to them with their sheep and ask them for something, but they will say to him, 'Return to us tomorrow.' God will destroy them during the night and will let the mountain fall on them, and He will transform the rest of them into monkeys and pigs and they will remain so till the Day of Resurrection." (al-Bukhārī, vol. 7, book 69, #494B)

In another version, also on the authority of Abū Mālik al-Ashᶜarī, The Messenger of God (Peace be upon him) said: "Most certainly, people from my Umma will consume liquor which they will describe with some other name. Over their heads will be playing musical instruments and singing girls. God will cause the earth to swallow them, and from among them He will transform into apes and pigs." (Ibn Majah, chapter 38, #4020)

Imran ibn Ḥusayn (God be pleased with him) narrated that the Messenger of God (Peace be upon him) said: "In this Umma will be earthquakes, disfiguration (of faces which will be transformed into apes and pigs) and showers of stone (descending on them from the heaven)." A man from among the Muslims said: "O Messenger of God! When will this be?" The Messenger of God (Peace be upon him) said: "When singing girls and musical instruments will become profuse and when liquor will be consumed (in abundance)." (al-Tirmidhī, *Jami'*, vol. 4, book 33, #2212)

ᶜAlī ibn Abī Ṭālib narrated that the Messenger of God said: "When my Umma does fifteen things, the afflictions will occur in it." It was said: "What are they O Messenger of God?" He said: "When Al-Maghnam (the spoils of war) are distributed (preferentially), trust is usurped, Zakah is a fine, a man obeys his wife and disobeys his mother, he is kind to his friend and abandons his father, voices are raised in the mosques, the leader of the people is the most despicable among them, the most honored man is the one whose evil the people are afraid of, intoxicants are drunk, silk is worn (by males), there is a fascination for singing slave-girls and music, and the end of this Umma curses its beginning. When that occurs, anticipate a red wind, collapsing of the earth, and transformation." (al-Tirmidhī, vol. 4, book 33, #2210)

Another variant on the authority of Abū Hurayra, who narrated that the Messenger of God said: "When Al-Fai' is distributed (preferentially), trust is a spoil of war, Zakat is a fine, knowledge is sought for other than the (sake of the) religion, a man obeys his wife and disobeys his mother, he is close to his friend and far from his father, voices are raised in the mosques, tribes are led by their wicked, the leader of the people is the most despicable among them, the most honored man is the one whose evil the people are afraid of, singing slave-girls and music spread, intoxicants are drunk, and the end of this Umma curses its beginning- then anticipate a red wind, earthquake, collapsing of the earth, transformation, Qadhf, and the signs follow in succession like gems of a necklace whose string is cut and so they fall in succession." (al-Tirmidhī, vol. 4, book 33, #2211)

ᶜĀ'isha (God be pleased with her) reported: "Abū Bakr came to see me and I had two girls with me from among the girls of the Ansar and they were singing what the Ansar recited to one another at the Battle of Buᶜath. They were not, however, singing girls. Upon this Abū Bakr exclaimed: What! (the playing of) this wind instrument of Satan in the house of the Messenger of God (Peace be upon him) and this too on ᶜId day? Upon this the Messenger of God (Peace be upon him) said: Abū Bakr, every people have a feast and it is our feast (so let them play on)." (Abū Muslim, book 4, #1938)

This *ḥadīth* has numerous variations and transmitters. According to one variant, the words are: "Two girls were playing upon a tambourine and singing." (*Sunan al-Nasa'i*, vol. 2, book 19, #1598)

Another variant, also on the authority of ᶜĀ'isha reads: ᶜĀ'isha (God be pleased with her), reported: "God's Messenger (Peace be upon him) came to my house while two girls were singing beside me the songs of Buᶜath (a story about the war between the Khazraj and the Aws before Islam). The Prophet (Peace be upon him) was laying down and turned his face away. Then Abū Bakr came and spoke to me harshly saying: 'Wind instruments of Satan near the Prophet (Peace be upon him)?' God's Messenger (Peace be upon him) turned his face towards him and said, 'Leave them.' When Abū Bakr became inattentive, I signaled to those girls to go out and they left." (al-Bukhārī, vol. 2, book 15, #70)

Another variant is: ᶜĀ'isha (God be pleased with her) reported: "Abū Bakr came to my house while two small Ansari girls were singing beside me the stories of the Ansar concerning the Day of Buᶜath. And they were not singers. Abū Bakr said in protest, 'Musical instruments of Satan in the house of God's Apostle!' It happened on the ᶜId day and God's Apostle (Peace be upon him) said, 'O Abū Bakr! There is an ᶜId for every nation and this is our ᶜId.'" (al-Bukhārī, vol. 2, book 15, #72)

Yet another is: ᶜĀ'isha (God be pleased with her) reported: "Abū Bakr came to see me and I had two girls with me from among the girls of the Ansar and they were singing what the Ansar recited to one another at the Battle of Buᶜath. They were not, however, singing girls. Upon this Abū Bakr said: What is (the playing of) this wind instrument of Satan in the house of the Messenger of God (Peace be upon him) and this too on ᶜId day? Upon this the Messenger of God (Peace be upon him) said: Abū Bakr, every people have a festival and it is our festival (so let them play on)." (Abū Muslim, book 4, #1940)

ᶜĀ'isha (God be pleased with her) reported: "It was the day of ᶜId, and Abyssinians were playing with shields and spears; so either I requested the Prophet (Peace be upon him) or he asked me whether I would like to see the performance. I replied in the affirmative. Then the Prophet (Peace be upon him) made me stand behind him and my cheek was touching his cheek and he was saying, 'Carry on! O Banū Arfida', until I grew tired. The Prophet (Peace be upon him) asked me: 'Is that enough?' I replied in the affirmative and he told me to leave." (al-Bukhārī, vol. 4, book 52, #155; and Abū Muslim, book 4, #1942)

Al-Rubai bint Muaᶜwidh reported that ᶜĀ'isha related: "The Prophet (Peace be upon him) came to me after consuming his marriage with me and sat down on my bed as you (the narrator) are sitting now, and small girls were beating the tambourine and singing in lamentation of my father who had been killed on the day of the battle of Badr. Then one of the girls said, 'There is a Prophet amongst us who knows what will happen tomorrow.' The Prophet (Peace be upon him) said (to her), 'Do not say this, but go on saying what you have spoken before.'" (al-Bukhārī, vol. 5, book 59, #336)

Saᶜid ibn Yarbu' al-Makhzumī reported: "The Prophet (Peace be upon him) said: on the day of the conquest of Mecca: There are four persons whom I shall not give protection in the sacred and non-sacred territory. He then named them. There were two singing girls of al-Maqis; one of them was killed and the other escaped and embraced Islam." (Abū Dāwūd, book 8, #2678)

ᶜAlī ibn Abī Ṭālib (God be pleased with him) reported: "There fell to my lot along with God's Messenger (Peace be upon him) an old she-camel from the spoils of Badr. God's Messenger (Peace be upon him) granted me another camel. I made them kneel down one day at the door of one of the Ansar, and I wanted to carry on them Idhkhir (a kind of grass) in order to sell. There was with me a goldsmith of the tribe of Qainuqa'. I sought to give a wedding feast (on the occasion of marriage with) Fatimah with the help of that (the price accrued from the sale of this grass). And Ḥamza ibn ᶜAbd al-Muṭṭalib was busy drinking in that house in the company of a singing girl who was singing to him. She said: Ḥamza, get up for slaughtering the fat she-camels. Ḥamza attacked them with the sword and cut off their humps and ripped their sides, and then took out their livers. I said to Ibn Shihāb: Did he take out anything from the hump? He said: He cut off the humps altogether. Ibn Shihāb reported ᶜAli having said: I saw this (horrible) sight and it shocked me, and I came to God's Messenger (Peace be upon him) and there was Zayd ibn Haritha with him and communicated to him this news. He went in the company of Zayd and I also went along with him, to Ḥamza and he expressed his anger at him. Ḥamza raised his eyes and said: Are you (not) but the slaves of my fathers? God's Messenger (Peace be upon him) turned back on his heels (on hearing this) until he went away from them." (Abū Muslim, book 23, #4881)

Anas (God be pleased with him) reported: "God's Messenger (Peace be upon him) had in one of his journeys his black slave who was called Anjashah along with him. He goaded by singing the songs of camel-driver. Thereupon God's Messenger (Peace be upon him) said: Anjashah, drive slowly as you are driving (the mounts which are carrying) 'glass vessels' (i.e. women)." (Abū Muslim, book 30, #5743)

It was narrated that Abū Umama said: "The Messenger of God, forbade selling or buying singing girls, and their wages, and consuming their price." (Ibn Majah, vol. 3, book 12, #2168)

> Variant on the authority of ᶜĀ'isha reads: "Verily, God hath made the singing girl unlawful and the selling of her and her price and teaching her."
>
> Another variant on the authority of Abū Umama reads: The Messenger of God (Peace be upon him) said: "Do not sell the female singers, nor purchase them, nor teach them (to sing). And there is no good in trade in them, and their prices are unlawful. It was about the likes of this that this Ayah was revealed: 'And among mankind is he who purchases idle talk to divert from the way of God (31:6).'" (al-Tirmidhī, book 5, #3195)

On Instruments

Nafīᶜ (God be pleased with him) narrated: "Once when ᶜAbdullāh ibn ᶜUmar (God be pleased with him) heard the sound of a shepherd's flute, he placed his fingers in both ears (to block the sound of the music), and he diverted his mount from that path. (As they rode on), he would say: 'O Nafīᶜ, can you still hear (the sound)?' I would say: 'Yes.' He would then continue riding. Only when I said: 'I can no longer hear it,' did he remove his fingers from his ears. Then he returned to the road. He then said: 'I saw The Messenger of God (Peace be upon him) doing like this when he had heard the flute of a shepherd.'" (Abū Dāwūd, book 36, #4906)

> Another variant reads: It was narrated that Mujahid said: "I was with Ibn ᶜUmar, and he heard the sound of a drum, so he put his fingers in his ears and turned away. He did that three times, then he said: 'This is what I saw the Messenger of God (Peace be upon him) do.'" (Ibn Majah, vol. 3, #1901)

ᶜAbdullāh ibn ᶜUmar (God be pleased with him) narrated: "Verily, The Prophet (Peace be upon him) made *ḥarām* liquor, gambling, the musical drum and the tambourine. And, every intoxicant is *ḥarām*." (Abū Dāwūd)

Ibn ᶜAbbās (God be pleased with him) narrated that The Messenger of God (Peace be upon him) said: "The deputation of ᶜAbd al-Qais asked (the Prophet): From which (vessels) should we drink? He (the Prophet) replied: Do not drink from pumpkins, vessels smeared with pitch, and hollow stumps, and steep dates in skins. They asked: Apostle of God, if it ferments? He replied: Infuse water in it. They asked: Apostle of God … (repeating the same words). He replied to them third or fourth time: Pour it away. He then said: God has forbidden me, or he said: He has forbidden me wine, game of chance and kūba (drums). He said: Every intoxicant is unlawful. Sufyān said: I asked ᶜAli ibn Badhima about kūba. He replied: Drum." (Abū Dāwūd, Book of Drinks, #3687)

Abū Hurayra (God be pleased with him) narrated that the Messenger of God (Peace be upon him) said: "The angels do not accompany travelers who have with them a dog and a bell." (Abū Muslim, Book of Clothes and Decorations, #5277)

> Another variant reads: Umm Habiba reported that The Prophet (Peace be upon him) said: "The angels do not go with a travelling company in which there is a bell." (Abū Dāwūd, book 8, #2548)

Bunanah, a female client of ᶜAbd al-Raḥmān ibn Hayyan al-Anṣārī told that when she was with ᶜĀ'isha, a girl wearing little bells was brought in to her. She ordered that they were not to bring her in where she was unless they cut off her little bells. She said: I heard the Prophet (Peace be upon him) say: The angels do not enter a house in which there is a bell. (Abū Dāwūd, book 29, #4219)

ᶜUmar ibn al-Khaṭṭāb (God be pleased with him) narrated: "Ibn al-Zubayr told that a woman client of theirs took al-Zubayr's daughter to ᶜUmar ibn al-Khaṭṭāb wearing bells on her legs. ᶜUmar cut them off and said that he had heard the Apostle of God (Peace be upon him) say: There is a devil along with each bell." (Abū Dāwūd, *Sunan*, book 29, #4218)

> Variation according to Abū Hurayra, who narrated that the Messenger of God (Peace be upon him) said: "The bell is among the musical instruments of shaitān." (Abū Muslim, Book of Clothes and Decorations, #5279)
>
> Another variant according to Abū Hurayra: The Apostle of God (Peace be upon him) was reported saying "The bell is a wooden wind musical instrument of Satan." (Abū Dāwūd, Book of Jihad, #2550)

ᶜAbdullāh ibn ᶜAmr ibn al-ᶜAs reported: "The Prophet (Peace be upon him) forbade wine (*khamr*), games of chance (*maysir*), drum (*kūba*), and wine made from millet (*ghubayrah*), saying: Every intoxicant is forbidden." (Abū Dāwūd, book 20, #3677) ᶜAbdullāh ibn ᶜAmr ibn al-ᶜAs narrated: "A woman came to the Prophet (Peace be upon him) and said: Apostle of God, I have taken a vow to play the tambourine over you.

He said: Fulfil your vow.

She said: And I have taken a vow to perform a sacrifice in such-a-such a place, a place in which people had performed sacrifices in pre-Islamic times.

He asked: For an Idol?

She replied: No.

He asked: For an image?

She replied: No.

He said: Fulfil your vow." (Abū Dāwūd, book 15, #3306)

On Singing and Listening

Abū Hurayra (God be pleased with him) reported God's Messenger (Peace be upon him) as saying. "God fixed the very portion of adultery which a man will indulge in. There would be no escape from it. The adultery of the eye is the lustful look and the adultery of the ears is listening to voluptuous (song or talk) and the adultery of the tongue is licentious speech and the adultery of the hand is the lustful grip (embrace) and the adultery of the feet is to walk (to the place) where he intends to commit adultery and the heart yearns and desires which he may or may not put into effect." (Abū Muslim, book 33, #6422)

Salām ibn Miskin, quoting an old man who witnessed Abū Waᶜil in a wedding feast, said: "They began to play, amuse and sing. He united the support of his hand round his knees that were drawn up, and said: I heard ᶜAbdullāh (Ibn Masᶜud) say: I heard the Apostle of God (Peace be upon him) say: Singing produces hypocrisy in the heart." (Abū Dāwūd, book 5, #4909)

Another variant is: Abū Hurayra (God be pleased with him) narrated that the Messenger of God (Peace be upon him) said: "Love for singing germinates hypocrisy in the heart just as water causes plants to grow."

This variant from the *Kaf al-Rua* states: Ibn Masᶜud (God be pleased with him) narrated that the Messenger of God (Peace be upon him) said: "Beware of listening to musical instruments and singing, for verily, both these acts germinate *nifāq* (hypocrisy) in the heart just as water causes vegetables to grow."

Ṣafwān ibn Umayya (God be pleased with him) narrated that ᶜAmr ibn Qurra said (to the Messenger of God—Peace be upon him): "I am very unfortunate. I do not see any way for acquiring my *rizq* except by means of my *duff*. Therefore, grant me permission to sing (with my *duff*) such songs which will be devoid of any immorality (evil)." The Messenger of God (Peace be upon him) replied: "I do not give you permission. There is no honor and no goodness (in what you are saying). O enemy of God! You are a liar. Most certainly, God has ordained for you *halāl rizq*, but you have chosen what God has made *ḥarām* for you in place of what He has made *halāl* for you of the sustenance He has decreed for you." (al-Ṭabarānī)

Abū Umāma (God be pleased with him) narrated that the Messenger of God (Peace be upon him) said: "When someone raises his voice with singing, God sends two shaitāns who sit on his shoulders striking his breast with their heels until he stops (singing)." (al-Ṭabarānī)

Kisan narrates that Muᶜāwiya (God be pleased with him) stated in his khutba: "Verily, the Messenger of God (Peace be upon him) forbade seven things, and I too forbid you from these things. Know that these things are: Loud wailing (on occasions of death), singing, pictures ..." (al-Ṭabarānī)

Abū Burza (God be pleased with him) narrated: "We were with the Prophet (Peace be upon him) on a journey when he heard two men singing. The one was responding to the other (by means of singing poetry). The Prophet (Peace be upon him) then said: 'Look who these two are.' They (the Sahabah) said: 'They are so and so (naming them).' The Messenger of God (Peace be upon him) then cursed, saying: 'O God! Cast them upside down in Jahanam.'" (*Majmū' al-Zawaᶜid*)

Qatāda (God be pleased with him) narrated that God gave to every Prophet that He had sent a beautiful feature and beautiful voice. Your Prophet (Peace be upon him) also had a beautiful feature and a beautiful voice. The Messenger of God (Peace be upon him) did not recite in a melodious tone as singers do. (al-Tirmidhī, chapter 43, #007 (303))

It was narrated that ᶜAmir bin Saᶜad said: "I entered upon Quraza ibn Kaᶜb and Abū Masᶜud al-Anṣārī during a wedding and there were some young girls singing. I said: 'You are two of the Companions of the Messenger of God who were present at Badr, and this is being done in your presence!' They said: 'Sit down if you want and listen with us, or if you want you can go away. We were granted a concession allowing entertainment at weddings.'" (*Sunan* al-Nasa'i, vol. 4, book 26, #3385)

It was narrated that Abū Balj said: "I heard Muḥammad ibn Hatib say: 'What differentiates between the lawful and the unlawful is the voice (singing).'" (*Sunan* al-Nasa'i, vol. 4, book 26, #3372)

> The version that precedes this one from the same volume and book, the injunction includes the tambourine: It was narrated that Muḥammad ibn Hatib said: "The Messenger of God (Peace be upon him) said: 'What differentiates between the lawful and the unlawful is the *duff*, and the voice (singing) for the wedding.'" (#3371)

It was narrated that Fadala ibn ᶜUbaid said "The Messenger of God (Peace be upon him) said: 'God listens more attentively to a man with a beautiful voice who recites Qur'an out loud than the master of a singing slave listens to his slave.'" (Ibn Majah, book 2, #1340)

Mukhannathūn

Abū Hurayra (God be pleased with him) reported: "A *mukhannath* who had dyed his hands and feet with henna was brought to the Prophet (Peace be upon him). He asked: What is the matter with this man? He was told: Apostle of God! He affects women's get-up. So he ordered regarding him and he was banished to al-Naqi'. The people said: Apostle of God! Should we not kill him? He said: I have been prohibited from killing people who pray. Abū Usama said: Naqi' is a region near Medina and not a Baqi'." (Abū Dāwūd, book 36, #4910)

ᶜĀ'isha narrated: "A *mukhannath* used to enter upon the wives of Prophet (Peace be upon him). They (the people) counted him among those who were free of physical needs. One day the Prophet (Peace be upon him) entered upon us when he was with one of his wives, and was describing the qualities of a woman, saying: When she comes forward, she comes forward with four (folds in her stomach), and when she goes backward, she goes backward with eight (folds in her stomach). The Prophet (Peace be upon him) said: Do I not see that this (man) knows what here lies. Then they (the wives) observed veil from him." (Abū Dāwūd, book 27, #4095)

Appendix II

A Brief Glossary of Music Terms

The list that follows, although by no means exhaustive, contains terms for music, instruments, and musicians found in medieval sources.

General Terms Used to Refer to Music and Song

ālat al-lahw:	Music, instruments of diversion, or "diverting things"
ālat al-ṭarab:	Music, that which inspires *ṭarab*
Ghinā':	Song, to sing
Maᶜāzif:	Instruments of diversion, entertainment instruments, later stringed instruments
Malāhī:	Music, diversion
Mūsīqā:	Music, that which is performed and also music theory
Samāᶜ:	To hear, to listen
Ṣawt:	Sound, music
Ṭarab:	The emotional transportation one experiences when hearing beautiful or compelling sound

The Act of Playing

Ḍaraba:	To strike, as with a plectrum on the lute or a drum
Laᶜiba:	To play games, childish or frivolous play, also to play music
Zammāra:	To blow into, play a pipe

Singers and Musicians

Jawārī:	Singing slave women, musical concubines
Mughanniyat/mughannūn:	Singers

Mukhannathūn:	Cross-gendered musicians and entertainers, usually men who dress and perform as women
Mūsīkār:	Singers, musicians, often used to refer to men
Muṭrib:	A musician, one who induces *ṭarab*
Qiyān:	Singing women, elite courtesans, and musicians

Stringed Instruments (Also Generalized as *Maᶜāzif*)

Barbaṭ:	Long-necked lute
Kīthāra, kītāra, kinnāra, kirān, muwattar, mizhar, lūra:	Lyres
Ṣanj, jank:	Harps
Ṭunbūr (also transliterated as *tambur/pandore*):	Another species of long-necked lute
ᶜŪd:	The lute, played with a plectrum

Percussion Instruments

Darabukka:	A type of drum
Dirridj:	A type of drum
Duff (pl. *dufūf*):	General term for tambourines; they can be round or square, with different materials for the drumhead, with or without jingles and bells
Duff murabbaᶜ:	A square tambourine, thought to have been a favored instrument of *mukhannathūn*
Jarasu:	Bells, whether worn on the ankles for dancing, large church bells, and bells used to decorate animals
Kabar:	A large drum
Kūba:	A large drum
Naqqāra, also *dabdāb/ dabbada* (pl. *dabādib*):	Kettledrums, used for battle and military processions
Qaḍib:	Wand or stick that is thumped on the ground to keep time and accompany song/recitation
Qasf:	Clapping
Sonaj:	Cymbals
Ṭabl (pl. *ṭabūl*):	General term for drums, usually used to refer to small hand-held drums

Winds

Būq:	Brass instruments, a trumpet
Diyānāy:	A type of flute
ᶜIrān mishtaq, *yaraᶜ*, *hanbaqa*, and *zanbaq*:	Probably types of winds, but what kind is uncertain
Kawal:	A type of flute
Mizmār:	Reed flute, usually used to refer to the double pipe or aulos
Nāy:	Flute
Quṣaba:	A type of reed pipe
Shabbāba:	A type of flute
Surnāy (also *surnā*, *zurnā*):	A smaller reed pipe
Zammāra:	Reed instrument, used to refer to a small bagpipe and reed flute

Notes

Introduction

1 His full name was Abū Ja^c^far Sa'ib ibn Yassar. See Henry George Farmer, *A History of Arabian Music to the 13th Century* (London: Luzac; reprint, 1995), 53–4.

2 Her name is sometimes transliterated as Djamila. See Abū'l faraj al-Iṣbahānī, *Kitab al-Aghānī* (Beirut: Dār Ṣader, 2004), in 25 vols., vol. VIII (Jamīla), 186. For an English summary of this famous event and her life, see Farmer, *A History of Arabian Music to the 13th Century*, 85–7. See also Amnon Shiloah, *Music in the World of Islam: A Socio-Cultural Study* (Detroit, MI: Wayne State University Press, 1995), 12–13.

3 A professional in the ancient and medieval Islamicate world was an individual who was hired for the purpose of music performance. Although many did have a form of formal training, the distinguishing feature of a professional was visibility. Professionals came from a variety of social backgrounds ranging from free to enslaved. In contrast, a nonprofessional might have the same level of skill and training, but performed only under socially prescribed settings, such as family and private gatherings of friends.

4 Use of "Islamicate" to reference cultures influenced by Islamic rule and cultural exchanges was proposed by the late Marshall Hodgson. See Marshall G. S. Hodgson, *The Venture of Islam: Conscience and History in a World Civilization*, 2 vols. (Chicago: Chicago University Press, 1974), vol. 1, 45.

5 There are several detailed, rich studies of medieval Islamicate performance practices and music theory available. I draw on them frequently and highly recommend them to those interested in doing a deeper dive into these areas.

6 Michael Chamberlain, *Knowledge and Social Practice in Medieval Damascus, 1190–1350* (Cambridge: Cambridge University Press, 1994), 21–2.

7 Hodgson, *The Venture of Islam*. See also Chamberlain, *Knowledge and Social Practice*, 9–10.

8 I borrow the term "asymmetrical dependencies" from the Bonn Center for Dependency and Slavery Studies, https://www.dependency.uni-bonn.de/en. Ira Berlin also defines slavery as a relationship which is constantly negotiated, even within chattel slavery. See Ira Berlin, *Generations of Captivity: A History of African-American Slaves* (Cambridge, MA: Harvard University Press, 2004).

9 Like the ancient Greeks, the Arabs equated male maturity and masculinity with having a beard. Children inhabited a gender-neutral space until their secondary sexual characteristics began to manifest. Young boys, along with singing women, were objects of desire, and references to their smooth faces and lithe bodies are staple images in wine and love poetry. See Khaled El-Rouayheb, *Before Homosexuality in the Arab-Islamic World, 1500–1800* (Chicago, IL: University of Chicago Press, 2005).

10 See ibid. for a detailed look at male relationships in the Islamicate world. Until recently, same-sex relationships among women were not studied as much as those among men. Sara Amer and others have shown that women took other women as lovers. Those women who were more dominant were considered "masculine," and it was believed they had outsized-pudenda that drove them to want to penetrate other women. See Sara Amer, "Medieval Arab Lesbians and Lesbian-Like Women," *Journal of the History of Sexuality* 18, no. 2 (May 2009): 215–36.

11 See Kecia Ali, *Marriage and Slavery in Early Islam* (Cambridge, MA: Harvard University Press, 2010), 23–5; Chapter 5, "Marriage and Dominion," especially 181–6. On p. 141, Ali points out how even the verb structures related to having sex or getting married are constructed in such a way that the masculine forms perform the action (e.g., "have sex with") while the feminine form only receives (literally, "is sexed").

12 This focus has been, in part, the result of limitations in the available documentary record; however, the documentary record does show women's quarters exerted considerable political influence. A number of formerly enslaved women maneuvered their way into marriage to caliphs, mothering rulers and contributing to affairs of state. The body of research on different women's quarters is too lengthy to list in full. See, for example, Leslie Peirce, *The Imperial Harem: Women and Sovereignty in the Ottoman Empire* (Oxford: Oxford University Press, 1993); Mary Ann Fay, *Unveiling the Harem: Elite Women and the Paradox of Seclusion in Eighteenth-Century Cairo*, Middle East Studies beyond Dominant Paradigms, Peter Gran, series ed. (Syracuse: Syracuse University Press, 2012); Marilyn Booth (ed.), *Harem Histories: Envisioning Places and Living Spaces* (Durham, NC: Duke University Press, 2010); Anne Walthall (ed.), *Servants of the Dynasty: Palace Women in World History* (Berkeley: University of Berkeley Press, 2008); Nadia Maria El-Cheikh, "The Qahramana in the Abbasid Court: Position and Functions," *Studia Islamica*, no. 97 (2003): 41–55; El-Cheikh, "Describing the Other to Get at the Self: Byzantine Women in Arabic Sources (8th–11th Centuries)," *Journal of the Economic and Social History of the Orient* 40, no. 2 (1997): 239–50; and El-Cheikh, "Revisiting the Abbasid Harems," *Journal of Middle East Women's Studies* 1, no. 3 (2005): 1–19. For earlier studies, see Nabia Abbott, "Women and the State in Early Islam," *Journal of Near Eastern Studies*

1, no. 3 (1942): 341–68; Abbott, "Women and the State on the Eve of Islam," *American Journal of Semitic Languages and Literatures* 58, no. 3 (1941): 259–84; and Leila Ahmed, "Western Ethnocentrism and Perceptions of the Harem," *Feminist Studies* 8, no. 3 (1982): 521–34. For literature, see Fedwa Malti-Douglas, *Woman's Body, Woman's Word: Gender and Discourse in Arabo-Islamic Writing* (Princeton, NJ: Princeton University Press, 1991). For performance practices, see Suzanne Meyers-Sawa, "The Role of Women in Musical Life: The Medieval Arabo-Islamic Courts," *Canadian Women's Studies* 8, no. 2 (1987): 93–5; and Meyers-Sawa, "Historical Issues of Gender and Music," in Virginia Danielson, Scott Marcus, and Dwight Reynolds (eds.), *The Garland Encyclopedia of Music: The Middle East* (New York: Routledge, 2002), 293–8.

13 I will discuss the complexity of the term "domestic" in Chapter 4.

14 Abū Dūnya, *Tracts on Listening to Music: Being the Dhamm al-Malāhī of Ibn Abi Dūnya*, The Royal Asiatic Society Translation Services, trans. James Robson (London: Royal Asiatic Society, 1937).

15 Such concerns also arise in earlier treatises on piety. Ibn Khurdādhbih's treatise *Kitāb al-lahw wa'l malāhī* (Book of Play and Musical Instruments) and *Kitāb al-Malāhī min qibal al-mūsīqā* (literally, Book of Instruments of Play, pertaining to music, but usually translated simply as Book of Musical Instruments) by Ibn Salama were written in the ninth century. Both are among the earliest treatises that discuss music. Though the authors are positive about singing and instrumental music, their guarded comments about the moral value of music indicate this was already subject to debate. For the modern Arabic editions, see Ibn Khurdādhbih, *Kitāb al-Lahw wa'l malāhī*. Nusūs wa darūs, 17 (Beirut: al-Matbaᶜa al-kātūlīkīya, 1961); and Ibn Salama, *Kitāb al-malāhī min qibal al-mūsīqā* (Cairo: al-Hayaʾ al-miṣriya al-ᶜammaʾ al-kitāb, 1984). For an English translation, see Henry George Farmer, "Ibn Khurdādhbih on Musical Instruments," *Journal of the Royal Asiatic Society of Great Britain and Ireland*, no. 3 (July 1928): 509–18; James Robson and H. G. Farmer. "The Kitāb al-Malāhī of Abū Ṭālib Al-Mufaḍḍal Ibn Salāma," *Journal of the Royal Asiatic Society of Great Britain and Ireland*, no. 2 (April 1938): 231–49. When referring to Ibn Salama's treatise, I use the translation as it also contains the page numbers for the Arabic manuscript.

16 Ibn Surayj was a *mukhannath*. See George Sawa, "'Ubayd Ibn Surayj," *Encyclopedia of Islam*, 3rd ed., http://dx.doi.org/10.1163/1573-3912_ei3_COM_32260 (accessed November 2019).

17 See S. El-Khoury, *The Function of Music in Islamic Culture in the Period up to 1100 AD* (General Egyptian Book Organization, 1984). El-Khoury outlines these conflicts clearly, albeit with a decided Eurocentric opinion that the Muslim (and therefore Semitic) temperament was somehow more susceptible to being emotionally influenced by music. See 50–5.

18 Along with the *shahada*, or profession of faith, the other pillars are to pray five times a day (*salat*), contribute to the communal good (*zakat*), perform the pilgrimage to Mecca (*hajj*), and fast for Ramadan.

19 Among the seminal studies of medieval Islamicate music are: Farmer, *A History of Arabian Music to the 13th Century*; and Julian Ribera, *Music in Ancient Arabia and Spain: La Musica De Las Cantigas*, trans. Eleanor Hague, abridged ed. (Stanford: Stanford University Press, 1929). Farmer included biographies of musicians based on the *Aghānī* in *History of Arabian Music*, but more detail is available in Stigelbauer, "Die Sangerinnen Am Abbasidenhof Um Die Zeit Des Kalifen al-Mutawakkil Nach Dem *Kitāb al-Aghānī* Des Abu'l Farag al-Iṣbahāni and Anderen Quellen Dargestellt" (dissertation, Universitat Wien, 1975). See also Eckhard Neubauer, *Musiker Am Hof Der Fruhen 'Abbasiden* (Frankfurt am Main: JW Goethe-Universitat, 1965); Hans Engel, *Die Stellung des Musikers im arabisch-islamischen Raum* (Bonn: Verlag für Systematische Musikwissenschaft, 1987); and Shiloah, *Music in the World of Islam: A Socio-Cultural Study*. For a compendium of singing girls and their books of songs, see Muḥammad Mestiri and Soumaya Mestiri, *La Femme Arabe Dans Le Livres Des Chants* (Fayard: Bibliotheque Maktaba, 2004); and F. Matthew Caswell, *The Slave Girls of Baghdad: The Qiyan in the Early Abbasid Era* (London: I.B. Tauris, 2011). For performance practice, the work of George Sawa is unparalleled. See in particular *Music Performance Practice in the Early Abbasid Era, 132–32-AH/750–932AD* (Toronto: Pontifical Institute of Medieval Studies, 1989) and the recently published *Musical and Socio-cultural Anecdotes from* Kitab al-Aghānī al-Kabir, Islamic History and Civilization, vol. 159 (Leiden: Brill, 2019).

20 This need to focus on translating those aspects of a literary corpus which are morally "good" or "of value" is best illustrated in a statement made by the Arabist D. S. Margoliouth in the preface to his wonderfully readable 1922 translation of al-Tanūkhi's memoirs:

> For one matter an apology must be added. A few stories have been omitted from the Arabic text on the ground of their obscenity, and some of those left there have not been translated in this. As my friend Mr. Kurd 'Ali in the Journal of the Academy of Damascus has found fault with this procedure, I venture to assign a reason. One of the educational authorities in Cairo pleaded the cause of expurgated editions on the ground that it was desirable to provide good literature in Arabic for those whose literary language it is; and many a work in classical Arabic contains matter which *is not desirable* for the young to see. It may be added that it is frequently of a sort which *has no scientific value either*; for there is nothing to be learned from e.g. the bulk of the matter contained in that *Baghdader Sittenbild* which Prof. Mez thought proper to publish. Now the *Table-Talk* is precisely

> the sort of book which, it might be hoped, would be read with interest, pleasure and appreciation in educated families in those countries where education is in Arabic. I should very much prefer that in such households the book might without danger be left about. (emphasis mine)

See Margoliouth, introduction to Al-Muhassin ibn al-Tanūkhi, *Table Talk of a Mesopotamian Judge*, trans. D. S. Margoliouth (London: Royal Asiatic Society, 1922), vii.

21 Despite his often pointed views of the importance of non-Western history, Farmer adhered to the Western consensus that the so-called Golden Age of Islam was over. He commented that the Arabs had made no progress musically since the fourteenth century since they had not developed written notation. See Farmer, "Clues for the Arabian Influence on European Musical Theory," *Journal of the Royal Asiatic Society* (1925): 79, and his notes from the Cairo Congress, found in Israel Katz, *Henry George Farmer and the First International Congress of Arab Music (Cairo 1932)* (Leiden: Brill, 2015), 243.

22 Dūnya, *Tracts on Listening to Music: Being the Dhamm al-Malāhī of Ibn Abi Dūnya.*

23 James Robson (1890–1981) served in the Middle East as a missionary for the Free Church of Scotland. On his return, he was appointed lecturer in Arabic at Glasgow University, and later professor of Arabic at Manchester University. At the time of his collaboration with Farmer, the manuscript of Ibn Khurdādhbih's treatise on music had not yet been found.

24 Michael Shank and David Lindberg, "Introduction to Medieval Science," in David C. Lindberg and Michael H. Shank (eds.), *The Cambridge History of Science: Medieval Science*, vol. 2 (Cambridge: Cambridge University Press, 2013), 1–2.

25 Ibid., 3.

26 Because there is no tradition of sacred music in Islam, defining music as sacred and secular makes little sense. To provide an anchor for categories of sounded expression, I use religious and nonreligious. Depending on context and content, there could be little differentiation between the two, along with decidedly gray areas between what constituted song over recitation. I discuss both in more detail here.

27 For my purposes, music discourses include the broader conversation related to music as well as those shifts in the language and concepts used to define music and musical expression in public (court, tavern) and private (women's quarters, Ṣūfi *dhikr*) audition.

28 There is no greater source on music and musicians in the tenth century than the *Kitāb al-Aghānī* (*Great Book of Songs*) of Abū'l faraj al-Iṣbahānī. Both al-Iṣbahānī and al-Iṣfahānī are used, but the former is more common. There are several Arabic editions, along with expert translations and commentary. I primarily consulted Abū'l faraj al-Iṣbahānī, *Kitab al-Aghānī*, 25 vols. (Beirut: Dār Ṣader, 2004), and

also Abū'l faraj al-Iṣbahānī, *Kitāb al-Aghānī*, 24 vols. (Turathina, Beirut: Dār al-Thaqāfah, 1955–61) and *Kitāb al-Aghānī*, 24 vols. (Cairo: Dār al-Kutub, 1927–74) when available. I refer to several different editions of al-Mas'ūdī's work: *Murūj al-dhahab wa'l maᶜādin al-jawhar*, 4 vols. (Beirut: Dār al-Andalus, 1965–66); *The Meadows of Gold: The Abbasids*, trans. Paul Lunde and Caroline Stone (London: Kegan Paul, 1989); and *Les Prairies D'or*, trans. Barbier de Meynard and Abel Pavet de Courteille, revised and corrected by Charles Pellat (Paris: Société asiatique, 1962).

29 Where Western perceptions of music may best align with medieval Islamicate thinking is our shared influences from Greek theories and philosophies of music, making thinkers such as al-Kindī (*c.* 800–870 CE/183–255 *H*), al-Fārābī (*c.* 870–950/1 CE/257–339 *H*), Ibn Sīnā (known as Avicenna in the West, *c.* 970–1037 CE/358–427 *H*), and al-Ghazālī (*c.* 1056–1111 CE/450–505 *H*), feel more familiar.

30 More so than Ibn Abi'l Dūnya, the influential Ḥanbali jurist Ibn Taymiyya (1263–1328 CE/661–728 *H*) has been held up as the exemplar of anti-Ṣūfi and anti-music sentiment, with all Ḥanbalis being painted with the same brush. This was not the case. Although Ibn Taymiyya was firmly against listening and his work has been used to reinforce bans on music and listening in some sects of fundamentalist Islam (most notably Wahhabism), he was possibly himself a Ṣūfi and his ideas were not shared by his Ḥanbalite colleagues. See Christopher Melchert, "The Ḥanbalia and the Early Ṣūfis," *Arabica* 48 (2001): 352–67.

31 NLI Ap. Ar. 158, 1–155ff.: *Majmūᶜ fi mas'alat al-samāᶜ wa'l malāhī* (A collection of treatises concerning music and musical instruments).

32 Farmer noted *taghbīr* is a form of cantillation. See *A History of Arabian Music to the 13th Century*, 33. Based on how the practice is discussed, *taghbīr* was a form of religious cantillation that could be melodic and embellished vocally. According to Edward Lane, *taghbīr* can mean: "a reciting of poetry, or verses, in the praising, or glorifying, of God, in which the performers trill, or quaver, and prolong, the voice." Edward Lane, *Lexicon, Arabic-English Lexicon*, 2 vols. (Cambridge: Islamic Texts Society Trust, 1984; reprint of 1863–93 edition), 2,223, section #2. See also Michael Cook's discussion of *al-Amr* by al-Khallāl and the discussions about music in pietistic texts in *Commanding Right and Forbidding Wrong in Islamic Thought* (Cambridge: Cambridge University Press, 2000), 93, note #52. Given how often *taghbīr* is noted in conjunction with instruments, it is possible the term came to reference a type of musical instrument. Since to render the different possible meanings of this term into English is cumbersome, I use the Arabic *taghbīr*.

33 Translations of the titles are my own except for #3 and #9, which are Amnon Shiloah's translations from the entries for these texts in *The theory of music in Arabic writings (c. 900–1900). Descriptive catalog of manuscripts in libraries of*

Egypt, Israel, Morocco, Russia, Tunisia, Uzbekistan, and supplement to B/X (B/Xa) Repertoire Internationel Des Sources Musicales (RISM) (Munich: G. Henle Verlag, 2003). Subsequent mention of the 2003 RISM will be shortened to RISM 2.

34 The text by Ibn Rajab is well over fifty pages and represents a compilation of his work. It is a very interesting treatise, touching on history, Islamic and Jewish law, with only passing mention of song and music. The second text by al-Khallāl is unrelated to music and listening.

35 To place in the dynastic timeline, the Mamlūk era (1250–1517 CE), followed the Ayyubid period (1171–1250 CE).

36 My approach to this balance is broad. I am not a book specialist, nor am I in any way an expert on Ṣūfism, Islamic law, or literature or setting out to create a translation. It is my hope experts in these areas will fill in those gaps as these texts are examined further.

37 Some prominent Orientalists in the first half of the twentieth century could be described as "pro-woman" and fairly balanced in their outlook, as in the work of Henry Farmer and Julian Ribera. There were a number of women engaged in Oriental scholarship and the colonial effort as well, from Lady Hester Stanhope to Gertrude Bell. Nabia Abbott, a respected scholar of Middle East Studies, authored several books and articles on women in the early Islamic world. She taught in the Oriental Institute at the University of Chicago in the 1940s.

38 For example, courtesans are frequently lumped in with prostitutes, whores, catamites, and concubines. Though they may share some of the sexual roles, they are not in the same social and financial relationship with men. See Chapter 3 for further discussion of courtesans.

39 Henry George Farmer was among the first to compile information about individual singing women as part of his study of early Arabian music history, *A History of Arabian Music to the 13th Century.*

40 Charles Pellat, *The Life and Works of Jāhiz*, trans. D. M. Hawke (Berkeley: University of California Press, 1969), 26.

41 Applying transgender to the *mukhannathūn* is not entirely accurate either. More on the *mukhannathūn* in the following chapters.

1 Music in the Near East before Islam

1 The definition for music and musicianship changed over time. For the sake of simplicity, I use the term "musician" to indicate an individual who performs in public and is known for their performance.

2 To use a simple example, a rock musician has different codes of performance than that of a member of a classical string quartet. The boundaries can be shaken

slightly, such as the Kronos Quartet playing Jimi Hendrix or Eddie van Halen playing classical music on electric guitar. The patrons of each genre may accept innovation and eccentricity, but within limitations. They might only accept it from specific artists or just the once, and prevent such deviance from expectations from expanding through the threat of withdrawing their patronage.

3 See chapter 6, "Religion," in Robert G. Hoyland, *Arabia and the Arabs: From the Bronze Age to the Coming of Islam* (London: Routledge, 2001), 139–66. For an argument that monotheism was more prevalent in pre-Islamic Arabia and Mesopotamia than previously thought, see G. R. Hawting, *The Idea of Idolatry and the Emergence of Islam: From Polemic to History*, Cambridge Studies in Islamic Civilization, ed. David Morgan, Virginian Aksan, Michael Brett, Michael Cook, Peter Jackson, Tarif Khalidi, Roy Mottahedeh, Basim Musallem, and Chase Robinson (Cambridge: Cambridge University Press, 1999).

4 There are many references to idols and gods being stolen or destroyed in the Judaic testament along with prohibitions against making images of the one God. For example, see Gen. 31:19, 30-35, 35:2-5, Exod. 20:4-6 (the commandment not to make an image of God or other gods), 32:1-35, 34:11-17, and Lev. 19:4. When the Philistines make off with the Ark of the Covenant after a vicious battle with the Hebrews, they mistakenly believe they have demoralized the enemy by capturing their God. The Philistines are soon plagued by mice and hemorrhoids, and none of their gods can help them. In desperation, they make an offering of five golden mice and five golden hemorrhoids and return the Ark with an offering of jewels. They are soon defeated in battle and the Ark is restored. See 1 Samuel 4–7.

5 As in the later Islamicate context, the division between religious and nonreligious sounding was often blurred in the Ancient Near East and cannot be defined as strict categories. In addition, the link between certain instruments and gender is still not entirely clear. Certainly, the use of particular instruments in the worship of certain gods and goddesses had an impact, but the reason why the tambourine, say, was linked to women is still uncertain. It was likely a combination of ritual association, in conjunction with genre requirements and, possibly, portability and construction. See, for example, Veronica Doubleday, "The Frame Drum in the Middle East: Women, Musical Instruments and Power," *Ethnomusicology* 43, no. 1 (1999): 101–34.

6 Poets and musicians in the ancient world relied on memory as the basis of performance. That reliance continued well into the medieval era. For memory in the medieval Western music tradition, see Anna Maria Busse-Berger, *Medieval Music and the Art of Memory* (Berkeley: University of California Press, 2005). There are many indications from the Arabic sources that such memory training was also common in the Islamicate world.

7 See studies into Greek music, for example, such as Stefan Hagel, *Ancient Greek Music: A New Technical History* (Cambridge: Cambridge University Press, 2009).

8 See Ann Suter, ed. *Lament: Studies in the Ancient Mediterranean and Beyond* (Oxford: Oxford University Press, 2008); and Ilse Seibert, *Woman in Ancient Near East*, trans. Marianne Herzfeld (Leipzig: Edition Leipzig, 1974). Lamentation poetry and song was the genre of women in pre-Islamic Arabia as well. For samples, see Abdullah al-Udhari, *Classical Poems by Arab Women: A Bilingual Anthology* (London: Saqi Books, 1999).

9 Women have long used music for work, telling stories, soothing children (lullabies), and educating young girls. See, for example, Doubleday, "The Frame Drum in the Middle East."

10 For music and musicians in the Ancient Near East, see John C. Franklin, "The Global Economy of Music in the Ancient Near East," in Joan Goodnick Westenholz (ed.), *Sounds of Ancient Music* (Jerusalem: Bible Lands Museum, 2007), 27–37. See also Franklin, *Kinyras: The Divine Lyre*, Hellenic Studies Series 70 (Washington, DC: Center for Hellenic Studies, 2016).

11 Dynastic Egyptian art is rife with images of women playing flutes and various types of stringed instruments, and there are textual references to women playing instruments in many settings. See Lise Manniche, *Music and Musicians in Ancient Egypt* (London: British Museum Press, 1991); and Carolyn Graves-Brown, *Dancing for Hathor: Women in Ancient Egypt* (London: Continuum, 2010). Greek texts and artworks reference *aulotrides* or "flute girls," who entertained at symposia and in taverns. The Greek *hetaerae* (courtesans) were often musically skilled. For flute girls and *hetarae*, see James Davidson, *Courtesans and Fishcakes* (New York: Harper Perennial, 1999). For a brief survey of sources linking contemporary performance practices of women to those of the Ancient Near East, see Doubleday, "The Frame Drum in the Middle East." See also Carol Meyers, "Of Drums and Damsels: Women's Performance in Ancient Israel," *Biblical Archaeologist* 54, no. 1 (1991): 16–27.

12 In 1 Sam. 18:6, 7, the women dance and play tambourine to welcome the victorious David home. See also the story of Jephthah and his daughter "meeting him with dancing and tambourines" in Judg. 11:34. For an example of contemporary use of the frame drum by women in Afghanistan, see Doubleday, "The Frame Drum in the Middle East."

13 See Manniche, *Music and Musicians in Ancient Egypt*; and Graves-Brown, *Dancing for Hathor*.

14 Manniche, *Music and Musicians in Ancient Egypt*. See also Franklin, "The Global Economy of Music."

15 The sistrum is a type of rattle associated with the worship of Hathor. See Manniche, *Music and Musicians in Ancient Egypt*, 85–6.

16 Medieval Arab historians credited the invention of the lute, or *ᶜūd*, to Lamech, and his son, Tubal (Jubal-Cain), is credited with inventing the drum and tambourine. This tradition is attested to in several sources, which I discuss further later. See Farmer, *A History of Arabian Music to the 13th Century*, 6–7.

17 See Manniche, *Music and Musicians in Ancient Egypt*, 108–99.

18 See ibid., 94–5, 99–100. These musicians are presumed blind because they are often represented as having deformed or slitted eyes. On the other hand, this might also have been the convention for rendering court musicians. Manniche makes a case for both possibilities. The rendering of the eyes might also have been a way to show the musician caught up in playing. It is not uncommon for musicians, especially those performing from memory, to shut their eyes while playing. Additionally, looking upon royalty and images of the gods while performing might not have been allowed. Therefore, the closed eyes could as readily be an indication of performance etiquette.

19 For example, in addition to Orpheus, there is the gruesome story of Marysas who was flayed and hung by Apollo for his hubris. Hephaestus is another example of a disabled artisan, and myths about Pythagoras, credited with inventing music, state he was blind.

20 One example is Ur Nanshe of Mari, of whom there is a delightfully ambiguous statue. The singer is depicted with hints of masculine and feminine traits, and their gender has been subject to debate. There were other known *gala* as well, and they appear in the literature, most famously in the epic *Inanna's Descent in to the Underworld*. That lamentation was a feminine art is further attested to by the fact that the Sumerian *gala* priests were also specialists in lamentation and sang in the "women's" language of Emesal. For the epic, see the Electronic Text Corpus of Sumerian Literature (ETCSL), http://etcsl.orinst.ox.ac.uk/ (last accessed July 2020). For discussion of women and lamentation, see the articles in Suter, *Lament*.

21 Castrati were popular temple attendants in a number of societies, and it is thought that Islamicate rulers adopted the use of eunuchs in civil service from Persia and India. For a detailed look at the priests of Cybele, see Will Roscoe, "Priests of the Goddess: Gender Transgression in Ancient Religion," *History of Religions* 35, no. 3 (1996): 195–230. See also Piotr O. Scholz, *Eunuchs and Castrati: A Cultural History*, trans. John A. Broadwin and Shelley L. Frisch (Princeton, NJ: Marcus Wiener, 2001), 93–123, for the *galli* and the cult of Cybele in the Hellenistic and Roman worlds. This book also offers an interesting history of the phenomenon of eunuchs and castrati in history from ancient to modern times.

22 The term *hijra* is a colonial artifact, and there are other preferred terms for this unique caste. In Pakistan, they are *khawaja sara*. I am indebted to Zulaika Khan, my former student, for her fine work challenging the Western model of gender and transgender when looking at *khawaja sara* and other non-Western gender

identities. See Mohammad Zakaria Khan, "In Translation/Transition: What Happens When *Hijra* and/or *Khawaja Sara* Meets Transgender?" (master's thesis, University of British Columbia, Vancouver, April 2019).

23 Music archeologists have been attempting to reconstruct ancient music texts for decades, with many different opinions about the nature of modes, performance, and rhythm in the Ancient Near East. The oldest known extant notation is on an Ugaritic tablet found in Ras Shamra in what is now Syria. The tablet dates from approximately 1400 BCE and has notation and lyrics in Hurrian, with instruction for performance. How this notation can be transcribed is an ongoing debate. See, for example, M. L. West, "The Babylonian Musical Notation and the Hurrian Melodic Texts," *Music & Letters* 75, no. 2 (1994): 161–79. Modern realizations have ranged from simple melodic sketches to full-blown performances with chorus.

24 Performance indications are noted in some Sumerian and Assyrian epics and poems. Although modal systems are referenced periodically, these instructions give only an outline and no solid indication of rhythm or melodic progression. See the introduction to Thorkild Jacobsen, *The Harps That Once … Sumerian Poetry in Translation* (New Haven, CT: Yale University Press, 1987), xiii–xiv.

25 See Manniche, *Music and Musicians in Ancient Egypt* for a survey of images in Egypt. For Sumer, see Julia Asher-Grave, "The Essential Body: Mesopotamian Conceptions of the Gendered Body," *Gender & History* 9, no. 3 (1997): 432–61. See also Seibert, *Women in Ancient Near East*. Though a bit dated, both books contain a number of images of musicians from the Ancient Near East and details as to where they are located.

26 Many gods were musicians and appreciated music, which was another reason for music being used in their ritual. In Greek mythology, the god Apollo is the most familiar musical god. Music in the hands of the gods could also be sinister, as in the later association of music, specifically the violin, with the Devil.

27 Representation of musicians and dancers could depict an actual event, but could just as well be symbolic. It would have been impractical, if not impossible, to depict the number of musicians used for large-scale entertainments, particularly when the record claims the use of one thousand musicians or more. Artworks in the Ancient Near East were produced at the request of a ruler or patron, and the artists likely never witnessed such events.

28 For discussion of images of musicians and performance practice versus symbolism, see Irit Ziffer, "Four New Belts from the Land of Ararat and the Feast of Women in Esther 1:9," in S. Parapola and R. M. Whiting (eds.), *Sex and Gender in the Ancient Near East*, two vols., vol. II, Proceedings of the 47th Recontre Assyriologique Internationale (Helsinki, Finland, July 2–6, 2001: Neo-Assyrian Text Corpus Project, 2001), 645–57.

29 For an overview of musical exchanges in Sumer, see Franklin, "The Global Economy of Music."

30 Numerology was a science in the Ancient Near East. At a basic level, the number of musicians in a group created a greater visual impact as well as display of wealth; however, numbers were also sacred and representational in their own right.

31 See West, "The Babylonian Musical Notation and the Hurrian Melodic Texts."

32 In the Middle East today, the audience is an important part of a performance. By shouting encouragement, clapping and otherwise participating in a concert event, the audience interacts with and often controls the performance. See A. J. Racy, *Making Music in the Arab World: The Culture and History of Tarab* (Cambridge: Cambridge University Press, 2004). See also George Sawa, "The Survival of Some Aspects of Medieval Arabic Performance Practice," *Ethnomusicology* 25, no. 1 (1981): 73–86.

33 See Olaf Kaper, "Rhythm and Recitation in Ancient Egypt" (paper presented at the *Musical Tradition in the Middle East: Reminiscences of a Distant Past*, Leiden University, The Netherlands, December 10–12, 2009). Musical practices which do not use or rely on written notation emphasize improvisation, memory, and oral transmission of performance techniques. In addition, musical cultures without specific written notation generally have an expanded sound palette and incorporate a broader variety of vocalizations and rhythmic diversions than those with written notation. Although notation allows for vertical, complex composition, it is limited in visually depicting different soundscapes. Vocal performance practice in the contemporary Middle East has a broader range of ornamentation and pitch variation available for decorating text, including the use of falsetto, bending and falling pitches, and stylized wails and sighs.

34 The ancient nature of some of the musical techniques described in the documentary record is attested to by early Islamic historians. See Sawa, "The Survival of Some Aspects of Medieval Arabic Performance Practice."

35 For one theory of mode based on the Hurrian fragment, see West, "The Babylonian Musical Notation and the Hurrian Melodic Texts." Other theories differ, as in the work of Theo Krispijn and Richard Dumbrill.

36 Sumerian poetry apparently did not use rhyme. Since it was sung-declaimed, there must have been a system for meter and rhythm but what that was is not apparent in the texts. See Jacobsen, introduction to *The Harps That Once*, xiv–xv. In contrast, according to the structure of extant poems and observations of outsiders, Egyptian poetry and song did have a system of rhythm and meter. See the introduction to Manniche, *Music and Musicians in Ancient Egypt*, 11.

37 See Jacobsen, introduction to *The Harps That Once*, viii–xiv.

38 By extending certain phrases or rhythms, even a scripted melody can, theoretically, be played indefinitely. See Ali Jihad Racy, "The Many Faces of Improvisation: The Arab *Taqsim* as a Musical Symbol," *Ethnomusicology* 44, no. 2 (2000): 302–20.

39 For example, see 1 Sam. 18:10, 19:9, for David playing the lyre and 18:6 for crowds playing "three stringed instruments," which could be lyres, harps, or zithers. See also 1 Chron. 15:16-29, for the procession leading the Ark back to the Temple. It is also theorized that the psalms were intended to have been performed in the Temple. Additional references from the Bible indicate use of lyres and lutes in court. For example, see 1 Kgs 10:12 for Solomon's gift of instruments, lyres, and lutes for the singers. See also David P. Wright, "Music and Dance in 2 Samuel 6," *Journal of Biblical Literature* 121, no. 2 (2002): 201–25. For references found in the poetry of ancient Sumer, see Jacobsen, introduction to *The Harps That Once*, viii–xiv. For the court, see Franklin, "The Global Economy of Music." For Egypt, see Manniche, *Music and Musicians in Ancient Egypt*. Perhaps the most familiar discussion of performance spaces is found in *De Architectura* (Ten Books on Architecture) by Vitruvius, regarding the acoustics of theaters in Book V.

40 There are several variations on a *ḥadith* of the Prophet Muḥammad taking his favorite wife, ᶜĀ'isha, to a celebration. Because she was a child, he put her on his shoulders so she could see the dancing, singing, and tambourine players. In another, there is a reference to ᶜĀ'isha listening to singers who were "not singing women." See Appendix I for variations on this tradition.

41 In Arabic, *Jarādatān*. See al-Jāḥiẓ, section 28, 23. See also Henry George Farmer, trans., *Music: The Priceless Jewel*, 2 vols., vol. 1 (Frankfurt am Main: Institute for the History of Arabic-Islamic Science at the Johann Wolfgang Goethe University, 1942; reprint, 1997), 11, Ibn Salama (Arabic edition), section 20, Robson and Farmer, 240, and Abū'l faraj al-Iṣbahānī, *Kitāb al-Aghānī*, vol. VIII, 327–31.

42 See Farmer, *A History of Arabian Music to the 13th Century*, 10–19.

43 See Everett K. Rowson, "The Effeminates of Early Medina," *Journal of the American Oriental Society* 111, no. 4 (1991): 671–93. *Ḥadīth* that mention *mukhannathūn* suggest the Prophet condemned them, but several are weak and have been interpreted widely. Some scholars assert the Prophet was condemning same-sex relations, whereas others suggest he was issuing a general warning. Rowson takes the position that the Prophet's condemnation of the *mukhannathūn* was less a condemnation of music, male musicians and same-sex relationships than trying to stop the practice of allowing these men in women's tents unsupervised. During the time of the Prophet, it seems that some men posed as *mukhannathūn* in order to gain access to women's tents to seduce the unwary or carry on illicit affairs. Rowson suggests that effeminate men had been considered "safe" and therefore functioned as entertainers and matchmakers, but could also have simply been enterprising Lotharios. See Appendix I for a selection of *ḥadīth* concerning *mukhannathūn*.

44 Ibid. Although unmasculine men were found in every culture of the ancient world and some, as in Sumer, held high rank, they remained sources of discomfort owning to assumptions about their sexuality. The proverbs about *gala* are not uniformly kind, Martial and Juvenal brutally mock sexually passive men as being unmasculine, and vehement screeds against effeminacy and same-sex passions can be found in the writings of early church fathers, such as Clement of Alexandria.

45 See the entry for *khanith* in Lane, *Lexicon*, vol. I, 814–15.

46 *Mukhannathūn* is often translated as effeminate or hermaphrodite. Although intersex is now the accepted term, in the past, use of hermaphrodite was a reflection of cultural standpoint. Similarly, since the root meaning of "hermaphrodite" means two forms in one body, this choice made sense to an audience well versed in Greek mythology. Given the influence of Greek philosophy and theory on Arabic thinking, the word "khunthawi" was used to mean hermaphroditic in the sense of blended forms, such as scale systems in music. See Henry George Farmer, "The Influence of Music: From Arabic Sources," in *Proceedings of the Musical Association, 52nd Session* (1925–6), 108.

47 "Hermaphrodite" was also used to reference eunuchs, as the meaning at the time included a lack of male genitalia in male bodies from birth or castration. See Robson, *Censure*, 40, n. 2.

48 See O. Wright, "Music and Verse," in A. F. L. Beeston, T. M Johnstone, R. B. Serjeant, and G. R. Smith (eds.), *Arabic Literature to the End of the Umayyad Period* (Cambridge: Cambridge University Press, 1983), 433–50.

49 See James T. Monroe, "Oral Composition in Pre-Islamic Poetry," *Journal of Arabic Literature* 3 (1972): 1–53.

50 See Mohammed A. Bamyeh, *The Social Origins of Islam: Mind, Economy, Discourse* (Minneapolis: University of Minnesota Press, 1999), 5–11. Baymeh uses the transition between "halting" and "movement" as a theoretical space, with the former being the exception. Both states are represented eloquently in the poetry literally and metaphorically, which, he suggests, became part of the social development of Islam.

51 From Suzanne Pinckney Stetkevytch, *The Mute Immortals Speak: Pre-Islamic Poetry and the Poetics of Ritual*, Myth and Poetics, ed. Gregory Nagy (Ithaca, NY: Cornell University Press, 1993), 10.

52 Genesis 1:1-3. The meaning of "spirit" in Hebrew is breath or wind. In Mesopotamian myth, the wind was a means to destroy the unknown. M. Jack Suggs, Katharine Doob Sakenfeld, and James R. Mueller (eds.), *The Oxford Study Bible* (New York: Oxford University Press, 1992), 11, n. 2.

53 John 1:1.

54 Scholars were expected to commit the Qur'an to memory, along with collections of *ḥadīth*, law, poetry, and literature. Students learned by listening to and reciting with their teachers.
55 Hoyland, *Arabia and the Arabs*, 204–11.
56 See Jonathan A. C. Brown, "The Social Context of Pre-Islamic Poetry: Poetic Imagery and Social Reality in the Muᶜallaqāt," *Arab Studies Quarterly* 25, no. 3 (2003): 29–50. See also Stetkevytch, *The Mute Immortals Speak*.
57 Farmer offers an overview of pre-Islamic music and instruments in chapter 1 of *History of Arabian Music to the 13th Century*, drawing on a variety of later historical sources. See ibid., 1–19.
58 Wright, "Music and Verse."
59 For speculation on pre-Islamic instrumental forms and song, see chapters 1 and 2 in Farmer, *A History of Arabian Music to the 13th Century*.
60 For a summary of sources attesting to feasts, see Hoyland, *Arabia and the Arabs*, 134–8.
61 This theme appears in the *fakhr* section of the poem, where the poet praises themselves, the tribe, and their accomplishments, or *madīḥ*, the courtly panegyric, which can replace the *fakhr*. See chapter 1 Stetkevytch, *The Mute Immortals Speak*. See also Suzanne Pinckney Stetkevytch, *The Poetics of Islamic Legitimacy: Myth, Gender, and Ceremony in the Classical Arabic Ode* (Bloomington: Indiana University Press, 2002), 4.
62 The *ᶜūd* was adapted from Persia during the first fifty to one hundred years of Islamic rule, and it appears to have had several different configurations. Early forms of the *ᶜūd* appear to have had a single course of at least four strings and could be played with the fingers or plectrum. Some were constructed of different woods and others were fretted.
63 Verses 59–60 from Stetkevytch, *The Mute Immortals Speak*, 15.
64 Quoted from Hoyland, *Arabia and the Arabs*, 138, after Lyall. See 134–8 for additional examples of feasting with musical entertainment.
65 A. J. Arberry, *The Seven Odes: The First Chapter in Arabic Literature* (London: G. Allen & Unwin; New York: Macmillan, 1957), 85–6.
66 Two of the better known pre-Islamic poets are Laila al-Akhyalia (d. *c.* 704 CE) and al-Khansa Tumadir bint ᶜAmr (d. after 644 CE). Although Laila lived into the Islamic era and was patronized by the Umayyads, some of her writing predates Islam. For the history of Laila and a selection of her songs, see al-Iṣbahānī, *Kitāb al-Aghānī*, vol. IX. Extracts of their poetry are also included in ᶜAbdullāh al-Udhari, *Classical Poems by Arab Women*. See also Hoyland, *Arabia and the Arabs*, 218. For an analysis of the thematic content and structure of select poems by women, see chapter 5 in Stetkevytch, *The Mute Immortals Speak*, 161–205.

67 The poems of Laila and Khansa are primarily laments. See chapter 5, Stetkevytch, *The Mute Immortals Speak.*

68 Ibid. See also Theresa Garulo, "Women in Medieval Classical Arabic Poetry," in Manuela and Randi Deguilhem Marin (eds.), *Writing the Feminine: Women in Arab Sources*, vol. I, The Islamic Mediterranean (London: I.B. Tauris, 2002), 25–40.

69 Poems attributed to women appear in a number of sources, some in fragments, some with different attributions, or rendered anonymous. The latter might have been because naming women in writing was not allowed. Another possibility is that if a poem was well known, there would be no need to record the name since it was already in the communal memory.

70 His annoyance was often contextual. In the case of the *ḥadīth* recited by ᶜĀ'isha about the Prophet's desire to silence a group of mourning women, he had, in fact, requested several times that they quiet down, which they refused to do. Rules about excessive wailing for the dead had been established, although they were not always obeyed. For this *ḥadīth*, see Nicholas Awde, ed., *Women in Islam: An Anthology from the Qur'an and Ḥadīths* (New York: St. Martin's, 2000), 29.

71 The musician Ibn Surayj was said to have enjoyed the elegists so much, he decided to become a singer so he could emulate them.

72 Umāma bint Kulaib, thought to be the daughter of Kulaib (d. 494 CE) who was the king of the Rabīᶜa people. He was murdered by Jassās, his brother-in-law, and cousin ᶜAmr. She is said to have recited this poem to her uncle, the poet Muhalhil, when he was drunk. From al-Udhari, *Classical Poems by Arab Women*, 42.

73 Khansa (d. 646 CE), a fragment of one of her laments to her brother, Sakhr. Ibid., 60.

74 For example, the lute and hand drums were associated with music, while instruments that accompanied poetry, including religious poetry, such as the *qaḍib* or wand, did not change a poetic recitation to song.

2 Musicianship and Performance

1 Damascus was the first capital of the early Islamicate states.

2 Enslaved concubines are referred to in the Qur'an as "those whom your right hand possesses." They appear in several verses in the Qur'an as members of the household, war captives, and allowable sexual subjects. See Sura 4 (al-Nisā'): 3, 24-25, 36; Sura 16 (al-Naḥl): 71; Sura 23 (al-Mu'minūn): 6; Sura 24 (al-Nūr): 31, 33, 58; Sura 33 (al-Aḥzāb): 50-52, 55; Sura 70 (al-Maᶜārij): 29-30.

3 The era between the eighth and tenth centuries is often referred to as the "Golden Age of Islam." Although this label is problematic, the intellectual and cultural achievements of the time were indeed outstanding.

4 For example, Ibn al-Washsha dedicates a full chapter to the malady of passion in *Muwashshā'*, and al-Jāḥiẓ similarly admonishes the reader to avoid passion in excess in the *Risālat al-Qiyān*.

5 Lois Ibsen al-Faruqi created a theoretical model outlining this shift in definition which she termed *handasah al-ṣawt* (engineering of music). Although her model is not without problems, it illustrates that definition of what sound genres constituted music was fluid and a topic of discussion in texts concerned with music, philosophy, poetry, and medicine. See Lois Ibsen al-Faruqi, "Music, Musicians and Muslim Law," *Asian Music* 17, no. 1 (1985): 3–36. For an analysis of the issues with al-Faruqi's model and another way of assessing these changes, see the introduction to Fadlou Shehadi, *Philosophies of Music in Medieval Islam* (New York: E.J. Brill, 1995).

6 I address these conversations in more detail in the second section.

7 In order for a scholar to earn the authority to teach a text, they had to have it memorized. Once authorized to teach, they were placed within the line of authority already attached to the text.

8 Mary Carruthers, *The Book of Memory: A Study of Memory in Medieval Culture* (Cambridge: Cambridge University Press, 1990), 10.

9 See Jonathan Bloom, "The Introduction of Paper to the Islamic Lands and the Development of the Illustrated Manuscript," *Muqarnas* 17 (2000): 17–23.

10 Caliphs and members of the aristocratic classes commissioned sculptures, tapestries, frescoes, and illuminations for manuscripts. One of the oldest and more complete copies of the *Aghānī*, for example, is an illuminated text created in the thirteenth century for the atabek of Mosul, Badr al-Dīn Lu'Lu'. For a discussion of the illuminations in this text, see D. H. Rice, "The *Aghānī* Miniatures and Religious Painting in Islam," *Burlington Magazine* 95, no. 601 (1953): 128–35. See also George Sawa, "The Differing Worlds of the Music Illuminator and the Music Historian in Islamic Medieval Manuscripts," *Imago Musicae* 6 (1989): 7–22.

11 Although there are books written on Western iconography and Islamic art, there is little on iconography and music in the Islamicate world. See Sawa, "The Differing Worlds of the Music Illuminator." Despite this lack, aspects of Western analysis—that is, symbolic, cultural uses of art—in conjunction with the methodology proposed by Sawa could lend much to our understanding of performance practice, instrumentation, and context in early Islamic representation.

12 For medieval learning and book culture, see George Maqdisi, "Muslim Institutions of Learning in Eleventh-Century Baghdad," *Bulletin of the School of Oriental and African Studies, University of London* 24, no. 1 (1961): 1–56; Jonathan Berkey, *The Transmission of Knowledge in Medieval Cairo* (Princeton, NJ: Princeton University Press, 1992); Michael Chamberlain, *Knowledge and Social Practice*; Konrad Hirschler, *The Written Word in the Medieval Arabic Lands* (Edinburgh: Edinburgh University Press, 2012); and Hirschler, *Medieval Damascus: Plurality and Diversity*

in an Arabic Library, Edinburgh Studies in Classical Islamic History and Culture, series ed. Carole Hillenbrand (Edinburgh: Edinburgh University Press, 2016).

13 Though such extensive quotation was an established and acceptable practice in Islamic literature, I suspect books were used similarly to Western medieval memory texts, such as *florilegium*, for retrieval of memorized information.

14 See Tayeb El-Hibri, *Reinterpreting Islamic Historiography: Harun al-Rashid and the Narrative of the 'Abbasid Caliphate*, Cambridge Studies in Islamic Civilization (Cambridge: Cambridge University Press, 1999). See also Tarif Khalidi, *Arabic Historical Thought in the Classical Period* (Cambridge: Cambridge University Press, 1994); and Chase Robinson, *Islamic Historiography* (Cambridge: Cambridge University Press, 2003).

15 The *isnād* is the chain of authority attached to a *ḥadīth* stating its lineage of transmission. A chain of authority is a literal chain of names leading back to the source of transmission. These often read "On the authority of so-and-so, it was related to me by so-and-so." The original source might be the Prophet himself, a companion, respected scholar, or member of the Prophet's family. How strong or verifiable the linkages are determine the strength of the *ḥadīth* and are typically ranked as strong or true, good, and weak. Strong *hadīth* are *ṣaḥīḥ*, whereas weak are *ḍaif*. Chains could be manufactured and manipulated, as could the *ḥadīth*, so there is speculation and disagreement as to the veracity of many *ḥadīth* and their transmitters.

16 Sometimes more is revealed in fantastic events and criticism than in presumed factual accounts. While the *1001 Nights* are not "true" or even a reflection of actual events, they reference many famous personalities (including Hārūn al-Rashīd, the poet Abū Nuwās, and several famous musicians) and give a sense of what types of stories were circulating for popular consumption.

17 For an extensive treatment of the history of the book and libraries in the medieval Islamicate world, see Hirschler, *The Written Word in the Medieval Arabic Lands*; and *Medieval Damascus*.

18 Even in writerly cultures such as ours, the interpretive aspect of performance lies in the hands of the performer. A musician learns by reading the score, but listens to other interpretations. Teachers still sing and talk through even the most familiar scores, and memorization is standard.

19 Male musicians were not called *qiyān* and women were not *mukhannathūn*, though both could be *mughanniyat/ūn*.

20 The term *mawlā* (pl. *mawālī*) implied a non-kin relationship with a family or employer. *Mawālī* are frequently rendered into English as clients, freedmen, and vassals, though *mawlā* is a complex term that renders translation difficult. As such, it cannot be assumed to mean the same thing in all cases nor does it encompass a homogenous group. I am indebted to Elizabeth Urban for this

insight and her work on the *mawālī*. Prior to Islam, *mawlā* was used to reference someone who was affiliated with, but not from, their tribe or clan group. Under Islam, the term came to mean a convert who, according to Jan Retso, did not have "affiliation to any tribe of the Islamic tribal federation." See Jan Retso, *The Arabs in Antiquity: Their History from the Assyrians to the Umayyads* (London: Routledge, 2003), 66. A number of male musicians who were not *mukhannathūn* in the early Islamic courts were *mawālī*. For the connection between male musicians and clientage, see Hilary Kilpatrick, "*Mawālī* and Music," in Monique Bernards and John Nawas (eds.), *Patronate and Patronage in Early and Classical Islam* (Leiden: Brill, 2005), 326–48. For *mukhannathūn* as musicians, see Rowson, "The Effeminates of Early Medina."

21 See Rowson, "The Effeminates of Early Medina."

22 Ibid.

23 See Amnon Shiloah, *Music in the World of Islam: A Socio-Cultural Study*, 35. Shiloah refers to these female patrons as the "Grand Ladies." Their protégés were predominantly free-born male clients, or *mawālī*. See also Farmer, *A History of Arabian Music to the 13th Century*.

24 See Shmuel Moreh, *Live Theater and Dramatic Literature in the Medieval Arab World* (New York: New York University Press, 1992).

25 See Sawa, *Music Performance Practice*. See also Lois Ibsen al-Faruqi, "The Nature of the Musical Art of Islamic Culture: A Theoretical and Empirical Study of Arabian Music" (dissertation, Syracuse University, 1974); and al-Faruqi, "Music, Musicians and Muslim Law." See also Shehadi, *Philosophies of Music in Medieval Islam*.

26 See, for example, Beverly Bossler, "Gender and Entertainment at the Song Court," in Anne Walthall (ed.), *Servants of the Dynasty* (Berkeley: University of California Press, 2008), 261–79.

27 *Aghānī*, vol. V, 154–259. See also Sawa, *Music Performance Practice*, 5.

28 For example, the celebrated singing woman Jamīla trained some of the first celebrity male musicians and *mukhannathūn*, including Ṭuways. See *Aghānī*, vol. II, 170. For Jamīla, see vol. VII, 124–48; the reference to Ṭuways is on 135. For their performance practices, see Sawa, *Music Performance Practice*.

29 In Western medieval philosophy, Boethius is best known for this perspective, inherited from the Greeks. Arab philosophers, such as al-Kindī, al-Fārābī, and Ibn Sīnā (Avicenna in the West), wrote extensively about music and music theory, though, with the exception of al-Fārābī, the place of the performing musician was secondary.

30 For example, the theorist al-Fārābī was a highly respected musician. In his *Great Book of Music*, he advocates practical musicianship and was clearly a performer. See Sawa, "The Survival of Some Aspects of Medieval Arabic Performance Practice"; and Sawa, *Rhythmic Theories and Practices in Arabic Writings to 339 AH/950 CE*

(Ottawa: Institute of Mediaeval Music, 2009). See also Farmer, *A History of Arabian Music to the 13th Century*, 175–7.

31 A similar distinction was made in the West, particularly as instrumental music and secular song developed in the eleventh century. The troubadours who appeared in the late eleventh century were careful to distinguish themselves from *jongleurs* or traveling entertainers. A troubadour could be a *jongleur*, but would not always so admit. When performing at court, a troubadour might have their songs performed for them. As instrumental prowess became more socially acceptable, they performed themselves.

32 See note 15 in the introduction.

33 The root of *maʿāzif* is عزف (*ʿazf*), meaning to play, to make music. In some uses, it references natural sounds, such as the wind and shifting sands; also the humming of *jinn*. See Lane, *Lexicon*, vol. II, 2035.

34 The root is لهو, not to be confused with لحو, which means to vilify, defame. See Lane, *Lexicon*, vol. II (Supplement), 3014. See also Hans Wehr, *The Hans Wehr Dictionary of Modern Written Arabic*, ed. J. M. Cowan (Urbana, IL: Spoken Language Services, 1994), 714.

35 The root is طرب, with the possible meanings pointing not just to emotional response, but to a heightened or, as Lane puts it, "lively" response. Lane also notes that *ṭariba* signified vocal embellishment—trills, quavering, elongation of syllables—in song and recitation. See Lane, *Lexicon*, vol. II, 1835–6. See also Racy, *Making Music in the Arab World.*

36 Musicians were *muṭrib*, or one who provokes *ṭarab*.

37 For the definition of *ālat al-ṭarab*, see Wehr, *Dictionary*, 649; and Lane, *Lexicon* 1835–6. Amnon Shiloah offers a brief discussion of the transformation of meaning for *ālat al-ṭarab* and *maʿāzif* in *Music in the World of Islam.* In his discussion of performance contexts in *Music Performance Practices in the Early Abbasid Era*, Sawa comments that "musicians initiated performances in direct response to their physical state (drunkenness) or emotional state" (127).

38 See Christopher Page, *The Owl and the Nightingale: Musical Life and Ideas in France 1100–1200* (Berkeley: University of California Press, 1990); and Page, *Voices and Instruments of the Middle Ages* (London: JM Dent, 1987).

39 See Farmer, *A History of Arabian Music to the 13th Century*, chapter 1, particularly pp. 13–14, for his comments on early songs and use of instrumental accompaniment.

40 In Arabic, عود. As with most Arabic roots, there is a wide variety of meaning available, with the one relevant to the instrument being wood or timber. See Lane, *Lexicon*, vol. II, 2190.

41 In Arabic, طنبور. Another term borrowed from Persian, which, according to Lane, is a lute with metal strings played with a plectrum. See Lane, *Lexicon*, vol. II, 1885.

42 In Arabic, بربط. Lane refers to this instrument as "the Persian lute." He suggests it is an Arabized word derived from two Persian words that combined mean "breast of the duck or goose." One possible reason why is that one places the instrument on the breast to play, another is it is simply a borrowed term. See Lane, *Lexicon*, vol. I, 179–80.

43 According to Ibn Khurdādhbih, the *kīthāra* and *lūra* were types of lyres. There is no mention in Lane. The *ṣanj* (صنج) was a form of cymbal, with jingles tied onto a tambourine and a kind of harp. See Lane, *Lexicon*, vol. II, 1731.

44 The Western instrument comes from the Arabian lute. Lute derives from the elision of the definite article "al" with "ᶜūd." It is spelled al-ᶜūd, but heard as "a'lud."

45 Today, the *ᶜūd* is played without frets and has five to seven double-coursed strings. See Robson and Farmer, "The Kitāb al-Malāhī of Abū Ṭālib Al-Mufaḍḍal Ibn Salāma," 242–3. See also Farmer, "The Structure of the Arabian and Persian Lute in the Middle Ages," *Journal of the Royal Asiatic Society* 71, no. 1 (1939): 41–51; and Curtis Bouterse, "Reconstructing the Medieval Arabic Lute: A Reconsideration of Farmer's 'Structure of the Arabic and Persian Lute,'" *Galpin Society Journal* 32 (May 1979): 2–9.

46 Lamech is a descendent of Cain and appears in Gen. 4:17-24. According to the Bible, Lamech's son, Jubal, is the "ancestor of those who play harp and pipe" (Gen. 4:21).

47 See Robson and Farmer, "The Kitāb al-Malāhī of Abū Ṭālib Al-Mufaḍḍal Ibn Salāma," 239.

48 Ibn Salama also suggests the *barbaṭ* had a skin belly.

49 There is no letter "p" in Arabic, suggesting the name pandore is a variant of *ṭunbūr*. According to Farmer, al-Mas'ūdī says the pandore was invented by the people of Sodom and Gomorrah, and the name derives from the combination of tunn = musical sound and bur = one destined to perdition. Alternatively, it could simply be descriptive of the shape, coming from dunn = tail and bara = lamb. Other related instruments are the buzuk, tar, sitar, balalaika.

50 Iconographic evidence suggests at least four strings. See Farmer, "Ud," *EI* X, 768–70.

51 Robson and Farmer, "The Kitāb al-Malāhī of Abū Ṭālib Al-Mufaḍḍal Ibn Salāma," 239–40.

52 There are many extant images of young male wine servers and dancers, with some of the loveliest found on Fatimid pottery. In the textile collection of the Cleveland Art Museum, there is a delightful fifteenth- to sixteenth-century Persian brocade featuring wine servers, dancers, and musicians playing the *barbaṭ* and *duff*, all wearing jaunty little Dutch hats.

53 For a detailed study of the Greek lyre, with connections to related instruments—*kinnor*, *kīthāra*—see Franklin, *Kinyras: The Divine Lyre*.

54 See Shiloah, "Kithara," *EI* 5, 234. He suggests the *lūra* was an amateur instrument, while the *kīthāra* was for professionals.

55 That it was a lyre is probably correct, given the history of this instrument in the Ancient Near East. For a detailed study of the *kinnor* and lyre in the ancient world, see the work of John Franklin, especially his monograph *Kinyras: The Divine Lyre*.

56 Robson and Farmer, "The Kitāb al-Malāhī of Abū Ṭālib Al-Mufaḍḍal Ibn Salāma," 241. That these instruments were in use is attested to by pre-Islamic and early Islamic poetry, and Ibn Salama references two poets from the *Muᶜallaqāt*. He states the *mizhar* is an early lute, but Farmer believes it was an early tambourine. According to Lane, however, the *mizhar* was a lute, see مزهر, Lane, *Lexicon*, vol. I, 1262. See Farmer, "Duff," 620; and Farmer, "Ud," 768. Regarding *kirān/karina*, Lane posits it is a possible reference to a blacksmith's fireplace, as in the bellows used to stoke the flame. The root of *qiyān* also refers to blacksmith and craft. See Lane, *Lexicon*, vol. II, 2637, section 10.

57 In Arabic, these are طبل and دف. See Lane, *Lexicon*, vol. II, 1828 and vol. I, 887–8, respectively. Both terms also mean to strike and beat, such as the beating of a bird's wings.

58 Farmer notes that Ṭuways played the *duff murabbaᶜ* or square tambourine, which suggests that the round version was more seemly. See Farmer, "Duff," *EI* 2, 620–1. Ibn Salama makes a passing reference to the *duff murabbaᶜ* as well.

59 The term *sonaj* is the plural of *sanj*, meaning cymbals and metallic jingles. *Jarasu* derives from the root جرس, which means a soft or gentle tone. It refers to all kinds of bells, including those for practical matters (such as those hung around an animal's neck) and for music. Bells could be played by ringing or striking the bell. See Lane, *Lexicon*, vol. I, 409–10.

60 Robson and Farmer, "The Kitāb al-Malāhī of Abū Ṭālib Al-Mufaḍḍal Ibn Salāma," 240. See Chapter 1, note 41 for other references to the Two Grasshoppers.

61 See Farmer, "Darabukka," *EI* 2, 135–6. The root for *dirrij* is درج, which can mean something that is rolled up, but also segmentation, as in taking steps or rungs on a ladder. Lane hints it was used to indicate something that is played, such as a stringed instrument; it was also used in the nineteenth century to indicate the fast bits of a song. Lane, *Lexicon*, vol. I, 867–70. See particularly دِرِّيجٌ and دَارِجٌ on p. 869. Given these meanings, I suggest *dirrij* may be a woodwind instrument, but also potentially a reference to the act of playing.

62 In Arabic, كوبة. The word possibly refers to the shape, like cup with no handle. Lane's entry also suggests *kūba* referred to the *barbaṭ*. See Lane, *Lexicon*, vol. II, 2635.

63 There was also a specific term for war drums and drum ensembles, the *ṭabl-khana*. See Farmer, "Tabl," *EI* X, 32–4, and "Tabl-khana," 34–8. The largest drum was called a *kus* (*kos*), plural, *kusat*. See also Lane, *Lexicon*, vol. II, 2638. Although it is not the

root for *ḍaraba* (to strike), ضرب, *darb*, is noted by Lane as another term for beating a drum, and he notes other variants that reference drums as دبدب, *dabdab*, and دردب, *dardab*. Lane, *Lexicon*, vol. I, 866.

64 From the root قضب, which means to cut off, as in prune or cut tree branches. See Lane, *Lexicon*, vol. II, 2537–8, especially p. 2538.

65 This is pure conjecture on my part, based on a passage in al-Ṭabarī's treatise. He comments on what forms of *samā*ᶜ are not acceptable, and the instruments include the ᶜ*ūd*, *ṭunbūr*, and this *sayeer*. Al-Ṭabarī also mentions the "rattling of the *qaḍib*." Thus, it is possible that some wands had rings or some other kind of decoration to add additional percussion. See al-Ṭabari, *Kitāb fīhi mas'alat fi'l radd* ᶜ*alā man yaqūl bi-jawāz al-samā*ᶜ *al-ghinā' wa'l raqṣ wa'l taghbīr* (Book refuting the opinions of those who allow listening to music, dance, and the *taghbīr*), Ap. Ar. 158/9, f.85a–91b. See p. 88a for mention of the سايار. Lane, *Lexicon*, vol. I, 4–1483 ,سير. See p. 1484 in particular. For rattling the *qaḍib*, see al-Ṭabari, *Kitāb fīhi mas'alat fi'l radd* ᶜ*alā man yaqūl bi-jawāz al-samā*ᶜ *al-ghinā' wa'l raqṣ wa'l taghbīr*, 86b.

66 From ناى, meaning a flute without a mouthpiece. The term and origin of the instrument is Persian. According to Wehr, such flutes were made of bamboo rather than wood and came in different sizes. Wehr, *Dictionary*, 1100. There is no corresponding entry in Lane.

67 The *quṣab* was a reed pipe, from the root قصب. See Wehr, *Dictionary*, 897; Lane, *Lexicon*, vol. II, 2529. This instrument is also referenced by al-Khallāl in *Al-amr bi'l ma*ᶜ*rūf wa'l-nahy* ᶜ*an al-munkar*.

68 Women musicians, specifically enslaved concubines, also played reed pipes, so the term *zammāra* came to be synonymous with prostitution (*zaniya*, زانية). Lane, *Lexicon*, vol. I, 1250. Given Greek influences on Islamicate culture, they could be akin to flute girls.

69 See Farmer, "Mizmār," *EI* VII, 206–10. The name derives from the same root as *mizmār*, زمر, meaning to pipe and play reed instruments. See Lane, *Lexicon*, vol. I, 1250.

70 *Surnāy* and *surnā* (*sorna*) are Persian. Along with *shabbāba*, neither are in Lane; however, the former is in Wehr. See the entry for شب on p. 527. The *zurna* is a reed pipe that is played in parts of Central Europe and North Africa today. Ibn Salama confirms *nāy*, *surnāy*, and *dunāy* are all of Persian origin. The root of the latter two is *nāy*, and the prefixes *sur*- and *du*- indicate the type of woodwind. All are borrowed from Persian.

71 Ibn Salama mentions a *dunāy* that could be a variation of this instrument.

72 The connection of pipes to David is found in the Psalms as well as a *ḥadīth*. According to one tradition, when the Prophet heard Abū Musa al-Ashri reciting, he said that he had been gifted with a pipe like David himself. Lane cites this tradition in the entry for *mizmār*. See Lane, *Lexicon*, vol. I, 1251. For an excellent

discussion of the origins of the *mizmār* and connections to King David, see David R. M. Irving, "Psalms, Islam, and Music: Dialogues and Divergence about David in Christian-Muslim Encounters of the Seventeenth Century," *Yale Journal of Music and Religion* 2, no. 1 (2016): 53–78.

73 Farmer suggests this is a misspelling or misinterpretation of *kirān*, or lute.

74 Farmer notes these are obscure, and I likewise could not locate these instruments in other sources or a clear connection to possible Arabic roots.

75 Farmer, "Ibn Khurdādhbih on Musical Instruments," 516.

76 See Farmer, "Urghan," *EI* X, 893–4. There were apparently two types of organ, hydraulic and pneumatic. The story of Hārūn al-Rashīd gifting an organ to Charlemagne is entertaining, but unfortunately only a legend.

77 A musician is occasionally referred to as a *muḍrab*, one who plays (literally, one who strikes). *Ḍaraba* is a poetic and flexible verb, from the root ضرب. For the full explication of the root, see Lane, *Lexicon*, vol. II, 1777–83, with reference to striking the lute noted on p. 1778. *Laᶜiba*, from the root لعب, means the physical act of play. Today, one uses *laᶜiba* to talk about playing an instrument as well as games. See Wehr, *Dictionary*, 1019–20. In the medieval sources, while *laᶜiba* is used occasionally in relation to playing an instrument, most often it refers to games (most commonly chess, backgammon, and various forms of wagering) and the play of children. See Lane, *Lexicon*, vol. II, 2661–3. Other words indicating the act of playing or making music are akin to *ḍaraba* in that they are descriptive of the act or effect, such as *ghinā'*, to sing.

78 Lane, *Lexicon*, vol. II, 1778.

79 See note 69.

80 Al-Ājurrī testily uses both terms to describe singing as diversion and the stupidity of playing the *mizmār*. See al-Ājurrī, *Al-jawāb ᶜan mas'alat al-samāᶜ*, 16a. Al-Maqdisī combines *lahw* and *laᶜiba* to reinforce his points along these lines. See al-Maqdisī, *Al-amr bi-itbāᶜ al-sunan wa ijtināb al-bidaᶜ*, microfilm, 35a, and 38a.

81 Al-Iṣbahānī is among the few authors who make a distinction between song and poetry, indicating a song or collection of songs with the heading *ṣawt*. He further titles anecdotes (*akhbār*) as "Songs of xx," which might include song texts as well as poems. For a detailed discussion of al-Iṣbahānī's use of *akhbār* and nuances between song and poetry in the *Aghānī*, see Hilary Kilpatrick, *Making the Great Book of Songs: Compilation and the Author's Craft in Abu'l Faraj al-Iṣbahānī's* Kitāb al-Aghānī (London: RoutledgeCurzon, 2003).

82 Don Randel provides a concise discussion in "Al-Farabi and the Role of Arabic Music Theory in the Latin Middle Ages," *Journal of the American Musicological Society* 9, no. 2 (1976): 181. Al-Ghazālī also describes the relationship of sound and text, with the point that one carries the other. See al-Ghazālī, MacDonald translation, Duncan B. Macdonald, "Emotional Religion in Islam as Affected by

Music and Singing," *Journal of the Royal Asiatic Society of Great Britain and Ireland* (April 1901): 195–252, part I. In their treatise on music and sound, the Ikhwān al-Safa likewise discusses the relationship between sound and text in metaphysical terms, including the uses of music to heal the sick. See Ikhwān al-Safa, *The Epistle on Music*, trans. Amnon Shiloah (Tel Aviv: Tel Aviv University, 1978).

83 Many medieval cultures did not make a clear distinction between musical sounding and spoken word, if at all. Salons incorporated music and poetry, with attendant discussion about what the distinction between song and poetry was. Those discussions are not prescriptive; rather such conversations depict what was going on in the moment. Many are aspirational, suggesting proper forms and behavior, and offer social commentary. See Julia Bray, "Men, Women and Slaves in Abbasid Society," in Leslie Brubaker and Julia M. H. Smith (eds.), *Gender in the Early Medieval World: East and West, 300–900* (Cambridge: Cambridge University Press, 2004), 121–46.

84 From the root جلس. For a brief article on singing girls at court and *majālis*, see Abd al-Kareem al-Heitty, "The Contrasting Spheres of Free Women and Jawari in the Literary Life of the Early Abbasid Caliphate," *Al-Masaq* 3 (1990): 31–51. See also Suleiman Haritani, *Al-jawārī wa'l qiyān fi al-mujtama*ᶜ *al-*ᶜ*Arabī al-Islamī (The Slave Women and Singing Girls: The Phenomenon of Slave Women, Clubs and Household Practice in the Arabic Islamic Courts)* (Damascus: Dār al-Ḥaṣad, 1997). For the *majlis*, see Dominic Brookshaw, "Palaces, Pavilions and Pleasure Gardens: The Context and Setting of the Medieval *Majlis*," *Middle Eastern Literatures, Incorporating Edebiyat* 6, no. 2 (2003): 199–223. For performance practice and history, see Sawa, *Music Performance Practice*.

85 For a description of the *majlis*, see Sawa, *Music Performance Practice*; and Brookshaw, "Palaces, Pavilions and Pleasure Gardens." For examples of musical humor, see George Sawa, "Musical Humor in the *Kitab al-Aghānī*," in Roger Savory and Dionisius Agius (eds.), *Logos Islamikos: Studia Islamica in Honorem Georgii Michaelis Wickens* (Toronto: Pontifical Institute of Medieval Studies, 1984), 35–50. Satirical, vulgar, and humorous poetry, plays, and stories comprised a subgenre of literature called *mujūn*. For a brief overview of *mujūn*, see Pellat, "Mudjun," *EI*, vol. VII, 304. See also Everett Rowson, "Two Homoerotic Narratives from Mamlūk Literature: al-Ṣafadī's *Law*ᶜ*at al-shākī* and Ibn Danīyāl's *al-Mutayyam*," and Franz Rosenthal, "Male and Female: Described and Compared," both in J. W. Wright and Everett K. Rowson (eds.), *Homoeroticism in Classical Arabic Literature* (New York: Columbia University Press, 1997), 158–91 and 24–54.

86 For example, during the eighteenth and nineteenth centuries, courtesans and noble women in France and India organized salons, and other cultures relied on women to serve as the focal point for artistic and intellectual gatherings.

87 See Sawa, *Music Performance Practice*; and Sawa, "The Status and Roles of the Secular Musicians in the *Kitāb al-Aghānī* (Book of Songs) of Abū al-Faraj al-Iṣbahānī (D.356AH/967AD)," *Asian Music* 17, no. 1 (1985): 69–82.

88 See Brookshaw, "Palaces, Pavilions and Pleasure Gardens." The *Aghānī* contains vivid detail about these gatherings, and Sawa discusses many in *Music Performance Practice*.

89 For a version of the story of the famous "yellow" *majlis* called by the caliph al-Mutawakkil, where everything, from the garden to the musicians, had to be yellow, see al-Tanūkhi, *Table Talk of a Mesopotamian Judge*, 160.

90 For example, al-Iṣbahānī will often introduce a song performance with a statement such as "and then xx took up the lute and sang the following" or a description of musicians settling their instruments in preparation to play.

91 El-Khoury, *The Function of Music in Islamic Culture in the Period up to 1100AD*, 123.

92 See in particular Shehadi, *Philosophies of Music in Medieval Islam*; Farmer, *A History of Arabian Music to the 13th Century*; and Farmer, "Greek Theorists of Music in Arabic Translation," *Isis* 13, no. 2 (1930): 325–33. See also Ikhwān al-Safa, *The Epistle on Music*; and Amnon Shiloah, "The Arabic Concept of Mode," *Journal of the American Musicological Society* 34, no. 1 (1981): 19–42.

93 For specifics on the history and development of Arabic mode, see Shiloah, "The Arabic Concept of Mode"; Farmer, "Greek Theorists of Music in Arabic Translation"; and Farmer, *A History of Arabian Music to the 13th Century*, 149–53.

94 Notation of a type is referred to in the *Kitāb al-Aghānī* and a few other music treatises, but, as far as I am aware, no one has successfully devised a method for reading it. Farmer included a sample image from a thirteenth-century treatise in *A History of Arabian Music to the 13th Century*, plate 3, facing 202.

95 Again, this is similar to uses of memory in the Western musical tradition. See Busse-Berger, *Medieval Music and the Art of Memory*. Since the majority of Arabian music was improvised, there was less of a need to memorize formulas for vertical composition (i.e., polyphony); however, musicians still needed to retain the melodic and rhythmic modes in memory, as well as the many possibilities for using them singly and in modulation.

96 Al-Fārābī devotes extensive commentary to the relationship of modes to meter and affect. See Sawa, *Rhythmic Theories and Practices in Arabic Writings to 339 AH/950 CE*.

97 There are hundreds of melodic and rhythmic modes, and each tradition and region has its own set. When systems overlap, modes might have different names and uses. For example, a particular mode that is used to uplift or represent a noble theme in one tradition might have a different connotation in another. See Racy, *Making Music in the Arab World*. For contemporary practices, see Johnny Farraj

and Sami Abu Shumays (eds.), *Arabic Maqam World*, http://www.maqamworld.com/ (last accessed December 2, 2019).

98 The classical Arabic music tradition continues to rely on oral transmission, owing to the subtlety of the modal system and the inadequacy of Western notation to capture the complicated degrees in pitch (quarter and microtonal) and rhythm.

99 See Sawa, *Music Performance Practice.*

100 Ibid.

101 Kilpatrick, *Making the Great Book of Songs*, 35.

102 The *Aghānī* is filled with such anecdotes. For a collection of some of the funnier (and more painful) anecdotes, see Sawa, "The Status and Roles of the Secular Musicians in the *Kitāb al-Aghānī*"; Sawa, "Musical Humor in the *Kitāb al-Aghānī*." See also chapters 5, 6, and 7 in Farmer, *A History of Arabian Music to the 13th Century*.

103 The limits, however, were broad. Many texts on love, sex, and wine reach well into what we consider vulgarity. Detailed study into their form and purpose has changed perceptions of *mujūn* and wine poetry.

104 Ibn al-Washsha dedicates several chapters to how to write a good letter and proper etiquette for sending poetry to one's lover in the *Muwashshā'*. See also Everett Rowson, "The Categorization of Gender and Sexual Irregularity in Medieval Arabic Vice Lists," in Julia Epstein and Kristina Straub (eds.), *Body Guards: The Cultural Politics of Gender Ambiguity* (New York: Routledge, 1991), 50–79.

105 I discuss these tensions further in Part II.

3 Patrons, Singing Women, *Mukhannathūn*, and Men

1 Brokering intimacy and effectively pimping out one's slaves for profit is the basis for al-Jāḥiẓ's social critique in the *Risālat al-Qiyān*. He outlines the lure of sex in sections 37–38 and 47 and how singing girls manipulate their lovers in section 48 and 51–52. Yet, he notes enslaved women have little power and are not fully to blame for their actions; rather, he implies their owners and trade in musical concubines are the true problems.

2 Ibid. Al-Jāḥiẓ provides trenchant commentary on the practice of loaning singing slave women for social gain in the *Risālat al-Qiyān*.

3 Along with the *Aghānī*, the memoirs of al-Tanūkhi are filled with details about social gatherings, the exchange of favors, including lending favored singing women for events.

4 Courtiers were expected to be able to cook, garden, speak and write well, hunt, dabble in poetry, and understand the language of flowers and scents. See Muḥammad Manazir Ahsan, *Social Life under the Abbasids* (London: Longman Group, 1979). See also Ibn al-Washsha, *Muwashshā', or al-zarf wa'l zurafa'*.

5 Ibn al-Washsha's *Muwashshā'* is an etiquette manual for the refined man, and includes helpful tips for refined women as well.

6 *Mukhannathūn* were infamous drinkers and singing women engaged in sexy banter with their clientele. There are plenty of stories in the *Aghānī* related to overindulgence, including vomiting in front of and on dignitaries, passing out, and fart jokes. For a few hilarious examples, see Sawa, "Musical Humor in the *Kitāb al-Aghānī*."

7 In addition to Ibrāhīm al-Mawṣilī, another musician famous for his outrageousness was Abū Dulāma, a jester and singer of African origin known for his rude humor and verses. See al-Ṭabarī, *The Early ᶜAbbasi Empire: The Sons and Grandsons of al-Mansur: The Reigns of al-Mahdi, al-Hadi and Harun al-Rashid*, vol. 2, trans. John Alden Williams (Cambridge: Cambridge University Press, 1989), 133, n. 322.

8 The story is available in English in al-Mas'ūdī, *The Meadows of Gold: The Abbasids*, 299.

9 See Chapter 2. See also Racy, *Making Music in the Arab World*.

10 Among its meanings, *wajd* refers to strong emotions and the ecstasy of passion. It means to receive, to come across, and have bestowed upon, particularly love, ecstasy, spiritual knowledge, and money. See Lane, *Lexicon*, vol. II, 2924–5; and Wehr, *Dictionary*, 1230–1. For *wajd* in *dhikr*, see Fritz Meier, "The Dervish Dance: An Attempt at an Overview," in *Essays on Islamic Piety and Mysticism*, trans. John O'Kane (Leiden: Brill, 1999), 23–48.

11 The permeable boundary between the gaze and desire are what James Davidson defined as the "economy of looking" in his discussion of *hetaerae*. Both Davidson and Khaled El-Rouayheb demonstrate how the unfettered and unmediated masculine gaze, like music performance and listening, could lead to excess. See Davidson, *Courtesans and Fishcakes*, 127–36; and El-Rouayheb, *Before Homosexuality*, 95–118.

12 El-Rouayheb, *Before Homosexuality*, 95–118.

13 From the root جرى.

14 For example, *surriya* and *hatheya*. Each term derives from a different root and is further differentiated from the terms for prostitute, such as *bigha'*.

15 The link of the word *qiyān* (قينة، قيان) to "singing girl" is elusive, which is mysterious in itself because Arabic is a highly organized and logical language. Among the possibilities are that it derives from the same root as the word for blacksmith (*kayn*), song (*ghinā'*), or perhaps from the Greek (*cano*). See Charles Pellat, "Kayna," in *Encyclopedia of Islam*, vol. IV, 820–4. See also Beeston's introduction to his translation of al-Jāḥiẓ, *The Epistle on the Singing Girls*, 2. For the root, see Wehr, *Dictionary*, 943. Although not completely the same, the root قنّ (*qanna*) also means servant. *Qayna* literally means "trained, technician," with the masculine form used to refer to a blacksmith. This link has been justified in a number of

ways. One suggestion is that because singing women were forming music or creating song, they were acting like a blacksmith who creates and forms metal. Another interesting possibility is that since musicians and blacksmiths were viewed at various times in the Ancient Near East as having mystical or shamanistic powers, this relationship carried over linguistically. See Christian Poche, "Music in Ancient Arabia from Archaeological and Written Sources," in Virginia Danielson, Scott Marcus, and Dwight Reynolds (eds.), *The Garland Encyclopedia of World Music: The Middle East* (New York: Routledge, 2002), 357–62.

16 These are the *Kitāb Moufākharat al-jawārī wa'l ghilmān* (The Debate of the Concubines and Catamites) and the *Risālat al-Qiyān* (The Epistle on the Singing Girls). The former is a delightfully vulgar debate as to whether it is more fun to have sex with women or boys, with detailed supporting evidence. Included are a number of truly filthy jokes, all of which are still hilarious.

17 Geisha translates as "arts person" and *ji* were artists-technicians. See Judith Zeitlin, "'Notes of Flesh' and the Courtesan's Song in Seventeenth-Century China," in Bonnie Gordon and Martha Feldman (eds.), *The Courtesan's Arts: Cross-Cultural Perspectives* (Oxford: Oxford University Press, 2006), 75–99, and the two articles devoted to the geisha in the same collection (223–52). These articles on Asian courtesanship are particularly relevant to understanding the roles of Islamicate singing women, especially similarities in their use in the culture and how they were represented in the literature.

18 Most standard dictionaries list concubine, prostitute, and courtesan as being synonymous. See, for example, the collection of definitions for "Courtesan," from different dictionaries aggregated at Dictionary.com: https://www.dictionary.com/browse/courtesan (last accessed December 5, 2019).

19 The term *courtisane*, the feminine of *courtier*, came into use in the sixteenth century and originally meant a woman of the court. It appeared in 1549 from the French as *courtisane* and in Italian as *cortigiana* (prostitute), literally, "woman of the court," feminine of *cortigiano* (one attached to a court), from *corte* (court) from Latin *cortem* (see court).

20 See Bonnie Gordon and Martha Feldman's introduction to *The Courtesan's Arts: Cross-Cultural Perspectives*, 6.

21 Sacred courtesans, sometimes called "sacred prostitutes," existed in several cultures. They were attached to places of worship as brides of the god and performed the *heirosgamos*, or sacred marriage, with men wishing to be blessed. There may have been a class of sacred courtesans in ancient Sumer, and the *devadasi* of India still exist today.

22 Courtesan instruments include flutes, lap harps, lutes, and bowed strings. These same instruments, and regional variations, are still associated with courtesans in China, Japan, Italy, and India. For example, see Regula Qureshi, "How Does Music

Mean? Embodied Memories and the Politics of Affect in the Indian 'Sarangi,'" *American Ethnologist* 27, no. 4 (2000): 805–38. See also Amelia Maciszewski, "Tawa'if, Tourism, and Tales: The Problematics of Twenty-First-Century Musical Patronage for North India's Courtesans," in Gordon and Feldman, *The Courtesan's Arts: Cross-Cultural Perspectives*, 332–51.

23 For example, the Japanese Floating World was purposefully placed outside of the city borders to reduce spiritual pollution, and brothels worldwide have always been relegated to specific areas. During times of plague, courtesans were exiled, tortured, and killed. The famous courtesan Veronica Franco was accused of witchcraft when Venice was devastated by plague, although she was later acquitted. See Margaret Rosenthal, *The Honest Courtesan: Veronica Franco, Citizen and Writer in Sixteenth-Century Venice* (Chicago: University of Chicago Press, 1993). See also Courtney Quaintance, "Defaming the Courtesan: Satire and Invective in Sixteenth-Century Italy," in Feldman and Gordon, *The Courtesan's Arts: Cross-Cultural Perspectives*, 199–208.

24 Men serving courtesans as instrumentalists, wigmakers, and dressers was common in several courtesan communities, such as in Mughal India and Edo-era Japan.

25 *Umm walad* could mean giving birth to a male child, but there are a number of references to concubines simply producing a healthy child, no specifics as to gender.

26 Evidence of their musical prowess is found throughout the *Aghānī*; however, one of the most concise accounts of the training (and exploitation) of singing women is found in the *Risālat al-Qiyān*. Ibn al-Washsha provides a detailed outline of their skills as well, though as a vice to be avoided. He dedicates several chapters of the *Muwashshā'* to the manipulation and emotional weapons employed by singing women as a warning to young swains who might be seduced. See Ibn Al-Washsha, *Muwashshā'*, chapter 20, "On the Character and Censure of Singing Slave Women, the Influence of the Ruses They Use in Seduction (of Young Men)"; Chapter 21, "Breaking the Bonds of Perfidious Love"; and Chapter 22, "Prohibition and Dangers of Passion."

27 See Meyers-Sawa, "The Role of Women in Musical Life: The Medieval Arabo-Islamic Courts." Al-Tanūkhi is a particularly good source for providing a glimpse into the status of entertainment houses and singing women. His memoirs include stories that range from sedate evenings in the company of an elite courtesan to wild parties with singing women in houses of ill repute.

28 Al-Jāḥiẓ, *Risālat al-Qiyān*, section 53, beginning of sections 54, 35.

29 Ibn al-Washsha, *Muwashshā'*, 134.

30 Al-Iṣbahānī, *Kitāb al-Aghānī*, vol. XV, 27.

31 Al-Jāḥiẓ, *Risālat al-Qiyān*, section 53, 35.

32 Ibid., 36.

33 See Basim Musallam, *Sex and Society in Islam* (Cambridge: Cambridge University Press, 1983); and Leila Ahmed, *Women and Gender in Islam: Historical Roots of a Modern Debate* (New Haven, CT: Yale University Press, 1992).

34 Enslaved women typically stood in as "temporary wives." In addition to visiting singing slave women, men would purchase slaves while traveling. Ibn Battuta, for example, purchased several slaves on his travels, reselling some and losing others. See Marina Tolmacheva, "Concubines on the Road: Ibn Battuta's Slave Women," in Matthew Gordon and Kathryn Hain (eds.), *Concubines and Courtesans: Women and Slavery in Islamic History* (Oxford: Oxford University Press, 2017), 163–89.

35 Fornication (*zinā*) is defined clearly in Islamic law, as is adultery. Basically, all sexual contact outside of marriage and legal concubinage, regardless of gender, age, species, and so forth, fell under the category of fornication. See Qur'an: 17:32, 24:2-3, 25:68. See also Rowson, "The Categorization of Gender and Sexual Irregularity in Medieval Arabic Vice Lists," 54–6.

36 See Awde, *Women in Islam: An Anthology from the Qur'an and Hadīths*, 112.

37 Ibid., 78–85, for a sampling of *ḥadīth* related to adultery and slaves.

38 See the introduction and James Davidson, "Making a Spectacle of Her(self)," in Gordon and Feldman, *The Courtesan's Arts: Cross-Cultural Perspectives*, 12, 29.

39 Ibn al-Washsha, *Muwashshā'*, 135–6.

40 Al-Jāḥiẓ, *Risālat al-Qiyān*, section 55, 35.

41 Ibid., section 58, 37.

42 See, for example, al-Tanūkhi, *Table Talk of a Mesopotamian Judge*, 102.

43 In many cultures of the ancient and medieval world, rape was recognized by law as an act of violence, with differing degrees of punishment based on the status of the victim. Because rape was effectively theft of property, punishment frequently was monetary, with a higher price paid for crimes against free women. Some of the most familiar laws from the ancient world are found in the Code of Hammurabi, Leviticus, and Deuteronomy. Rape was prohibited by religious law in the Abrahamic traditions, but a woman was not considered a victim if raped by husband or owner as enslaved concubine. The crime lay in violation of another person's female property. Punishment for rape could be severe in Islamicate society, including protections for unfree women.

44 Al-Jāḥiẓ, *Risālat al-Qiyān*, 20. In this section, he describes an enslaved woman being sexually assaulted. Al-Mas'ūdī relates a version of a popular story about a prince so enamored of his slave woman, she took over his every thought and he was advised to have her killed to save himself. He did so by having her drowned.

45 As noted earlier, courtesans in other cultures were jailed, beaten, and exiled during times of social stress, plus they were sources of violent fantasies. See the introduction, in Gordon and Feldman, *The Courtesan's Arts: Cross-Cultural*

Perspectives, 11; and Quaintance, "Defaming the Courtesan," in Gordon and Feldman, *The Courtesan's Arts: Cross-Cultural Perspectives*,

46 Although it was rash to have a party, get drunk, and behave stupidly during times of political uncertainty and war, some diehards held parties as political acts. Parties took place on the battlefield, during sieges, and in defiance of caliphal edict. Al-Mas'ūdī and al-Tanūkhi have a number of stories of people partying in the face of adversity, with some receiving grudging respect for their audacity.

47 For example, Abū Nuwās (756–814 CE/170–99 H), considered one of the greatest classical Arab poets, wrote famously of his love for men and young boys.

48 *Ghilmān* were young, beardless serving boys who could be either enslaved or free. *Sāqī* were wine-servers and cupbearers who were often young boys, but could also be young girls. Much like Greek *ephebes*, *sāqī* and *ghilmān* were objects of desire and sexually available. For discussion of *ephebes* and desire in ancient Greece, see Davidson, *Courtesans and Fishcakes*. For homoerotic admiration of *ghilmān* and *sāqī*, see Khaled El-Rouayheb, *Before Homosexuality*. For an exploration of the homoerotic in medieval Arabic literature, see the essays in Wright and Rowson, *Homoeroticism in Classical Arabic Literature*, particularly Rosenthal's discussion of the *Kitāb Moufākharat al-jawārī wa'l ghilmān* and related texts in "Male and Female: Described and Compared," 24–54. See also Stephen O. Murray and William Roscoe (eds.), *Islamic Homosexualities: Culture, History, and Literature* (New York: New York University Press, 1997); and Joseph Massad, *Desiring Arabs* (Chicago, IL: University of Chicago Press, 2007).

49 See Amer, "Medieval Arab Lesbians and Lesbian-Like Women." In accounts about the women's quarters, such as in the *Kama Sutra*, there was tacit understanding that women might get bored and turn to one another for sexual gratification. Some manuals on governing the women's quarters speak to this possibility and how women could lose their taste for men entirely if their sexual needs were neglected (by men) for too long.

50 For gender-bending in the Islamicate courts, see Everett Rowson, "Gender Irregularity as Entertainment: Institutionalized Transvestism at the Caliphal Court in Medieval Baghdad," in Sharon Farmer and Carol Braun Pasternack (eds.), *Gender and Difference in the Middle Ages* (Minneapolis: University of Minnesota Press, 2003), 45–72; and Rowson, "The Categorization of Gender and Sexual Irregularity in Medieval Arabic Vice Lists." See also Amer, "Medieval Arab Lesbians and Lesbian-Like Women."

51 See the *Kitāb Moufākharat al-jawārī wa'l ghilmān* (Beirut: Dar al-Makshuf, 1957). An English translation is available in *Sobriety and Mirth: A Selection of the Shorter Writings by Al-Jāhiz*, The Keagan Paul Arabia Library, trans. Jim Colville (London: Routledge, 2013). The *Aghānī* records many bawdy songs, and the genres of *mujūn* and wine poetry illuminate the humor and proclivities of the Abbasid

court. For an amusing collection of erotic stories from the *Aghānī*, see George Sawa (trans and ed.), *Erotica, Love and Humor in Arabia: Spicy Stories from The Book of Songs by al-Isfahani* (Jefferson, NC: McFarland, 2016).

52 Al-Jāḥiẓ also wrote a satirical debate called "On the Superiority of the Belly to the Back" (*Kitāb fi tafdil al-bafn ᶜala al-zahr*), a translation of which is also available in *Sobriety and Mirth*. For a discussion of the purpose of Arabic debates of jest and earnest (*al-jidd wa'l-hazl*) and the two mock debates noted earlier, see Geert Jan Van Gelder, "Arabic Debates of Jest and Earnest," in G. J. Reinink and H. L. J. Vanstiphout (eds.), *Dispute Poems and Dialogues in the Ancient and Mediaeval Near East* (Leuven: Peeters Press and Department Orientalistiek, 1991), 199–211.

53 Ali, *Marriage and Slavery*, chapter 5, 181–6.

54 Some medieval Islamicate scholars asserted listening made men effeminate. I will discuss this connection further in Part II.

55 For example, the *mukhannath* al-Dalāl specialized in outrageous behavior, which only made him more in demand. How many of his affairs were with men as well as women cannot be verified, but he apparently got around. See *Aghānī*, IV, 59–73.

56 It was conjectured al-Dalāl was the cause, as he was purportedly canoodling with the governor's daughter. Rowson provides a summary of the story in "The Effeminates of Early Medina." The full story, plus information about al-Dalāl, begins in *Aghānī*, IV, 59–73.

57 Rowson, "The Effeminates of Early Medina." More on Ṭuways in the next section.

58 See note 23.

59 For example, the caliph Hārūn al-Rashīd's (763 or 768–809 CE/148–93 H) half brother, Ibrāhīm ibn al-Mahdī (779–839 CE/162–224 H), was famous as a patron and accomplished musician.

60 See Moreh, *Live Theater and Dramatic Literature in the Medieval Arab World.*

61 See Sawa "The Status and Roles of the Secular Musicians in the *Kitāb al-Aghānī* (Book of Songs)."

62 I discuss these musicians and their social and music performance in more detail later.

4 Slavery and Gender

1 Edward Said, *Orientalism* (New York: Random House, 1979); and Said, *Culture and Imperialism* (New York: Vintage Books, 1993).

2 This perception is noted by Bernard Lewis in *Race and Slavery in the Middle East: An Historical Enquiry* (Oxford: Oxford University Press, 1990). It is useful to note that several European travelers, including Lady Montagu, also lauded

the seclusion of women and the harem in Ottoman society as being beneficial to women and a good means of regulating morality.

3 Ehud Toledano points out that comparing institutions of slavery is inherently Eurocentric. When an institution of slavery is rated according to severity, it places a moral value judgment on the institution as a whole within the community being studied. See Toledano, *As If Silent and Absent: Bonds of Enslavement in the Islamic Middle East* (New Haven, CT: Yale University Press, 2007).

4 Ibid.

5 See, for example, Martha Roth, "Women and the Law," in Mark W. Chavalas (ed.), *Women in the Ancient Near East: A Sourcebook* (London: Routledge, 2014), 144–74; and E. G. Pulleyblank, "The Origins and Nature of Chattel Slavery in China," *Journal of the Economic and Social History of the Orient* 1, no. 2 (April 1958): 185–220. See also David Brion Davis, *Slavery and Human Progress* (Oxford: Oxford University Press, 1984), 32–3.

6 See William Clarence-Smith, *Islam and the Abolition of Slavery* (Oxford: Oxford University Press, 2006), 22–48, for a discussion of the legal positions on slavery in the major schools of Islamic jurisprudence. I purposefully use colonialism here as a general term. European colonialism has had the biggest impact on recent history; however, colonization of one people by another is an ancient practice. The early Islamicate dynasties colonized conquered regions through imposition of Arabic as the state language and Islam as the state religion, though for hundreds of years religious tolerance was the norm. Discussions about manumission first arose in the early Islamicate era as each school of jurisprudence took a position on whether or not slavery was allowable and what legal rights a slave might have.

7 As noted in the introduction, this term is borrowed from the Bonn Center for Dependency and Slavery Studies, https://www.dependency.uni-bonn.de/en.

8 According to current knowledge, medieval documents concerned with the slave trade, slave rights and manumission, and the experience of slavery were written by men.

9 The series of revolts by the Zanj in the ninth century, for example, were among the most successful slave rebellions in history. Al-Ṭabarī provides an account of the revolt in the *Histories*. For a deft accounting of the Zanj revolt and analysis, see Davis, *Slavery and Human Progress*, chapters 1 and 2. Davis offers a thoughtful discussion of race and the Islamicate slave trade in chapter 4.

10 William Fitzgerald provides a helpful discussion of love and friendship between the enslaved and the slaver in ancient Rome as represented in the literature. See *Slavery and the Roman Literary Imagination* (Cambridge: Cambridge University Press, 2000).

11 For the anachronistic use of slaves and agency, see Laura Culbertson (ed.), *Slaves and Households in the Near East*, Papers from the Oriental Institute Seminar,

"Slaves and Households in the Near East," Oriental Institute at the University of Chicago, March 5–6, 2010 (Chicago: Oriental Institute at the University of Chicago, 2011): 11–12. Rather than "agency," I use "access" to indicate the passage of people along free and unfree states.

12 Sura 24:33 says: "And if any of your slaves ask for a deed in writing (to enable them to earn their freedom for a certain sum) give them such a deed."

13 See J. Alexander, "Islam, Archaeology and Slavery in Africa," *World Archaeology* 33, no. 1 (2001): 44–60.

14 Sura 4:3 provides guidance regarding how many wives and concubines a man may have: "Marry women of your choice, two, or three or four, but if ye fear that ye shall not be able to deal justly with them, then only one, or (a captive) that which your right hand possesses" (فوحدة أو ما ملكت أيميكم). In Ali's translation of the Qur'an, he delicately refers to these women as "handmaidens," taking pains in several footnotes to indicate that slavery has been abolished and the religion gave slaves rights. See Abdullah Yusef Ali, *The Meaning of the Holy Qur'an*, 9th ed. (Beltsville, MD: Amana, 1997).

15 The term *raqabah* (رقبة) is found in Sura 90:13 (al-Balad), in reference to the virtues that help one become a better Muslim: "It is freeing the bondsman." *raqabah* derives from the root رقب. According to Lane, it can also mean something or someone who is assigned to another person. See Lane, *Lexicon*, vol. I, 1133–4.

16 See Ramon Harvey, "Slavery, Indenture and Freedom: Exegesis of the *'Mukātaba* Verse' (Q. 24:33) in Early Islam," *Journal of Qur'anic Studies* 21, no. 2 (2019): 68–107. The author suggests that the institution of slavery in the early period shifted from a personal relationship to one overseen by the state, necessitating social structures and therefore a stronger legal foundation.

17 Ibid. I suspect some of the intent behind these laws were to entrap people, as the discussion of when the person is free—at time the contract is signed or when paid—wavers between promoting manumission and manipulating loyalty.

18 These terms are racist epithets in some countries today, such as Morocco and India. For a summary of the Arabic terms for slave and unfree over time, see R. Brunschvig, "'Abd," in *Encyclopedia of Islam*, vol. I, 24–40. See also Chouki El Hamel, *Black Morocco: A History of Race, Slavery and Islam* (Cambridge: Cambridge University Press, 2014), for an excellent study of how certain terms became racialized in North Africa.

19 The root is حر. See Lane, *Lexicon*, vol. I, 538–40, for a comprehensive overview of the possible uses for *ḥurr*; and Wehr, *Dictionary*, 193–4, for an abbreviated outline.

20 Sura 5:89 states: "Allah will not call you to account for what is futile in your oaths, but he will call you to account for your deliberate oaths. For expiation, feed ten indigent persons, on a scale of the average for the food of your families, or clothe them, or give a slave his freedom" (Ali, *The Meaning of the Holy Qur'an*,

276). The term for liberating slaves is *taḥrīr*, derived from the same root, حر. *Taḥrīr* also appears in reference to freeing slaves to atone for divorce in Sura 58:3 (al-Mujādilah).

21 Sura 90:2 (al-Balad): "And thou art a freeman of this city." Ali chooses "freeman" for *ḥilūn*, deriving from the root h-l (حل), which is a stretch based on other uses. Arberry translates the term as "lodgers," and among the many other options are to be settled, legitimate, and to be at liberty. See A. J. Arberry (trans.), *The Koran Interpreted* (New York: Simon & Schuster, 1996), 339. The word *halāl* comes from the same root and refers to what is allowable. In essence, this term can be read as "legitimate or lawful," but just as easily "someone who has settled" as in a traveler settling into a community. As such, it is not a term used specifically to indicate the state of freedom. See Lane, *Lexicon*, vol. I, 619–20.

22 Such non-choices tied to survival are integral to human trafficking today as well, and bartering women for political gain through marriage and other kin ties was common globally well into the twentieth century. With the rise of racialized slavery in the sixteenth century and plantation slavery in the Americas, the essential humanity of slaves was eradicated, allowing for absolute denial of rights and dehumanization. See Davis, *Slavery and Human Progress*; and David Livingstone Smith, *Less than Human: Why We Demean, Enslave, and Exterminate Others* (New York: St. Martin's, 2011).

23 Women and children continue to comprise 50 percent of all trafficking victims globally today.

24 The primary sources for Islamic slavery are numerous and diverse, including literature, histories, treatises, legal rulings, and slave manuals. For a sampling of extant texts, see Brunschvig, "'Abd"; and Lewis, *Race and Slavery in the Middle East*.

25 For an overview of gifting and diplomacy, see Anthony Cutler, "Gifts and Gift Exchange as Aspects of the Byzantine, Arab and Related Economies," *Dumbarton Oaks Papers* 55 (2001): 247–87; and El-Cheikh, "Describing the Other to Get at the Self: Byzantine Women in Arabic Sources (8th–11th Centuries)."

26 Brunschvig, "'Abd."

27 Enslaved men were used as generals, secretaries, and advisors, and some rose to hold important governmental offices. Enslaved women also exerted enormous political influence and some became queens, gave birth to caliphs, and ruled from behind the scenes. See Fatima Mernissi, *The Forgotten Queens of Islam*, trans. Mary Jo Lakeland (Minneapolis: University of Minnesota Press, 1993); and Ahmed, *Women and Gender in Islam*. See also El-Cheikh, "Revisiting the Abbasid Harems"; and al-Heitty, "The Contrasting Spheres of Free Women and Jawari."

28 Carol Graham connects conversations about slavery to purity in al-Andalus through Ibn Garcia's commentary on Arab obsession with genealogy, pointing out that slavery was the messy underbelly of society, structurally and ethnically.

Graham also notes the role of singing slave women in those intersections. See Carol Graham, "The Meaning of Slavery and Identity in Al-Andalus: The Epistle of Ibn Garcia," *Arab Studies Journal* 3, no. 1 (1995): 68–79.

29 For an analysis of origins for enslaved women, see Pernilla Myrne, *Narrative, Gender and Authority in Abbasid Literature on Women*, Orientalia et Africana Gothoburgensia, no. 22 (Goteburg, Sweden: Edita Vastra, 2010).

30 For African slave trade in the first two hundred years of the Islamic states, see E. Savage, "Berbers and Blacks: Ibadi Slave Traffic in Eighth-Century North Africa," *Journal of African History* 33, no. 3 (1992): 351–68. See also the collected essays in Gwen Campbell, Suzanne Miers, and Joseph Miller (eds.), *Women and Slavery: Africa, the Indian Ocean World and the Medieval North Atlantic*, vol. I, "Women and Slavery" (Athens: Ohio University Press, 2007); and Humphrey Fisher, *Slavery in the History of Muslim Black Africa* (New York: New York University Press, 2001).

31 Port cities frequently had a slave market of some type, as did major cities along trade routes. In the eighth century, Venice was major port for slave trade between Europe and the East.

32 There are many references to buyers being tricked by slavers in literature and poetry as well, often with humorous consequences. For an example of how to pick a good slave, see al-Jāḥiẓ, *Risālat al-Qiyān*, 24. The physician Ibn Buṭlan wrote a tract on how to pick a slave, and the tricks slavers used to hide flaws and ill health.

33 Eunuchs had value as scribes, harem guards and in other civic duties, so their trade was more brisk near major urban centers or governmental seats. See Clarence-Smith, *Islam and the Abolition of Slavery*, 46–7. Technically, mutilation was not allowed by Islam, so castrations took place on the fringes of the Islamicate states. Like major slave markets, castration centers were in cities and ports. Enslaved men and boys were trafficked to centers near slave markets because they had a higher chance of survival than if the operation was performed before transport or at point of capture. Verdun served as a preparation, that is, castration, center for enslaved men, and there were such centers in Spain as well. There were several procedures used, all potentially lethal, with the two most common being one in which the testicles were cut or removed so that an individual was rendered sterile, and the horrific extreme in which the genitals were completely removed, referred to as being "made level with the belly."

34 Male slaves were sometimes given the name Kātib, if they were a scribe, or called al-Yunān (from Greece).

35 See Toledano, *As If Silent and Absent: Bonds of Enslavement in the Islamic Middle East*, 67. The classic study of erasure and social death is Orlando Patterson, *Slavery and Social Death: A Comparative Study* (Cambridge, MA: Harvard University Press, 1982).

36 For example, the singing women ᶜArīb became ᶜArīb al-Ma'mūniyya when freed.

37 There are many well-known queen mothers in history, such as Umm Muqtadir. The record is fuzzier when tracing *qiyān* and concubines. One famous example of a queen mother is Jodha Bai, the wife of the Mughal king Jahangir. She was a Rajput princess and Hindu whom he married for political reasons. According to legend, they loved one another fiercely, but there is no clear evidence she actually existed, as she is not referenced in court documents or records. For names and honorifics, see Ruby Lal, "Mughal Palace Women," in Walthall, *Servants of the Dynasty*, 96–114; and Nadia Maria El-Cheikh, "Caliphal Harems, Household Harems: Baghdad in the Fourth Century of the Islamic Era," in Booth, *Harem Histories: Envisioning Places and Living Spaces*, 87–103.

38 One example of this type arrangement appears in Genesis in the Judaic Testament. Abram and his wife Sarai take in a slave woman, Hagar, for the purpose of getting a male heir. Hagar's successful production of Ishmael improves her status in the family, and Abram later adopts her son as one of his heirs. See also Clarence-Smith, *Islam and the Abolition of Slavery*, 24.

39 Of the most notorious was the caliph al-Muqtadir (reigned 908–32 CE/295–320 *H*), whose mother ran the show. He ascended the throne as a child, and his father, al-Muᶜtaḍid (860–902 CE/245–89 *H*), had dire predictions that the women would rule him. As it turned out, this was the case. Al-Muqtadir loved to drink and play with his enslaved concubines and gave them whatever he wanted. Al-Tanūkhi has many anecdotes about the Queen Mother, as well as the prediction that al-Muqtadir would lose his power to the women. For the latter, see al-Tanūkhi, *Table Talk of a Mesopotamian Judge*, 154. For power politics in al-Muqtadir's court, see El-Cheikh, "The Qahramana in the Abbasid Court: Position and Functions."

40 See, for example, Francesca Bray, "Technics and Civilization in Late Imperial China: An Essay in the Cultural History of Technology." *Osiris* 13 Beyond Joseph Needham: Science, Technology and Medicine in East and Southeast Asia (1998): 22.

41 Although subsequent studies have also discussed this shift in the power structure in more detail, Goldziher is among the first to make this point in his article on the *shuᶜūbiyya*. See Ignaz Goldziher, "The Shu'ubiyya," in *Muslim Studies (Muhammedanische Studien)*, 2 vols.; vol. 1, trans. S. M. Stern (London: George Allen and Unwin, 1967), 137–63. Goldziher points out that the Umayyads were much harsher about preserving Arab lineage, which eased under the Abbasids. As the lineage of the mother became less important, the role—Goldziher says "dignity"—of women lessened. By diminishing the importance of the mother's line, enslaved mothers and dilution of the bloodline became allowable without

besmirching the dignity of the father's line, thus placing emphasis on lineage through the father.

42 See Goldziher, "Arab and 'Adjam," in *Muslim Studies (Muhammedanische Studien)*, 98–136. To be born the child of a slave was to dilute the tribal hierarchy. Enslaved people, however, were understood not to have responsibility over their actions. Goldziher comments that "Muḥammad taught that an immoral slave woman received only half the punishment that would apply to a freeborn woman in a similar case." Sura 4:25 states: "And from this derives the principle that the hadd of a slave must always be only half the punishment prescribed for a free person" (117–18).

43 See El-Cheikh, "Describing the Other to Get at the Self: Byzantine Women in Arabic Sources (8th–11th Centuries)."

44 Without a full understanding as to what various terms related to ethnicity, skin color, and origin meant in the medieval Islamicate world, what real impact they had on the perception of musicians is open to speculation. Their inclusion in descriptions of musicians and performances, however, suggests that *ethnos* and geographic origin were part of conversations about music.

5 Literary Performance of Music and Reading Musical Identity

1 Such skills are emphasized in Ibn al-Washsha's *Book of Brocade*, discussed earlier. See also Ahsan, *Social Life under the Abbasids*; and Anwar Chejne, "The Boon Companion in Early 'Abbasid Times," *Journal of the American Oriental Society* 85, no. 3 (1965): 327–35.

2 *Vida* means "life" in Occitan.

3 Since composition included improvisation and collaboration, when sources list works attributed to a specific musician, they refer to what songs that person had composed and memorized.

4 Like *vidas*, those narratives that omit biographical material could mean that the author simply did not have the information as well as the possibility it was assumed the reader would know the salient details already.

5 The singular is *khabar* (pl. *akhbār*), which means report, anecdote. For a detailed study of the use of *akhbār* (within medieval Arabic literature), see Hilary Kilpatrick, "Context and the Enhancement of the Meaning of *akhbār* in the *Kitab al-Aghānī*," *Arabica* 38, no. 3 (1991): 351–68; and Kilpatrick, *Making the Great Book of Songs*, chapter 5.

6 In the *Aghānī*, for example, al-Iṣbahānī includes biographical outlines and narratives, but since his intent was to educate the reader about the most important songs of the past and his own time, focus on the performance itself was essential.

His narratives often include basic biographical information, but the biography functions more as a reference point so the reader will have a context for the stories and performances that follow.

7 See Matthew Gordon, "The Place of Competition: The Careers of Arib al-Ma'mūniya and Ulayya bint al-Mahdi, Sisters in Song," in James Montgomery (ed.), *Occasional Papers of the School of Abbasid Studies*, Orientalia Lovaniensia Analecta, no. 135 (Leuven: Peeters, 2004), 61–81; and Boaz Shoshan, "High Culture and Popular Culture in Medieval Islam," *Studia Islamica* 73 (1991): 67–107.

8 Ibrāhīm al-Mawṣilī is a well-documented example of a musician who flaunted the rules and got into considerable trouble as a result. His anecdotes, as I comment on further later, are filled with questionable exploits and scandal. He was saved by his skill, charm, wealth, and powerful friendships, particularly that of Hārūn al-Rashīd.

9 Such stories appear in several of the treatises examined in the following chapters.

10 Marriage to a former slaver shifted women musicians out of the public gaze, although this change in status may only have moved their performance to the private sphere. There are few stories about former singing women being freed for marriage, however.

11 Ibn al-Washsha included tips for the refined woman in the *Muwashshā'* such as proper dress, comportment, and how to write suitable poetry.

12 For example, ᶜUlayya bint al-Mahdī. Tragic stories, such as that of Maḥbūba, who refused to renounce her love and loyalty of the caliph al-Mutawakkil, are also both warnings and examples.

13 See Gordon, "The Place of Competition."

14 One can find a wealth of similar examples in Greek and Roman literature, in which women, soldiers, and enslaved peoples comment on their fate.

15 See Farmer, *A History of Arabian Music to the 13th Century*, 52. For remarks and anecdotes about Ṭuways, see *Aghānī*, II, 170–7. There is a brief biography of Ṭuways in vol. IV, 38, but it is only a recapitulation of the basic details. For a discussion of this mislabeled section, see Kilpatrick, *Making the Great Book of Songs*, 265 and 405, n. 6 in appendix II.

16 The *Rashīdūn*, or Rightly Guided, were the first four rulers of the Islamic community after the death of the Prophet Muḥammad. They were Abū Bakr (632–4 CE), ᶜUmar ibn al-Khaṭṭāb (634–44 CE), ᶜUthmān ibn ᶜAffān (644–56 CE), and ᶜAli ibn Abī Ṭālib (656–61 CE).

17 As noted previously, some scholars asserted that listening to music made one effeminate. Al-Dalāl's exploits are relayed in *Aghānī*, IV, 59–73.

18 Rowson, "The Effeminates of Early Medina." Other *mukhannathūn* of Medina continued their careers after exile. Narratives related to gender-ambiguous entertainers often have them express defiance, crack jokes, and even confront the audience.

19 There are many stories about Ibn Jāmi[c] in the *Aghānī*, with the main entry in vol. VI, 68–92. See also Kilpatrick, *Making the Great Book of* Songs, 212. Interestingly, while other important celebrity musicians such as Ibrāhīm ibn al-Mahdī, Ibrāhīm al-Mawṣilī, and Isḥāq al-Mawṣilī (who has the longest biography) have entries in the *Fihrist*, Ibn Jāmi[c] does not.
20 Farmer, *A History of Arabian Music to the 13th Century*, 113.
21 Sawa includes several examples in *Music Performance Practice*, 125, 163–5, 180.
22 The main article about him and his life is in *Aghānī*, vol. 5, 169–277. The entry for his son begins in the same volume at p. 278.
23 The nobility of their family is reported on the authority of Isḥāq, *Aghānī*, vol. 5, 169.
24 Al-Nadīm states Ibrāhīm's father was named Māhān, but he changed it to Maymūn. *Fihrist*, 307. The *Aghānī* also notes his name change: *Aghānī*, vol. 5, 169–70.
25 J. W. Fück, "Ibrāhīm al-Mawṣilī," *EI*, vol. III, 996.
26 *Aghānī*, vol. 5, 172.
27 The same Siyāṭ who was Ibn Jāmi[c]'s stepfather. Farmer, *History*, 116–17.
28 Farmer, *A History of Arabian Music to the 13th Century*, 119.
29 The *Aghānī* reports on both, vol. 5, 177–8. Regardless, Ibrāhīm received an enormous sum in compensation from al-Hādī. See also Fück, "Ibrāhīm al-Mawṣilī," *EI*, vol. III, 996.
30 *Aghānī*, vol. 5, 177–8.
31 The statement made by Ibrāhīm's son Isḥāq is: "handsome women are now being trained to sing, when before it was the black and yellow girls." Cited in Lewis, *Race and Slavery in the Middle East*. For the original story, see the Brunnow edition of the *Kitāb al-Aghānī*, vol. 5, 9. The same story is told in Ibn Khurdādhbih, *Kitāb al-Lahw wa'l malāhī*, 24, with this variation: "Ishaq said: At first, those (women) chosen to be trained in singing were black and yellow girls until the rule of Walid bin Yazid. Then, handsome and noble (or Iraq) were taught." Based on this variant, the distinction made is ethnicity and class. Goldziher reads this story as being less about race than differentiating skin color, although it is difficult not to see the undertone of racial categorization and potential biases. Needless to say, these trainees were enslaved, further suggesting a profit motive and market preferences.
32 Zalzal has an interval named after him, called the "zalzal third." See Farmer, *A History of Arabian Music to the 13th Century*, 118–19.
33 Fück, "Ibrāhīm al-Mawṣilī," *EI*, vol. III, 996.
34 References to and songs by Isḥāq al-Mawṣilī are found throughout the *Aghānī*. His main entry is in vol. V, 52–131.
35 J. W. Fück, "Ishak ibn Ibrāhīm al-Mawṣilī," *EI* vol. 4, 110–11.

36 Al-Nadīm includes a comment by al-Suli that Isḥāq had five siblings, although only two became musicians.

37 Kilpatrick, *Making the Great Book of Songs*, 126, n. 119, 242.

38 For example, in one story, Isḥāq al-Mawṣilī conceals his instrument behind a curtain, only bringing it out when it is time to play. Sawa discusses this episode in "Status and Roles of the Secular Musicians," 74–5.

39 Farmer quotes the story from the *Aghānī* in *A History of Arabian Music to the 13th Century*, 124.

40 Fück, "Ishak ibn Ibrāhīm al-Mawṣilī," *EI* vol. 4, 111. He was a *fakīh* and allowed to assist at Friday prayer.

41 Al-Nadīm, *Fihrist*, 308.

42 Ibn al-Aᶜrābī (*c.* 760–846 CE /142–231 H) was a philologist. See Fück, "Ishak ibn Ibrāhīm al-Mawṣilī," *EI* vol. 4, 111.

43 Al-Nadīm, *Fihrist*, 309. One was on *qiyān*, the other on *qiyān* of the Hijaz.

44 Ibid., 363. Isḥāq al-Mawṣilī is on the same list as ᶜUlayya bint al-Mahdī and other *qiyān*. Since the caliph al-Ma'mūn is also in the list, it is not exclusively a list of works by women and slaves as the title of the list states.

45 Isḥāq al-Mawṣilī appears as an authority and transmitter of poetry (*rāwī*) or judge (*qāḍī*) throughout al-Ṭabarī's *Histories*, in situations as various as the building of Baghdad and affirming an aspect of the question of succession during the reign of al-Manṣūr (reigned 754–75 CE/136–58 H). When al-Ṭabarī indicates an anecdote is on the authority of Isḥāq, he does not refer to him as a musician. See, for example, al-Ṭabarī, *The Early 'Abbasi Empire: The Reign of 'Abu Jaᶜfar al-Mansur (AD 754–775)*, vol. 1, trans. John Alden Williams (Cambridge: Cambridge University Press, 1988), 178, 198.

46 Al-Nadīm, *Fihrist*, 253. This page number is listed erroneously under Ibrāhīm al-Mawṣilī in the index of p. 1043. The account of Ibrāhīm al-Mawṣilī begins on 307. Ibrāhīm ibn al-Mahdī is the first entry in the second section of the third chapter, and is noted as "the first genius among the Banū al-Abbas and the children of the caliphs to become prominent."

47 For an overview of Ibrāhīm ibn al-Mahdī's brief and unsuccessful sojourn into politics, see D. Sourdel, "Ibrāhīm ibn al-Mahdī," *EI* vol. III, 987–8.

48 Ibid.

49 Farmer refers to this as a conflict between Classicists and Romanticists—a clunky analogy but comprehensible to a Western readership. Sawa discusses the differences in style in detail in *Music Performance Practices*.

50 Farmer, *A History of Arabian Music to the 13th Century*, 119–21.

51 Her *akhbār* is in *Aghānī*, vol. XVII, 80–6.

52 Given this range, Badhl either started quite young or died early in al-Muᶜtaṣim's reign. See Kilpatrick, *Making the Great Book of Songs*, 328. See also Farmer, *A History of Arabian Music to the 13th Century*, 119, 134.

53 Farmer, *A History of Arabian Music to the 13th Century*, 134. In the *Aghānī*, the comment specifically indicates enslaved women, *jāriya*. See vol. XVII, 81.

54 Farmer, *A History of Arabian Music to the 13th Century*, 134.

55 According to al-Iṣbahānī, these were recorded without performance indications. See Kilpatrick, *Making the Great Book of Songs*, 51. The story is in *Aghānī*, vol. XVII, 82.

56 Kilpatrick, *Making the Great Book of Songs*, 126–7.

57 Ibid., 242. Farmer also notes this story without the details, stating that her memory was so sharp "even Isḥāq al-Mawṣilī stood abashed." *A History of Arabian Music to the 13th Century*, 134. See also *Aghānī*, vol. XVII, 84.

58 Farmer states both possibilities.

59 The entry dedicated to her life and work comments frequently on the number of songs she knew, all in the thousands.

60 Her *akhbār* is in *Aghānī*, vol. X, 199–226, 2002 edition.

61 Information about Maknūna, who is described as an *umm walad*, is noted in the *Aghānī*, vol X, 199. She is referred to as a *jāriya*, not a *qayna*.

62 Ibid., 200.

63 Neubauer, "'Ullayah bint al-Mahdī," *EI* vol. X, 810.

64 Ibid. See al-Nadīm, *Fihrist*, 361. ᶜUlayya is mentioned in the list entitled "Women: The Free and the Slaves" as having written twenty leaves. According to al-Nadīm, one leaf contained twenty lines on each side of the sheet.

65 Her main entry in the *Aghānī* is in vol. XXI, starting on p. 54.

66 For detailed analysis of the life and role of ᶜArīb, including a full translation of her *akhbār* from the *Aghānī*, see Myrne, *Narrative, Gender and Authority in Abbasid Literature on Women* and appendix 2, 272–98. See also Matthew Gordon, "'Arib al-Ma'mūniya: A Third/Ninth Century Abbasid Courtesan," in Neguin Yavari, Lawrence G. Potter, and Jean-Marc Ran Oppenheim (eds.), *Views from the Edge: Essays in Honor of Richard W. Bulliet* (New York: Columbia University Press, 2004), 86–100; Gordon, "The Place of Competition"; and Gordon, "ᶜArib al-Ma'mūniyah," in Michael Cooperson and Shawkat Toorawa (eds.), *Arabic Literary Culture, 500–925* (Farmington Hills, MI: Thomson Gale, 2004), 85–90. I use Myrne's excellent translation for this section.

67 See Gordon, "ᶜArib al-Ma'mūniya: A Third/Ninth Century Abbasid Courtesan."

68 Myrne, *Narrative, Gender and Authority in Abbasid Literature on Women*, Appendix 2, 272. For the Arabic, see *Aghānī*, vol. XXI, 53. The *ᶜūd* is not mentioned by name in the Arabic; instead, *ḍaraba*, to strike, is used.

69 See Gordon, "ᶜArib al-Mamuniyyah: A Third/Ninth Century Abbasid Courtesan," 87; and Myrne, *Narrative, Gender and Authority in Abbasid Literature on Women*, appendix 2, section 13, p. 277.

70 According to one story, an observer remarked that ᶜArīb's feet reminded him of Jaᶜfar's as a means of proof of his parentage. See Myrne, *Narrative, Gender and Authority in Abbasid Literature on Women*, appendix 2, section 14, p. 277. See also Gordon, "Arib al-Mamuniyyah: A Third/Ninth Century Abbasid Courtesan," 87.

71 The Barmakid family were intimates of the court during the early Abbasid era, holding several important positions and wielding considerable power. Jaᶜfar's father was Yaḥya ibn Khālid al-Barmaki (d. 806 CE/190 *H*), who was the tutor and later vizier for Hārūn al-Rashīd. Jaᶜfar was purportedly al-Rashīd's favorite and possibly his lover. According to the histories, when al-Rashīd returned from pilgrimage, he suddenly rounded up key members of the Barmakid family and destroyed them. There are many stories and speculations about the rise and fall of the Barmakids, but for a succinct overview, see D. Sourdel, "al-Baramika," in *Encyclopedia of Islam*, vol. 1, 1033–6.

72 Gordon, "ᶜArib al-Mamuniyyah: A Third/Ninth Century Abbasid Courtesan"; Myrne, *Narrative, Gender and Authority in Abbasid Literature on Women*, appendix 2, 273–4.

73 Myrne, *Narrative, Gender and Authority in Abbasid Literature on Women*, appendix 2, section 44, p. 290. This brief section notes that ᶜArīb was 14 during the rule of al-Amīn.

74 Ibid., appendix 2, sections 8, 9, and 58. For information about al-Hishāmi, see p. 274, n. 2.

75 Ibid., appendix 2, 274.

76 Ibid., appendix 2, section 58, p. 296.

77 For a sampling of song titles, see ibid., appendix 2, sections 9 and 58.

78 There are four mentions of *wustā*, paired with different rhythmic modes. *Wustā* means middle and refers to the middle finger and middle fret on the *ᶜūd*. For a detailed discussion of this mode, see Sawa, *Music Performance Practice*, 75–6; and Owen Wright, "Ibn Munajim and the Early Arabian Modes," *Galpin Society Journal* 19 (1966): 27–48.

79 Myrne, *Narrative, Gender and Authority in Abbasid Literature on Women*, appendix 2, 273. A foot is a unit of metrical measure, usually including one stressed and one unstressed syllable.

80 ᶜArīb is far earthier, saying: "Eight of them have fucked me, but the only of them I desired was al-Mu'tazz." She was likely in her sixties at this point. ᶜArīb has several ribald comments on sex and men sprinkled throughout her biography. Along with al-Mu'tazz (866–9 CE), the caliphs 'Arīb served under were: al-Amīn (809–13 CE), al-Ma'mūn (813–33 CE), al-Muᶜtaṣim (833–42 CE), al-Wāthiq (842–7 CE),

al-Mutawakkil (847–61 CE), al-Muntaṣir (861–2 CE), and al-Mustaᶜīn (862–6 CE). She also survived the caliphs al-Muhtadī (869–70 CE) and al-Muᶜtamid (870–92 CE) and died during the reign of al-Muᶜtaḍid (892–902 CE). See Myrne, *Narrative, Gender and Authority in Abbasid Literature on Women*, appendix 2, section 43 and n. 1, p. 288.

81 See Gordon, "ᶜArib al-Ma'mūniya: A Third/Ninth Century Abbasid Courtesan," for an analysis of ᶜArīb's voice and social status through the lens of these stories.

82 Providing guests and patrons with sexual companions was practiced by wealthy women slavers as well as men. As mentioned previously, training singing women included music and seduction, if not outright prostitution. The training of courtesans in other cultures comments on the sexual availability and bidding for the virginity of new courtesans by patrons. Comely and virginal *jawārī* were similarly prized, yielding high profits for slavers.

83 See al-Tanūkhi, *Table Talk of a Mesopotamian Judge*, 144–6.

84 Her *akhbār* is in *Aghānī*, XV, 79–85.

85 See Farmer, *A History of Arabian Music to the 13th Century*, 135.

86 One finds similar representations of courtesans in medieval India, Japan, and China. The memoirs of Sei Shonagon, Lady Murasaki, and the famous story of the *47 Ronin* in Japan share these character types. Likewise, the stories of Ming-era writer Feng Meng Long in China and famous operas like *The Peony Pavilion* all share these archetypes. The figure of the courtesan and courtesan culture is central to the nineteenth-century Urdu novel *Umrao Jan Ada* by Mirza Ruswa.

87 For example, when al-Jāḥiẓ names two singing women, he does so in defense of singing based purely on their talent. Similarly, Ibn al-Washsha quotes several singing women speaking about their own vices to support his view that they are willfully destructive.

88 Al-Ṭabarī, *Early Abbasi*, vol. II, 179.

89 Ibid.

90 Al-Ṭabarī, *Al-Mansur and al-Mahdi A.D. 763–786/A.H. 146–169*, vol. 29, trans. Hugh Kennedy (New York: New York University Press, 1990), 120–1. In the Williams translation, *Early Abbasi Empire*, vol. II, 23.

91 Ibid. The second anecdote is: "According to Asmaᶜi: Ashᶜab said to his son, ᶜUbaydah, 'I think that I will expel you from my house and banish you,' and he asked, 'Why, O father?,' and his father replied 'I am the best of God's creatures in earning a loaf of bread, and you are my son and you have reached this age of maturity and you are still in my household and have not earned anything.' His son said, 'I do earn, but I am like the banana tree that does not bear fruit until its mother dies.'"

92 For the development of Arabhood and Arabization from late antiquity to the eighth century, see Hoyland, *Arabia and the Arabs*, 229–47.

93 See Shoshan, "High Culture and Popular Culture in Medieval Islam," 67–107.

6 Politics of Listening

1 Given the number of stories and consistency in details, parties were common and some undoubtedly became wild.

2 The four major schools of Islamic jurisprudence that developed in the ninth century are the Ḥanbali, after Ibn Ḥanbal (780–855 CE); Ḥanafī, after Abū Ḥanifa (*c.* 699–767 CE); Mālikī, after Mālik ibn Anas (*c.* 715–95 CE); and Shāfiʿī's, after al-Shāfiʿī (767–820 CE). All the schools differ in terms of legal methodology, points of law, and uses of *ḥadīth* and logic in determining legal decisions.

3 See Megan Reid, *Law and Piety in Medieval Islam* (Cambridge: Cambridge University Press, 2013). Daniella Talmon-Heller also provides valuable insight into piety and how it was expressed through an examination of documentary evidence from Ayyubid Syria. See *Islamic Piety in Medieval Syria: Mosques, Cemeteries and Sermons under the Zangid and Ayyubids (1146–1260)*, vol. 7, Jerusalem Studies in Religion and Culture (Leiden: Brill, 2007).

4 Megan Reid states:

> Islamic society, ideally, strives to make it easy for people to live cleanly and without hypocrisy. It seeks to protect Muslims as well as to regulate their behavior. As custodians of legal knowledge, the jurists and judges not only served as arbiters of correct action but were also expected to be its exemplars, and to this extent their behavior was always public: the qadi and public administration of justice, nor were the private lives of legal scholars spared public scrutiny. These men were therefore self-regulators, and in this capacity the pious among them helped to define the patters of social avoidance that became prevalent in the medieval period, since they were charged with negotiating for others the situations they themselves often feared. (See ibid., 131)

5 See Gordon, "The Place of Competition."

6 A close, if somewhat unusual, analogy lies in the process of deep learning in AI. In order to teach a machine to reproduce a painting by Van Gogh, for example, one must feed it every scrap of information about Van Gogh's work. Logically, one would assume that the computer would then reproduce replicas of Van Gogh and produce familiar images—called "deepfakes"—based on Van Gogh's style. Although that can be the case, the interpretation by the computer can be completely unexpected, resulting in strange, fanciful interpretations of Van Gogh. To make things more interesting, AI specialists are not certain what exactly is happening in the middle as the machine "thinks" about the information and interprets the

request of the user. I am indebted to Dr. Jon Whitney for sharing his expertise in deep learning, aesthetics, and AI and giving me a fruitful way to think about this metaphysical phenomenon.

7 See Fritz Meier, "The Dervish Dance: An Attempt at an Overview," in *Essays on Islamic Piety and Mysticism*, trans. John O'Kane (Leiden: Brill, 1999), 23–48. Gifting clothing was an ancient practice and a frequent means of showing approval in the Islamicate courts. Gifts of clothing could be planned, as in a patron ordering a rich cloak for a favored courtier, or a spontaneous show of affection. There are numerous records of patrons giving clothing to musicians, often with descriptions of the cost, fabric, embroidery, and other key details. Due to the hierarchy of the courts and sumptuary laws, certain colors and styles were allowed only for certain people, making such gifts even more important.

8 This number is higher when one includes variations, many of which have minimal differences. See Appendix I for a list of select *ḥadīth* on listening and sample variations.

9 This *ḥadīth* serves a dual purpose in that it invokes the danger of hypocrisy in the individual as well as the Hypocrites who attempted to dismantle the Muslim community. See Appendix I.

10 Because there might be many variations on one *ḥadīth*, some versions of popular texts, such as Ibn Abi'l Dūnya's *Censure*, existed in an abridged form. That version has fewer variations on the same *ḥadīth* and abbreviated authentication; possibly intended to be a useful, easily accessed reference.

11 Arberry's translation from *The Koran Interpreted*, 112. In this verse, *lahw* (لهو) is used for diversion and expanded to include music. Ibn Abi'l Dūnya is among the first to stress this definition for *lahw* in the *Censure of Instruments of Diversion*, and al-Ājurrī is the first to explicitly cite 31:6 in relation to listening in *Response to the Question about Listening*.

12 See Reid, *Law and Piety*. See also Cook, *Commanding Right and Forbidding Wrong in Islamic Thought*.

13 For example, Abū'l Ṭayyib al-Ṭabari grumbles that music is stupid. I discuss his treatise in the following chapter.

14 James Robson's 1937 translation remains the only available English translation of the *Censure*.

15 The work of the Ṣūfi philosopher al-Ghazālī, also translated by a Western scholar, has a more familiar writing style and is sympathetic to music. For an English translation of the section on music from the *Iḥyā' ᶜUlūm al-Dīn* (The Revival of the Religious Sciences), published in three parts, see Duncan B. Macdonald, "Emotional Religion in Islam as Affected by Music and Singing," *Journal of the Royal Asiatic Society of Great Britain and Ireland* (April 1901): 195–252; Macdonald, "Emotional Religion in Islam as Affected by Music and Singing,"

Journal of the Royal Asiatic Society of Great Britain and Ireland (October 1901): 705–48; and Macdonald, "Emotional Religion in Islam as Affected by Music and Singing," *Journal of the Royal Asiatic Society of Great Britain and Ireland* (January 1902): 1–28.

16 Other scholars use terms such as "puritanical" and "conservative" to describe Ibn Abi'l Dūnya's tone and moral stance on music. Although Ibn Abi'l Dūnya is taking a conservative position, these labels imply he is a crank to be dismissed.

17 Discussions of *samāᶜ* are sometimes categorized as a literary subgenre. I am not convinced it was distinct from pietistic and legal literature during the medieval era.

18 Presumably, playing music was already in the realm of illegal for those against *samāᶜ* as there are few injunctions to stop playing music. The main focus is on what to do if one happens to hear instruments being played.

19 For education and the importance of oral transmission of texts, see George Maqdisi, "Muslim Institutions of Learning in Eleventh-Century Baghdad"; and Berkey, *The Transmission of Knowledge in Medieval Cairo*. Although scholars and students collected books, hearing a text by the author and reciting back to a teacher was still preferred well into the fifteenth century. Students traveled to libraries to copy books and made notes in the margins. Medieval learners understood that memorization or owning a copy of a book was not enough; a text needed to be parsed with a master and written in the hand of the learner to gain full value from the contents. See Berkey, *The Transmission of Knowledge in Medieval Cairo*, 24–34. For *samāᶜ* in the context of learning, see p. 33.

20 For *samāᶜat*, see R. Sellheim, "Samāᶜ," *EI*, new ed., vol. VIII, 1019–20.

21 See During, "Samāᶜ," in *EI*, vol. VIII, 1018–19.

22 Secondary studies of Ṣūfism attest to the variety in meaning for *samāᶜ* from the treatises. See, for example, the essays in Frederick De Jong and Bernd Radtke (eds), *Islamic Mysticism Contested: Thirteen Centuries of Controversies and Polemics* (Leiden: Brill, 1999).

23 See Nathan Hofer, *The Popularisation of Ṣufism in Ayyubid and Mamluk Egypt (1173–1325)* (Edinburgh: Edinburgh University Press, 2015), 3–7; and Reid, *Law and Piety*, 5–6, for a discussion of Ṣūfism in modern scholarship. See also Richard McGregor, "The Problem of Ṣūfism," *Mamlūk Studies Review* XIII, no. 2 (2009): 69–83.

24 Reid, *Law and Piety*, 5–6; Hofer, *The Popularisation of Ṣūfism*, 3–7. Joseph van Ess offers a concise summation of changes in perception in "Ṣūfism and Its Opponents: Reflections on Topoi, Tribulations, and Transformations," in De Jong and Radtke, *Islamic Mysticism Contested*, 22–44.

25 Hofer, *The Popularisation of Ṣūfism*, 8.

26 Ibid., 25.

27 Ibid., 11.

28 Ibid., 6.

29 See Boaz Shoshan's studies of popular culture in medieval Cairo. Shoshan, "High Culture and Popular Culture in Medieval Islam"; and his book-length study *Popular Culture in Medieval Cairo* (Cambridge: Cambridge University Press, 1993).

30 This confusion is seen in the treatises themselves, as different scholars attempt to define what constitutes popular sound genres and who is listening to them.

31 L. Massignon-(B. Radtke), "Tasawwuf," *EI*, vol. X, 313–17. At its simplest definition, "ṣūfi" derives from form V of the root صوف, which is the word for wool. Ṣūfis are also referred to as taṣawwuf, mutaṣawwuf. Early Ṣūfi were ascetics, renouncing the trappings of the world; hence the wearing of rough wool. Poverty was also the mark of a Ṣūfi. In the eighth century, Ṣūfis begin to emerge as a distinct group, some exhibiting "anti-nomian, antisocial and anti-governmental tendencies." Ṣūfis were concerned about the inner as well as external relationship with God, and sought ways to become closer to the divine. Because Ṣūfis embraced poverty, they are also referred to generically as *faqīr* (Arabic) or *dervish* (Persian).

32 Meier, "The Dervish Dance: An Attempt at an Overview," 189–219.

33 See Talmon-Heller, *Islamic Piety*; and Daphna Ephrat and Hatim Mahamid, "The Creation of Ṣūfi Spheres in Medieval Damascus (mid-6th/12th to mid-8th/14th). *Journal of the Royal Asiatic Society* 3.25.2 (2015): 189–208, particularly 197. See also Hofer's discussion of the relationship of the Ṣūfi *khanqah* to the state in *Popularisation of Ṣūfism* (35–60).

34 Ephrat and Mahamid, "The Creation of Ṣūfi Spheres," 201.

35 Joseph van Ess comments that

> in the third century philosophy and metaphysics still lay beyond the horizon of mysticism, whereas in the eighth century, they can be found everywhere. In the third century, the visionary element, though it did exist, was usually left unmentioned when it came to public statements; in the eighth century, it is an important element of mystical self-understanding. In the third century, Ṣūfism did not yet belong to the canon of religious disciplines; in the eighth century, it sometimes overshadows theology and jurisprudence. In the third century the authorities and the government were normally suspicious of it; in the eighth century they rather seek its support. (Introduction to De Jong and Radtke, *Islamic Mysticism Contested*, 36–7)

36 See Bashir Shahzad, *Ṣūfi Bodies: Religion and Society in Medieval Islam* (New York: Columbia University Press, 2011), 68–77.

37 Ibid. Shahzad discusses how *samā*ᶜ and *dhikr* are different practices, but intersect. *Dhikr* follows a certain order and can be silent or sounded. The latter can inspire *samā*ᶜ for another—that is, someone hears prayers or melodic sounding-music

from someone engaged in *dhikr*. See also Kenneth Avery, *A Psychology of Ṣūfī Samāᶜ: Listening and Altered States* (London: RoutledgeCurzon, 2004).

38 Fritz Meier, "Khurasan and the End of Classic Ṣūfism," in John O'Kane (trans.), *Essays on Islamic Mysticism and Piety* (Leiden: Brill, 1999), 189–219.

39 Based on comments in treatises concerned with *samāᶜ* about what kind of music was going on in some *dhikr* and *samāᶜ*, it appears singing women and young boys were hired for *samāᶜ* sessions. Al-Ghazālī comments that singing women sang to Ṣūfis and trained to do so early on. See Macdonald, "Emotional Religion in Islam as Affected by Music and Singing" (April 1901): 203. See also Meier, "A Book of Etiquette for Ṣūfis," in John O'Kane (trans.), *Essays on Islamic Mysticism and Piety* (Leiden: Brill, 1999), 49–92, which includes a brief translation of a thirteenth-century Ṣūfi manual. Music and the possible dangers—including hiring attractive singers—are noted on pp. 60–6. See also Meier, "The Dervish Dance: An Attempt at an Overview," 23–48.

40 Sara Amer discusses *naẓar* in "Medieval Arab Lesbians." See also Fritz Meier, "Introduction," *Essays on Islamic Mysticism and Piety*, 20; Meier, "An Important Manuscript Find for Sufism," 153; and Meier, "The Priority of Faith and Thinking Well of Others," 643. See El-Rouayheb, *Before Homosexuality*, 111–18, for discussions about *naẓar* that continued into the nineteenth century.

41 References to Ṣūfis gazing upon beautiful singing men and boys are found in later medieval treatises, although how much of this really took place is hard to say. For example, Hofer also mentions *samāᶜ* sessions as part of regular functions at the *khanqah*. In one story, a Ṣūfi brings a beardless young man to a *samāᶜ* and embraces him, calling him by a name of God (*The Popularisation of Ṣūfism*, 67); in another, a singer, named al-Qawwāl (lit. the Singer, from *qawwāl*) is so moving in his performance, people die when they hear him (74).

42 Although generally supportive of *samāᶜ*, Al-Ghazālī points to five cases where listening is unlawful: (1) in the person producing it (particularly a woman or beardless youth); (2) in the instrument used (tambourines with jingles, stringed instruments, pipes, and instruments associated with the *mukhannathūn*); (3) content of the poetry (satirical, sensual description of a woman or just filthy); (4) in the listener (especially hot-blooded young men who will be tempted or moved to love/lust after the musician); and (5) the commonality of creation (essentially, pursuing it for the thrill of pursuit, regardless of intent). Macdonald, "Emotional Religion in Islam as Affected by Music and Singing" (April 1901): 235–42.

43 Kenneth Avery discusses several examples in *A Psychology of Ṣūfī Samāᶜ: Listening and Altered States*. See also Meier, "A Book of Etiquette for Ṣūfis," 49–92; and Meier, "The Dervish Dance: An Attempt at an Overview," 23–48.

44 Ahmet Karamustafa, *God's Unruly Friends: Dervish Groups in the Islamic Later Middle Period, 1200–1550* (Salt Lake City: University of Utah Press, 1994), 51–6. The association of Persia with unlawful music making becomes stronger in later *samā*ᶜ treatises, possibly reinforced by these assumptions about the origins of certain Ṣūfi groups.

45 The most familiar place to find Qalandars and Haydaris is the *1001 Nights*.

46 There are also analogues to odd behavior in other mystic systems, including Hasidism. The desire to perform an "intense act" in order to be closer to—and to honor—God can be expressed in a variety of physical ways, including ecstatic dance, music, speaking in tongues, and acrobatics. For one example from twentieth-century Hasidism, see Zvi Leshem, "Flipping into Ecstasy: Towards a Syncopal Understanding of Mystical Hasidic Somersaults," *Studia Judaica* 17, no. 1 (2014): 157–84. I am grateful to Dr. Leshem for sharing his expertise in mystic traditions in Judaism and pointing me to his article. Intense acts are controversial in other mystic systems, although still employed in Ṣūfism, Hasidism, and some Christian sects.

47 For an analysis of the radical dervish communities and return of asceticism from 1200 to 1550, see Karamustafa, *God's Unruly Friends*.

48 As noted earlier, there are many important schools of Islamic jurisprudence, but the four major schools that arose in the eighth and ninth centuries are the Shāfiᶜī, Mālikī, Ḥanafi, and Ḥanbali. A medieval legal scholar would study one school or *madhab*, but could hold opinions and expertise in others, or even switch to a different school if they found it more aligned with their thinking.

49 See van Ess, "Ṣūfism and Its Opponents: Reflections on Topoi, Tribulations, and Transformations," in De Jong and Radtke, *Islamic Mysticism Contested*, 29–31. He offers a concise outline of how Ḥanbalism was not antagonistic to Ṣūfism in the medieval period. Since Ḥanbalism is now associated with Wahhabism—and contemporary fundamentalists are hostile to Ṣūfism—it is assumed this has always been the case.

50 For an overview of the origin and tenets of Ḥanbalism, see Laoust, "Hanbilia," *EI*, vol. III, 158–62. For the relationship between Ṣūfism and Ḥanbalism, see George Maqdisi, "The Ḥanbali School and Ṣūfism," *BAEO* 15 (1979) 115–26. See also Christopher Melchert, "The Ḥanbalia and the Early Ṣūfis," *Arabica* 48 (2001): 352–67 for the parallel growth of early Ṣūfism and Ḥanbalism. Melchert makes a strong case for the nascent Ḥanbalis and Ṣūfis coexisting through the evidence of early Ḥanbali *tabaqat*, showing that these groups interacted neutrally in general, despite select condemnation and ideological clashes.

51 Melchert, "The Ḥanbalia and the Early Ṣūfis," 355, 365. The treatise by al-Khallāl has this title, and variations of the concept of "commanding the right and forbidding wrong" are woven into the titles of several of the other texts, which I discuss in the next chapter.

52 See Cook, *Commanding Right and Forbidding Wrong in Islamic Thought*. In chapter 2 ("Koran and Koranic Exegesis," 13–31), Cook provides an outline of the verses from which this injunction comes and different interpretations.

53 For these approaches in the context of Ḥanbalism, see Cook, "Ibn Ḥanbal," in *Commanding Right and Forbidding Wrong in Islamic Thought*, chapter 5, 87–113. He further provides a detailed analysis of al-Khallāl's standpoint and the problem of listening to sound genres. Chapters 6 and 7 go into the Ḥanbalites of Baghdad and Damascus, showing how these questions were addressed from the tenth to the fourteenth centuries.

54 Cook, *Commanding Right and Forbidding Wrong in Islamic Thought*. Reid considers the difficulty of choosing the right path in terms of bodily devotions (abstinence, washing) throughout *Law and Piety*. See also Ephrat and Mahamid, "The Creation of Ṣūfi Spheres."

55 The acquisition of knowledge (*ᶜilm*) was linked to religious observation, as the student was enjoined to enter their lesson in a state of cleanliness and ritual purity. See Reid, *Law and Piety*, 9–10; Chamberlain, *Knowledge and Social Practice*, 125–51; and Berkey, *Transmission of Knowledge in Medieval Cairo*, 3–5.

7 Discomfort and Censure: The Case against *Samāᶜ*

1 The *ṭablkhane*, sometimes transliterated as *ṭabl-khana*, was a drum ensemble. It used specific types of drums, usually for the military, to play a genre specific to the ensemble called *nawba*. The *ṭabl* and *nakkāra* (also transliterated as *naqqāra* or kettledrum) were the main instruments. Such drum ensembles are noted in the pre-Islamic sources as being employed for battle. Under the Umayyads and Abbasids, drum ensembles added *mizmār* and horns. The ensemble was an emblem of rule and used to announce and/or celebrate the investment and achievements of rulers. See Farmer, "Tabl-khana," *EI*, vol. X, 34–8.

2 See Appendix I. Because the bell was of such concern, adding bells and jingles to *dufūf* made them more morally lethal.

3 See al-Sakhāwī, *al-Ḍaw' al-lāmiᶜ*, 12 vols (Cairo: Bab al-Haq, 1935), 80. Shiloah also has a brief summation and bibliography for what little is known about Ibn Burayd in his entry (052) in *The Theory of Music in Arabic Writings (c. 900–1900): Descriptive Catalog of Manuscripts in Libraries of Egypt, Israel, Morocco, Russia, Tunisia, Uzbekistan, and Supplement to B/X* (B/Xa) Repertoire Internationel Des Sources Musicales (RISM) (Munich: G. Henle Verlag, 2003), 94–5. Subsequent references to the 2003 RISM will be RISM 2.

4 Margoliouth, "Kadiriyya," *EI*, vol. IV, 380–3. See also RISM 2, entry on Ibn Burayd. The Qādiriyya are still around today, with several subsects. In North Africa, for

example, there is a subsect of this order called Jilalism, which the Gnawa follow. It is a mystic order syncretized with pre-Islamic traditions. The Gnawa are descended from formerly enslaved people and are known for their rich musical traditions.

5 His name is sometimes transliterated as al-Jili or Djilānī. Because the early Qādiriyya accorded sainthood and ascribed miracles to ᶜAbd al-Qāḍīr al-Jilānī, he has since been deified. Even after his death, he was thought to work miracles from the grave. This practice sparked criticism, however. Ibn Taymiyya mentions al-Jilānī as "among the saints of his time who still appeared to people, being in reality impersonated by demons." See Ephrat and Mahamid, "The Creation of Ṣūfi Spheres," 194–5, 318.

6 The Banū Qudama, of which Diya al-Dīn (al-Maqdisī) was a member, had other members who studied with al-Jilānī.

7 See Fritz Meier, "The Sumadiyya in Damascus," in John O'Kane (trans.), *Essays on Islamic Piety and Mysticism* (Leiden: Brill, 1999), 283–307, particularly 302. See also Carl Brockelmann, *Geschichte der Arabischen Litteratur*, 2 vols (Weimar: E. Felber, 1898–1902), vol. II, 122, #24. Subsequent references to Brockelmann will be abbreviated as "Br." Brockelmann gives Ibn Burayd's name as Ibrāhīm ibn Ali ibn A (Ahmad?) ibn Buraid al-Qāḍiri (d. 1475). The text under his name is: *Mafatih al matalib waraqabat al-talib*, Berlin 3361 (subscript 2). See Br II, 149, but there is no mention of the lost treatise. He lists a treatise that refers to *ṣawt*, however, in section II (Encyclopedia and Polyhistory), under a heading for Shāfi'ī and followers of same.

8 Meier, "The Sumadiyya in Damascus." Meier gives Ibn Burayd's name as Ibrāhīm ibn 'Ali ibn Aḥmad ibn Burayd al-Dayrī al-Ḥalabī al-Qāhirī al-Dimashqī al-Shāfiᶜī al-Qāḍirī (1413–75 CE/816–80 *H*) and confirms the existence of the treatise related to the Sumadiyya drum, called *Al-naṣīḥa li-dafᶜ al-faḍīḥa* (302). His article also discusses the drum specific to the Sumadiyya, its origins and use, including references to Sumadiyya playing it in the Umayyad Mosque. In the Sumadiyya traditions, the special drum was linked to the Battle of Acre as well as other key events and personages in their order. Later, the original drum was brought out only for special occasions.

9 See Jonathan Berkey's, *The Transmission of Knowledge in Medieval Cairo*; and Chamberlain, *Knowledge and Social Practice*.

10 See Talmon-Heller, *Islamic Piety*, 59–85, with note on Ṣūfi and *samāᶜ* (78–85). See also Jonathan Berkey, *Popular Preaching and Religious Authority in the Medieval Islamic Near East* (Seattle: University of Washington Press, 2001); and Chamberlain, *Knowledge and Social Practice*.

11 A comparison of the al-Ẓāhiriyya manuscripts to those in the NLI might give more insight into who copied them, and if Ibn Burayd contributed copies himself. Unfortunately, that is currently not possible. Most of the library holdings were transferred to the modern al-Assad library around 2009–10.

12 How the collection came to be in the National Library of Israel is another fascinating question. I consider the possible modern history in my article "*Samāᶜ* Intertwined in Practice: Eight Treatises from the 9th to the 15th Centuries," in Reinhard Strohm (ed.), *The Music Road: Coherence and Diversity in Music from the Mediterranean to India*, Proceedings of the British Academy, no. 223 (Oxford: Oxford University Press, 2019), 126–47.

13 These comments are presumably by him, though there are some variations in the writing suggesting later commentators.

14 The title given in the NLI catalogue is *Majmūᶜ fi mas'alat al-samāᶜ wa'l-malāhī* (A collection of treatises concerning music and musical instruments). The protective cover in which the book is kept has the following title: *Majmūᶜ Ibn Burayd al-Qāḍirī, fi mas'alat al-samāᶜ wa ma yasbihūm al-malāhī* (A collection of Ibn Burayd al-Qāḍrī of treatises concerning listening and condemnation of musical instruments).

15 Although the *shuᶜūbiyya* movement was on the wane by the ninth century, it is possible the conflation of music with Persia and other foreign influences was derived, in part, from this movement. For a discussion of the movement, see Ignaz Goldziher, "The Shu'ubiyya" and "The Shu'ubiyya and Its Manifestation in Scholarship," in *Muslim Studies (Muhammedanische Studien)*. See also Roy Mottahedeh, "The Shu'ubiyah Controversy and the Social History of Early Islamic Iran," *International Journal of Middle East Studies* 7, no. 2 (1976): 161–82.

16 See M. J. Kister, "'Exert yourselves, O Banū Arfida!': Some Notes on Entertainment in the Islamic Tradition," *Jerusalem Studies in Arabic and Islam* 23 (1999): 67. This story is in the treatise by Diya al-Dīn. Kister is among the few scholars to take a closer look at the NLI collection, and his article gives a quick overview of the key arguments used against *samāᶜ*.

17 Goldziher makes note that "fanatics asserted the Persians were descended from Lot" in his article on "'Arab and ᶜAdjam," in *Muslim Studies (Muhammedanische Studien)*, 135, n. 4, citing p. 8 of Ibn Badrūn. In addition, al-Mas'ūdī states that some people think the Persians were the offspring of Lot, through his children Rabbatha and Zaᶜritha. He, however, does not agree. See al-Mas'ūdī, *Les Prairies D'or*, vol. 1, chapter 23, 211.

18 By this time, the caliphate had moved to Samarra, but al-Muwaffaq remained in Baghdad. Al-Muᶜtaḍid was the last Abbasid to rule the empire independently. He was considered abstemious by nature, pious and not as given to courtly excess as some of his predecessors.

19 See R. A. Kimber, "Ibn Abi'l Dunya," in Julie Meisami and Paul Starkey (eds.), *Routledge Encyclopedia of Arabic Literature* (New York: Routledge, 2010), 304.

20 "[Ibn Abi'l Dūnya] was well-regarded as a traditionalist, and composed over a hundred books, mostly of a religiously edifying character promoting

abstemiousness and simplicity of living, virtues for which he himself was respected. He could be entertaining as well as solemn, and reduced al-Muwaffaq to helpless laughter on occasion" (ibid.). There is also a poem attributed to him in the *Muwashshā'*, and apparently al-Tanūkhi referred to Ibn Abi'l Dūnya's books for some of his anecdotes.

21 See Robson, introduction to Abū Dūnya's treatise in *Tracts on Listening to Music*, 15. The missing books are: *Censure of Envy* (*Dhamm al-ḥasad*), *Censure of the World* (*Dhamm al-dūnya*), *Censure of Anger* (*Dhamm al-ghaḍab*), *Censure of Slander* (*Dhamm al-ghība*), *Censure of Obscenity* (*Dhamm al-faḥsh*), and *Censure of Intoxicants* (*Dhamm al-muskir*). Robson attributes his catalog of Ibn Abi'l Dūnya's work to the Arabist Alfred Wiener. Brockelmann lists forty-three works by Ibn Abi'l Dūnya, and subsequent research has shown that many more of Ibn Abi'l Dūnya's works exist. See Leonard Librande, "Ibn Abi al-Dunyā: Certainty and Morality," *Studia Islamica* 100/101 (2005): 5–42; and Leah Kinberg, *Morality in the Guise of Dreams: A Critical Edition of Kitāb al-Manām of Ibn Abi al-Dūnya*, vol. XVIII, Islamic Philosophy, Theology and Science, ed. H. Daiber and D. Pingree (Leiden: E.J. Brill, 1994).

22 The popularity of his work is attested to by the survival of a number of his books as well as references to his popularity sprinkled throughout other books. That his work is still appealing is seen in the recent revival and publication of a number of his works. See Librande, "Ibn Abi al-Dunyā: Certainty and Morality," 5–11.

23 Ibid., 12.

24 Robson and Shiloah also make this suggestion.

25 Shoshan, "High Culture and Popular Culture in Medieval Islam."

26 For discussion of these genres, see Reid, *Law and Piety*; and Cook, *Commanding Right and Forbidding Wrong in Islamic Thought*. Throughout the treatise, at no point does Ibn Abi'l Dūnya offer his own opinion; rather, he lets the *ḥadīth* and selected exegetical commentary speak for him. His only additions are in the form of brief comments interspersed with the *ḥadīth* intended to illuminate a particular point and clarify a given anecdote or *ḥadīth*, which is consistent with the *zuhd* writing style.

27 See Librande, "Ibn Abi al-Dūnya: Certainty and Morality," 8–9.

28 Ibid. See also Kinberg, *Morality in the Guise of Dreams*.

29 Ibn Abi'l Dūnya refers to himself only once in the Berlin text, identified as "the sheik," at the beginning of a long commentary wherein he clarifies fifteen unlawful acts that will bring affliction. In the NLI text, he himself appears as an authority.

30 Ap. Ar. 158/8, f. 73a–84b, in the NLI collection. Robson's translation includes the Arabic, except the pagination matches the English, and therefore proceeds from left to right. For a modern Arabic edition, see Ibn Abi'l Dūnya, *Dhamm al-Malāhī* (al-Qāhira: Dār al-Itiṣām, 1987). For locations of the other manuscript copies, see

the entry for Ibn Abi'l Dūnya in Amnon Shiloah, *The Theory of Music in Arabic Writings (c. 900–1900): Descriptive Catalogue of Manuscripts in Libraries of Europe and the USA*, Repertoire Internationel Des Sources Musicales (RISM) (Munich: G. Henle Verlag, 1979). Subsequent references to the 1979 RISM will be RISM 1. Ibn Abi'l Dūnya also has a reference in RISM 2 which lists holdings of his work outside of Europe.

31 The abridged version is the basis for Robson's 1937 translation and the more recent Arabic edition. Whether Ibn Abi'l Dūnya abridged the *Censure* himself—or expanded it to include more variants—is unknown.

32 The Arabic for "the *qaināt* are the singing girls" reads القينات الجواري المغنيات (al-qaināt al-jawārī al-mughanniyat). The translation is "the singing women, the singing slave concubines." The incipit is identical in both the Berlin and NLI manuscripts, although this sentence is written along the margin of the first page in the NLI version.

33 As in Judaism, pigs are unclean animals and apes are close to humans; therefore, both are unlawful. Robson cites the Qur'an as a source for this prophecy; however, the Qur'an only refers to behaving as apes as an act of transgression, rather than actual transformation. See 2:65, 7:166 for examples. Though some of the *ḥadīth* transmitters may have meant actual transformation, the Arabic term Dūnya uses, مسخ, also means spiritual metamorphosis and falsity. See the modern Arabic edition, Ibn Abi'l Dūnya, *Dhamm al-Malāhī*, 32, n. 1.

34 Robson, *Censure*, 29; Ibn Abi'l Dūnya, *Dhamm al-Malāhī*, 43, 52. The *ḥadīth* has many variants, but essentially states the Prophet cursed women who imitated men and men who imitated women.

35 Ibn Abi'l al-Dūnya uses the Arabic for "one who prefers anal sex with men in the passive position," اللوطي (*lūṭī*), which comes from the name Lot: لوط. The infamous story of Lot and the men of Sodom and Gomorrah is also part of Islamic exegesis. *Liwāṭ* did not strictly mean same-sex preference in the modern construct of "homosexuality," although it does denote a sexual preference of being the passive partner. Those with this preference are *lūṭi*. For a discussion of this linguistic distinction, see Rowson, "The Categorization of Gender and Sexual Irregularity in Medieval Arabic Vice Lists"; and El-Rouayheb, *Before Homosexuality*. For a detailed discussion of *liwāṭ* within Islamic law, see Jonathan Brown, "A Pre-Modern Defense of the *hadīths* on Sodomy: An Annotated Translation and Analysis of al-Suyuti's *Attaining the Hoped For in Service of the Messenger(s)*," *American Journal of Islamic Social Sciences* 34, no. 3 (2017): 1–44.

36 Robson, *Censure*, 40. Rendering controversial language into Latin or putting ellipses in their place was common practice in nineteenth- and early-twentieth-century translations of Arabic, Greek, and Persian literature. For example, some editions of the comedies of Aristophanes used Latin or replaced questionable

language with ellipses. Given that Aristophanes is quite filthy, such editing choices makes his work incomprehensible in translation.

37 Laoust, "Hanabilia," *EI*, vol. III, 158–62, which includes a brief discussion of al-Khallāl and his importance as a compiler of Ḥanbali teachings. Laoust, "Al-Khallal," *EI*, vol. IV, 989–90; and Laoust, *Les Schismes dans L'Islam* (Paris: Payot, 1965), 116–17, 125. See also Zaiuddin Ahmad, "Abū Bakr Al-Khallāl—The Compiler of the Teachings of Imām Ahmad b. Ḥanbal," *Islamic Studies* 9, no. 3 (1970): 245–54; and Cook, *Commanding Right and Forbidding Wrong in Islamic Thought*, 87–100.

38 Laoust, "Hanabilia."

39 Ibid.

40 Ibid. This text is referenced in Br. Supplement 1, 311.

41 Ap. Ar. 158/4, f. 38a–58a, in the NLI collection. One modern edition of *al-Amr* is edited by ʿAbd al-Qāḍir Ahmed ᶜAta (Cairo, 1975.) Cook provides a brief assessment of this edition in a detailed footnote, noting it is useful, if unscholarly and missing elements. He also compared it with a copy made of the version in Ap. Ar. 158. See Cook, *Commanding Right and Forbidding Wrong in Islamic Thought*, 88.

42 Shiloah, RISM 2, 124–5.

43 Laoust describes its tone as offering "a strong criticism of the life of luxury and ease enjoyed by the caliphal circles and the Turkish amirs which formed part of them." Laoust, "al-Khallal."

44 Cook, *Commanding Right and Forbidding Wrong in Islamic Thought*, 87–113.

45 Al-Khallāl, *al-Amr*, mention of *jāriya*, 46a; *qiyān*, 49a and b; *mughanniyat*, 53a; and *mukhannathūn*, 57a.

46 See Shiloah, RISM 2, 124–5; and Cook, *Commanding Right and Forbidding Wrong in Islamic Thought*, 98.

47 This section starts at the bottom of 54a in the NLI manuscript.

48 Mohammad Marmaduke Pickthall (trans.), *The Meaning of the Glorious Koran* (Hyderabad-Deccan: Government Central Press, 1938), https://www.sacred-texts.com/isl/pick/037.htm. These verses have a number of possible translations. Arberry translates it as: "Nay, thou marvellest; than they scoff, and when reminded do not remember." Arberry, *The Koran Interpreted*, 150. Ali renders it thus: "Truly thou dost marvel, while they ridicule. And when they are admonished, pay no heed." Ali, *The Meaning of the Holy Qu'ran*, 1138. In the manuscript, it is at the bottom of 55a.

49 See Lane, *Lexicon*, vol. II, 1956–8. See also Wehr, *Dictionary*, 691.

50 Al-Ājurrī does not have his own entry in the *Encyclopedia of Islam*, although he is mentioned in *EI2* in Laoust's entry under Hanabila, vol. III, 159. In this section, Laoust notes that al-Ājurrī is "claimed at the same time by Ḥanbalism and Shafism

… his *al-Sharia* shows obvious affinities with the professions of faith in the Ḥanbali style." See also Laoust, *Les Schismes dans L'Islam*, 174.

51 Ibn Khallikan, *Wafiyat al-a'yan wa-anba abna al-zaman*, 8 vols., ed. Ihsan ᶜAbbas Wadād Qādī and ᶜIzz al-Dīn ᶜUmar Aḥmad (Beirut: Dār Ṣader , 1968–94). Al-Ājurrī is listed under Abū Bakr (p. 84 in the concordance, vol. 8), 4:292–3, 5:256, 7:330. His biographic entry is in vol. 4.

52 See *Fihrist*, index, p. 1055, and his brief entry in chapter 6, section 3, p. 526. He is in the section of adherents of al-Shāfiᶜī and their books, full name given as Muḥammad ibn al-Husayn ibn ᶜUbayd Allah al-Ājurrī Abū Bakr, noted as a Shāfiᶜī jurist who lived in Mecca and died in 970 CE.

53 Ap. Ar. 158/1, f. 1a–10a, in the NLI collection. There are two other known extant copies, one in Syria (formerly in the al-Ẓāhiriyya library, probably now in al-Assad) and the other in the Baladiyya Library in Alexandria, Egypt (ET-AB ms. 2127d). There is another manuscript in the Egyptian collection, #052 in RISM, and it is a copy of Ibn Burayd's treatise. See Shiloah, RISM 2, 39–41.

54 Al-Ājurrī, *al-Jawāb*, 2b.

55 In 4a, he clarifies that *jawārī* are instrumentalists who sing, literally "enslaved women who strike song," using a form of *ḍaraba*.

56 Al-Ājurrī also wrote a book condemning *liwāṭ*. See Brown, "A pre-Modern Defense," 2, n. 1.

57 He uses *jawārī* for "purchase of slave women singers."

58 Noted at the bottom of 4b.

59 See also Sawa, *Music Performance Practice*, 149.

60 At the top of 5a.

61 Al-Ājurrī, *al-Jawāb*, 5b.

62 This page also has a marginal note, possibly a correction, halfway down the page, that says "in the heart."

63 Ibid., 6b.

64 Ibid., 7b.

65 Ibid., begins on 8b.

66 See George Maqdisi, "Muslim Institutions of Learning in Eleventh-Century Baghdad," 12–13. Apparently, Ibn ᶜAkīl was appointed when Abū'l Ṭayyib was semiretired at the age of 80.

67 J. Wakin, "Abu'l-Tayyeb Tabari," *Encyclopedia Iranica*, I/4, 390; an updated version is available online at http://www.iranicaonline.org/articles/abul-tayyeb-tabari (accessed February 2, 2014). See also E. Chaumont, "Al-Ṭabarī," *EI*, 2nd ed., vol. X, 15–16.

68 Maqdisi, "Muslim Institutions of Learning in Eleventh-Century Baghdad," 23–4.

69 See al-Ghazālī, Macdonald, "Emotional Religion in Islam as Affected by Music and Singing," 200–202.

70 Ibid. J. Wakin, "Abu'l-Tayyeb Tabari," *Encyclopedia Iranica*; and E. Chaumont, "Al-Ṭabarī," *EI*, 2nd ed., vol. X, 15–16.

71 See *Encyclopedia Iranica* and *EI* for his works. He has two entries in RISM 2, 112 and 113, 177–9.

72 Ap. Ar. 158/9, f.85a–91b, in the NLI collection. There is no modern edition or translation of the *Kitāb fīhi mas'alat*.

73 Abū'l Ṭayyib's treatise is also on similar paper as the *Censure*—slightly rougher and less polished than the others—with the same number of lines per page, approximately twenty-nine to thirty. All the other treatises have nineteen lines per page. There are several marginal comments, including one lengthy notation that takes up a lot of space on 85a. Sadly, the paper was cut down at some point, cutting off some of the text.

74 As in the other treatises, chapters and topics within each text are indicated in red ink.

75 Abū'l Ṭayyib, bottom of 84b.

76 He uses *mamlūk* and *jāriya* to refer to slaves. In his discussion of *samā*ᶜ, al-Ghazālī references this quotation, citing Abū'l Ṭayyib as the source. See Macdonald, "Emotional Religion in Islam as Affected by Music and Singing," (April 1091):199–201.

77 Abū'l Ṭayyib, bottom of 86b.

78 Abū'l Ṭayyib, 87a. See bottom of the page for various consequences.

79 Abū'l Ṭayyib, beginning of 88b.

80 Abū'l Ṭayyib, 85a. This is a blunt criticism of some Ṣūfi practices of embellishing sacred poetry and accompanying recitation.

81 Abū'l Ṭayyib, 89a.

82 Br I, 398, no. 14, states Diya al-Dīn was born 569/1173 in Dair al-Mubarak; he died in 643/1245. He studied in 595/1197 in Egypt, then in Baghdad, where he heard al-Gauzi (Jawzi?) in 597/1200 (s. 500), and in Hamadan. In 600/1203 he went to Damascus. Brockelmann lists three other books attributed to him.

83 Talmon-Heller, *Islamic Piety*. See also Daniella Talmon-Heller, "The Shaykh and the Community: Popular Ḥanbalite Islam in 12th–13th Century Jabal Nablus and Jabal Qaysūn," *Studia Islamica* 79 (1994): 103–20. This article focuses on three works by Diya al-Dīn and the role of the sheik in the community. Her translation of selections from the biographies Diya al-Dīn wrote on people from his community are in "*The Cited Tales of the Wondrous Doings of the Shaykhs of the Holy Land* by Diya al-Dīn Abu 'Abd Allah Muḥammad b. 'Abd al-Wahid al-Maqdisī (569/1173–643/1245): Text, Translation and Commentary," *Crusades* 1 (2002): 111–54.

84 Talmon-Heller, *Islamic Piety*, 121.

85 Talmon-Heller, "*Wondrous Doings*," 150. See also Talmon-Heller, *Islamic Piety*.

86 See Talmon-Heller, "*Wondrous Doings*," 148–9. She notes that although the Ḥanbali position was that no musical instruments were allowed, the general viewpoint was that tambourines were acceptable at weddings (149, citation #141).

87 Ap. Ar. 158/3, f. 21a–37b, in NLI collection. Diya al-Dīn's entry in RISM 2 is on pp. 132–3. There is no modern edition of *Al-amr bi-itbāᶜ al-sunan wa ijtināb al-bidaᶜ*.

88 Diya al-Dīn, 21a.

89 Ibid., 21b.

90 Diya al-Dīn's concerns point to the kinds of music used in some *dhikr* and *samāᶜ*, particularly that singers were hired for *samāᶜ* sessions. Such concerns are noted in some Ṣūfi manuals. See, for example, Meier, "A Book of Etiquette for Ṣūfis," 49–92.

91 Junayd (d. 910 CE) was a major early Ṣūfi mystic who was originally from Persia and later settled in Baghdad. He was among the adherents to the "sober" direction, which implies he would not have approved of the *dhikr* and *samāᶜ* used by other Ṣūfis.

92 See Shiloah's outline of the treatise in RISM 2 and Kister, " 'Exert Yourselves, O Banū Arfida!' " for a discussion of this story. The story begins on p. 35a of the manuscript.

93 Thankfully, Dr. Arjan Post of Utrecht University has filled this gap. I am grateful to Dr. Post for generously sharing his work on al-Wāsiṭī from his dissertation, "The Journey of a Taymiyyan Ṣūfi: Ṣūfism through the Eyes of ʿImād al-Dīn Aḥmad al-Wāsiṭī (d. 711/1311)," recently published by Brill as *The Journeys of a Taymiyyan Ṣūfi: Ṣūfism through the Eyes of ʿImād al-Dīn Aḥmad al-Wāsiṭī (d. 711/1311)*, Studies in Sufism, Band 6 (Leiden: Brill, 2020). For the slender information available prior, see Laoust, *Les Schismes dans L'Islam*, 274. See also Br II, 208, which lists him as al-Wāsiṭī al-Ḥanbali Imad al-Dīn l'Abbas bin al-Arif al-Hizami (d. 711/1311) and notes two extant books (Transliteration from Br): *Muhtasar al-sira an-nabawiya*, Auszugaus b. Hisham (1, 141), mss in Berl. 9566/7; *Miftah tariq al-muhibbin wabab al-uns birabb al-ᶜalamin al-mu'addi ila ahwal al-muqarrabin*, Mystic, Kairo II, 177. Brockelmann further notes that there is a fragment of an answer to a theological question on listening, which could be the same texts as in the NLI collection. Al-Wāsiṭī also wrote a work entitled *al-Tadhkirat*, which Brockelmann does not mention.

94 His name is sometimes transliterated as "Al-Wassiti."

95 The Shādhilīyya order, originating with the Moroccan sheik Abū al-Ḥasan al-Shādhilī in the thirteenth century, was popular in Egypt and North Africa. See P. Lory, "Shādhiliyya," *EI*, http://dx.doi.org/10.1163/1573-3912_islam_SIM_6736 (accessed December 27, 2019).

96 See Arjan Post, "A Taymiyyan Ṣūfi's Refutation of the Akbarian School: ʿImād al-Dīn Aḥmad al-Wāsiṭī's (d. 711/1311) *Lawāmiʿ l-istirshād*," in Kristof D'hulster,

Gino Schallenbergh, and Jo Van Steenbergen (eds.), *CHESFAME Proceedings IX* (Leuven: Peeters, 2019), 309–25.

97 Ibid.

98 See Henry George Farmer, *The Sources of Arabian Music; an Annotated Bibliography of Arabic Manuscripts Which Deal with the Theory, Practice, and History of Arabian Music from the Eighth to the Seventeenth Century* (Leiden: E.J. Brill, 1965), 262.

99 The question is Ap. Ar. 158, f. 62a–62b, and answer is f. 64a–72b. Al-Wāsiṭī is listed twice in RISM 2, entries 123 and 124, 197–9, with his name spelled two different ways. There are no modern editions of either text.

100 The title page is on 62a, question on 62b.

101 The blank page, 63b, has two lines of text, written upside down and in pencil, suggesting it might be a modern notation. I asked my colleague Dr. Pernilla Myrne for her assistance in deciphering it, and she interpreted it as a scrap of poetry, likely modern. There is at least one other penciled notation in the book—that noting the catalog number of Ibn Abi'l Dūnya's *Censure* held in Berlin—so this notation might be a modern doodle.

102 Al-Wāsiṭī, 64a.

103 As with the other dates used by the authors these are in *hijra* years in the manuscript. I have rendered them into Common Era here.

104 Shiloah offers a deft summary of each chapter in RISM2, 197–9.

105 See 72a for gazing at young men and the excitement of *naẓar* when enhanced by playing the *duff* and singing.

106 Kamal Salibi, "Ibn Djama'a," *EI*, vol. III, 748–9.

107 Ibid. For a detailed summation of the Banū Jamā'a and the different family branches to the sixteenth century, see Kamal Salibi, "The Banū Jamā'a: A Dynasty of Shāfi'ite Jurists during the Mamlūk Era," *Studia Islamica* 9 (1958): 97–109. A more recent study of the family after the sixteenth century is Elizabeth Sirriyeh, "Whatever Happened to the Banū Jamā'a? The Tail of a Scholarly Family in Ottoman Syria," *British Journal of Middle Eastern Studies* 28, no. 1 (2001): 55–65.

108 Burhān al-Dīn oversaw the initial restoration. For images and a brief summary, see Yusuf al-Natsheh, "Minbar of Burhān al-Dīn," in *Discover Islamic Art*, Museum With No Frontiers, http://islamicart.museumwnf.org/database_item.php?id=monument;ISL;pa;Mon01;32;en&pageD=N (last accessed September 16, 2020).

109 Burhān al-Dīn has two entries in RISM 1, 160–2, listing two texts related to music. In RISM 2, his entry is on 104–5.

110 See Farmer, *The Source of Arabian Music*, 286. The catalogue number given by Farmer for the Berlin treatise is 5510. Br II, 112, #14, notes it as Berl. 5511, as does Shiloah, RISM 1, 161.

111 Ap Ar 158, f.11a–20a. There is no modern edition of the treatise.

112 Burhān al-Dīn, 11a. The title page has the lecture title in red ink and states: "From the qāḍī and learned man of religion, Ibn Jamāᶜa, an answer given while he was lecturing in Jerusalem in the year 772." The copy date is given at the end of the treatise.

113 See Meier, "The Sumadiyya in Damascus," 283–307.

114 Kister offers a summation of Burhān al-Dīn's opinions in "'Exert Yourselves, O Banū Arfida!'" 67, 71.

115 The phrase is *ghanihū al-mughiyya ḍaraba*, roughly, singers striking song. Use of *ḍaraba* implies song accompanied by drum and lute.

116 Ibid.

117 Burhān al-Dīn, 16b.

118 Ibid., 18a.

119 Ibid.

120 Ibid., 19a. See RISM 2 for a concise overview.

121 The Hypocrites were a faction who converted to Islam but contested the Prophet and his teachings. Their criticism led others to believe their conversion was skin deep and they secretly did not believe. Therefore, hypocrisy is a major sin, and references to it refer to both the early history of Islam and personal practice of religion.

122 See Reid, *Law and Piety*, 147. What was considered filthy, and the extension of purity (*tahara*), was subject to much confusion and discussion.

123 See George Sawa's magisterial study of uses and theories of rhythm in *Rhythmic Theories and Practices in Arabic Writings to 339 AH/950 CE*. See also Yaron Klein, "Musical Instruments as Objects of Meaning in Classical Arabic Poetry and Philosophy" (dissertation, Harvard University, 2008).

124 In addition to clapping and the sounds of their bodies, many dance traditions use instruments. Examples include the subtle unfurling of a fan in traditional Chinese and Japanese dance and use of percussion in bhangra.

125 Use of a prop in storytelling is still common. For example, in Damascus, Syria, one could hear a storyteller on certain nights in a teashop, who emphasized his narrative with well-timed whacks on the table with a sword. Even if one did not know what the story was, his performance made the story exciting to hear.

126 See Reid, *Law and Piety*.

8 Reflections

1 Al-Jāḥiẓ comments on the imposition of the veil in the *Risālat al-Qiyān*. Although he is writing satire, he cites precedent supporting more autonomy for women in the past.

Appendix I

1 The topic of music is under discussion in some circles today, and there are a number of contemporary articles and commentary that invoke many of the same *ḥadīth* found in the NLI treatises. Along with the treatises themselves, an article by Sautush Shaitaan for *Majlis* (vol. 16, no. 6, http://themajlis.net/Article146.html) handily pulls many *ḥadīth* concerning music together.

2 That is not to say they are more true or authentic, however. Some well-known reciters of *ḥadīth* were known to have changed the story to suit their own opinion, and some simply made up new traditions. See G. H. A. Juynboll, *Muslim Tradition: Studies in Chronology, Provenance and Authorship of Early Hadith*, Cambridge Studies in Islamic Civilization, ed. Michael Cook, Martin Hinds, Albert Hourani, Roy Mottahedeh, and Josef van Ess (Cambridge: Cambridge University Press, 1983).

Bibliography

Abbreviations

Br Brockelmann
EI Encyclopedia of Islam
RISM 1 Répertoire International des Sources Musicales—*RISM (1979)*
RISM 2 RISM (2003)

Manuscripts

Ap. Ar. 158/1, f. 1a–10a, al-Ājurrī: *Al-jawāb ᶜan mas'alat al-samāᶜ* (Response to the question regarding listening).

Ap. Ar. 158/2, f. 11a–20a, Ibn Jamā'a: *Suwwāl sālahu shakhṣ min al-fuqarā'* (Response to a *faqīr*).

Ap. Ar. 158/3, f. 21a–37b, al-Maqdisī: *Al-amr bi-itbāᶜ al-sunan wa ijtināb al-bidaᶜ* (The command to follow established laws and avoid heresy).

Ap. Ar. 158/4, f. 38a–58a, al-Khallāl: *Al-amr bi'l maᶜrūf wa'l-nahy ᶜan al-munkar* (Commanding the proper and condemnation of the improper).

Ap. Ar. 158/5, f. 58b–61b, al-Khallāl: *Kitāb al-qirā ᶜan al-qabūr.*

Ap. Ar. 158/6, f. 62a–62b, al-Wāsiṭī: *Mas'alat fi al-samāᶜ* (Question regarding *samāᶜ*).

Ap. Ar. 158/7, f. 64a–72b, al-Wāsiṭī: *Al-bulghat wa'l iqnaᶜ fi ḥill shubhat mas'alat al-samāᶜ* (The exaggeration and persuasion of those who declare *samāᶜ* is permitted).

Ap. Ar. 158/8, f. 73a–84b, Ibn Abi'l-Dūnya: *Dhamm al-Malāhī* (Censure of instruments of diversion).

Ap. Ar. 158/9, f. 85a–91b, al-Ṭabari: *Kitāb fihi mas'alat fi'l radd ᶜalā man yaqūl bi-jawāz al-samāᶜ al-ghinā' wa'l raqṣ wa'l taghbīr* (Book refuting the opinions of those who allow listening to music, dance, and the *taghbīr*).

Ap. Ar. 158/1, f. 92a–155b, Ibn Rajab: *Fū'ayn min Kalām Ibn Rajab* (A collection of teachings by Ibn Rajab).

Primary Sources

Ali, Abdullah Yusef. *The Meaning of the Holy Qur'an*, 9th ed. Beltsville, MD: Amana, 1997.

al-Andalusi, Said ibn Ahmad. *Tabaqat al-Umam* (The Categories of Nations). History of Science Series, no. 5. Translated by Sema'an I. Salem and Alok Kumar. Austin, TX: University of Austin Press, 1991.

Arberry, A. J., trans. *The Koran Interpreted*. New York: Simon & Schuster, 1996.

Arberry, A. J. *The Seven Odes: The First Chapter in Arabic Literature*. London: G. Allen & Unwin, 1957.

Dūnya, Abū. *Tracts on Listening to Music: Being the Dhamm al-Malāhī of Ibn Abi Dūnya*. Translated by James Robson, The Royal Asiatic Society Translation Services. London: Royal Asiatic Society, 1937.

al-Ghazālī, Abū Hamid Muḥammad ibn Muḥammad al-Tusi. *Kitāb ihya ᶜulum al-dīn*. Miṣr: Al-Matba al-Amira al-Sharfeyya, 1908–10.

Hadith Collection Online. http://hadithcollection.com/.

Ibn Abi'l Dūnya, Abū Bakr 'Abdullāh ibn Muḥammad ibn Sufyān. *Dhamm al-Malāhī*. al-Qāhira: Dār al-Itiṣām, 1987.

Ibn al-Sāᶜī. *Consorts of the Caliphs*. The Library of Arabic Literature. Translated by Shawkat Toowara. New York: New York University Press, 2015.

Ibn al-Washsha, Abū Ṭayib ibn Muḥammad ibn Isḥāq. *Le Livre De Brocart (The Book of Brocades)*. Translated by Siham Bouhlal. Paris: Editions Gallimard, 2004.

Ibn al-Washsha, Abū Ṭayib ibn Muḥammad ibn Isḥāq. *Muwashshā', or al-zarf wa'l zurafa'*. Beirut: Dar Sadr, 1960.

Ibn ᶜAbd Rabbih. *The Unique Necklace (Al-ᶜIqd al-Farid)*. 2 vols. Translated by Issa J. Boullata. Reading: Garnet, 2006.

Ibn Khaldun. *The Muqaddimah, an Introduction to History*. Translated by Franz Rosenthal. Edited and abridged by N. J. Dawood. Vol. 160, Bollingen Series. Princeton, NJ: Princeton University Press, 1969.

Ibn Khallikan. *Wafiyat al-a'yan wa-anba abna al-zamān*. 8 vols. Edited by Ihsan ᶜAbbas Wadād Qādī and ᶜIzz al-Dīn ᶜUmar Aḥmad. Beirut: Dār Ṣader, 1968–94.

Ibn Khurdādhbih. *Mukhtār Kitāb al-Lahw wa'l Malāhī*. Nusūs wa darūs, 17. Beirut: al-Matbaᶜa al-kātūlīkīya, 1961.

Ibn Salama. *Kitāb al-Malāhī min qibal al-mūsīqā*. Cairo: al-Haya' al-miṣriya al-ᶜamma' al-kitāb, 1984.

al-Iṣbahānī, Abū'l faraj. *Kitāb al-Aghānī*. 24 vols. Cairo: Dār al-Kutub, 1927–74.

al-Iṣbahānī, Abū'l faraj. *Kitāb al-Aghānī*. 24 vols. Turathina, Beirut: Dār al-Thaqāfah, 1955–61.

al-Iṣbahānī, Abū'l faraj. *Kitāb al-Aghānī*. 25 Vols. Beirut: Dār Ṣader, 2004.

al-Jāḥiẓ. *The Epistle on the Singing Girls*. Translated by A. F. L. Beeston. Edited by Kamal Abu Deeb, Approaches to Arabic Literature. Warminster: Aris & Phillips, 1980.

al-Jāḥiẓ. *Nine Essays of al-Jāhiz*. Translated by William M. Hutchins. Vol. 53, American University Studies, Series VII, Theology and Religion. New York: Peter Lang, 1989.

al-Jāḥiẓ. *Sobriety and Mirth: A Selection of the Shorter Writings by Al-Jahiz*. The Keagan Paul Arabia Library. Translated by Jim Colville. London: Routledge, 2013.

al-Kalbī, Hishām ibn. *The Book of Idols (Kitāb al-Asman)*. Translated by Nabih Feris. Princeton, NJ: Princeton University Press, 1952.

al-Mas'ūdī. *Les Prairies D'or*. Translated by Barbier de Meynard and Abel Pavet de Courteille. Revised and corrected by Charles Pellat. Paris: Société asiatique, 1962.

al-Mas'ūdī. *The Meadows of Gold: The Abbasids*. Translated by Paul Lunde and Caroline Stone. London: Kegan Paul, 1989.

al-Mas'ūdī. *Murūj al-Dhahab wa maᶜādin al-jawhar*. 4 vols. Beirut: Dār al-Andalus, 1965–66.

Muflihun. https://muflihun.com/.

al-Muqaddasī. *The Best Divisions for Knowledge of the Regions* (Ahsan al-Taqasim fi Ma'rifat al-Aqalim). Centre for Muslim Contribution to Civilization. Translated by Basil Anthony Collins. Reading: Garnet, 1994.

al-Nadīm. *The Fihrist of Ibn al-Nadīm: A 10th Century Survey of Muslim Culture*. 2 vols. Records of Civilization, Sources and Titles. Translated by Bayard Dodge. Edited by Bayard Dodge. New York: Columbia University Press, 1970.

Pickthall, M. M. (Mohammad Marmaduke), trans. *The Meaning of the Glorious Koran*. Hyderabad Deccan: Government Central Press, 1938. https://www.sacred-texts.com/isl/pick/index.htm.

al-Sabi, Hilal. *Rusum Dar l-Khilafah (the Rules and Regulations of the ᶜAbbasid Court)*. Unesco Collection of Representative Works, Arabic Series. Translated by Elie A. Salem, Beirut: Lebanese Commission for the Translation of Great Works, 1977.

al-Safa, Ikhwān. *The Epistle on Music*. Translated by Amnon Shiloah. Tel Aviv: Tel Aviv University, 1978.

al-Sakhāwī. *al-Ḍaw' al-lāmiᶜ*. 12 vols. Cairo: Bab al-Haq, 1935.

al-Ṭabarī. *The Early ᶜAbbasi Empire: The Reign of Abu Jaᶜfar al-Mansur (AD 754–775)*. 2 vols. Vol. 1. Translated by John Alden Williams. Cambridge: Cambridge University Press, 1988.

al-Ṭabarī. *The Early ᶜAbbasi Empire: The Sons and Grandsons of al-Mansur. The Reigns of al-Mahdi, al-Hadi and Harun al-Rashid*. 2 vols. Vol. 2. Translated by John Alden Williams. Cambridge: Cambridge University Press, 1989.

al-Ṭabarī. *Al-Mansur and al-Mahdi A.D. 763–786/A.H. 146–169*. Vol. 29. Translated by Hugh Kennedy. New York: New York University Press, 1990.

al-Tanūkhi, al-Muhassin ibn Ali. *Nishwār al-muḥaḍārah*. Vol. 2. Beirut: Dār al-Kutub, 2004.

al-Tanūkhi, al-Muhassin ibn Ali. *Table Talk of a Mesopotamian Judge*. Translated by D. S. Margoliouth. London: Royal Asiatic Society, 1922.

Secondary Sources

Abbott, Nabia. *Two Queens of Baghdad*. Chicago, IL: University of Chicago Press, 1946.

Abbott, Nabia. "Women and the State in Early Islam." *Journal of Near Eastern Studies* 1, no. 3 (1942): 341–68.

Abbott, Nabia. "Women and the State on the Eve of Islam." *American Journal of Semitic Languages and Literatures* 58, no. 3 (1941): 259–84.

Abu-Lughod, Lila. *Women and Gender in Islam: Historical Roots of a Modern Debate.* New Haven, CT: Yale University Press, 1992.

Ahmad, Zaiuddin. "Abū Bakr Al-Khallāl—The Compiler of the Teachings of Imām Aḥmad b. Ḥanbal." *Islamic Studies* 9, no. 3 (1970): 245–54.

Ahmed, Leila. "Western Ethnocentrism and Perceptions of the Harem." *Feminist Studies* 8, no. 3 (1982): 521–34.

Ahmed, Leila. *Women and Gender in Islam: Historical Roots of a Modern Debate.* New Haven, CT: Yale University Press, 1992.

Ahsan, Muḥammad Manazir. *Social Life under the Abbasids.* London: Longman Group, 1979.

Alexander, J. "Islam, Archaeology and Slavery in Africa." *World Archaeology* 33, no. 1 (2001): 44–60.

Ali, Kecia. *Marriage and Slavery in Early Islam.* Cambridge, MA: Harvard University Press, 2010.

Amit, Gish. "Ownerless Objects? The Story of the Books the Palestinians Left behind in 1948." *Jerusalem Quarterly* no. 33 (2008): 7–20.

Anawati, G. "Science." In *The Cambridge History of Islam*, edited by P. M. Holt, Ann K. S. Lambton, and Bernard Lewis, 741–79. Cambridge: Cambridge University Press, 1977.

Asher-Grave, Julia. "The Essential Body: Mesopotamian Conceptions of the Gendered Body." *Gender & History* 9, no. 3 (1997): 432–61.

Avery, Kenneth. *A Psychology of Ṣūfi samāᶜ: Listening and Altered States.* London: RoutledgeCurzon, 2004.

Awde, Nicholas, ed. *Women in Islam: An Anthology from the Qur'an and Ḥadīths.* New York: St. Martin's, 2000.

Bamyeh, Mohammed A. *The Social Origins of Islam: Mind, Economy, Discourse.* Minneapolis: University of Minnesota Press, 1999.

Berkey, Jonathan P. *Popular Preaching and Religious Authority in the Medieval Islamic Near East.* Seattle: University of Washington Press, 2001.

Berkey, Jonathan P. *The Transmission of Knowledge in Medieval Cairo.* Princeton, NJ: Princeton University Press, 1992.

Berlin, Ira. *Generations of Captivity: A History of African-American Slaves.* Cambridge, MA: Harvard University Press, 2004.

Bloom, Jonathan M. "The Introduction of Paper to the Islamic Lands and the Development of the Illustrated Manuscript." *Muqarnas* 17 (2000): 17–23.

Bossler, Beverly. "Gender and Entertainment at the Song Court." In *Servants of the Dynasty*, edited by Anne Walthall, 261–79. Berkeley: University of California Press, 2008.

Bouterse, Curtis. "Reconstructing the Medieval Arabic Lute: A Reconsideration of Farmer's 'Structure of the Arabic and Persian Lute.'" *Galpin Society Journal* 32 (May 1979): 2–9.

Braude, Benjamin. "The Sons of Noah and the Construction of Ethnic and Geographical Identities in the Medieval and Early Modern Periods." *William and Mary Quarterly* 54, no. 1 (1997): 103–42.

Bray, Francesca. "Technics and Civilization in Late Imperial China: An Essay in the Cultural History of Technology." *Osiris* 13. Beyond Joseph Needham: Science, Technology and Medicine in East and Southeast Asia (1998): 11–33.

Bray, Julia. "Men, Women and Slaves in Abbasid Society." In *Gender in the Early Medieval World: East and West, 300–900*, edited by Leslie Brubaker and Julia M.H. Smith, 121–46. Cambridge: Cambridge University Press, 2004.

Brockelmann, Carl. *Geschichte der Arabischen Litteratur*. 2 vols. Weimar: E. Felber, 1898–1902.

Brookshaw, Dominic. "Palaces, Pavilions and Pleasure Gardens: The Context and Setting of the Medieval *Majlis*." *Middle Eastern Literatures, Incorporating Edebiyat* 6, no. 2 (2003): 199–223.

Brown, Jonathan A. C. "A Pre-Modern Defense of the *ḥadīth*s on Sodomy: An Annotated Translation and Analysis of al-Suyuti's *Attaining the Hoped for in Service of the Messenger(s)*." *American Journal of Islamic Social Sciences* 34, no. 3 (2017): 1–44.

Brown, Jonathan A. C. "The Social Context of Pre-Islamic Poetry: Poetic Imagery and Social Reality in the Mu'allaqat." *Arab Studies Quarterly* 25, no. 3 (2003): 29–50.

Brunschvig, R. "'Abd." *EI*, vol. I: 24–40.

Busse-Berger, Anna Maria. *Medieval Music and the Art of Memory*. Berkeley: University of California Press, 2005.

Calder, Norman. *Interpretation and Jurisprudence in Medieval Islam*. Edited by Jawid Mojaddedi and Andrew Rippin. Aldershot, Hampshire: Ashgate Variorum Collected Studies, 2006.

Campbell, Gwen, Suzanne Miers, and Joseph Miller, eds. *Women and Slavery: Africa, the Indian Ocean World and the Medieval North Atlantic*. Vol. I, "Women and Slavery." Athens: Ohio University Press, 2007.

Carruthers, Mary. *The Book of Memory: A Study of Memory in Medieval Culture*. Cambridge: Cambridge University Press, 1990.

Caswell, F. Matthew. *The Slave Girls of Baghdad: The Qiyan in the Early Abbasid Era*. London: I.B. Tauris, 2011.

Chamberlain, Michael. *Knowledge and Social Practice in Medieval Damascus, 1190–1350*. Cambridge: Cambridge University Press, 1994.

Chaumont, E. "Al-Ṭabarī." *EI*, vol. X: 15–16.

Chavalas, Mark W., ed. *Women in the Ancient Near East: A Sourcebook*. London: Routledge, 2014.

Chejne, Anwar. "The Boon Companion in Early 'Abbasid Times." *Journal of the American Oriental Society* 85, no. 3 (1965): 327–35.

Clarence-Smith, William. *Islam and the Abolition of Slavery*. Oxford: Oxford University Press, 2006.

Cook, Michael. *Commanding Right and Forbidding Wrong in Islamic Thought*. Cambridge: Cambridge University Press, 2000.

Culbertson, Laura, ed. *Slaves and Households in the Near East*. Papers from the Oriental Institute Seminar, "Slaves and Households in the Near East," Oriental Institute at the University of Chicago, March 5–6, 2010. Chicago: Oriental Institute at the University of Chicago, 2011.

Cutler, Anthony. "Gifts and Gift Exchange as Aspects of the Byzantine, Arab and Related Economies." *Dumbarton Oaks Papers* 55 (2001): 247–87.

Davidson, James. *Courtesans and Fishcakes: The Consuming Passions of Classical Athens*. New York: Harper Perennial, 1999.

Davidson, James. "Making a Spectacle of Her(self): The Greek Courtesan and the Art of the Present." In *The Courtesan's Arts: Cross-Cultural Perspectives*, edited by Martha Feldman and Bonnie Gordon, 29–51. Oxford: Oxford University Press, 2006.

Davis, David Brion. *Slavery and Human Progress*. Oxford: Oxford University Press, 1984.

De Jong, Frederick, and Bernd Radtke, eds. *Islamic Mysticism Contested: Thirteen Centuries of Controversies and Polemics*. Leiden: Brill, 1999.

Doubleday, Veronica. "The Frame Drum in the Middle East: Women, Musical Instruments and Power." *Ethnomusicology* 43, no. 1 (1999): 101–34.

Downer, Leslie. *Women of the Pleasure Quarters: The Secret History of the Geisha*. New York: Broadway Books, 2001.

Drory, Rina. "The Abbasid Construction of the Jahiliyyah: Cultural Authority in the Making." *Studia Islamica* 1, no. 83 (1996): 33–49.

During, J. "Samāᶜ." *EI*, vol. VIII: 1018–19.

El-Cheikh, Nadia Maria. "Caliphal Harems, Household Harems: Baghdad in the Fourth Century of the Islamic Era." In *Harem Histories: Envisioning Places and Living Spaces*, edited by Marilyn Booth, 87–103. Durham: Duke University Press, 2010.

El-Cheikh, Nadia Maria. "Describing the Other to Get at the Self: Byzantine Women in Arabic Sources (8th–11th Centuries)." *Journal of the Economic and Social History of the Orient* 40, no. 2 (1997): 239–50.

El-Cheikh, Nadia Maria. "The Qahramana in the Abbasid Court: Position and Functions." *Studia Islamica*, no. 97 (2003): 41–55.

El-Cheikh, Nadia Maria. "Revisiting the Abbasid Harems." *Journal of Middle East Women's Studies* 1, no. 3 (2005): 1–19.

El-Cheikh, Nadia Maria. *Women, Islam and Abbasid History*. Harvard: Harvard University Press, 2015.

El-Hamel, Chouki. *Black Morocco: A History of Race, Slavery and Islam*. Cambridge: Cambridge University Press, 2014.

El-Hibri, Tayeb. *Reinterpreting Islamic Historiography: Harun al-Rashid and the Narrative of the ʿAbbasid Caliphate*. Cambridge Studies in Islamic Civilization. Cambridge: Cambridge University Press, 1999.

El-Khoury, S. *The Function of Music in Islamic Culture in the Period up to 1100 AD*. General Egyptian Book Organization, 1984.

El-Rouayheb, Khaled. *Before Homosexuality in the Arab-Islamic World, 1500–1800*. Chicago, IL: University of Chicago Press, 2005.

Engel, Hans. *Die Stellung des Musikers im arabisch-islamischen Raum*. Bonn: Verlag für Systematische Musikwissenschaft, 1987.

Ephrat, Daphna, and Hatim Mahamid. "The Creation of Ṣūfi Spheres in Medieval Damascus (Mid-6th/12th to Mid-8th/14th). *Journal of the Royal Asiatic Society* 3.25.2 (2015): 189–208.

Farmer, Henry George. *Al-Fārābī's Arabic-Latin Writings on Music*. London: Hinrichsen Edition, 1965.

Farmer, Henry George. "Clues for the Arabian Influence on European Musical Theory." *Journal of the Royal Asiatic Society* 57, no. 1 (1925): 61–80.

Farmer, Henry George. "Duff." *EI*, vol. II: 620–1.

Farmer, Henry George. "Greek Theorists of Music in Arabic Translation." *Isis* 13, no. 2 (1930): 325–33.

Farmer, Henry George. *A History of Arabian Music to the 13th Century*. London: Luzac; repr., 1995.

Farmer, Henry George. "Ibn Khurdādhbih on Musical Instruments." *Journal of the Royal Asiatic Society of Great Britain and Ireland*, no. 3 (July 1928): 509–18.

Farmer, Henry George, trans., Music: *The Priceless Jewel*, 2 vols., vol. 1. Frankfurt am Main: Institute for the History of Arabic-Islamic Science at the Johann Wolfgang Goethe University, 1942; reprint, 1997.

Farmer, Henry George. *The Sources of Arabian Music; an Annotated Bibliography of Arabic Manuscripts Which Deal with the Theory, Practice, and History of Arabian Music from the Eighth to the Seventeenth Century*. Leiden: EJ Brill, 1965.

Farmer, Henry George. "The Structure of the Arabian and Persian Lute in the Middle Ages." *Journal of the Royal Asiatic Society* 71, no. 1 (1939): 41–51.

Farmer, Henry George. "Tabl-Khana." *EI*, vol X: 34–8.

Farmer, Henry George. "Ud." *EI*, vol. X: 768–70.

al-Faruqi, Lois Ibsen. "Music, Musicians and Muslim Law." *Asian Music* 17, no. 1 (1985): 3–36.

al-Faruqi, Lois Ibsen. "The Nature of the Musical Art of Islamic Culture: A Theoretical and Empirical Study of Arabian Music." Dissertation, Syracuse University, 1974.

al-Faruqi, Lois Ibsen. "Structural Segments in the Islamic Arts: The Musical 'Translation' of a Characteristic of the Literary and Visual Arts." *Asian Music* 16, no. 1 (1985): 59–82.

Fay, Mary Ann. *Unveiling the Harem: Elite Women and the Paradox of Seclusion in Eighteenth-Century Cairo*. Middle East Studies Beyond Dominant Paradigms, Peter Gran, series ed. Syracuse: Syracuse University Press, 2012.

Feldman, Martha, and Bonnie Gordon, eds. *The Courtesan's Arts: Cross-Cultural Perspectives*. Oxford: Oxford University Press, 2006.

Fisher, Humphrey. *Slavery in the History of Muslim Black Africa*. New York: New York University Press, 2001.

Fitzgerald, William. *Slavery and the Roman Literary Imagination*. Cambridge: Cambridge University Press, 2000.

Franklin, John C. "The Global Economy of Music in the Ancient Near East." In *Sounds of Ancient Music*, edited by Joan Goodnick Westenholz, 27–37. Jerusalem: Bible Lands Museum, 2007.

Franklin, John C. *Kinyras: The Divine Lyre*. Hellenic Studies Series 70. Washington, DC: Center for Hellenic Studies, 2016.

Garulo, Theresa. "Women in Medieval Classical Arabic Poetry." In *Writing the Feminine: Women in Arab Sources*, vol. I, The Islamic Mediterranean, edited by Manuela and Randi Deguilhem Marin, 25–40. London: I.B. Tauris, 2002.

Goldziher, Ignaz. *Muslim Studies (Muhammedanische Studien)*. 2 vols. Vol. 1. Translated by S. M. Stern. London: George Allen and Unwin, 1967.

Gordon, Matthew. "Arib al-Ma'mūniya: A Third/Ninth Century Abbasid Courtesan." In *Views from the Edge: Essays in Honor of Richard W. Bulliet*, edited by Neguin Yavari, Lawrence G. Potter, and Jean-Marc Ran Oppenheim, 86–100. New York: Columbia University Press, 2004.

Gordon, Matthew. "Arīb al-Ma'mūniyah." In *Arabic Literary Culture, 500–925*, edited by Michael Cooperson and Shawkat Toorawa, 85–90. Farmington Hills, MI: Thomson Gale, 2004.

Gordon, Matthew. "The Place of Competition: The Careers of Arib al-Ma'mūniya and Ulayya bint al-Mahdi, Sisters in Song." In *Occasional Papers of the School of Abbasid Studies*, Orientalia Lovaniensia Analecta, no. 135, edited by James Montgomery, 61–81. Leuven: Peeters, 2004.

Gordon, Matthew. "Yearning and Disquiet: al-Jāḥiẓ and the *Risālat al-Qiyan*." In *Al-Jāhiz: A Muslim Humanist for our Time*, edited by Armin Heinemann, John L. Meloy, and Tarif Khalidi, 253–68. Wurzburg: Ergon-Verlag, 2009.

Graham, Carol. "The Meaning of Slavery and Identity in Al-Andalus: The Epistle of Ibn Garcia." *Arab Studies Journal* 3, no. 1 (1995): 68–79.

Graves-Brown, Carolyn. *Dancing for Hathor: Women in Ancient Egypt*. London: Continuum, 2010.

Gribetz, Arthur. "The Samāᶜ Controversy: Ṣūfi Vs Legalist." *Studia Islamica* 74 (1991): 43–62.

Hagel, Stefan. *Ancient Greek Music: A New Technical History*. Cambridge: Cambridge University Press, 2009.

Hallaq, Wael. *Law and Legal Theory in Classical and Medieval Islam*. Aldershot, Hampshire: Ashgate Variorum Collected Studies, 1994.

Hambly, Gavin R. G., ed. *Women in the Medieval Islamic World*. New York: St. Martin's, 1998.

Hanne, Eric J. "Women, Power, and the Eleventh and Twelfth Century Abbasid Court." *Hawwa: Journal of Women of the Middle East and the Islamic World* 3, no.1 (2005): 80–110.

Haritani, Suleiman. *Al-jawārī wa'l qiyān fi al-mujtama*ᶜ *al-*ᶜ*Arabī al-Islamī (The Slave Women and Singing Girls: The Phenomenon of Slave Women, Clubs and Household Practice in the Arabic Islamic Courts)*. Damascus: Dār al-Ḥaṣad, 1997.

Harvey, Ramon. "Slavery, Indenture and Freedom: Exegesis of the '*Muktāba* Verse' (Q. 24:33) in Early Islam." *Journal of Qur'anic Studies* 21, no. 2 (2019): 68–107.

Hawting, G. R. *The Idea of Idolatry and the Emergence of Islam: From Polemic to History*. Cambridge Studies in Islamic Civilization. Edited by David Morgan, Virginian Aksan, Michael Brett, Michael Cook, Peter Jackson, Tarif Khalidi, Roy Mottahedeh, Basim Musallem, and Chase Robinson. Cambridge: Cambridge University Press, 1999.

al-Heitty, Abd al-Kareem. "The Contrasting Spheres of Free Women and Jawari in the Literary Life of the Early Abbasid Caliphate." *Al-Masaq* 3 (1990): 31–51.

Hirschler, Konrad. *Medieval Damascus: Plurality and Diversity in an Arabic Library*. Edinburgh Studies in Classical Islamic History and Culture. Series ed. Carole Hillenbrand. Edinburgh: Edinburgh University Press, 2016.

Hirschler, Konrad. *The Written Word in the Medieval Arabic Lands*. Edinburgh: Edinburgh University Press, 2012.

Hodgson, Marshall G. S. *The Venture of Islam: Conscience and History in a World Civilization*. 2 vols. Chicago, IL: Chicago University Press, 1974.

Hofer, Nathan. *The Popularisation of Ṣūfism in Ayyubid and Mamluk Egypt (1173–1325)*. Edinburgh: Edinburgh University Press, 2015.

Hoyland, Robert G. *Arabia and the Arabs: From the Bronze Age to the Coming of Islam*. London: Routledge, 2001.

Irving, David R. M. "Psalms, Islam, and Music: Dialogues and Divergence about David in Christian-Muslim Encounters of the Seventeenth Century." *Yale Journal of Music and Religion* 2, no. 1 (2016): 53–78.

Jacobsen, Thorkild. *The Harps That Once … Sumerian Poetry in Translation*. New Haven, CT: Yale University Press, 1987.

Juynboll, G. H. A. *Muslim Tradition: Studies in Chronology, Provenance and Authorship of Early Hadith*. Cambridge Studies in Islamic Civilization. Edited by Michael Cook, Martin Hinds, Albert Hourani, Roy Mottahedeh, and Josef van Ess. Cambridge: Cambridge University Press, 1983.

Kaper, Olaf. "Rhythm and Recitation in Ancient Egypt." Paper presented at the Musical Tradition in the Middle East: Reminiscences of A Distant Past, Leiden University, The Netherlands, December 10–12, 2009.

Karamustafa, Ahmet. *God's Unruly Friends: Dervish Groups in the Islamic Later Middle Period, 1200–1550*. Salt Lake City: University of Utah Press, 1994.

Katz, Israel. *Henry George Farmer and the First International Congress of Arab Music (Cairo 1932)*. With Sheila Craik and foreword by Amnon Shiloah. Leiden: Brill, 2015.

Khalidi, Tarif. *Arabic Historical Thought in the Classical Period*. Cambridge: Cambridge University Press, 1994.

Khalidi, Tarif. *Islamic Historiography: The Histories of Mas'ūdi*. Albany: State University of New York Press, 1975.

Khan, Zulaika (Mohammad Zakaria). "In Translation/Transition: What Happens When *Hijra* and/or *Khawaja Sara* Meets Transgender?" Master's thesis, University of British Columbia, Vancouver, April 2019.

Kilpatrick, Hilary. *Making the Great Book of Songs: Compilation and the Author's Craft in Abu'l Faraj al-Iṣbahānī's Kitāb al-Aghānī*. London: RoutledgeCurzon, 2003.

Kilpatrick, Hilary. "*Mawālī* and Music." In *Patronate and Patronage in Early and Classical Islam*, edited by Monique Bernards and John Nawas, 326–48. Leiden: Brill, 2005.

Kimber, R. A. "Ibn Abi'l Dūnya." In *Routledge Encyclopedia of Arabic Literature*, edited by Julie Meisami and Paul Starkey, 304. New York: Routledge, 2010.

Kinberg, Leah. *Morality in the Guise of Dreams: A Critical Edition of Kitāb al-Manam of Ibn Abi al-Dūnya*. Vol. XVIII, Islamic Philosophy, Theology and Science. Edited by H. Daiber and D. Pingree. Leiden: Brill, 1994.

Kister, M. J. "'Exert yourselves, O Banū Arfida!': Some Notes on Entertainment in the Islamic Tradition." *Jerusalem Studies in Arabic and Islam* 23 (1999): 53–78.

Klein, Yaron. "Musical Instruments as Objects of Meaning in Classical Arabic Poetry and Philosophy." Dissertation, Harvard University, 2008.

Lal, Ruby. "Mughal Palace Women." In *Servants of the Dynasty*, edited by Anne Walthall, 96–114. Berkeley: University of California Press, 2008.

Lane, Edward. *Arabic-English Lexicon*. 2 vols. Cambridge: Islamic Texts Society Trust, 1984; reprint of 1863–93 ed.

Laoust, Henri. "Al-Khallāl." *EI*, vol. IV: 989–90.

Laoust, Henri. "Hanabilia." *EI*, vol. III: 158–62.

Laoust, Henri. *Les Schismes dans L'Islam*. Paris: Payot, 1965.

Leshem Zvi. "Flipping into Ecstasy: Towards a Syncopal Understanding of Mystical Hasidic Somersaults." *Studia Judaica* 17, no. 1 (2014): 157–84.

Lewis, Bernard. *Race and Slavery in the Middle East: An Historical Enquiry*. Oxford: Oxford University Press, 1990.

Librande, Leonarde. "Ibn Abi al-Dunyā: Certainty and Morality." *Studia Islamica* 100/101 (2005): 5–42.

Librande, Leonarde. "The Need to Know: Al-Ājurrī's *Kitāb Farḍ Ṭalab Al-ᶜIlm*." *Bulletin d'Etudes Orientales* XIV (1993–94): 89–159.

Lindberg, David C., and Michael H. Shank, eds. *The Cambridge History of Science: Medieval Science*. Vol. 2. Cambridge: Cambridge University Press, 2013.

Lory, P. "Shādhiliyya." *EI*, 2nd ed. Accessed December 27, 2019. http://dx.doi.org/10.1163/1573-3912_islam_SIM_6736.

Macdonald, Duncan B. "Emotional Religion in Islam as Affected by Music and Singing." *Journal of the Royal Asiatic Society of Great Britain and Ireland* (April 1901): 195–252.

Macdonald, Duncan B. "Emotional Religion in Islam as Affected by Music and Singing." *Journal of the Royal Asiatic Society of Great Britain and Ireland* (October 1901): 705–48.

Macdonald, Duncan B. "Emotional Religion in Islam as Affected by Music and Singing." *Journal of the Royal Asiatic Society of Great Britain and Ireland* (January 1902): 1–28.

Maciszewski, Amelia. "Tawa'if, Tourism, and Tales: The Problematics of Twenty-First-Century Musical Patronage for North India's Courtesans." In *The Courtesan's Arts: Cross-Cultural Perspectives*, edited by Bonnie Gordon and Martha Feldman, 332–51. Oxford: Oxford University Press, 2006.

Malti-Douglas, Fedwa. *Woman's Body, Woman's Word: Gender and Discourse in Arabo-Islamic Writing*. Princeton, NJ: Princeton University Press, 1991.

Manniche, Lise. *Music and Musicians in Ancient Egypt*. London: British Museum Press, 1991.

Maqdisi, George. "The Ḥanbali School and Ṣūfism." *BAEO* 15 (1979) 115–26.

Maqdisi, George. "Muslim Institutions of Learning in Eleventh-Century Baghdad." *Bulletin of the School of Oriental and African Studies, University of London* 24, no. 1 (1961): 1–56.

Margoliouth, D. S. "Kadiriyya." *EI*, vol. IV: 380–3.

Massad, Joseph. *Desiring Arabs*. Chicago, IL: University of Chicago Press, 2007.

Massignon, L. (B. Radtke). "Tasawwuf." *EI*, vol. X: 313–17.

McGregor, Richard. "The Problem of Ṣūfism." *Mamlūk Studies Review* XIII, no. 2 (2009): 69–83.

Meier, Fritz. *Essays on Islamic Piety and Mysticism*. Translated by John O'Kane. Leiden: Brill, 1999.

Melchert, Christopher. "The Ḥanbalia and the Early Ṣūfis." *Arabica* 48 (2001): 352–67.

Mermelstein, Hannah. "Overdue Books: Returning Palestine's 'Abandoned Property' of 1948." *Jerusalem Quarterly* 47 (2011): 46–64.

Mernissi, Fatima. *The Forgotten Queens of Islam*. Translated by Mary Jo Lakeland. Minneapolis: University of Minnesota Press, 1993.

Mernissi, Fatima. *Women and Islam: An Historical and Theological Enquiry*. Translated by Mary Jo Lakeland. Oxford: Basil Blackwell, 1991.

Mestiri, Muḥammad, and Soumaya Mestiri. *La Femme Arabe Dans Le Livres Des Chants*. Fayard: Bibliothetque Maktaba, 2004.

Meyers, Carol. "Of Drums and Damsels: Women's Performance in Ancient Israel." *Biblical Archaeologist* 54, no. 1 (1991): 16–27.

Meyers-Sawa, Suzanne. "Historical Issues of Gender and Music." In *The Garland Encyclopedia of Music: The Middle East*, edited by Virginia Danielson, Scott Marcus, and Dwight Reynolds, 293–98. New York: Routledge, 2002.

Meyers-Sawa, Suzanne. "The Role of Women in Musical Life: The Medieval Arabo-Islamic Courts." *Canadian Women's Studies* 8, no. 2 (1987): 93–5.

Michalowski, Piotr. "Love or Death? Observations on the Role of the Gala in Ur III Ceremonial Life." *Journal of Cuneiform Studies* 58 (2006): 49–61.

Monroe, James T. "Oral Composition in Pre-Islamic Poetry." *Journal of Arabic Literature* 3 (1972): 1–53.

Moreh, Shmuel. *Live Theater and Dramatic Literature in the Medieval Arab World.* New York: New York University Press, 1992.

Mottahedeh, Roy. *Loyalty and Leadership in an Early Islamic Society*. London: I.B. Tauris; revised ed. January 2001.

Mottahedeh, Roy. "The Shu'ubiyah Controversy and the Social History of Early Islamic Iran." *International Journal of Middle East Studies* 7, no. 2 (1976): 161–82.

Murray, Stephen O., and William Roscoe, eds. *Islamic Homosexualities: Culture, History, and Literature*. New York: New York University Press, 1997.

Musallam, Basim. *Sex and Society in Islam*. Cambridge: Cambridge University Press, 1983.

Myrne, Pernilla. *Narrative, Gender and Authority in Abbasid Literature on Women.* Orientalia et Africana Gothoburgensia, no. 22. Goteburg, Sweden: Edita Vastra, 2010.

al-Natsheh, Yusuf. "Minbar of Burhān al-Dīn." In *Discover Islamic Art*, Museum With No Frontiers. http://islamicart.museumwnf.org/database_item.php?id=monument;ISL;pa;Mon01;32;en&pageD=N.

Neubauer, Eckhard. *Musiker Am Hof Der Fruhen ᶜAbbasiden*. Frankfurt am Main: JW Goethe-Universitat, 1965.

Nielson, Lisa. "Gender and the Politics of Music in the Early Islamic Courts." *Early Music History* 31 (2012): 233–59.

Nielson, Lisa. "*Samāᶜ* intertwined in Practice: Eight Treatises from the 9th to the 15th Centuries." In *The Music Road: Coherence and Diversity in Music from the Mediterranean to India*, edited by Reinhard Strohm. *Proceedings of the British Academy*, no. 223, 126–47. Oxford: Oxford University Press, 2019.

Nielson, Lisa. "Visibility and Performance: Courtesans in the Early Islamicate Courts (661–950 CE)." In *Concubines and Courtesans: Women and Slavery in Islamic History*, edited by Matthew Gordon and Kathryn Hain, 75–99. Oxford: Oxford University Press, 2017.

Page, Christopher. *The Owl and the Nightingale: Musical Life and Ideas in France 1100–1200*. Berkeley: University of California Press, 1990.

Page, Christopher. *Voices and Instruments of the Middle Ages*. London: JM Dent, 1987.

Patterson, Orlando. *Slavery and Social Death: A Comparative Study*. Cambridge, MA: Harvard University Press, 1982.

Peirce, Leslie. *The Imperial Harem: Women and Sovereignty in the Ottoman Empire.* Oxford: Oxford University Press, 1993.

Pellat, Charles. "Kayna." In *EI*, vol. IV, 820–4.

Pellat, Charles. *The Life and Works of Jāhiz.* Translated by D. M. Hawke. Berkeley: University of California Press, 1969.

Pellat, Charles. "Mudjun." *EI*, vol. VII: 304.

Poche, Christian. "Music in Ancient Arabia from Archaeological and Written Sources." In *The Garland Encyclopedia of World Music: The Middle East*, edited by Virginia Danielson, Scott Marcus, and Dwight Reynolds, 357–62. New York: Routledge, 2002.

Post, Arjan. *The Journeys of a Taymiyyan Ṣūfi: Ṣūfism through the Eyes of ʿImād al-Dīn Aḥmad al-Wāsiṭī (d. 711/1311).* Studies in Sufism, Band 6. Leiden: Brill, 2020.

Post, Arjan. "A Taymiyyan Ṣūfi's Refutation of the Akbarian School: ʿImād al-Dīn Aḥmad al-Wāsiṭī's (d. 711/1311) *Lawāmiʿ l-istirshād.*" In *CHESFAME* Proceedings IX, edited by Kristof D'hulster, Gino Schallenbergh, and Jo Van Steenbergen, 309–25. Leuven: Peeters, 2019.

Pouzet, Louis. "Prises de position autour du 'samāᶜ' en Orient musulman au VIIe/XIIIe siècle." *Studia Islamica* 57 (1983): 119–34.

Pulleyblank, E. G. "The Origins and Nature of Chattel Slavery in China." *Journal of the Economic and Social History of the Orient* 1, no. 2 (April 1958): 185–220.

Quaintance, Courtney. "Defaming the Courtesan: Satire and Invective in Sixteenth-Century Italy." In *The Courtesan's Arts*, edited by Martha Feldman and Bonnie Gordon, 199–208. Oxford: Oxford University Press, 2006.

Qureshi, Regula. "How Does Music Mean? Embodied Memories and the Politics of Affect in the Indian 'Sarangi.'" *American Ethnologist* 27, no. 4 (2000): 805–38.

Racy, Ali Jihad. *Making Music in the Arab World: The Culture and History of Tarab.* Cambridge: Cambridge University Press, 2004.

Racy, Ali Jihad. "The Many Faces of Improvisation: The Arab *Taqsim* as a Musical Symbol." *Ethnomusicology* 44, no. 2 (2000): 302–20.

Randel, Don. "Al-Farabi and the Role of Arabic Music Theory in the Latin Middle Ages." *Journal of the American Musicological Society* 9, no. 2 (1976): 173–88.

Raven, W. "Al-Washsha." *EI*, vol. XI: 160–1.

Reid, Megan H. *Law and Piety in Medieval Islam.* Cambridge: Cambridge University Press, 2013.

Retso, Jan. *The Arabs in Antiquity: Their History from the Assyrians to the Umayyads.* London: Routledge, 2003.

Rice, D. H. "The *Aghānī* Miniatures and Religious Painting in Islam." *Burlington Magazine* 95, no. 601 (1953): 128–35.

Robinson, Chase. *Islamic Historiography.* Cambridge: Cambridge University Press, 2003.

Robson, James, and H. G. Farmer. "The Kitāb al-Malahi of Abū Talib Al-Mufaddal Ibn Salāma." *Journal of the Royal Asiatic Society of Great Britain and Ireland*, no. 2 (April 1938): 231–49.

Roscoe, William. "Priests of the Goddess: Gender Transgression in Ancient Religion." *History of Religions* 35, no. 3 (1996): 195–230.

Rosenthal, Franz. "Male and Female: Described and Compared." In *Homoeroticism in Classical Arabic Literature*, edited by J. W. Wright and Everett K. Rowson, 24–54. New York: Columbia University Press, 1997.

Rosenthal, Margaret. *The Honest Courtesan: Veronica Franco, Citizen and Writer in Sixteenth-Century Venice*. Chicago, IL: University of Chicago Press, 1993.

Roth, Martha. "Women and the Law." In *Women in the Ancient Near East: A Sourcebook*, edited by Mark W. Chavalas, 144–74. London: Routledge, 2014.

Rowson, Everett K. "The Categorization of Gender and Sexual Irregularity in Medieval Arabic Vice Lists." In *Body Guards: The Cultural Politics of Gender Ambiguity*, edited by Julia Epstein and Kristina Straub, 50–79. New York: Routledge, 1991.

Rowson, Everett K. "The Effeminates of Early Medina." *Journal of the American Oriental Society* 111, no. 4 (1991): 23.

Rowson, Everett K. "Gender Irregularity as Entertainment: Institutionalized Transvestism at the Caliphal Court in Medieval Baghdad." In *Gender and Difference in the Middle Ages*, edited by Sharon and Carol Braun Pasternack Farmer, 45–72. Minneapolis: University of Minnesota Press, 2003.

Rowson, Everett K. "Two Homoerotic Narratives from Mamlūk Literature: al-Ṣafadī's *Lawᶜat al-shākī* and Ibn Ḍāniyāl's *al-Mutayyam*." In *Homoeroticism in Classical Arabic Literature*, edited by J. W. Wright and Everett K. Rowson, 158–91. New York: Columbia University Press, 1997.

Said, Edward. *Culture and Imperialism*. New York: Vintage Books, 1993.

Said, Edward. *Orientalism*. New York: Random House, 1979.

Salibi, Kamal. "The Banū Jamā'a: A Dynasty of Shāfiᶜīte Jurists in the Mamlūk Period." *Studia Islamica* 9 (1958): 97–109.

Salibi, Kamal. "Ibn Djama'a." *EI*, vol. III: 748–9.

Savage, E. "Berbers and Blacks: Ibadi Slave Traffic in Eighth-Century North Africa." *Journal of African History* 33, no. 3 (1992): 351–68.

Sawa, George. "The Differing Worlds of the Music Illuminator and the Music Historian in Islamic Medieval Manuscripts." *Imago Musicae* 6 (1989): 7–22.

Sawa, George, trans. and ed. *Erotica, Love and Humor in Arabia: Spicy Stories from The Book of Songs by al-Isfahani*. Jefferson, NC: McFarland, 2016.

Sawa, George. *Music Performance Practice in the Early Abbasid Era, 132-32-AH/750–932 AD*. Toronto: Pontifical Institute of Medieval Studies, 1989.

Sawa, George. *Musical and Socio-Cultural Anecdotes from* "Kitāb al-Aghānī al-Kabīr." Islamic History and Civilization, vol. 159. Leiden: Brill, 2019.

Sawa, George. "Musical Humor in the *Kitāb al-Aghānī*." In *Logos Islamikos: Studia Islamica in Honorem Georgii Michaelis Wickens*, edited by Rodger and Dionisius Agius Savory, 35–50. Toronto: Pontifical Institute of Medieval Studies, 1984.

Sawa, George. *Rhythmic Theories and Practices in Arabic Writings to 339 AH/950CE*. Ottawa: Institute of Mediaeval Music, 2009.

Sawa, George. "The Status and Roles of the Secular Musicians in the *Kitāb al-Aghānī* (Book of Songs) of Abū al-Faraj al-Iṣbahānī (D.356AH/967AD)." *Asian Music* 17, no. 1 (1985): 69–82.

Sawa, George. "The Survival of Some Aspects of Medieval Arabic Performance Practice." *Ethnomusicology* 25, no. 1 (1981): 73–86.

Sawa, George. "'Ubayd Ibn Surayj." *EI*, 3rd ed. Accessed November 2019. http://dx.doi.org/10.1163/1573-3912_ei3_COM_32260.

Scarabel, Angelo, ed. "The Qadiriyya Order." *Journal of Ṣūfi Studies*, 2 vols. (2000). Dedicated to Alexandre Popovic.

Scheper, Karin. *The Techniques of Islamic Bookbinding*. Leiden: Brill, 2015.

Scholz, Piotr O. *Eunuchs and Castrati: A Cultural History*. Translated by John A. Broadwin and Shelley L. Frisch. Princeton, NJ: Marcus Wiener, 2001.

Seibert, Ilse. *Women in Ancient Near East*. Translated by Marianne Herzfeld. Leipzig: Edition Leipzig, 1974.

Sellheim, R. "Samāc." *EI*, vol. VIII: 1019–20.

Shahzad, Bashir. *Ṣūfi Bodies: Religion and Society in Medieval Islam*. New York: Columbia University Press, 2011.

Shehadi, Fadlou. *Philosophies of Music in Medieval Islam*. New York: E.J. Brill, 1995.

Shiloah, Amnon. "The Arabic Concept of Mode." *Journal of the American Musicological Society* 34, no. 1 (1981): 19–42.

Shiloah, Amnon. "Music and Religion in Islam." *Acta Musicologica* 69, no. 2 (1997): 143–55.

Shiloah, Amnon. *Music in the World of Islam: A Socio-Cultural Study*. Detroit: Wayne State University Press, 1995.

Shiloah, Amnon. *The Theory of Music in Arabic Writings (c. 900–1900): Descriptive Catalog of Manuscripts in Libraries of Egypt, Israel, Morocco, Russia, Tunisia, Uzbekistan, and Supplement to B/X*. (B/Xa) Repertoire Internationel Des Sources Musicales (RISM). Munich: G. Henle Verlag, 2003.

Shiloah, Amnon. *The Theory of Music in Arabic Writings (c. 900–1900): Descriptive Catalogue of Manuscripts in Libraries of Europe and the USA*. Repertoire Internationel Des Sources Musicales (RISM). Munich: G. Henle Verlag, 1979.

Shoshan, Boaz. "High Culture and Popular Culture in Medieval Islam." *Studia Islamica* 73 (1991): 67–107.

Shoshan, Boaz. *Popular Culture in Medieval Cairo*. Cambridge: Cambridge University Press, 1993.

Sirriyeh, Elizabeth. "Whatever Happened to the Banū Jamā'a? The Tail of a Scholarly Family in Ottoman Syria." *British Journal of Middle Eastern Studies* 28, no. 1 (2001): 55–65.

Sourdel, D. "al-Baramika." *EI*, vol. I: 1033–6.

Sourdel, D. "Ibrāhīm ibn al-Mahdi." *EI*, vol. III: 987–8.

Stetkevytch, Suzanne Pinckney. *The Mute Immortals Speak: Pre-Islamic Poetry and the Poetics of Ritual.* Myth and Poetics. Edited by Gregory Nagy. Ithaca, NY: Cornell University Press, 1993.

Stetkevytch, Suzanne Pinckney. *The Poetics of Islamic Legitimacy: Myth, Gender, and Ceremony in the Classical Arabic Ode.* Bloomington: Indiana University Press, 2002.

Stigelbauer, Michael. *Die Sangerinnen am Abbasidenhof um Die Zeit Des Kalifen al-Mutawakkil Nach Dem* Kitāb al-Aghānī *Des Abu'l Farag al-Isbahani and Anderen Quellen Dargestellt.* Dissertation, Universitat Wien, 1975.

Stowasser, Barbara Freyer. *Women in the Qur'an, Traditions and Interpretation.* New York: Oxford University Press, 1994.

Suggs, M. Jack, Katharine Doob Sakenfeld, and James R. Mueller, eds. *The Oxford Study Bible.* New York: Oxford University Press, 1992.

Suter, Ann, ed. *Lament: Studies in the Ancient Mediterranean and Beyond.* Oxford: Oxford University Press, 2008.

Talmon-Heller, Daniella. "*The Cited Tales of the Wondrous Doings of the Shaykhs of the Holy Land* by Diya al-Dīn Abu 'Abd Allah Muḥammad b. ᶜAbd al-Wahid al-Maqdisī (569/1173–643/1245): Text, Translation and Commentary." *Crusades* 1 (2002): 111–54.

Talmon-Heller, Daniella. *Islamic Piety in Medieval Syria: Mosques, Cemeteries and Sermons under the Zangid and Ayyubids (1146–1260).* Jerusalem Studies in Religion and Culture, vol. 7. Leiden: Brill, 2007.

Talmon-Heller, Daniella. "The Shaykh and the Community: Popular Ḥanbalite Islam in 12th-13th Century Jabal Nablus and Jabal Qaysūn." *Studia Islamica* 79 (1994): 103–20.

Toledano, Ehud. *As If Silent and Absent: Bonds of Enslavement in the Islamic Middle East.* New Haven, CT: Yale University Press, 2007.

Tolmacheva, Marina. "Concubines on the Road: Ibn Battuta's Slave Women." In *Concubines and Courtesans: Women and Slavery in Islamic History*, edited by Matthew Gordon and Kathryn Hain, 163–89. Oxford: Oxford University Press, 2017.

al-Udhari, ᶜAbdullāh. *Classical Poems by Arab Women: A Bilingual Anthology.* London: Saqi Books, 1999.

Van Gelder, Geert Jan. "Arabic Debates of Jest and Earnest." In *Dispute Poems and Dialogues in the Ancient and Mediaeval Near East*, edited by G. J. Reinink and H. L. J. Vanstiphout, 199–211. Leuven: Peeters Press and Department Orientalistiek, 1991.

Wakin, J. "Abu'l-Tayyeb Tabari." *Encyclopedia Iranica*, vol. 1: 390. Accessed September 17, 2020. http://www.iranicaonline.org/articles/abul-tayyeb-tabari.

Wehr, Hans. "Arabic-English Dictionary." In *The Hans Wehr Dictionary of Modern Written Arabic*, edited by J. M Cowan. Urbana, IL: Spoken Language Services, 1994.

Wright, David P. "Music and Dance in 2 Samuel 6." *Journal of Biblical Literature* 121, no. 2 (2002): 201–25.

Wright, O. "Ibn Munajim and the Early Arabian Modes." *Galpin Society Journal* 19 (1966): 27–48.

Wright, O. "Music and Verse." In *Arabic Literature to the End of the Umayyad Period*, edited by A. F. L. Beeston, T. M Johnstone, R. B. Serjeant, and G. R. Smith, 433–50. Cambridge: Cambridge University Press, 1983.

Zeitlin, Judith. "'Notes of Flesh' and the Courtesan's Song in Seventeenth-Century China." In *The Courtesan's Arts: Cross-Cultural Perspectives*, edited by Martha Feldman and Bonnie Gordon, 75–99. Oxford: Oxford University Press, 2006.

Ziffer, Irit. "Four New Belts from the Land of Ararat and the Feast of Women in Esther 1:9." In *Sex and Gender in the Ancient Near East*, edited by S. Parapola and R. M. Whiting, vol. II, 645–57. *Proceedings of the 47th Recontre Assyriologique Internationale*, Helsinki, Finland, July 2–6, 2001: Neo-Assyrian Text Corpus Project, 2001.

Index

Note: Page numbers followed by "n" indicates endnotes in the text.